Constructing Cassandra

Constructing Cassandra

REFRAMING INTELLIGENCE FAILURE AT THE CIA,

1947–2001

Milo Jones and Philippe Silberzahn

Stanford Security Studies
An Imprint of Stanford University Press
Stanford, California

Stanford University Press
Stanford, California

Special discounts for bulk quantities of Stanford Security Studies are available to
corporations, professional associations, and other organizations. For details and
discount information, contact the special sales department of Stanford University Press.
Tel: (650) 736-1782, Fax: (650) 736-1784

Printed in the United States of America on acid-free, archival-quality paper

Library of Congress Cataloging-in-Publication Data

Jones, Milo, author.
    Constructing Cassandra : reframing intelligence failure at the CIA, 1947–2001 /
Milo Jones and Philippe Silberzahn.
        pages cm
    Includes bibliographical references and index.
    ISBN 978-0-8047-8580-8 (cloth : alk. paper)
    1. United States. Central Intelligence Agency—History. 2. Intelligence service—
United States—History. I. Silberzahn, Philippe, author. II. Title.
    JK468.I6J7 2013
    327.1273009'045—dc23
                                                        2013010527
Typeset by Thompson Type in 10/14 Minion

ISBN: 978-0-8047-8715-4 (electronic)

CONTENTS

PREFACE AND ACKNOWLEDGMENTS

THIS BOOK IS THE RESULT of a unique collaboration between Milo Jones (on whose research it is based) and Philippe Silberzahn.

Both Milo and Philippe would like to thank (in alphabetical order): Dr. Albena Azmanoza, Fiona Buckland, Ignacio Corrachano, Dr. Christopher Daase, Daniel Gastel, Jeremy Ghez, A. Edward Gottesman, Dr. Kent Grayson, Lisel Hintz, the late Alan P. Jones Jr., Edith H. Jones, Dr. Elizabeth B. Jones, Frances C. Jones, Dr. Amanda Klekowski von Koppenfels, Bernhard Kerres, Dr. Mitchell Leimon, the late Dr. William Melczer, Ewa Moncure, Dr. Philippe Monin, Dr. Michael Palo, Prof. Richard Portes, Alastair Ross, Dr. Blair A. Ruble, Dr. Eitan Shamir, Dr. Jamie Shea, Nassim Nicholas Taleb, Dr. Mark Teeter, and Dr. Jarrod Wiener; they also thank Allen Thomson, the late Christine Zummer, and other CIA employees (past and present) and members of the AFIO who wish to remain anonymous.

Milo dedicates this book to his wife Ewa, daughter Emily, and to U.S. Marines, past, present and future: *Semper Fi.*

Philippe dedicates this book to his wife Chittima, daughter Margaux, and son Antoine.

ABBREVIATIONS

COSPO: Community Open Source Program Office
CTC: Counterterrorism center (CIA)
DCI: Director of Central Intelligence, head of the CIA
DDCI: Deputy Director of Central Intelligence
DI: Directorate of Intelligence
DIA: Defense Intelligence Agency
DO: Directorate of Operations
DOD: Department of Defense
HUMINT: Human Intelligence
IC: Intelligence Community
IMINT: Image Intelligence
INR: Bureau of Intelligence and Research (State Department)
MASINT: Measurement and Signature Intelligence
NIC: National Intelligence Council
NIE: National Intelligence Estimate
NSC: National Security Council
OIG: Office of Inspector General (CIA)
OSINT: Open-source Intelligence
SIGINT: Signal Intelligence
SNIE: Special National Intelligence Estimate
SOVA: Office of Soviet Analysis (CIA)

Constructing Cassandra

INTRODUCTION

OVERTURE

On September 22, 1947, in response to the rapidly escalating Cold War, U.S. President Harry Truman created the Central Intelligence Agency (CIA). In the dry language of the National Security Act of 1947, the core responsibility of the agency was "to correlate and evaluate the intelligence relating to national security, and to provide for the appropriate dissemination of such intelligence within the government."[1] Washington shorthand for the CIA's mission was "to prevent another Pearl Harbor"[2]—obviously a remit to give strategic warning, not to thwart further attacks by the Japanese Imperial Navy. In short, the CIA was charged with preventing strategic surprises to the United States in the realm of foreign affairs. The agency's multiple failures to meet that demanding charge—at tremendous cost—are the subject of this book.

In 1962, for example, the CIA's estimate of the likelihood that the Soviets would place nuclear missiles in Cuba proved completely wrong. The agency's misjudgment was not simply a question, as chief analyst Sherman Kent put it, of coming down "on the wrong side" in a single intelligence estimate.[3] It was a fundamental misreading of the intentions and logistical capabilities of the USSR. It included a failure to learn facts that, had they been known, could have proved crucial to the risk calculations made by President Kennedy's team following the discovery of the missiles. The agency missed, for example, that the USSR had managed to slip both the missiles' nuclear warheads *and* tactical nuclear weapons into Cuba—a facet of the crisis that put the United States and the Soviets closer to a nuclear holocaust than either side recognized at the time.[4] Agency analysts made these misjudgments despite vigorous warnings about the probability of the USSR positioning missiles in Cuba, warnings provided months before the rockets were discovered.

Sixteen years later, in 1978, Iran was a key U.S. ally. Samuel Huntington was a staff member of President Carter's National Security Council (NSC). In September of that year, when the Iranian Army shot and killed peaceful demonstrators in the "Jaleh Square massacre," indicators of a revolutionary climate soared. Huntington asked the CIA for an assessment of a post-shah Iran. In response, the agency sent him "a discussion of the Iranian constitution and the chances of creating a regency council for a transition within the Pahlavi dynasty,"[5] with no mention of the immensely popular but exiled Ayatollah Khomeini or of any potential revolution. The year before, the CIA's formal sixty-page Iran estimate concluded, "The Shah will be an active participant in Iranian political life well into the 1980s," saying that there would "be no radical change in Iranian political behavior in the near future."[6] For several years before the Islamic Revolution, however, businessmen had noted that Iranians were sending record amounts of money out of the country. Private business risk management services were also questioning the stability of Iran. Moreover, in the spring of 1978, the French newspaper *Le Monde* ran a series of articles detailing grave trouble for the shah. French and Israeli intelligence also detected Iran's revolutionary rumblings well in advance. Nevertheless, the agency was caught off guard.

Eleven years later, in 1989, the CIA's original raison d'être, the Soviet empire, started collapsing. According to former DCI—director of central intelligence, as the head of the CIA is called—Stansfield Turner, the CIA's corporate view missed this event "by a mile."[7] In large part, this was because for decades the agency's understanding of the Soviet economy was seriously flawed. The CIA, for example, put Soviet military spending at 11 to 15 percent of GNP (gross national product)[8] between 1975 and 1980; after the breakup of the USSR, it was clear that this estimate was approximately one-third as large as the actual figures.[9] In other words, for decades the agency underestimated the military burden on the economy of the primary U.S. global competitor by a factor of 200 percent. The CIA also underrated the fact that its main target was a multiethnic empire and that—in the colorful metaphor of a one-time chief analyst of the KGB—"the Soviet Union resembled a chocolate bar: it was creased with the furrowed lines of future division, as if for the convenience of its consumers."[10] Instead, for decades Langley[11] ignored émigré analysts telling them both that they were seriously overestimating the size of the USSR's economy and that the centrifugal forces of nationalism in Soviet republics were increasing.

Some ten years later, the head of the CIA's "bin Ladin unit," Michael Scheuer, struggled to raise the alarm within the CIA about the danger posed by al Qa'ida.[12] In 1999, in desperation, Scheuer went outside his usual chain of command and sent an e-mail about the group directly to DCI George Tenet. Within days, Scheuer was relieved of his duties, made a junior agency librarian, and given no substantive work. As the 9/11 Commission revealed, despite producing numerous individual reports dealing with al-Qa'ida and bin Ladin,[13] prior to September 11, 2001, the CIA provided no complete portrayals of the group's strategy or of the extent of its involvement in past terrorist attacks.[14] The last National Intelligence Estimate (NIE) to focus on foreign terrorism had been in 1997; it devoted three sentences to bin Ladin, and it did not mention al-Qa'ida at all.[15]

In short, by September 12, 2001, fifty-four years and countless billions of dollars[16] after it was founded, it was clear that the CIA would not be a cure-all for America's "Pearl Harbor problem."

A NEW APPROACH TO AN OLD QUESTION

This book takes a new approach to an old question:[17] How do strategic surprises occur? More explicitly, it offers a new way of understanding strategic surprises experienced by the United States between 1947 and 2001 by looking at the agency charged with preventing such surprises, the CIA.

The word *understand* as opposed to *explain* is carefully chosen in the previous sentence. There is a tradition in the so-called social sciences[18] that approaches the human realm as natural scientists treat nature, as "outsiders." This positivist approach is usually identified with "explaining" social phenomena. The alternative approach is used here. It takes an insider's view of the human realm; it seeks to comprehend what events mean (as distinct from unearthing any laws of nature). That approach seeks "understanding,"[19] as opposed to explanation. As the following argument develops, it will become clear that this distinction is more than linguistic hairsplitting. In fact, it goes straight to the heart of the epistemology of this book—what can we know about surprise and intelligence analysis, how we can know it, and what are the implications of our knowledge and our ignorance?

It is important to emphasize that this book is not a "gotcha-style" attack on the dedicated men and women of the agency. It does not underestimate the difficulty of their task, and it tries to avoid hindsight bias. Instead, it is an attempt by two outsiders to take a fresh approach to understanding how the CIA repeatedly failed to provide effective strategic warning over this period and to make these intelligence failures informative in order to improve analysis. Toward that end it examines the four strategic surprises already listed, the CIA itself, and Cassandras—those from both inside and outside the agency whose warnings were ignored.

In the same spirit, before going any further, we should define other key terminology used in this book. When we say *intelligence analysis*, we're using the term as shorthand to indicate all the activities related to designating, acquiring, evaluating, and distilling information into a finished intelligence "product." Popular imagination tends to associate the work of the CIA with Hollywood characters like James Bond. While the agency has a clandestine service (historically called the Directorate of Operations) carrying out some covert operations and human intelligence gathering that would correspond to the less lurid aspects of the Hollywood characterization, this book is concerned with all forms of intelligence gathering, synthesis, and analysis. During the period dealt with here, this work was carried out by the Directorate of Intelligence (DI), which employed thousands of analysts to that end. Rather than the attention-grabbing espionage and direct political action activities of the CIA, therefore, this book focuses on the seemingly mundane office-bound tasks of the agency, making much so-called espionage literature irrelevant. In other words, we are concerned with people who think rather than shoot or service dead drops for a living. These CIA analysts, as described for instance by intelligence veteran Thomas Fingar, are "information workers" who work in many ways like industry analysts in banks, strategic planning departments, or market research firms: They process large amounts of information and try to make sense of it to produce recommendations for policy—or decision makers. The difference with their civilian equivalent is that CIA analysts largely deal with secret information and that the stakes are higher as they involve U.S. national security and the fate of other nations. This book only incidentally addresses other aspects of intelligence work, such as protecting the integrity of the intelligence process from penetration by adversaries (that is, counterintelligence), or political intervention (otherwise known—even when overt—as covert action).[20] Sometimes, for the sake of variety, we'll use the abbreviation DI to stand in for CIA units performing this analytical activity.[21]

Strategic surprise is what academics call a "contested concept" because surprise and warning are sometimes matters of opinion and always matters of degree. In fact, the definition of strategic surprise has a profound impact on the lines of reasoning people use to understand it. Here, *strategic surprise* is defined as "the sudden realization that one has been operating on the basis of an erroneous threat assessment that results in a failure to anticipate a grave threat to 'vital' national interests."[22]

Notice several features of this definition. First, it emphasizes the failure by the victim of surprise as opposed to factors like skillful deception by the initiators of the surprise. Second, the inclusion of the words *grave threat to "vital" national interests* keeps this analysis firmly fixed on strategic, as opposed to tactical, surprise. The CIA makes the distinction between the two adjectives in this way: Whereas a *tactical* surprise might involve a specific incident that endangers U.S. interests, a *strategic* surprise involves "important changes in the character or level of security threats" to U.S. vital interests.[23] Most crucially, this definition of strategic surprise incorporates "erroneous threat assessment," thus opening the door to consideration of surprises stemming *both* from the deliberate actions of enemies (such as surprise attacks) *and* from unanticipated events (for example, revolutions; such diffuse phenomenon with no definitive initiators are called "mysteries" in intelligence literature). This definition would not surprise most people, but it differs sharply from that used by most books about strategic surprises. It differs because the vast majority of works—which will here be called the "orthodox school" of strategic surprise—focus almost exclusively on surprise *attacks*. In so doing, our definition shifts our focus away from the culminating event of the surprise (be it an attack, a revolution, or the collapse of an empire) and on to the logically prior antecedent conditions before the surprise: a previous misunderstanding of reality that people in the business would call an "erroneous threat assessment."

Why use such an expansive definition of strategic surprise? We do so because it flows logically from the remit of the CIA. The agency exists to provide general strategic warning to U.S. policy makers, that is, to prevent surprises. The National Security Act of 1947 that established the agency does not mention "attacks." It simply says the CIA should "correlate and evaluate the intelligence relating to national security" and provide such intelligence to the rest of the government. More importantly, the CIA itself usually accepts the view that their remit is to prevent strategic surprises of all sorts, not just attacks. Sherman Kent, the pioneer of analysis at the CIA, wrote in *Strategic Intelligence for American World Policy* (a foundation document for American intelligence analysts, published in 1949), that intelligence is "the knowledge which our highly placed civilians and military men must have *to safeguard the national welfare*."[24] Fifty years later, the CIA's Office of Public Affairs, in *A Consumer's Guide to Intelligence*, observed: "Reduced to its simplest terms, intelligence is knowledge and foreknowledge of the world around us—the prelude to decisions and action by US policymakers."[25] After the September 11, 2001, attacks (hereafter, 9/11), an internal CIA publication said, "The central mission of intelligence analysis is to warn US officials about dangers to national security interests and to alert them to perceived openings to advance US policy objectives."[26] Quite clearly, therefore, a definition of strategic surprise that takes in more than merely surprise attacks seems a fair place to start. After the Iranian Revolution or the collapse of the USSR, no responsible CIA analyst could say, "These events were not surprise attacks, so foreseeing them wasn't my job." Though not attacks, these events had a bearing on U.S. national security, and clearly any meaningful definition of surprise should encompass them.

THE CHALLENGE OF CASSANDRAS

How about the "Cassandras" of this book's title? The term derives from *The Iliad*, in which Cassandra, the daughter of Hecuba and Priam (king of Troy), was given the gift of prophecy by Apollo in an attempt to win her favors. When he was refused, the god could not withdraw his original gift, so Apollo ensured that though Cassandra would retain her ability to prophesy, she would never be believed. She accurately foretold the fall of Troy but was duly ignored. Accordingly, we use the term *Cassandra* to refer to an individual who anticipated the approximate course of events that comprised a strategic surprise but was nevertheless ignored. We see the ability to identify a Cassandra in each of the four cases as evidence that the surprise in question could have been anticipated by the CIA as a whole because it was indeed anticipated by some, and therefore the surprise did not occur because it was impossible to imagine.[27] These Cassandras reframe what is often an exercise in finger pointing into a problem of the sociology of knowledge. Sometimes these Cassandras were outside the agency (for example, businesspeople, foreign intelligence operatives, or émigré economists), and sometimes they were inside the agency but were still sidelined or ignored.

A few examples will help clarify and limit our definition of a Cassandra. After any major surprise, many individuals claim to have foreseen it. To qualify as a Cassandra here requires that someone anticipate a strategic surprise based on a *reasoned threat assessment*. The fact that a Tom Clancy novel prior to 2001 included an airplane suicide attack, for example, does not qualify Clancy as a Cassandra about 9/11. Moreover, the stall-keepers in Pakistani bazaars who sold calendars emblazoned "Look Out America, Usama Is Coming"[28] in 2000 also do not qualify. They were expressing as much a wish as a forecast (though such anecdotes *do* offer limited clues to the puzzle at hand and are sometimes used for that purpose in the argument to follow). Cassandras need to meet us halfway epistemologically—psychics channeling Nostradamus and biblical "scholars" finding evidence of "end times" need not apply.

As we'll see, however, the former head of the CIA's bin Ladin station—Michael Scheuer, whom 9/11 Commission staffers nicknamed "the Prophet"[29]—*does* qualify as a Cassandra. Scheuer gave the right warning (he "anticipated the approximate course of events") for the right reasons ("on the basis of a reasoned threat assessment"). In so doing, he acted as a foil to the mainstream views of the rest of the agency, and thereby his case helps us understand how strategic surprises occur.

Don't think that this means that all Cassandras are "hawks" about threats. The contrast that their assessments provide can cut both ways. A study of the Cassandras in the case of the collapse of the USSR highlight erroneous threat perception in the opposite direction: They offered far smaller (that is, more accurate) estimates of the Soviet Union's GNP and forecast societal instability when the CIA was calling the USSR stable and talking about its future in decades.

To mix literary metaphors, up to now intelligence literature has treated Cassandras as Rosencrantz and Guildenstern appear in *Hamlet*, walk-on figures outside the main tragedy. Most postsurprise accounts mention such people only anecdotally or as a curious aside. In contrast, this work takes Cassandras seriously and tries to treat them systematically. It does not—Tom Stoppard–like[30]—make Cassandras the sole center of the action, but it does argue that they provide valuable contrast. They do so because they illustrate how persistent attributes of the CIA's identity and culture shaped the interpretation of evidence and how such filters removed signals that might have prevented strategic surprises. They belie the idea that these surprises were in some sense "inevitable" and thereby expose the analytical process of the CIA to constructive scrutiny.

PREVAILING EXPLANATIONS OF STRATEGIC SURPRISES

Prevailing explanations of strategic surprises concentrate on—and lay the majority of the "blame" on—intelligence *consumers* (such as political or military leaders) rather than intelligence *producers* like the CIA.[31] This book concentrates on the CIA, and therefore most issues raised by what is called the "warning–response problem" (for example, blaming the consumer) are outside its scope. After all, if the case is made successfully that the CIA itself is surprised, then the warning–response problem is moot. What concerns us is how intelligence producers—those organizations like the CIA with a specific remit to prevent surprise—fail to give adequate warning.

When scholars *do* address the contribution of intelligence producers to surprise, two tendencies reveal themselves: They either create a journalistic narrative of error within the producer without advancing an explicit theory of surprise, or they create intermediate-level theories based on psychology, organizational behavior, and so on. When you survey the topic, however, you find that these theories rarely flatly contradict one another, but they are not fully compatible, complete, or satisfying in isolation.

Specifically, prevailing intermediate explanations of surprise fall into three main categories. The first takes an organizational behavior perspective and is best represented by *Essence of Decision*,[32] the landmark work of Graham Allison on the Cuban missile crisis, which has had a substantial impact on thinking about the topic. Allison explains the crisis through three different models: the rational actor, organizational behavior, and governmental politics. His "Model Two" (organizational behavior) is especially pertinent to the argument made here because it evolved to account for the role of organizational culture, and it explored slightly how culture can affect intelligence analysis. Allison opened (although he did not fully investigate) the questions of where organizations derive their preferences and how organizations relate to their environment. Allison's Model Three, "governmental" or "bureaucratic" politics, has also contributed richly to the literature on strategic surprise, though usually from the perspective of failures among competing agencies to cooperate, share information, or act as impediments to warning transmission and reception. Discussions of the "politicization" of intelligence are variations on this theme, and some scholars advance variants as "institutional" explanations for surprise.

On a practical level, however, bureaucratic politics models break down as an explanation because attempts to reform intelligence structures exactly address such problems and have repeatedly been found wanting. Following Israel's 1973 intelligence failure before the Yom Kippur War, for example, the Agranat Commission produced proposals for institutional reform that amounted to copying the U.S. institutional arrangement at the same time—which had failed in precisely the same way.

The second category of intermediate explanations takes a psychological perspective. Scholars such as Robert Jervis and Richards Heuer advance the importance of psychological factors in strategic surprise and stress the role of "heuristic" shortcuts in "cold"—or cognitive—processing of information: how humans introduce biases into analysis because of their beliefs, prior experiences, and existing expectations and the individual's current cognitive "set" or agenda. Jervis also explored "hot"—or affective—mental processes: how humans' needs and emotional states alter how they process information through motivational biases. Irving Janis's work on "groupthink," stressing the emotional dynamics and pressures of small groups, also largely dealt with "hot" mental processes. Psychological explanations, however, have four limitations. First, their focus is on the moment of information processing by either analysts or decision makers. As a result, while necessary and illuminating for understanding isolated elements of strategic surprises, they are not sufficient to explain the phenomenon as a whole. This is because issues need to be considered earlier in the intelligence cycle, that is, at the tasking (what to search for) and collection stages, even before analysis (as we see with the work of Roberta Wohlstetter in the following discussion). Second, much of the psychologically oriented literature is built around *individual* analysis and decisions. However, intelligence is a group process, so collective dynamics must be captured. As anyone familiar with systems theory knows, systems can have properties that none of their individual components intends. Third, when psychological theories concentrate on the "hot" biases, they do not effectively bring to the fore long-term processes of cumulative causation in a structured manner. The Cassandras we identify were not ignored in the heat of the moment but in a sustained way. Fourth and perhaps most important, the role that one particular, historically grounded, and continually reinforced identity or culture plays in patterns and failures in analysis is left unaddressed in psychological literature.

The third category of intermediate explanations of surprise takes a "cybernetic"—that is, systemic, information-centered—perspective by looking at the issues regarding information available on a surprise. Here, the difficulty of anticipating strategic surprises is ascribed to a "signal-to-noise" problem, or the inability to pick out so-called weak signals that foretell such surprises. This theory was advanced in a groundbreaking study of Pearl Harbor[33] by Roberta Wohlstetter. Wohlstetter advanced the idea that the Japanese attack did not succeed because of a lack of information: "At the time of Pearl Harbor the circumstances of collection in the sense of access to a huge variety of data were . . . close to ideal." Analytical problems, she wrote, arose not from too little information but from the inability to glean "information" from mere "data." (Contemporary proponents of technical fixes to intelligence like "total information awareness" please take note!) Moreover, Wohlstetter wrote, "The job of lifting signals out of a confusion of noise is an activity that is very much aided by hypotheses." We believe that Wohlstetter's insight about the role of hypotheses is key to understanding strategic surprise but also believe that up to now the question of *how* hypotheses are generated and discarded has not been systematically addressed.

In the field of intelligence, the difficulty of the wrong, insufficient, or non-existent hypothesis is often described as that of "solving the wrong puzzle." In prior works about surprise, the wrong puzzle, or "failure of imagination," has been a deus ex machina after the surprise has already happened. It has become an "exogenous phenomenon," not analyzed in detail, explained away as an imponderable or simply ignored as an embarrassment. In the pages that follow, however, we will document that it is the culture and identity of the intelligence-producing agency that ultimately shapes, constrains, and generates the problem of the wrong puzzle and therefore that any complete understanding of strategic surprise must address identity and culture.

Richard Betts, who might be called the dean of strategic surprise, does not dispute the intermediate explanations named in the preceding paragraphs but takes a fatalistic stand and maintains that intelligence failures are inevitable. His reasoning is grounded in what he calls "paradoxes of perception." These paradoxes consist of the irresolvable trade-offs and dilemmas inherent in attempts to improve strategic warning. For instance, making warning systems more sensitive reduces the risk of surprise but increases the number of false alarms, which in turn reduces sensitivity.[34] This played out in the Yom Kippur War, for instance, where the Egyptians repeatedly held threatening exercises near the border and then drew back. Betts's insights may indeed be true, but they should not prevent analytical failures from being instructive, and they say nothing about the problem of the wrong puzzle.

In a notable departure from mainstream analysis of surprise, Ofira Seliktar, in a work on the Iranian Revolution,[35] argued intelligence failures can best be understood in terms of Thomas Kuhn's ideas of the role of paradigms in revolutionary changes in knowledge. In a second work, she showed how Kuhn's ideas help understand the U.S. foreign policy establishment surprise at the demise of the USSR. Seliktar's approach was directionally correct, and Chapters 3 and 4 owe much to her scholarship. Kuhn's paradigm approach, however, was developed to address the discovery of and theorizing about natural facts, so the wholesale application of a Kuhnian approach to an activity mostly concerned with social facts—intelligence analysis—is problematic. To get to the bottom of strategic surprise, intelligence analysis must be placed firmly in the realm of social facts, and then a specific linkage must be established between the culture and identity of an intelligence producer like the CIA and the formation and rejection of the hypotheses used to filter information.

Some existing intermediate explanations of strategic surprise ignore factors of cultural and identity altogether or treat them superficially, simply labeling an intelligence producer's culture as "dysfunctional" or not fit for the purpose. None looks at the *specific* identity and culture of intelligence producers over time and how those factors bound which and what type of surprises occur. In contrast, this book brings culture and identity to the foreground. It views intelligence analysis and strategic surprise as permeated by social facts and thus firmly in the grip of the identity and culture of the intelligence producer. It presents a model of surprise that focuses on the internal makeup of the CIA, including the identities of analysts and elements of Langley's organizational culture. It suggests that by examining these features of the agency and contrasting them with those who offered reasoned warning prior to each surprise—the Cassandras—we can arrive at a better, more unified understanding of strategic surprise generally. As a result, instead of shrugging our intellectual shoulders about future "failures of imagination," strategic surprises can become informative.

A UNIFIED UNDERSTANDING OF INTELLIGENCE FAILURE

The unified understanding of intelligence failure that this book seeks to provide is not in conflict with the prevailing intermediate explanations of strategic surprise just sketched, but it is logically prior to them. It is logically prior because it shows the genesis of the antecedent conditions that enable these narrower theories of strategic surprise to operate. It also has the virtue of parsimony.

The argument here is that because all strategic surprises have their origins in erroneous threat assessments and rejected or unformed hypotheses, one can find in the CIA's identity and culture common attributes that link them. Such an approach allows one to cut through some of the rhetorical devices employed following strategic surprises to mask errors in threat assessment. Following the collapse of the USSR, for example, one veteran intelligence official disingenuously asked, "Gorbachev himself and even his KGB didn't know, so how could the CIA?"[36] The answer, of course, is that the collapse, while not a certainty, was at least foreseeable as a possibility but not foreseen by the CIA for reasons that we will explore.

In a nutshell, this book begins with the fairly commonplace observation that the culture and identity of an organization shapes its members' perceptions and questions, affects what they notice, and changes how they interact with their environment, screening from view some parts of "reality" and magnifying others. It argues that this process inevitably frames and constrains the CIA's threat perception and thus is an underlying cause of strategic surprises. In the language of social science, this is called a "social constructivist" approach.

Such an approach allows us to use the broad definition of strategic surprise discussed in the preceding paragraphs. That definition (encompassing a revolution, the sudden demise of an empire, a surprise maneuver, and a surprise attack) allows a distinctive systematic comparison of four diverse surprises, two rooted in "secrets" and two in "mysteries." Previous comparisons of such varied surprises have been anecdotal and partial, lumping them into uninformative categories like "intelligence blunders."[37] A social constructivist approach to surprise also allows a detailed and methodically consistent look at Cassandras' role in these surprises in the general phenomenon of strategic surprise. It also allows us to weigh in with new perspectives on each case study and on strategic surprise as a whole. This new perspective concludes that a "diverse" group of strategic surprises actually have common roots: the identity and internal culture of the CIA. It illuminates these events and shows that surprises were not—as is frequently asserted—solely outside Langley (resident in the inherent unpredictability of events) nor necessarily to be found looking at obtuse, indifferent, or overworked intelligence consumers.

The commonalities discovered highlight that the information filters imposed by identity and culture both distort tasking (that is, deciding what questions the CIA should be answering) and then impede "course correction" of threat assessment. In other words, it brings to center stage what intelligence expert Jeffrey Cooper calls "the problem of the wrong puzzle"[38] in intelligence analysis. Cooper quotes a classic intelligence aphorism: "You rarely find what you're not looking for, and you usually do find what you are looking for." If the wrong puzzles are pondered, all the other parts of the intelligence process are useless (or worse: The irrelevant information that they provide wastes resources, and results in false confidence).

This model of an identity and culture-induced negative feedback loop in threat assessment leads to another conclusion: Understanding of strategic surprise in light of identity and culture is logically prior to previous proximate, partial, and overlapping explanations. Such a unified theory makes strategic surprises informative again, as it opens the door to a better understanding of the relationships among culture, identity, and intelligence failures. Before blaming surprises on intelligence consumers, intelligence producers must demonstrate that it is not features of their identity and culture that are responsible for the poor-quality warning. If Cassandras are shown to have offered high-quality warning but have been marginalized in the intelligence production process, understanding the surprise needs to focus first on the intelligence producer (the warner), not the intelligence consumer (the warnee). This is another way of saying that although the Washington aphorism that Thomas Fingar mentions—that there are only "policy successes" and "intelligence failures"[39]—may be true, that does not mean that there are no intelligence failures. In other words, we simply detail at the level of a particular agency some of the social mechanisms by which what the strategist and scholar Edward Luttwak recently called "strategic autism"[40] occurs.

This book cannot dispose of allegations (more often hinted at than stated) that the CIA knew more than it was willing to say to intelligence consumers about the strategic surprises discussed in the following pages. *Constructing Cassandra* takes the commonsense approach that if either the agency admits it was surprised by an event (for example, the Iranian Revolution) or documentation exists to back claims by high-level intelligence consumers that the CIA did not warn them, then the CIA failed. After all, the agency's responsibility is not to "know but don't tell"—it is to provide strategic warning, and each of the following case studies provides substantial evidence that the CIA was surprised before exploring how that surprise occurred.

Similarly, a moment's thought generates the observation that the same qualities of identity and culture that offer an understanding of the intelligence failures outlined in the following pages also offer an understanding of many of the CIA's intelligence successes. These successes—"prevented surprises"— constitute the "dark matter" of any work on intelligence failure. Here, though we acknowledge that intelligence successes are the logical flip side of failures, the CIA's many successes stay in the background. They stay in the background because any "sample" of successes is tainted by the practical fact that an unknown number of successes are secret and became "nonevents" in the public record and that this is true because of the logical problem that successful prevention frequently leads to a self-altering prediction.[41]

RECOMMENDATIONS

This book provides no easy answers to the problem of strategic surprise. It does, however, conclude with some practical recommendations for both the CIA and policy makers who rely on the agency. In part, we believe that our diagnosis of how strategic surprises arise helps fulfill our self-assigned task to make intelligence failures informative again. A unified understanding of surprises that allows for the validity and explanatory power of past approaches to the subject, while at the same time exposing the commonality among surprises, can only improve analytical efforts. We hope that an understanding of surprise based on identity and culture is a partially effective inoculation against future surprise or at least the start of a fresh reflection on the subject at the CIA and beyond.

Beyond that new understanding, we offer some practical actions that flow logically from our analysis. The most consequential of these changes may seem trivial at first glance: We suggest a seemingly modest addition to the so-called intelligence cycle (the iconic process diagram of how U.S. intelligence works), discussed in the following pages. It has been criticized,[42] but it endures both in the CIA's thinking and in its communication with the outside world.[43] In the pages that follow, the intelligence cycle is used as a lens to focus on how identity and culture influence the full spectrum of CIA activities. The change we suggest—begin the cycle with "hypotheses," not "tasking"—may seem minor but could have far-reaching consequences.

Why add hypotheses as an explicit step in the intelligence cycle? For the CIA, such a change would accomplish three things. First, it would perpetually reinject intellect into a cycle that too easily becomes a bureaucratic process diagram. That in itself might help cut the Gordian knot that tasking has become. Second, and related to that point, this change makes refreshing hypotheses and revising assumptions an explicit, inescapable, and ongoing part of intelligence work. This may help prevent the sort of negative synergy between unquestioned hypotheses and intelligence collection and analysis that we document; it also works toward questions of "solving the wrong puzzle," discussed in the following pages. Third, hypotheses in the intelligence cycle might assist the agency when intelligence consumers demand only answers; we document in the following pages the destructiveness of making the focus of the CIA's work a mere mirror-image pursuit of answers to intelligence consumers' questions. It keeps Langley in the question-asking instead of only the answer-fetching business.

For policy makers, this change to the intelligence cycle would have two effects. First, it would perpetually remind the consumers of CIA information that hypotheses are the key mechanism by which analysts separate the "signal" of information from the background "noise" of data and events. This awareness of the ultimate importance of ideas in the agency's work would in turn reinforce the second effect: The addition of hypotheses to the intelligence cycle would remind policy makers that the work of the CIA is ambiguity, probabilities, and forecasts, not exact scientific predictions.

Several other practical recommendations to prevent strategic surprises flow from the new understanding of the subject presented here. These are best explained in detail at the end of our analysis, but in summary these are as follows.

For the CIA
1. Enforce diversity at the CIA for practical, not moral, reasons. We find that the homogeneity of the CIA personnel severely hobbles its central mission.
2. Recognize that tasking is a wicked problem for intellectual as well as bureaucratic reasons. We propose a six-step intelligence cycle beginning

with hypotheses instead of tasking partly because we believe that tasking is far more—or *should be far more*—intellectually complex than it has often been credited with being.

3. Educate, don't simply "train," analysts; ideas matter, and while there is no quick fix for the lack of ontological, epistemological, and methodological self-awareness that *Constructing Cassandra* documents, exposure to the full complexity of the dilemmas of "social science" is essential.

4. Drop the "customers" mind-set; our cases repeatedly show that this attitude leads into a wilderness of mirror imaging[44] of the customers' unconscious ignorance.

For Policy Makers

1. Accept that the CIA delivers forecasts, not predictions; part of why we recommend the addition of "hypotheses" to the intelligence cycle is exactly to keep this fact before your eyes.

2. Understand how to use CIA analysts. In keeping with the previous recommendation, understand that agency analysts are there to help you plumb the depth of an issue, not to function as infallible oracles that draw on veiled (but knowable) secrets; their statements are laced with qualifiers as a result of intellectual integrity and self-awareness.

3. Cultivate and monitor your own Cassandras; the very nature of the social and intellectual processes that we document ensure that Cassandras will occur, and the need to listen to diverse voices is not a reflection of failure by the CIA but a natural consequence of the social construction of strategic surprise.

Our suggestions will not cure everything that ails the CIA or prevent every possible strategic surprise. They would, however, offer more substantive improvements to analysis at the agency than either mindless CIA bashing or proposals that rely on the rearrangement of bureaucratic boxes that currently passes for "debate" about intelligence reform in Washington.

1 THE WORK OF INTELLIGENCE

THIS CHAPTER HAS FOUR SECTIONS. The first section makes the case that intelligence is a social problem, a recognition that has significant implications for the work of the CIA. The second section introduces the theoretical viewpoint, social constructivism, and explains why it is well suited to investigate the CIA's work. In sum, this is because intelligence work happens not merely in the minds of individual analysts but in a distinctive community, the CIA. This section also spends time illuminating the details of exactly what is meant by "intelligence work," especially "intelligence analysis," to demonstrate its essentially social nature. The third section introduces a crucial distinction between two types of strategic surprises, secrets and mysteries. The fourth and final section introduces the intelligence cycle, a model that we use to examine the impact of the CIA's identity and culture on its work.

THE SOCIAL FOUNDATIONS OF INTELLIGENCE

Explicit recognition of the social nature of intelligence analysis has emerged only in the last few years. In the following pages, however, we examine the actual process of intelligence analysis in detail and expose it as an almost entirely social process and therefore one well suited to a social constructivist examination. Time spent laboring over the social nature of intelligence analysis in this section illuminates an activity that those outside the world of intelligence have difficulty picturing precisely. A close look at the actual processes of analysis here also introduces documentary material that Chapter 2 draws on to elucidate the social mechanisms that create and maintain the agency's identity.

Anecdotal accounts of both intelligence analysis and of specific strategic surprises have always contained accounts of social interactions, but scholars and practitioners have explicitly recognized the essentially social nature of intelligence analysis only in the last few years.[1] The literature targeting improved analysis has usually consisted either of collections of practical analytic techniques for the individual analyst (essentially, what an individual "should do") or descriptions of the various psychological traps to which individual analysts are prone (essentially, what an individual "should not do"). One can observe this social void in both CIA publications about intelligence analysis and in external sources.

The slighting of the essentially social basis of U.S. intelligence analysis began at its birth. Sherman Kent, in *Strategic Intelligence for American World Policy*, describes a seven-step process of intelligence analysis. None of Kent's analytical steps overtly recognizes the social nature of analysis. Quite the contrary: Step One of Kent's process of analysis reads, "1. The appearance of a problem requiring the attention of a strategic intelligence staff."[2] Note a peculiar thing about this step: The problem to be analyzed simply "appears"—the analyst and the agency as a whole are unproblematically presented by the exogenous environment with this problem; *they do not participate in its definition or creation.*

This uncritical, deus ex machina introduction of a discrete intelligence problem is even more peculiar considering Step Two of Kent's process: "2. Analysis of this problem to discover which facets of it are of actual importance to the U.S., and which of several lines of approach are most likely to be useful to its governmental consumers." Clearly, Kent is describing an essentially social process as unproblematically as if intelligence issues were atomic particles.

For the readers of his book, Kent's positivistic approach is not a surprise. In the preceding paragraphs (by the man, one may note, called "the godfather of National Intelligence Estimates," after whom the CIA's school for analysts is named, and whose "Principles of Intelligence Analysis" analysts still use in training), Kent says:

> A medieval philosopher would have been content to get his truth by extrapolating from Holy Writ, an African chieftain by consultation with his witch doctor, or a mystic like Hitler from communion with his intuitive self. But we insist, and have insisted for generations, that truth is to be approached, if not attained, through research guided by a systematic method. In the social sci-

ences which largely constitute the subject matter of strategic intelligence, there is such a method. It is much like the method of the physical sciences. It is not the same method but it is a method none the less.[3]

Kent then elucidates in a footnote the qualification to this naked positivism made in the final sentence quoted above: namely, that in the social science there is "enormous difficulty" in "running controlled and repetitive experiments." This idea, while true, does not reveal any appreciation by Kent for the distinction between natural and social facts or any insight into the social nature of analysis.

One might object that Kent's book is a 1950s relic. As far as its attitudes to social facts are concerned, it is not. To offer but one example, Abram Shulsky and Gary Schmitt's *Silent Warfare: Understanding the World of Intelligence*, a 2002 book still widely respected among analysts and used in many courses on intelligence, says:

> Analysis refers to the process of transforming bits and pieces of information that are collected in whatever fashion into something that is usable by policy makers and military commanders. The result, or "intelligence product," can take the form of short memorandums, elaborate formal reports, briefings, or any other means of presenting information.[4]

Silent Warfare then goes on to describe cryptanalysis, telemetry analysis, photo interpretation, and the production of scientific and technical intelligence, military intelligence, political intelligence, and economic and (even) "social" intelligence (sic) without addressing the social aspects of the analytical process. The closest that the authors come to acknowledging that the analytical process *is* a social process is through such asides as, "In some cases, such as the production of economic and political intelligence, the techniques [of analysis] are not distinguishable from those of the corresponding social sciences" (p. 52). Such asides hardly go to the heart of the epistemological problems raised by the approach described in the preceding paragraphs.

In the same way, one of the CIA's attempts to improve analysis, the oft-cited volume Richards Heuer's *The Psychology of Intelligence Analysis* pulls together articles written in the Directorate of Intelligence's in-house journal, written between 1978 and 1986. Here, too, the focus is almost entirely on the internal cognitive challenges to the individual analyst, at one point comparing the analyst to a "chess master."[5] The analyst exists in splendid, endogenous isolation, handed discrete, exogenous "problems" from on high. The analyst works in isolation: The second sentence of chapter 1 of Heuer's magnum opus begins with *"Intelligence analysis is fundamentally a mental process . . ."*

The single (partial) exception to that generalization is in itself revealing. In the final section, "Improving Intelligence Analysis," Heuer acknowledges the need for CIA personnel to have "exposure to alternative mind-sets." He writes:

> The realities of bureaucratic life produce strong pressures for conformity. Management needs to make a conscious effort to ensure that well-reasoned competing views have the opportunity to surface within the Intelligence Community. Analysts need to enjoy a sense of security, so that partially developed new ideas may be expressed and bounced off others as sounding boards with minimal fear of criticism for deviating from established orthodoxy . . . [Management should promote] the kinds of activities that confront analysts with alternative perspectives—consultation with outside experts, analytical debates, competitive analysis, devil's advocates, gaming, and interdisciplinary brainstorming.[6]

These measures seem like an implicit acknowledgment that intelligence analysis is a social activity. One must realize, however, that Heuer's remarks aim to aid *individual* analysts to keep an "open mind." Observe in this passage that *management* needs to make this effort and that only "well-reasoned" competing views should have the opportunity to surface to challenge "orthodoxy." Observe too that it is the "sense of security" of the *individual* analyst that needs nurturing and that it is *individual* analysts who need "confronting" with "alternative viewpoints." One can conclude, therefore, that the essentially dynamic, social aspects of analysis are ignored, and recommendations are made to improve the analytical performance of individual CIA "chess players,"[7] who are conceived in isolation from the chess board, pieces, or rules.

In the same manner, in *Anticipating Surprise: Analysis for Strategic Warning*, a 1970s manual for training analysts at the CIA (called "mandatory reading for intelligence analysts whose job it was to forecast threats to the United States" during the Cold War) also largely ignores the social nature of intelligence analysis. In it, the social nature of the analytical process gets a nod but little more, and the focus remains on individual judgments made (seemingly) in a social void.[8]

A change comes in Robert Clark's *Intelligence Analysis: A Target-Centric Approach*, published in 2004. This work is mostly a toolbox of analytical techniques written by a veteran CIA analyst and executive in the Directorate of

Intelligence. It does not raise larger issues of problem formation and definition in analysis, but at least it dwells on the activity's social aspects: Three sections clearly address the "ideal" analyst's social attributes, or "interpersonal skills." These are the "analyst as team player," the "analyst as advocate," and the "analyst as communicator." The description offered of ideal individual analysts, for example, states that:

> They are persuasive. They enjoy interacting with people and teaching others how the analytical game is played. They choose their words with care, and when they speak, customers listen and respect their opinions. They are highly regarded by their peers and can organize and work with a team on analysis. But they have the courage to stand alone in their judgments. They are good, and they know it. Their self-confidence, like that of the Israeli intelligence analyst who spotted the oncoming Yom Kippur attack, tends to perturb their superiors.[9]

Note that this description ends with these *social* traits in an analyst underscored as a factor in preventing a strategic surprise! Clark goes on to state: "The process of getting an answer, especially on complex intelligence problems, is fundamentally a *social* one." Unfortunately, however, the hypothesis is not pursued further![10]

The following year (2005), in the beginning of his pathbreaking anthropological study of intelligence analysis, Dr. Rob Johnston (a Director of Central Intelligence postdoctoral research fellow at the CIA's Center for the Study of Intelligence), finally defined intelligence analysis in a social manner: "Intelligence analysis is the application of individual and collective cognitive methods to weigh data and test hypotheses within a secret *socio-cultural context*."[11] He did so while introducing the results of a two-year study to "investigate analytic culture, methodology, error and failure within the Intelligence Community," in the course of which he conducted 489 interviews, "direct participant observations," and focus groups. Johnston concludes his introduction to the analysis process thus: "My work during this study convinced me of the importance of making explicit something that is *not well described in the literature, namely, the very interactive, dynamic, and social nature of intelligence analysis*."

Johnston's volume offers abundant evidence to confirm the essentially social nature not just of intelligence work generally but of intelligence analysis at the CIA. In fact, Johnston says, "Despite the seemingly private and psychological nature of analysis as defined in the literature, what I found was a great deal of *informal, yet purposeful collaboration* during which individuals began to make sense of raw data *by negotiating meaning among the historical record, their peers, and their supervisors.*" He then offers even more detail by describing a typical description of the analytic process in the words of a CIA analyst:

> When a request comes in from a consumer to answer some question, the first thing I do is read up on the analytic line. [I] check the previous publications and the data. Then, I read through the question again and find where there are links to previous products. When I think I have an answer, I get together with my group and ask them what they think. We talk about it for a while and come to some consensus on its meaning and the best way to answer the consumer's questions. I write it up, pass it around here, and send it out for review.[12]

This description neatly brings us to further evidence that intelligence analysis is essentially social: the "review process." The review process—so key to the CIA's analytical work—is clearly social, not merely individual and cerebral. Both for that reason and because of its centrality to the CIA's work as a whole, the review process is worth understanding in detail.

Evidence of the Social Nature of Analysis:
The Review Process

Martin Petersen opens his 2005 *Studies in Intelligence* article, "Making the Analytic Review Process Work," with the words, "If there is a first principle in producing written intelligence, it is that finished intelligence is a *corporate product*, not a personal one."[13] This article provides rich fodder for a social constructivist analysis of strategic surprise because it further exposes the social nature of the CIA's analytical work.

Petersen begins by reminding his CIA audience that the review process in intelligence analysis is not mere bureaucratic pettifogging, and it is more than editing: "Editing is NOT review. Editing is a mechanical task that should be accomplished by the first-level reviewer or by a staff. Review is about thinking, about questioning evidence and judgments. It focuses on the soundness of the analytic points that are being made and the quality of the supporting evidence." In this view, "review" in intelligence might resemble review of a physics problem by a more experienced physicist. After an analysis is finished, for example, "The drafter's supervisor is almost always the first-level reviewer";

this supervisor "bears the greatest responsibility—after the author—for the substantive accuracy of the piece." Use of the words *supervisor* and *responsibility* implies a culture recognizes that hierarchy, but so far it remains at least debatable whether review is purely social.

A second level of review of the analysis then occurs, and this level of review is more clearly social: We not only have further mentions of responsibility, but a relationship—closeness to the policy maker—is cited as a virtue (the greater significance of which is explored in Chapter 2). In addition, Petersen continues, one of the key questions that the second-level reviewer must ask is about *consistency*: "Is this piece consistent not only with previous work on this topic but also with other analysis being done in the issue group?" Such a question foregrounds the social nature of intelligence analysis, as it strongly implies that consistency with other, past analysis is a screen through which an analytical piece must pass to get to the next level. Natural sciences, however, recognize neither "arguments from authority" nor a majority consensus to settle disputes—those are usually used to settle social, not scientific questions. Next, Petersen explains the third level of review:

> The third-level review should be done by the office director or the staff of a senior officer in the organization. *On a particularly sensitive piece, both may weigh in* . . . Like earlier reviews, the third level needs to ponder core tradecraft questions: is it clear what is known and not known and what the level of confidence is? What assumptions underpin the analysis? *And does the piece address policymaker concerns? . . . is it consistent with other work being done in the organization? . . . The third-level reviewer should focus most on whether the right questions have been asked* and what the key variables are.

From this passage, there can be little doubt that at the CIA analysis is not an individual but an intensely social activity. The focus is on consistency, and the policy makers' concerns overwhelmingly point to a subjective process. The culture of a hierarchical attitude to review of intelligence analysis finds an echo in the earlier, "tasking" phase of the intelligence cycle—what "facts" should get collected for analysis. Former DCI Allen Dulles says:

> The matters that interest an intelligence service are so numerous and diverse that some order must be established in the process of collecting information. This is logically the responsibility of the intelligence headquarters. *It alone has the world picture and knows what the requirements of our government are from*

day to day and month to month . . . It also establishes priorities among these objectives according to their relative urgency. Soviet ICBMs will take priority over their steel production. Whether or not Communist China would go to war over Laos will take priority over the political shading of a new regime in the Middle East.[14]

Dulles is clearly (but largely unconsciously) talking about a social process of problem formulation here, and he is miles away from Kent's ideal of the exogenous "appearance"[15] of an intelligence problem. Perhaps this passage explains why Petersen's article enjoins his CIA audience that "reviewers must be open to discussing substantive differences raised by analysts. Although the final say goes to the reviewers, the process should be a dialogue not a decree." Analysts, on the other hand, should not dissimulate but instead "respect the experience, perspective, and expertise of the reviewers, and accept that the final say belongs to them." In sum, review is obviously both a key part of intelligence analysis and a demonstrably social process.

Further evidence of the social nature of intelligence analysis appears in another recent work sponsored by the CIA, Jeffrey Cooper's *Curing Analytical Pathologies: Pathways to Improved Intelligence Analysis.* Here, Cooper suggests that intelligence failures like that surrounding 9/11 and misjudgments regarding weapons of mass destruction (WMD) in Iraq "resulted from deep-seated, closely-linked, interrelated 'systemic pathologies.'"[16] Although he does not take an explicitly constructivist or even cultural approach, Cooper does compare the Intelligence Community as a whole (as opposed to the CIA alone) to a "complex adaptive system" and dissects the failings of this system on the level of the Intelligence Community as a whole, the individual analysts and analytic units and organizations.

Cultural Evidence of the Social Nature of Analysis

In addition to this process-driven evidence for the social nature of intelligence, there is cultural evidence. As early as 1955, there was clear evidence of a sense of community and shared customs within the CIA: the rules, norms, and practices of a culture. Here, for example, is Sherman Kent writing that year, in the inaugural issue of *Studies in Intelligence* (which itself is evidence of and a contributor to that culture). In a missive to his colleagues entitled "The Need for an Intelligence Literature," Kent wrote:

We have orderly and standardized ways of doing things. We do most things the right way almost automatically . . . Most important of all, we have within us a feeling of common enterprise and a good sense of mission . . . Intelligence . . . has developed a recognized methodology; it has developed a vocabulary; it has developed a body of theory and doctrine; it has elaborate and refined techniques.[17]

This passage is a pellucid depiction of a community with a common operating culture. Such a characterization makes sense (as early as Max Weber, it was recognized that bureaucracies not only embody certain modern values and have distinct agenda, but they also have behavioral dispositions and distinctive cultures) and is easily supported by further evidence. There is even, for example, a collection of articles from *Studies in Intelligence* whose title recognizes these mores: "Law and Custom of the National Intelligence Estimate: An Examination of the Theory and Some Recollections Concerning the Practice of the Art."

Items like these also offer proof that the CIA was a distinct epistemic community in the period under review. Ernst Haas defines an epistemic community as "a network of professionals with recognized expertise and competence in a particular domain and an authoritative claim to policy-relevant knowledge within that domain or issue area."[18] In such communities, he adds, "Cultural standards and social arrangements interpenetrate around a primary commitment to epistemic criteria in knowledge production and application," which further strengthens the case for a social constructivist analysis.

THE METHODOLOGY OF SOCIAL CONSTRUCTIVISM

As already mentioned, despite the social nature of intelligence work, no one has ever used social constructivism to study strategic surprises. But that raises some questions—How does constructivism work? More important, what advantages does it confer?

As an operational methodology, constructivism explores a group's rules (explicit statements telling people what they *should* do), norms (informal, unwritten rules), practices (actual behavior in light of rules and norms), institutions (stable—but not fixed—patterns of rules and practices), and structures (consistent patterns of the rules, practices, institutions, and norms, and the intended and unintended consequences of all of them).[19] Taken together, these elements ultimately constitute a society or community with a distinct identity and culture.

Constructivism is different from traditional cultural analysis because of its clear focus on the dynamic interaction between agent and structure.

According to political scientist Valerie Hudson, "Culture shapes practice in both the long and the short term. At the moment of action, culture provides the elements of grammar that define the situation, that reveal motives, and that set forth a strategy for success."[20] However—crucially—viewed through constructivism, the CIA's culture not only becomes a generator of preferences but also "a vehicle for the perpetuation of values and preferences."[21] The identity and culture at Langley not only create a set of behavioral dispositions and fix meanings, but they also perpetuate and participate in constant re-creation of those meanings and dispositions.[22] The significance of this distinction becomes clear in Chapter 2, which outlines the many social mechanisms that both create and maintain the CIA's culture and identity over several decades.

Besides its emphasis on the social interaction between agent and structure, there are at least five further advantages of using a social constructivist approach to scrutinize the CIA and strategic surprises.

The first advantage is its holistic quality, its ability to make it "feasible to theorize about matters that seem unrelated because the concepts and propositions normally used to talk about such matters are also unrelated."[23] Constructivism's recognition of multiple pathways and directions of interdependence means one can advance an approach to strategic surprise that encompasses a wide variety of factors and processes within the CIA and then link the resulting identity and culture to a pattern of outcomes formed by a series of historically unique events: intelligence failures leading to strategic surprises. When trying to generate a theory covering complex, discrete events over a period of fifty-four years, this is a methodological strength.

The second advantage of constructivism is its emphasis on the reproduction of existing social structures and on how structures transform agents. Because of this, we can account for continuity *and* change. Rejecting exogenously determined static structures provides us with a distinct advantage when investigating an entity that, while always a recognizable whole, has been in constant organizational flux since it began. Since an act of Congress created the CIA in 1947, there have been countless reforms and changes to its structure and bureaucracy.[24] Purely bureaucratic, organizational, or other structural methodologies cannot easily account for continuity in such an entity. Their relative inflexibility leaves the theories of surprise that these approaches generate open to attack for ahistorical neglect of detail concerning the constantly shifting boxes and lines of authority in the organizational chart of the entity always called "the CIA."

Similarly, because the composition of America's foreign policy analysis agencies, governmental actors, intelligence targets, intellectual climate, and external political circumstances have varied considerably between 1947 and 2001, a pure strategic culture approach is also an imperfect way to examine strategic surprise. This book "views culture as an *evolving* system of shared meaning that governs perceptions, communications and actions . . . Culture shapes practice in both the long and the short term."[25] Constructivism labels the generally stable but never final patterns shaped by intersubjective processes "institutions" and acknowledges that these both suit *and shape* agent's actions over time: Hence, change (intentional and unintentional, even unconscious, change) is *expected*. Because one of the social mechanisms discussed in Chapter 2 involves the CIA's interactions with the "consumers" of its analysis and with other parts of the Intelligence Community, a methodological provision for some development of the *Weltanschauung* (worldview) of both CIA employees and their "customers" is extremely important. It allows the analysis here to address a varied set of phenomena: preexisting categories used by the Intelligence Community (secrets and mysteries) and examples of surprise that the CIA itself takes as paradigmatic of each category (attacks and social upheaval).

This iterative aspect of the relationship between a culture and its environment that constructivism captures so well is especially useful because intelligence work often involves the *interaction* of an analytical community with the threat over time: It is rarely a one-time assessment of one side or another.[26] Cornell's Peter Katzenstein says it best: With constructivism, culture "refers both to a set of evaluative standards, such as norms and values, and to cognitive standards, such as rules or models defining what entities and actors exist in a system *and how they operate and interrelate*."[27]

The third advantage of constructivism is that the origin of the puzzle that this book addresses is partly the presence after each U.S. strategic surprise of Cassandras (that is, individuals inside or outside the agency who anticipated the approximate course of events that comprised a strategic surprise based on reasoned threat assessments that differed sharply from those of the CIA). Constructivism opens the door to exploring the idea that "rules yield rule."[28] As such, it offers tools to investigate the puzzle of why some analytical voices are left crying in the intelligence wilderness, and how the "epistemic community"[29] of the CIA systematically excludes certain people and ideas. Chapter 2 describes several coercive elements (both overt and subtle) within the social mechanisms that create and maintain the identity and culture of the CIA.

The fourth advantage of constructivism is that it embraces unintended consequences: The linchpin of this book's hypothesis is that strategic surprise is an unintended consequence of four key characteristics of the CIA's identity and culture. A constructivist approach allows a structural analysis of practices that highlights "possibility conditions"[30] rather than the discrete choices emphasized by positivist structural models. As international relations scholar Nicholas Onuf writes, "Agents often make choices that have consequences, for themselves and others, that they had not anticipated . . . Unintended consequences frequently form stable patterns with respect to their effect on agents."[31] Strategic surprises are such a pattern: This book argues that the intersubjective social processes and the CIA agents' (no pun intended) choices within them produce assessments of the outside world that sometimes result in strategic surprises. These choices about identity and culture create what Michael Barnett and Martha Finnemore have called in other organizations "pathologies"[32] that become the wellspring of strategic surprises.

Take "mind-set," for example. Using the prevailing CIA mind-set, many strategic questions are defined and analyzed efficiently. However, as one CIA postsurprise review puts it—without questioning the deeper origins of the problem—"the basic trade-off for mind-set [in intelligence analysis] is much like that for nuclear power plants: it works wonders to get production out—in between disasters."[33] Here, we trace the CIA's mind-set back to the intersubjective social processes that create it: As Chapter 2 discusses, it allows one to sustain Seliktar's "Kuhnian paradigm model" of mystery-based failure (at least as a metaphor: The aforementioned distinction between natural and social facts must be remembered), with the orthodox theories of secrets-based intelligence surprises.

This raises the final strength of constructivism applied to this topic. It offers the ability to explore with exactitude the social mechanisms that generate the CIA's identity and culture and see the resulting attributes of identity and culture at work in the cases creating erroneous threat assessments and "constructing the Cassandras" and also allows a theoretical reach across previous attempts to explain or understand strategic surprise—it allows one to create a unified theory of strategic surprise (that is, one that encompasses many levels of analysis and types of explanation). It achieves this theoretical reach in part because it frequently asks questions that are "distal" (here used to indicate logically prior) to those asked by other approaches.[34] This combination of theoretical depth and breadth allows it to generate a way of understanding that both endorses and transcends existing explanations of strategic surprise. It allows one, for example, to acknowledge the strengths of Jervis's and others' work on misperception[35] and Seliktar's paradigm model, while at the same time extending and relating this mode of understanding to others.

STRATEGIC SURPRISES: SECRETS AND MYSTERIES

In both the literature and practice of intelligence analysis, a distinction is made between secrets and mysteries. In Hollywood's view of intelligence, secrets are the CIA's raison d'être—clandestinely obtaining plans, blueprints, maps, or hidden facts from an opponent. For our purposes, the central point is made by intelligence experts Bruce Berkowitz and Allan Goodman: "Secrets," they say, are "facts that actually exist, but which the opponent is trying to hide."[36] In the real world, while obtaining secrets matters to the CIA (in fact, as is argued here, sometimes matters too much!), Hollywood grossly exaggerates their importance. Secrets have never been the sole focus of the agency's work: "Mysteries" also bear on the tasks that intelligence agencies are charged with because so many of their tasks involve prediction (either explicitly or implicitly).

The difficulty, as Gregory Treverton points out, is that a secret is like a puzzle, and "puzzles are relatively stable."[37] Such puzzles can also be relatively value free: Either a cache of nerve gas exists, or it does not. Moreover, in the realm of secrets, an insightful adage obtains: "If a critical piece is missing one day, it usually remains valuable the next." Mysteries, in contrast, pose a "question that has no definitive answer because the answer is contingent." The answers to mysteries cannot be definitively answered through a covert—or overt—operation; they can only be "framed by identifying the critical factors and applying some sense of how they have interacted in the past and might interact in the future." The distinction is vital to our thesis because it seems to argue in favor of the division of the world that the orthodox school of strategic surprise has always advocated, that is, that strategic surprises that stem from mysteries and those that stem from secrets are of such a different character that they cannot be analyzed together. The argument here is that, because all strategic surprises have their origins in erroneous threat assessments, one can find common features that link them (and thus also arrive at a theory of strategic surprise logically prior to any of the orthodox school's explanations of secrets-based surprises). In favor of this approach is that, while it is logically necessary and methodologically useful to distinguish between the two surprise types, no strategic surprises are "pure types"; that is, strategic surprises invariably contain elements that stem from both sources.

One aspect of the CIA's miscalculation about Iran's stability that illustrates this point is that prior to the shah's exile the agency was ignorant of his grave medical condition—a secret that he kept from even his most trusted advisors. Nevertheless, it is difficult to make the case that the Iranian Revolution was foreseeable primarily through the acquisition of the shah's recent medical records. The revolutionary events of 1979 were a multicausal and at times randomly determined set of events that remain to this day a mystery in many respects.

Moreover, to say that something is a mystery is different from saying that it was *unforeseeable* or that better warnings could not have been provided through the acquisition of both secret and nonsecret information. The introduction to this chapter mentioned that a frequent defense of the CIA's analytical performance following a strategic surprise is to disown the "mysteries business" entirely or to muddle the logical distinction between mysteries and secrets. For the first case study, a great example of this phenomenon is the rationalization given former DCI Richard Helms (who was also ambassador to Iran from 1973 to 1976). After the Iranian Revolution, Helms conceded, "Certainly it would have been useful to have advance knowledge . . . But the participants in the uprising did not themselves have that foreknowledge. It is thus questionable whether more contacts with religious and bazaar elements would have provided it."[38] Helms here implies that CIA's threat assessments look better when "even the participants didn't know what would happen."

In the same manner, Ken Adelman, a member of the Pentagon's Defense Policy Board, in an interview with National Public Radio in 2002, trots out a similar defense for the CIA's performance regarding the implosion of the USSR: "Mikhail Gorbachev shaking up the Communist system through *perestroika* and *glasnost* was out there for everyone to see, but it was a *mystery* how it would all play out. *Gorbachev himself and even his KGB didn't know, so how could the CIA?*"[39]

Of course, mysteries are contingent events that no one can predict with absolute certainty. As we explore, however, this manner of defending the agency's record—especially concerning these two particular strategic surprises—is disingenuous, especially coming from men with intelligence backgrounds. We demonstrate decisively that such intellectual humility was in short supply at CIA *prior* to these mysterious events. Indeed, ab ovo Sherman Kent asserted that the prediction of mysteries in human affairs is "a feasible intelligence task, provided that intelligence learns to use the methods being developed in the social sciences."[40] Enormous predictive hubris contemporary to these events and—ironically—linked to erroneous threat assessments, is documented in the following discussion.

Furthermore, statements such as these set up the straw man of absolute precision and omniscience as the only criterion by which to judge the CIA's record. It has been clear since 1947 that one of the CIA's main roles is to serve as a "safety valve" to "help reduce uncertainty about potential threats as well as a source for identifying opportunities to promote the national interests."[41] Helms's and Adelman's arguments intentionally obscure the simple distinction made by Paul Saffo, a prominent expert on prediction, between "accurate" and "effective" forecasts: Effective forecasts need not be completely accurate, but they "define the cone of uncertainty," that is, they effectively "delineate the possibilities that extend from a particular moment or event" and "tell you what you need to know to take meaningful action in the present."[42] In the language of strategic surprise, Saffo argues for a high-quality warning.

Intelligence consumers share this view. Zbigniew Brzezinski, who served as U.S. national security advisor to President Carter from 1977 to 1981, puts it with characteristic clarity in his memoirs: "Failure [in Iran] was not so much a matter of particular intelligence reports or even specific policies"; instead it was "a deeper intellectual misjudgment of a central historical reality."[43] As a *Washington Post* editorial opined in December 1979, "What is the purpose of intelligence . . . if not to arm policy-makers with the best available materials of decision? Helms' dismissal of what greater professionalism might have produced in Tehran turns the intelligence creed upside down."[44]

George Allen produced a similar view reflecting on almost twenty years of working on another intelligence failure, the Vietnam War: "Intelligence," Allen says, must

> . . . detect and report incipient trends and patterns, anticipate changes, be "ahead of the curve." Intelligence staffs should never be satisfied with merely reporting, analyzing and interpreting what *has* happened; they must concern themselves with what *is* happening now, and *where it seems likely to take us*.[45]

Finally there is the view of Richard Betts: "Warning need not be conclusive to be credible, assuming that its function is to alert leaders to danger even if the evidence does not warrant firm prediction."[46] With mysteries, absolute precision and omniscience is not expected of the CIA; adequate strategic warning about various possibilities is.

The second, related, misuse of the mysteries/secrets distinction can be dealt with summarily: the reframing of secrets *as* mysteries. As an example, one particularly egregious mischaracterization relating to 9/11 suffices —from Gregory Treverton, an expert, and a senior terrorism policy analyst at RAND Corporation. In a 2007 article, Treverton says, "Until the 9/11 hijackers actually boarded their airplanes, their plan was a *mystery*, the clues to which were buried in too much 'noise'—too many threat scenarios."[47] The reply to this statement is to contrast the shah's knowledge of likely future events in late 1978, or Gorbachev's knowledge of future events in 1988, with Usama bin Ladin's knowledge of likely events in the summer of 2001 (or, in keeping with our other secrets case, with Khrushchev's knowledge of Soviet plans for Cuba in the summer of 1962). Obviously, the epistemological gap is immense: The former two involve genuine contingency and the interaction of an immense number of agents and structures; the latter two involve advanced plans and clearly delineated chains of human intention and agency. The first two cases are things that "nobody can know for certain," while the latter two primarily involve "bits of information that exist somewhere but to which one does not have direct access."[48] Intentionally clouding the distinction prevents lucid thinking about these problems and thus does an active disservice to revealing how such strategic surprises occur. Conversely, if the epistemological distinction between a mystery and a secret is not clear to the CIA's partisans, then the lack of methodological self-awareness at the CIA documented below runs even deeper than is alleged here.

To close this section—and as a prelude to the Iran case—the thoughts of another intelligence consumer, Gary Sick (principle NSC aide for Iran in the White House during the revolution), are worthy of reflection. In a section of his memoirs entitled "From Chess Board to Hurricane," Sick wrote:

> The classic model of foreign policy decision making is the chessboard, but the Iranian crisis was not in any sense comparable to a chess game. A chess game involves two opponents competing over a well-defined territory according to agreed rules, with the ability to observe each move as it takes place. The

process is incremental, goal-oriented, competitive and fundamentally rational, although the greatest players display creativity and boldness as well. Governments are organized to deal with chesslike questions. They examine the position of players, consider the relevant factors and evaluate available options. There is another model of decision-making that is more of a hurricane model . . . A hurricane is not a calculated act, and its internal logic can produce some whimsical twists and turns. Careful observation and a knowledge of historical patterns are helpful but seldom conclusive . . . [Of course] the Iranian revolution was not a force of nature. It was "man-made" in the sense that it was the tumultuous outcome of decades of accumulated human acts, encouraged and exploited by various men for their own political objectives. Unlike a hurricane, the revolution was susceptible to some measure of human manipulation and crude adjustment.[49]

A political hurricane can also, if the right "barometers" are watched, be at least foreseen as a *possibility*, but in 1979 the CIA's attention was elsewhere, for reasons we describe.

In the cases that follow, this section's excursus into the distinction between mysteries and secrets—the unknowable and the knowable—is a point of reference for determining which elements of strategic surprises can be laid fairly at the door of the CIA's identity and culture.

FRAMING THE WORK OF INTELLIGENCE: THE INTELLIGENCE CYCLE

To examine the social nature of intelligence work requires a framework. The framework employed in this book is well known to intelligence practitioners,[50] the so-called intelligence cycle. It is reproduced schematically in Figure 1.1. The intelligence cycle seeks to represent distinct steps in intelligence activities, and as we move through each case it enables us to understand better how identity and culture make specific surprises possible.

Defining the Steps

The intelligence cycle is a five-step process. The first step (though as a cycle, it is conceived of as iterative, and thus "first" is actually a misnomer)[51] involves planning what intelligence is desired; in the shorthand of this book this is called "tasking." The items of intelligence desired are then—one hopes—gathered; this is henceforth called "collection." Logically enough, analysis and processing (that is, the scrutiny and transformation of the data collected

Figure 1.1. The intelligence cycle.

into usable forms, for example, by translating foreign-language documents) are then performed; this is henceforth called "analysis." The final steps are the creation of intelligence reports or "products" for the agency's "consumers" and the delivery of these to end users; these are henceforth called "production" and "dissemination." The only aspect of this part of the cycle that deserves special mention here is that it is that information might be "sanitized," that is, have its origins disguised to protect the method or source from which it was collected.

While the cycle as a whole is a serviceable framework for exploring the cases that follow, dissemination problems frequently fall outside the scope of this book because they involve entities far removed from the CIA. For that reason, the production and dissemination sections in each of the following case studies are short in comparison to those on tasking, collection, and analysis. Production and dissemination issues are interesting but all too often take our analysis outside the walls of the CIA and therefore out of scope. In any case, such issues become moot if (thanks to processes in the previous three parts of the cycle), no warning was issued. That is the case made in each of the following examples.

A Deeper Look at the Intelligence Cycle

We use the intelligence cycle not because it is an exact representation of the intelligence process—it is not—but because it is an organizational aid to dis-

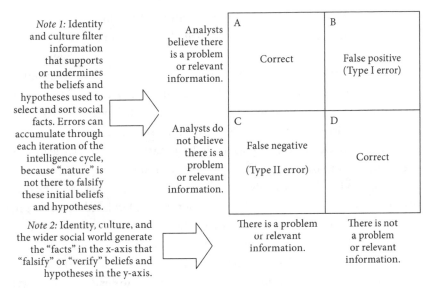

Note 1: Identity and culture filter information that supports or undermines the beliefs and hypotheses used to select and sort social facts. Errors can accumulate through each iteration of the intelligence cycle, because "nature" is not there to falsify these initial beliefs and hypotheses.

Note 2: Identity, culture, and the wider social world generate the "facts" in the x-axis that "falsify" or "verify" beliefs and hypotheses in the y-axis.

Figure 1.2. Type I and Type II errors in a world of social facts: Alchemy, not science.

cover and isolate specific failings at the CIA that tie the qualities of the CIA's identity and culture identified in Chapter 2 (homogeneity, scientism, an excessive regard for secrets, and a drive for consensus) to the strategic surprise examined. In other words, the cycle is a tool to disaggregate the contributory elements of surprises to lay bare their ultimate origins in Chapter 2's elements of identity and culture.

Figure 1.2 helps the reader visualize how errors accumulate as a result of this filtering. It also shows how many of the problems that intelligence analysis addresses are "mutually constitutive." Through each iteration of the intelligence cycle, analysts either reject true hypotheses or accept false hypotheses; in the language of statistics, they commit "type I" and "type II" errors (where false negatives and false positives are called type I and type II errors, respectively).[52] Figure 1.2 illustrates a logical truism: When Cassandras say there is a problem (or information relevant to a problem available from certain approaches or sources), they are correct in cell C but incorrect in cell D. Conversely, when CIA analysts say there is no problem (or no information relevant to a problem available from certain approaches or sources), they are correct in cell B but incorrect in cell A. In each case study, one can witness both types of errors accumulate through the cycle. Both types of errors play a role in each phase of the intelligence cycle in reinforcing the problem of the "wrong puzzle."

Notes 1 and 2 in Figure 1.2, however, call attention to two things. First, identity and culture-generated filters help analysts select and sort social facts, because belief plays a central role in that process (the y-axis in Figure 1.2).[53] This is the heart of Kuhn's "paradigm" idea and also Roberta Wohlstetter's thesis about strategic surprise when she writes the "job of lifting signals out of a confusion of noise is an activity that *is very much aided by hypotheses.*"[54] The question of course becomes *how* these hypotheses arise, and it is usually not discussed. Here we assert that they are in large part a function of the identity and culture of the analyst and his or her organization.

Second, in intelligence analysis—unlike in the natural sciences—the identity and culture of both the analysts and of the world at large also affect the x-axis, that is, they help create many of the "facts" used to verify the hypotheses of the y-axis. This phenomenon goes beyond the notions that "the questions you choose affect the answers you get":[55] It is that, in the world of social facts, sometimes the questions you choose help to *generate* the answers you get. Over time, the course of events affects analysts' thinking, and analysts' thinking affects the course of events. Many facts in intelligence analysis exist only as a result of thinking participants, and that leaves the deductive-nomological model of science in a shambles: Rather than social science, intelligence analysts are often engaged in social alchemy because their thinking can change the essential properties of the elements that they study.[56]

Figure 1.3 brings these abstract notions to bear on the first two case studies. It summarizes the linkages between the persistent attributes of the identity and culture of the CIA and those parts of the intelligence cycle where they offer the greatest power to understand surprises involving mysteries.

Intelligence cycle phase	Feature of the CIA's identity and culture			
	Homogeneity	Scientism	Secret	Consensus
Tasking	█	█	█	█
Collection	█	█	█	
Analysis	█	█	█	█
Production and dissemination			█	█

Figure 1.3. Features of identity and culture versus key distortions of the intelligence cycle—mysteries.

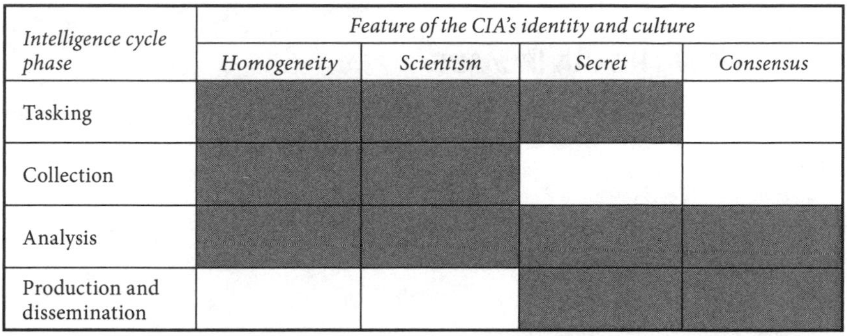

Intelligence cycle phase	Feature of the CIA's identity and culture			
	Homogeneity	Scientism	Secret	Consensus
Tasking	■	■	■	
Collection	■	■		
Analysis	■	■	■	■
Production and dissemination			■	■

Figure 1.4. Features of identity and culture versus key distortions of the intelligence cycle—secrets.

Where a block is filled in Figure 1.3, the corresponding characteristic can be inferred as a contributory factor to distortions in that phase of the intelligence cycle. Both case studies offer evidence of that characteristic's role in each portion of the cycle involving a mystery-based surprise. Similarly, Figure 1.4 summarizes the linkages for surprises involving secrets.

Before closing this section, the attention of the reader is drawn to the fact that Figure 1.3 and Figure 1.4 are merely indicative—the linkages portrayed in them are general; these charts are decidedly not an attempt to capture precisely the intersubjective variables of identity and culture in the manner of a periodic table and assign to them a unidirectional causal role. Instead, they are intended as a rough guide, a semi-impressionistic map of where particular aspects of the CIA's identity and culture exercise the greatest effects on the intelligence cycle. Using them, one must bear in mind both that properties of identity and culture are not always separable explanatory variables and that the cycle itself is an imperfect map of the intelligence process. In addition, as a reminder, the cycle itself is iterative, so that errors in each phase—but especially in initial tasking—can be self-reinforcing.

2 HOW THE CIA IS MADE

CONSTANTS OF THE CIA'S IDENTITY AND CULTURE

This chapter addresses fundamental questions: What have been the persistent traits of the CIA's identity and culture? How have these features affected the CIA's work? This identity and culture are best summed up by four persistent traits. These traits are homogeneity of personnel, scientism (sometimes manifested as the reification of "objectivity" and "reason"), a preference for "secrets" over other categories of information, and a tendency to be captivated by consensus. As we shall see, working in concert, these traits bear on the strategic surprises that we seek to understand.

Homogeneity of Personnel

The first consistent attribute of the CIA's identity and culture from 1947 until 2001 is homogeneity of its personnel in terms of race, sex, ethnicity, and class background (relative both to the rest of America and to the world as a whole).

At least one expert—Markus Wolf, former head of East Germany's Foreign Intelligence Bureau—speculates that perhaps "the predominance of WASP, East Coast Americans in the CIA" was a form of "protective mechanism against betrayal" through a "strong collegial feeling."[1] An inspector general's study of CIA recruitment found that

> [In 1964] the Office of National Estimates had no black, Jewish, or women professionals, and only a few Catholics. In 1967, . . . it was revealed that there were fewer than 20 African Americans among the approximately 12,000 non-clerical CIA employees. According to a former CIA case officer and recruiter,

the agency was not hiring African-Americans, Latinos, or other minorities in the 1960s, a habit that continued through the 1980s . . . Until 1975, the IC openly barred the employment of homosexuals . . . [Moreover, residual distrust of gays still pervades the Agency].[2]

In June of 1979, legal action began against the CIA charging that the agency had "willfully violated the Equal Pay Act of 1963" by failing to promote female operations officers; the agency settled the case in June of 1980, worried that it would "put the Agency's entire personnel system on trial," and agreed to the substance of the women's complaint.[3] Two similar sex discrimination lawsuits were brought against the CIA in 1994 that resulted in congressional hearings[4] and ended with the agency paying out almost a million dollars in back pay.[5]

And what happened in the next decade? At a November 1999 CIA-sponsored conference, "U.S. Intelligence and the End of the Cold War," of the thirty-five speakers and presenters, thirty-four were white males. The one exception was a white female who introduced a dinner speaker. Of the approximately 300 people who attended the conference, fewer than five were not white, and only a handful were women.[6] In other words, the CIA was consistently far more uniform in sex, ethnicity, and class background (given that the vast majority of analysts had at least one degree) than U.S. society as a whole.[7] We see in the 9/11 case that Cassandra Michael Scheuer's CIA colleagues derisively called the bin Ladin Unit "The Manson family,"[8] both for his fervor *and* because the unit was filled disproportionately with young female analysts.

Further support for this aspect of the CIA's identity and culture can be found in a 1999 statement by DCI Tenet. In a passage almost custom made to draw attention to the interactions between the social mechanisms discussed in the previous paragraphs with one another, Tenet's statement was titled "On Diversity." First, he acknowledged the need for a more diverse workforce at the CIA in terms of race, sex, and background. Then, Tenet justifies this goal partly because "having a more diverse workforce will help us serve our customers better."[9] The diversity mandate that Tenet imposed came from the Clinton administration, however, and it was the wrong thing at the wrong time. Instead of trying to beef up Arab-speaking operatives and ensuring the cognitive diversity of DI analysts, Tenet wasted time and effort to fill simplistic U.S.-centric diversity quotas. More than reflecting the diversity of the U.S. society, what the CIA needed to do was reflect the diversity of the U.S. engagement around the world. The issue here is not one of professional efficiency versus the social mandate that everything needs to look like the "real America." It is that heterogeneity is necessary because people with different backgrounds will be better at figuring out foreign cultures rather than projecting an American type of rationality on foreign actors. Put otherwise, the case for diversity at the CIA is practical (a matter of the sociology of knowledge) and not moral.

Scientism

The second consistent characteristic of the CIA's identity and culture is a tendency toward scientism and the consistent reification of "objectivity" or "reason." Scientism is "an exaggerated trust in the efficacy of the methods of natural science applied to all areas of investigation (as in philosophy, the social sciences, and the humanities)" (Merriam-Webster). All four of the social mechanisms discussed in the following pages (self-selection, active selection, socialization, and mirror imaging) seem to contribute to this pervasive characteristic of the CIA's identity and culture.

The first piece of evidence for this characteristic was prefigured in earlier: Sherman Kent's volume *Strategic Intelligence for America World Policy*. Recall that Kent maintains, "[We] insist, and have insisted for generations, that truth is to be approached, if not attained, through research guided by a systematic method. In the social sciences which very largely constitute the subject matter of strategic intelligence, there is such a method. *It is much like the method of the physical sciences*."[10] Kent's only disclaimer separating social sciences from physical sciences was the former's frequent lack of practical experiments. Kent made other contributions in this direction, however, as he also pioneered the "vocabulary of false precision," a social mechanism discussed in the following paragraphs (including his dismissive use of the term *poets* for those who made nonquantified judgments in his classic essay, "Words of Estimative Probability"[11]). Other deep background factors already mentioned (for example, the self-definition of intelligence interpreters as "analysts") contribute, too, as does the "wisdom literature" that Kent established at Langley.

On the other hand, it is important to recall that Kent's "scientific" approach reflected the zeitgeist of 1950s America. As Ron Robin's *The Making of the Cold War Enemy: Culture and Politics in the Military Industrial Complex* conveys, in the 1950s and early 1960s, behaviorists in the United States fetishized statistics and numbers and, when forced to use words, shoehorned them into tight jargon, "the linguistic equivalent of numerical precision."[12] Significant here is the fact that as a result the social mechanisms introduced below (for example, relative isolation; mirror-imaging the customer and other members of the Intelligence Community), this 1950s positivist mind-set *persisted* at the CIA. In "Intelligence for the 1980s," DCI William Colby wrote:

> A new discipline specifically designed for intelligence analysts must be re-
> fined, and the process of research and development has already begun. It will
> step beyond academic analysis through new techniques to project future prob-
> abilities rather than explain the past. Experiments in this new discipline are
> by no means limited to the official Intelligence Community, as they take place
> in information science research centers, among political risk analysts, and in
> the projections of the Club of Rome, the Global 2000 study, and others.[13]

In other words, long after the reputation of efforts like that of the Club of Rome et al. had shrunk to almost vanishing in the social sciences, such approaches permeated the CIA. We have already cited Johnston's *Studies* article, "Developing a Taxonomy of Intelligence Analysis Variables." Now consider the editor's note that preceded it:

> By distilling a list of the variables that affect analytic reasoning, the author
> aims to move the tradecraft of intelligence analysis closer to a science. A care-
> fully prepared taxonomy can become a structure for heightening awareness
> of analytic biases, sorting available data, identifying information gaps, and
> stimulating new approaches to the understanding of unfolding events, ulti-
> mately increasing the sophistication of analytic judgments.[14]

The idea that the various entries in this table are social rather than natural facts is entirely absent. Johnston himself introduces his final taxonomic product by quoting the eighteenth-century pioneer of biological classification, Linnaeus: "The first step of science is to know one thing from another. This knowledge consists in their specific distinctions; but in order that it may be fixed and permanent distinct names must be given to different things, and those names must be recorded and remembered."[15] The resulting unselfcon-scious taxonomy presents social facts like so many types of naturally occurring frogs and birds. This naively positivistic approach continued largely unquestioned through 9/11. The first explicit critique of it in the CIA itself appeared only in 2005 in *Curing Analytical Pathologies: Pathways to Improved Intelligence Analysis* by Jeffrey R. Cooper. The author says that the CIA's "Myth of 'Scientific Methodology,'" and its "strong cultural orientation towards an 'evidence-based scientism,'" are deeply ingrained. He wrote:

> Many well-informed outside commentators and intelligence profession-
> als continue to talk about the "science of analysis," and only some of them
> are truly aware of the shaky foundations of this belief or of its real implica-
> tions. But this talk of a "science of analysis" is a conceit, *partly engendered
> by Sherman Kent's dominating view of intelligence analysis as a counterpart
> of the scientific method.* The reality is otherwise; analysis falls far short of be-
> ing a "scientific method" in the common, but usually misunderstood, sense.
> Moreover, this view of science itself is "scientism," which fails to recognize the
> important role of less "rational" and less "scientific" elements, such as imagi-
> nation and intuition.[16]

Note again, though, that this internal criticism occurs *four years after* 9/11. Did this "scientific" attitude appear in day-to-day analysis in the de-cades before the attacks? According to a CIA guide, "Warnings of Revolu-tion," published in 1980, a "discerning analyst would have recognized the warnings of the [French] revolution at least a year prior to the fall of the Bas-tille."[17] Our first case reveals the rich irony of this predictive hubris: "Warn-ings of Revolution" was published the year *after* the CIA was surprised by the revolution in Iran (and a decade before our second case, the demise of the Soviet Union)!

Similarly, the following discussion of mirror imaging of targets pro-vides evidence for a consistent spillover of narrow expectations of "reason-able" or "reasoned" behavior by CIA analysts to their opponents. Another facet of this trait of the agency's identity and culture is the famous American "intelligence–policy divide" (one of Turner's distinctive traits, also known as the "Kent Doctrine"). This doctrine asserts that CIA analysis must (and can!) always be "separate" from "policy making" and never slip into "advocacy."[18] A thirty-five-year veteran of the CIA calls the divide a "Red Line" and says, "The 'Red Line' is a warning to intelligence officers that, in order to maintain cred-ibility with the policy community, they need to limit their role to informing policy discussions rather than expressing a policy preference."[19]

However, as Seliktar observes, "The so-called Kent Doctrine [of the intelligence-policy divide] . . . exuded a strong positivist belief in a 'rational' political universe that experts could objectively analyze by parsing political reality in a detached and dispassionate way."[20] The notion of a "Red Line," an intelligence–policy divide, is entirely innocent of the idea that, as bureaucrats classify and organize information and knowledge, they exercise power and choice,[21] much less that those choices might have practical consequences later.

Consider some of the practical consequences of such epistemological naiveté. The group that bombed the World Trade Center in 1993 was for years afterward referred to by the head of the CIA's Counterterrorism Center (CTC) as "ad hoc terrorists"[22]—a group that spontaneously came together for a one-time operation rather than "al-Qa'ida"; CIA documents going to the NSC (when they referred to bin Ladin at all) called him the "terrorist financier Usama bin Laden."[23] To cite another example, the crucial Special NIE (SNIE) requested by President Kennedy just days before the USSR's missiles were discovered (issued September 19, 1962) stated that "the Soviets would not do anything so uncharacteristic, *provocative* and *unrewarding*"[24] as place missiles in Cuba. Policy choices are inescapably embedded in textual decisions, and the CIA's cherished notion of an intelligence–policy divide actively obscures such choices and reinforces a flawed self-image of analysts doing "science."

The social mechanism of isolation further maintained scientism and a reification of "objectivity." Westerfield ascribes Dulles's decision to move the CIA out of Washington to the Langley "campus" as contributing to "analysts [becoming] more royalist than the king" [that is, Sherman Kent] and helping them "to idealize their own objectivity and keep policymakers at arm's length."[25] As a result, in 2004 the *New York Times* could comment:

> For decades, the U.S. Intelligence Community has propagated the myth that it possesses analytical methods that must be insulated pristinely from the hurly-burly world of politics. *The CIA has portrayed itself as, and been treated as, a sort of National Weather Service of global affairs. It has relied on this aura of scientific objectivity for its prestige*, and to justify its large budgets, despite a record studded with error.[26]

Apart from confirmation that the CIA cultivates an aura of scientific objectivity for its prestige, in this quotation we also see mirror imaging of intelligence consumers reinforcing this phenomenon.

One can imagine the methodological and epistemological gymnastics required to try to sustain this particular form of "objectivity" in any but the most mundane analytical situations. Nevertheless, the CIA has fought to preserve this intellectual fossil. It even crops up in articles about improving intelligence analysis. In "Fixing the Problem of Analytical Mindsets: Alternative

Analysis," a veteran analyst writes, "*One difficulty with this sort of outside-the-box analysis* [that might otherwise improve the CIA's performance] *is that it can blur the line between intelligence analysis and policy advocacy.*"[27] Such evidence of intellectual tenacity in clinging to an artificial intelligence–policy divide is perhaps the best indicator of the epistemological and methodological limits imposed by the culture and identity of the agency.

In sum, there is more than ample evidence that scientism and the reification of "objectivity" and "reason" is a powerful, pervasive, and continuous feature of the CIA's identity and culture from its genesis to 2001.

The Preference for Secrets

The idea that the CIA prefers secrets over other forms of information is developed in our discussion of the social mechanisms of self-selection below, in some aspects of socialization (including induction, isolation, compartmentalization, and secrecy) and in exploring mirror imaging of its consumers, community, and main targets. However, the word *prefer* does not fully convey the strength of this component of Langley's identity and culture. Instead of a mere preference, what one discovers in examining the identity and culture of the CIA across time is an abiding "belief that *only clandestinely obtained information can be reliable*, and that it is precisely the secrecy in which it is obtained which guarantees this reliability and makes it more credible than other more overt sources of information."[28]

The most powerful generators of this belief might be during the preselection phase, in which candidates are drawn to what one CIA veteran calls "The Power of Secret Knowing."[29] What is indubitable, however, is that stress on secrecy begins—and has always begun since the CIA has existed—with the active selection mechanism. The background investigations, polygraph examinations, and nonverbal messages noted in the discussion of the active selection mechanism below make this factor abundantly clear. In a 1963 passage, for example, Allen Dulles stresses, "Every employee signs an oath which binds him not to divulge anything he learns or does in the course of employment to any unauthorized person . . . What this means is that an employee cannot discuss the substance of his daily work with his wife or his friends."[30] The day-to-day socializing effects of compartmentalization and the daily security rituals of "tradecraft" constantly reinforce this message.

Robert Gates, who went on to become DCI, recalls that when he joined the agency in 1969 a "culture, and ethic of secrecy" emanated from the Directorate of Operations (DO) and permeated the entire organization. He writes of his DO colleagues:

> For them, secrecy is not a convenience or a bureaucratic matter, but the essential tool of their craft—without it, sources are executed, operations fail, case officers' careers are cut short, and sometimes they and their agents die. Their culture, their ethic were the CIA's in 1969. They ran the Agency bureaucratically and *dominated it psychologically.* And few question the rightness of that.[31]

Secrecy was fetishized right up through 9/11, with the installation of new safes and security procedures at the CTC to keep information from analysts. Even the CIA term "open source intelligence" is indicative of the pervasiveness of this cultural attribute. Treverton in the 1990s could call this term a "relic of the Cold War" that in and of itself betrays a preference for secret information: "There is one other source besides intelligence's specialized INTs [such as SIGINT, or signal intelligence; HUMINT, or human intelligence; and so on]: everything else. That 'everything else' equals open source." While he notes that the Intelligence Community created the Community Open Source Program Office (COSPO) "as a focal point for innovation in using open sources" by the late 1990s, "COSPO was to be wound down as intelligence returned to a *preoccupation with secrets.*"[32]

There is also that basic fact that, while some security *is* necessary, it is not the *only* thing that is necessary to intelligence work, especially in those aspects that closely resemble social science. As Rob Johnston summarized:

> Secrecy and efficacy conflict. Secrecy interferes with analytical effectiveness by limiting access to information and sources that may be necessary for accurate or predictive analysis. In turn, openness interferes with security by degrading the value of information sources and by revealing specific sources and methods . . . Between [the extremes of perfect secrecy and perfect openness] there is some notional point where secrecy and openness converge to create optimal performance trade-off. *My perception is that, within the Intelligence Community, more organizational emphasis is placed on secrecy than on effectiveness.*[33]

Without a doubt, a cult of secrets is part of the identity and culture of the CIA. DCI Tenet had a fondness for the phrase "we steal secrets," to summarize the work of the agency in public speeches.[34] More evidence for this trait manifests itself through "overclassification," in which items receive a higher classification (say, "secret" instead of "confidential") than they objectively merit in an effort to raise their status.[35] A recent *Studies* article states, "Too many policymakers and intelligence officers mistake secrecy for intelligence and assume that information covertly acquired is superior to that obtained openly." Underlining the mechanism of self-selection, the article laments that recent CIA recruiting literature suggests to applicants: "You can be on the sidelines, *reading about global events in the newspaper*. Or you can be at the heart of world-shaping events [in the CIA]."[36] The brochure proposes a world divided between those who read newspapers and are "on the sidelines" and those with access to "intelligence" within the agency.

This attribute of the CIA's identity and culture led an exasperated former staff director of the House Intelligence Committee to bluntly tell a CIA deputy director: "We don't give you brownie points for collecting intelligence by the hardest means available."[37] The cultural penchant for secrets has even become something of a joke at the CIA. A former member of the National Intelligence Council (NIC) reminisces, "At the NIC, we used to quip that if academics sometimes did better than intelligence analysts, it was because the former weren't denied access to open sources!"[38]

In short, there is generous evidence that several distinct social mechanisms produce in the CIA a privileged regard for "secrets" and that this fact is a key part of the culture and identity of its members. As the cases of surprise in the later chapters make clear, it is a culture and identity that at times distorts the business of intelligence, which is defined by the CIA itself as "knowledge and foreknowledge of the world around us . . . that helps consumers, either civilian leaders or military commanders, to consider alternative options and outcomes."[39]

The Drive for Consensus

The fourth and final characteristic of the CIA's culture and identity explored in this book is that it is "consensus driven." This trait does not encompass merely Irving Janis's groupthink (though it does not exclude it): Groupthink is a "hot" psychological process; "consensus driven" takes that in and then includes a colder process of winnowing of information inside the CIA so that it neither disagrees with precedents set by the agency's prior positions nor dismays other agencies or intelligence consumers. It is enabled in part by the veneer of collegiality already discussed.

While the idea that the CIA particularly is consensus driven should come as no surprise given its coordinating mandate, this characteristic nevertheless merits examination in strengthening this book's argument. Recall Martin Petersen's words: "If there is a first principle in producing written intelligence, it is that finished intelligence is a corporate product, not a personal one."[40] What form does this drive for a corporate product take?

We posit that this drive for consensus at CIA springs from three social mechanisms: active selection, certain aspects of socialization, and the mirror imaging of both the consumer of intelligence and the wider U.S. Intelligence Community. It is more than a mere bureaucratic imperative; it is rather a key feature of the CIA's identity and culture that plays a role in each of the four examples of strategic surprise provided in the following pages. As the initial evidence for this assertion, consider the following interview with an analyst, which provides a "typical description of the analytic process":

> When a request comes in from a consumer to answer some question, the first thing I do is *read up on the analytic line.* [I] check the previous publications and the data. Then, I read through the question again and find where there are links to previous [Intelligence Community] products. When I think I have an answer, *I get together with my group and ask them what they think.* We talk about it for a while and come to some consensus on its meaning and the best way to answer the consumer's questions. I write it up, *pass it around here,* and send it out for review.[41]

In the highlighted passages, the analyst is evidently stressing the primacy of the corporate CIA views on a topic (along with providing yet more evidence in favor of intelligence analysis as a social process, and an example of mirroring the customer that Chapter 2 discusses). Cooper restates this idea more broadly: "The validity of the earlier judgments expressed in finished products is especially important because of the common practice of 'layering,' that is, using previous, formally coordinated products as the starting point for new assessments and estimates."[42] From that evidence, the conclusion that the CIA's is a highly consensus-driven culture is inescapable. DCI Robert Gates's address to analysts shortly after he was confirmed in 1992 (discussed below) is another example.

We not only have anecdotal evidence for the prizing of consensus above other values in analysis. There is also evidence that social pressure not to be an analytical "outlier" exists in the work environment. One CIA veteran remembers:

> As a result of the extensive coordination required to write them, NIEs and SNIEs were sometimes criticized for being the "lowest common denominator" judgments available in the analytical community. Nevertheless, they were broadly considered the analytical professions most prestigious products . . . In some circles, an analyst could not convincingly claim the status of a proven veteran until he or she had participated in an NIE or a SNIE.[43]

Note in this passage the link between "the 'lowest common denominator' judgments" and "the professions most prestigious products." There is no need to introduce the hot-box small-group dynamics of groupthink to see a consensus-driven culture existing at the CIA.

Roger George, a veteran analyst, agrees. He writes, "Trying to argue against the current analytical line can be seen as undermining teamwork or even a sign of personal self-promotion."[44] This is evident in the "game of footnotes" discussed later in this chapter and its role in channeling dissent, along with all the data supplied to CIA by the 800-pound gorilla of the DOD (Department of Defense). Bill Gertz writes that satisfaction of bureaucratic superiors at the CIA is more important than superior analysis for those who wish to get ahead. Then there was Gentry's claim that managers used staff psychiatrists at Langley's Office of Security to pressure individuals over issues of analytic substance.[45]

A quick example of this trait's role in threat assessment (discussed at greater length in the following paragraphs) was described by a retired CIA officer with whom the authors corresponded. This source reported how in 1984 the chief of the Soviet Economy Division at the CIA had forcefully argued that the USSR would soon face a Hobson's choice in the coming five-year plan between "guns and butter." The former analyst reported, however, "The problem here was that in 1984 *the rest of the community—especially the DOD—was not willing to even entertain such an idea*,"[46] so the chief's argument didn't make it into CIA assessments. Here, CIA culture anticipated (that is, mirrored) the objections of another Intelligence Community member (that is, the DOD) and in so doing was complicit in a "discourse failure"[47] (that is, an erroneous threat assessment) prior to a strategic surprise (the downfall of the USSR).

In conclusion, influential social structures like the review and coordination process, combined with powerful social mechanisms like self- and active selection, ersatz collegiality, and mirror imaging produce a culture and identity in the CIA that is strongly consensus driven at the expense of other values and viewpoints (notwithstanding the demonstrated pretense to the contrary).

Conclusion

This section set out to find what have been persistent features of the resulting identity and culture of the CIA. These were found to be homogeneity of personnel, scientism and the reification of narrow forms of objectivity and reason, a preference for secret over openly obtained information, and a drive for consensus.

SOCIAL MECHANISMS THAT CREATE AND MAINTAIN THE CIA'S IDENTITY AND CULTURE

In the previous section, we identified four key traits of the CIA's identity and culture and examined how they distort the intelligence cycle, the very work of the CIA. The question then is, What are the origins of these features? We argue that these lie in the social mechanisms developed by the organization. As management scholar Catherine Tinsley writes in the specific context of intelligence analysis, "People are often unaware of the extent to which their thoughts and behavior have been shaped by their social context."[48] We identify eleven such mechanisms, grouped into four main categories,[49] that are involved in constructing the identity and culture of the analytical arm of the CIA. These four social mechanisms are: (1) the self-selection of personnel working in intelligence; (2) the active selection of personnel by the CIA; (3) various socialization processes that follow selection (that is, aspects of the internal operating environment, so-called social diffusion[50] mechanism for creating norms in a culture); and (4) various "mirror-imaging" processes by the agency of its "customers," the Intelligence Community as a whole (that is, other agencies such as the NSA [National Security Agency], FBI [Federal Bureau of Investigation], and the armed services), and its assigned "targets" or adversaries. Figure 2.1 summarizes the four social mechanisms discussed and links them to the four perennial features of the CIA that enable strategic surprise.

The first column of the table in Figure 2.1 includes the subparts of two of the social mechanisms discussed, socialization and mirror imaging. Let's take a closer look at these mechanisms.

Self-Selection of Personnel

The first social mechanism plays its role outside of the formal organizational boundaries of the CIA: the self-selection by candidates to work there. No one

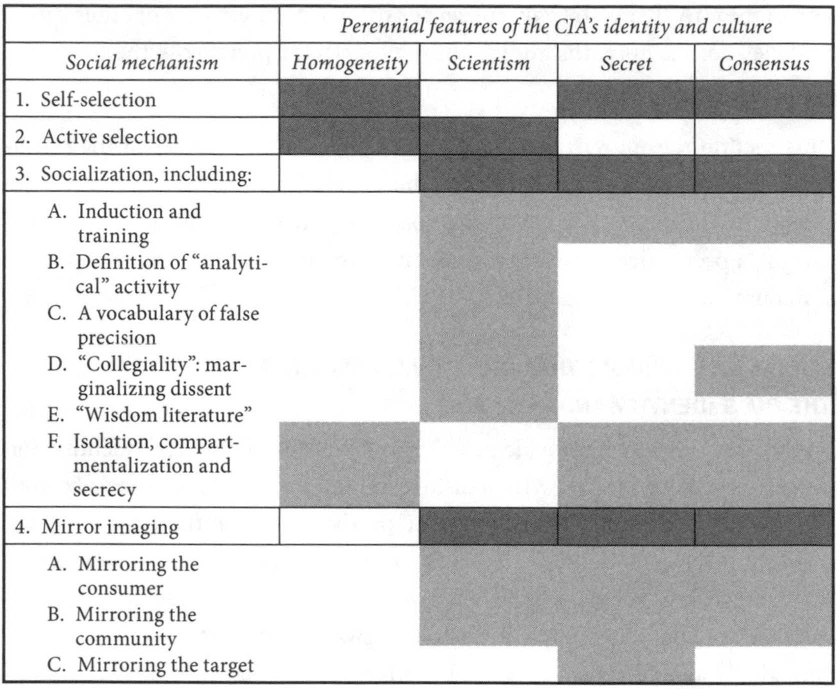

Social mechanism	Perennial features of the CIA's identity and culture			
	Homogeneity	Scientism	Secret	Consensus
1. Self-selection				
2. Active selection				
3. Socialization, including:				

A. Induction and training
   B. Definition of "analytical" activity
   C. A vocabulary of false precision
   D. "Collegiality": marginalizing dissent
   E. "Wisdom literature"
   F. Isolation, compartmentalization and secrecy				

4. Mirror imaging				

A. Mirroring the consumer
   B. Mirroring the community
   C. Mirroring the target				

Figure 2.1. Perennial features of the CIA's identity and culture and the related social mechanisms that create and maintain them.

enters the CIA involuntarily or (given the security checks and other procedures described in the following discussion) without knowing it. The identification of the role of this mechanism in the creation and perpetuation of the agency's identity and culture is entirely in keeping with Paul Kowert and Jeffrey Legro's idea that the first question determining group belongingness is not "Do I like these other individuals?" but "Who am I?" Everyone working at the CIA has sought it out, just as others have more or less actively avoided it. This assertion is easy to document. In his memoir *The Craft of Intelligence*, for example, Allen Dulles describes self-selection in his outline of the character traits of the average CIA volunteer in the early 1960s:

> What motivates a man to devote himself to the craft of intelligence? One way to answer the question is to look at some of the people who make up the ranks of American intelligence today and see how they got there . . . What all these men had in common was an awareness of the conflict that exists in the world today, a conviction that the United States is involved in this conflict, that the

peace and well-being of the world are endangered, and that it is worth trying to do something about these things.[51]

Clearly, all of these men consciously "self-selected." Similarly, in 1999 Stafford Thomas said in his study on the CIA's bureaucratic dimensions that "commitment to national loyalty," "public service," and "self-sacrifice"[52] motivate the CIA's applicants and that these traits were reflected in CIA application forms.

While consistent with U.S. government practice, a self-selecting, openly conducted recruitment of personnel to work at the CIA is not the only logical or practical possibility.[53] Indeed, it is in sharp contrast to the Soviet/Russian intelligence agencies' methods throughout the period in question. Vladimir Putin, for example, recounts that when he originally approached the KGB[54] about working for them, he was told, "We don't take people who come to us on their own initiative." Only after seven years did the KGB then approach *him* about working there.[55] The apogee (nadir?) of this approach was taken by Soviet Military Intelligence, the GRU,[56] in which a defector recounted in 1985 that "any volunteer would be arrested at once and subjected to a long and very painful interrogation."[57]

This contrast throws into relief another form of self-selection that the Soviet Union and the CIA's other adversaries also did not contend against: Most talents useful in intelligence work command a higher monetary premium elsewhere in American society. The result is that, though some people self-select for intelligence work, others do the opposite for reasons transcending simple ideology. This competition has qualitative effects. As Bruce Berkowitz and Allan Goodman point out,

> George Soros has earned billions of dollars through his ability to analyze exchange rates a half step ahead of the rest of the world. Do we really expect a civil servant in the bowels of the intelligence bureaucracy to do better, and if so, why is he or she working for the government? Can the US government attract the caliber of analyst that one finds at Goldman Sachs, Credit Suisse/First Boston, Merrill Lynch, or any other investment firms?[58]

Especially after the Cold War ended, they add, it took a certain type of person to choose to labor as a "civil servant in the bowels of the intelligence bureaucracy" as an intelligence analyst rather than in a well-paid private sector job.[59] The self-selection, both positive and negative, that occurred in the talent pool from which American intelligence draws very much mirrors U.S. society (as did the reverse approach taken by Soviet intelligence agencies). It also ensured, however, that people with a certain *Weltanschauung* and not others were the raw material from which the culture and identity of the Directorate of Intelligence was constructed. Clearly, this powerful social mechanism shaped the identity and culture of the CIA from 1947 to 2001.

Active Selection of Personnel

The next social mechanism that operates to form the identity and culture of the CIA is the active selection process, and it too exerts powerful pressures; it is a variation on fairly standard "in-group/out-group differentiation"[60] mechanisms for creating norms, cultures, and group identities. To understand this mechanism, one must picture the distinctive aspects of CIA recruitment. As Rob Johnston describes,

> Potential CIA analysts must submit to a thorough background investigation, a polygraph examination, and financial and credit reviews. Further, a battery of psychological and medical exams must be passed prior to a formal employment offer. The timeframe for the background check eliminates the possibility of a rapid hiring decision.

Johnston then writes, "Even more important are the nonverbal messages sent to the recruit that this is a position of secrecy and high importance."[61] CIA acculturation begins immediately, even before a final offer is made.

The distinctive aspects of the CIA selection process are a significant contributor to Langley's identity and culture, and many other agencies in the U.S. Intelligence Community share them. Two other distinctive factors shape active selection at the CIA, however. Both of these features have dramatically affected the agency over time: the class composition of the CIA's early members and the CIA's peculiar approach to émigrés.

The CIA's "social tone" (and thus one input in its selection process) was set early on: From 1940s to at least the late 1960s it disproportionably favored white Anglo-Saxon Protestant (WASP) East Coast "establishment types" (given the immense—but still largely unacknowledged—covert role of British intelligence in establishing several of the CIA's predecessors,[62] this is hardly surprising).

CIA employees who worked in counterintelligence at the FBI in the 1960s, for example, found the general atmosphere of the former was "tonier." The man who unmasked KGB agent "Kim" Philby found that, in comparison to the FBI, by joining the CIA he was stepping into "an organization of academics and Wall Street attorneys. Many of the men he met were heirs to considerable family fortunes . . . [the FBI man felt that he] was crossing the tracks, joining the establishment."[63]

Robert Gates recounts how he perceived this aspect of the agency's culture and identity when he joined the CIA in 1969. Gates, aware of the caricature of the CIA as a "conservative" institution, stresses in his memoir that the CIA that he joined in the 1970s was not a "conservative, Cold War monolith." During the Vietnam War, for example, he remembers that "not only was antiwar sentiment strong at the Agency, we were also influenced by the counterculture . . . Antiwar and anti-Nixon posters and bumper stickers festooned CIA office walls." Tellingly, Gates goes on to say that during Director William Casey's tenure in the Reagan administration:

> More and more, the recruitment process for the clandestine service had led to new officers who looked very much like the people who recruited them—white, mostly Anglo-Saxon; middle and upper class; liberal arts college graduates; mostly entering in their mid to late twenties; engaging hail fellows well-met. Few non-Caucasians, few women. Few ethnics, even of recent European background. In other words, not even as much diversity as there was among those who had helped create the CIA . . . in the late 1940s . . . By 1981, the [DO] had become a closed circle, and a bureaucratic one at that. No one who failed to fit the mold could get in.[64]

Gates is clearly discussing a social process resulting in homogeneity, at least among CIA collectors of human intelligence. Moreover (as discussed with the cultural features that result from these mechanisms), according to one recent article, at the CIA in 2001 one still found a "systematic distrust of people who do not fit preconceived notions of patriotic Americans. From its inception, the Intelligence Community [has been] staffed by the white male Protestant elite, not only because that was the class in power, but because that elite saw itself as the guarantor and protector of American values and ethics."[65]

Too much can be made of the tonier aspects of the CIA. According to Dino Brugioni, for example, who was a senior official at the CIA's National Photographic Interpretation Center, under DCI John McCone (in charge of the agency during the Cuban Missile Crisis), the Eastern establishment feel of the agency was salted with technocrats who fell outside this profile. He says, "New men, with family names unfamiliar to the Eastern establishment, began to move into positions of prominence in the Agency. They were experts in such disciplines as optics, electronics, chemistry, physics, engineering and photography."[66] What is noteworthy about his comment, however, is that it is clear that the "new men" represented a change great enough to be noticed and commented on and also that the technocrats described would reinforce other cultural tendencies that we find in the following discussion.

Still, Callum's phrase a "systematic distrust of people who do not fit pre-conceived notions of patriotic Americans" leads directly to the second distinctive factor shaping active selection of CIA personnel: the systematic exclusion of émigrés. The overt reasons given for their exclusion from the Community were security concerns, and this approach to émigrés continued at full tilt at least through the controversial tenure of James Jesus Angleton as chief of counterintelligence (that is, from 1954 to 1974). As one sympathetic scholar observes, "Angleton recognized that the KGB had vast resources to devote to the narrow task of penetration, and the opportunities for gaining that advantage were limited and easily countered: avoid employing personnel with a Russian background or those vulnerable to an appeal to patriotism; never underestimate the call of Mother Russia."[67] We will see, however, that this fine-meshed counterintelligence filter on recruitment has immeasurably contributed to the homogeneity of personnel—a trait of the agency's identity and culture that is bound up with the erroneous threat assessments that result in strategic surprises (and—importantly—not only with respect to the USSR).

A second, more subtle, reason for the exclusion of émigrés, particularly after the shift in the national mood with respect to communist infiltrators in government after the mid-1960s, was that many émigrés were bitter about aspects of the system that they had fled. Their attitude is understandable, but because the CIA was always striving to forge a scientific approach to analysis (documented in the following discussion), émigrés were considered "too ideological/not objective enough" to be suited to the "dispassionate" business of the CIA analyst.[68]

We see, then, that processes of active selection at CIA can be described collectively as a mechanism in which the various apparatuses of security (security checks, polygraphs, and the like) are paramount but that also included some class elements that had their genesis in the CIA's social origins in U.S. society. Some elements of these processes were independent of security concerns. Others, particularly the exclusion of émigrés, reinforced them. Like the other social mechanisms discussed in this section, active selection reveals how the CIA's identity and culture were created and maintained. This finding is entirely in keeping with the well-documented "in-group/out-group differentiation" mechanism previously mentioned for creating norms, cultures, and group identities.

Socialization

Induction and Training. Just as with workers in any other trade, once the Directorate of Intelligence recruits analysts into the CIA, they are socialized into their work place, thus beginning the process of the "social diffusion"[69] of norm creation. One might expect the first aspect of this socialization process would be formal training—certainly, there is an extensive training program for officers in the DO. It is also clear that intelligence analysts think of themselves as professionals. The social mechanism described by "induction and training," however, does not reflect this ideal.

Contrary to commonly held beliefs of how one becomes a professional, for over sixty years there was no systematic new analysts' training program at the CIA. Former analyst Stephen Marrin quotes Jeffrey Cooper about this unprofessional phenomenon as follows:

> Intelligence remains a "craft culture" operating within a guild and apprenticeship system—in fact, self-consciously referring to "tradecraft" for example. Such a culture builds pragmatically on accreted practices that were successful in the past, lacks the strong formal epistemology of a true discipline, and is reliant on implicit transmission of often-tacit expertise and domain knowledge to novices.[70]

Speaking of the 1970s—but bemoaning the same problem in the present—Agrell makes a similar point, saying intelligence analysis then was "a kind of semi-profession, resembling an early form of organized skills like a medieval guild. Here the secrets of the craft were transferred from master to apprentice through a process of initiation and sharing of silent knowledge. The craft was not developed but reproduced; its knowledge was static and the process cyclic."[71] Cooper concurs, calling training at the Directorate of Intelligence a "guild system" (and adding that as of 2005, the system for producing apprentices was "broken").[72] In support of these broad assertions, until the year 2000, there was no formal, comprehensive beginner's analytical training course at the CIA.

Tying back to the previous social mechanism described—active selection—a uniform human resources process for hiring analysts has also never existed:

> Most analysts were hired by the individual Directorate of Intelligence offices, assigned to "groups" which cover specific geographic areas, and then assigned a functional specialty . . . such as political, military, economic, leadership, scientific, technical and weapons intelligence.[73]

As an author with personal experience noted in a 2002 paper, "In fact, CIA analysts have been hired and assigned a desk at CIA headquarters without any analytic training whatsoever, with two or four weeks of analytic training coming six months or so later."[74] Another community insider, former staff director of the House Permanent Select Committee on Intelligence Mark Lowenthal, put it this way: "[The CIA does not] do a lot of training . . . They say, 'Congratulations, you're the Mali analyst, have a nice day.'"[75] In fact:

> The training process usually relied upon the analyst's prior formal education combined with an initial period of sink-or-swim adaptation to the DI. The sink-or-swim analogy is used frequently inside the CIA to describe its junior analyst acculturation. In May 2001, the Kent School's former dean likened previous DI training to being thrown into the deep end of a pool, and added that if the training or mentoring "missed," the analyst "floundered."[76]

This passage raises an important point: Informal induction and training are no less powerful influences shaping the culture and identity at CIA than a formal training program would be. As the sociologist Pierre Bourdieu famously summarized, when it comes to culture, "What goes without saying, comes without saying," and purely on-the-job training for analysts—no matter how good their starting qualifications—by their CIA colleagues and superiors is likely to usher in and sustain a large number of unexamined social practices, analytical methodologies and cultural norms. As we see in Chapter 3's exploration of the strategic surprise of the collapse of the shah of Iran's regime, at least one eminent scholar has concluded that a "conscious epistemology would have helped analysts and their consumers understand the implications of developmentalism and dependency on forecasting political change."[77] Such epistemological awareness certainly does not form in the informal approach to "training" described.

The "craft culture" operating within a "guild and apprenticeship system" continued throughout analysts' careers throughout most of the period in question: Only in 2000 was an analysts' training school established and a career track for a "Senior Analytic Service to promote in-depth work on multifaceted issues" implemented.[78] Some piecemeal formal training—some undoubtedly of high quality—also took place at the agency. From 1986 to 2002, for example, senior members of the Intelligence Community (from both the CIA and other agencies) attended an executive program run by Harvard's John F. Kennedy School of Government, which ran once or twice a year for one to three weeks. However, because these courses were "in-house" (that is, closed to community outsiders) and because the average attendee typically had twelve to twenty years of experience before attending,[79] it seems unlikely that such training would be a "transformative experience" for analytical methods employed by, not to mention the identity and culture of, the CIA.

The Definition of the Intelligence Activity.   Having dealt with two basic, even prosaic, aspects of identity formation among intelligence analysts (self- and active selection), and the initial phases of socialization (induction and training), it is time to dig deeper and unearth a factor at the CIA that initially seems esoteric: the term *intelligence analyst* itself and some of the accompanying vocabulary that analysts encounter from their first days at Langley. The very name of the role—*analyst*—and the word used to describe their core activity—*analysis*—must obviously lie at the core of the identity of CIA intelligence workers. Analysis is also a separate step in the intelligence cycle (described fully in Chapter 1).

Unfortunately, the term also provides evidence for a privileging of reductionist thinking: Both words have their root in the Greek *Analyein*, "to break up." As CIA Asia affairs analyst Josh Kerbel says in a 2004 journal article, "Although reductionism is usually associated with Newton, who, in effect, codified it in his laws of motion, the term is rooted in Greek philosophy and Aristotle, who emphasized 'illumination through disaggregation.'"[80] As the same article points out, however, while such an approach works well for linear problems (in which a system's behavior is the sum of its discrete parts; for example, the motion of a planet), it does *not* work well for systems that are not "genuinely reducible," systems that do not change or adapt their fundamental behavior as interaction occurs between their component parts (for example, human societies). As with the problem of self-selection, however, other approaches are possible. Kerbel continues:

> It is worth noting that Chinese thought—at least that thought freed of Marxist-Leninist ideology—appears significantly less inclined toward reductionism than most Western intellectual approaches. This, in turn, points to contrasting

US and Chinese approaches to foreign policy. Henry Kissinger has written that "Americans think in terms of concrete solutions to specific problems. The Chinese think in terms of a process that has no precise culmination.[81]

Kerbel concludes that for studying the real world (which, as a nonlinear system is "not rocket science; it's more complex") the CIA needs intelligence "synthesists" in addition to analysts, and suggests that "a good symbolic starting point for CIA might be modification of the Kent School's name to read: The Sherman Kent School for Intelligence Analysis and Synthesis."[82] Indeed, as we argue in Chapters 3 and 4, when the strategic surprise in question is a mystery (that is, a contingent event like the fall of the shah of Iran or the implosion of the Soviet Union), it is exactly this lack of synthesis—and the underlying scientism that the term *analyst* implies—that is partly to blame for a fundamental misapprehension of some analytical problems. Thus, the very name of a core part of the intelligence cycle—analysis—and title analysts constitute both a symptom and a cause among many of the key attributes of the agency's identity and culture.

The Vocabulary of False Precision.   As Peter Katzenstein notes in *The Culture of National Security*, norms can emerge in a culture from the process of communication itself: Norms can simply evolve through communication, and they can also emerge because certain communication practices are consciously promoted.[83] At the CIA, an excellent example of this phenomenon is the special vocabulary that members of the Directorate of Intelligence employ in the course of their "tradecraft" (a term coined by Dulles). It is a set of promoted norms that further reinforces a mind-set constantly driving for Newtonian certainty and reducibility. Sherman Kent originally set this norm in motion at the CIA. In his essay, "Words of Estimative Probability" (originally published in the Fall 1964 issue of *Studies in Intelligence*), Kent admits a number of tries at making the language of CIA assessments more "scientific and exact":

> We began to think in terms of a chart that would show the mathematical odds equivalent to words and phrases of probability. Our starter was a pretty complicated affair. We approached its construction from the wrong end. Namely, we began with 11 words or phrases that seemed to convey a feeling of 11 different orders of probability and then attached numerical odds to them.[84]

Admitting failure with this complex "Swiss watch" approach, Kent then describes a revised chart "set down in its classical simplicity." Thus, a 93 percent likelihood (give or take about 6 percent) would translate into "almost certain," a 75 percent likelihood (give or take about 12 percent) would translate into "probable," and a 50 percent likelihood (give or take about 10 percent) would translate into "chances about even."

While Kent admits in this article that "I [later] dropped all thought of getting an agreed airtight vocabulary of estimative expressions, let alone reproducing the chart in the rear of every NIE," nevertheless, "I did continue harassing actions and in the course of making a nuisance of myself to associates and colleagues did pick up some useful converts." And what is the problem of gaining acceptance for such linguistic laws? "What slowed me up in the first instance was the firm and reasoned resistance of some of my colleagues. Quite figuratively I am going to call them the 'poets'—as opposed to the 'mathematicians'—in my circle of associates." Kent then adds, "If the term conveys a modicum of disapprobation on my part, that is what I want it to do."[85] (Without running too far ahead of the overall argument of this book, we can wryly note here that Osama bin Ladin frequently addressed his threats to the United States quite literally in poetic verse: It is not too much of a stretch to conclude that the intellectual DNA of the CIA might make it more likely to puzzle over—or ignore—such a figure).

It is clear in the following pages that Kent's "physics envy" and drive for "precision" in language—in which one can detect a strong denial of the distinction between social and natural facts—left a powerful legacy in the CIA's analytical community, the consequences of which are found among the key persistent features of identity and culture.[86]

"Collegiality," "Coordination," and the Marginalization of Dissent. Any discussion of high-level policy-making should address the question of the degree and role of "collegiality" in day-to-day operations. In the late 1920s, the sociologist Max Weber introduced the idea that rationally specialized functional collegiality was a necessary counterweight to nineteenth-century hierarchal bureaucracies when "well-considered decisions" were more important than "quick and consistent" decisions.[87]

Given the CIA's mission to coordinate "all source intelligence" (that is, HUMINT, SIGINT, MASINT, IMINT)[88] gathered by the myriad agencies that make up the community, a certain degree of collegiality with respect to other agencies is indeed indispensable. For that reason, the CIA has always sought to foster and to project collegiality as a part of its culture and identity. DCI Robert Gates, for example, describes a 1980s "cadre of analysts accustomed to 'gentlemanly discourse'"[89] that DCI Casey's blunt Wall Street–style questions sometimes transgressed. Further evidence of an outward atmosphere of collegiality and an ostensive openness to "polite dissent" is evident from the earliest period of the CIA's existence in a Kent article describing the purpose of the agency's in-house journal, *Studies in Intelligence*. This literature's role as a socializing mechanism is dealt with later in this chapter, but here the reader should note that in 1955, in the inaugural essay describing the intent of the journal, the "Father of Analysis" wrote:

> The literature I have in mind will, among other things, be an *elevated debate*. For example, I see a Major X write an essay on the theory of indicators and print it and have it circulated. I see a Mr. B brood over this essay and write a review of it. I see a Commander C reading both the preceding documents and reviewing them both. I then see a revitalized discussion among the people of the indicator business.[90]

Kent seems here to be recalling his (somewhat idealized?) past in the history department at Yale. There is powerful evidence, though, to conclude that this "elevated debate" has always been more an aspiration than a reality at the agency. It is certainly specious to say that dissent is encouraged at the CIA in the way it is in academia.[91] Evidence to support this conclusion is easy to discover. Collegiality is defined, after all, as "shared power and authority vested among colleagues" (Houghton-Mifflin's *American Heritage Dictionary*). In Petersen's description of the CIA review process noted above, equality is not in evidence. He writes:

> The third-level review should be done by the *office director or the staff of a senior officer* in the organization. *On a particularly sensitive piece, both may weigh in* . . . does the piece address policymaker concerns? . . . is it consistent with other work being done in the organization? . . . The third-level reviewer should focus most on *whether the right questions have been asked* and what the key variables are.[92]

Here, the review process could easily be used as a socialization mechanism for the censorship of ideas, despite a veneer of collegiality. The phrase *the right questions* has multiple meanings. It can refer to the logical structure of an argument, but it can also imply that "appropriate" and "inappropriate" information is passing through a social filter.

There are other mechanisms for filtering ideas beneath a collegial veneer. Kent describes how once a document had been through review, the primary mechanism for registering dissent in NIEs was the footnote. NIEs are important pieces of evidence in the cases we studied, so let us examine briefly Kent's short memoir-style essay, "Law and Custom of the National Intelligence Estimate: An Examination of the Theory and Some Recollections Concerning the Practice of the Art." The title, of course (that is, "Law and Custom"), points to a distinct internal culture. Even more revealing is the CIA phenomenon known as "taking a footnote" that Kent discusses at some length. He says:

> At least two other limitations on the rights of the dissenter became accepted. One was that he did not have the license to point out in a footnote that he had once been forced to dissent on behalf of a viewpoint which had since gained currency within the community. The "I told you so" and "if you'd only listened to me" motifs were rather strongly discouraged as footnote material. Just as strongly discouraged were footnote formulations which impugned the sanity and morals of those who held to the text. I recall Mr. Dulles once explaining his objection with: "If you write a footnote such as you propose, I will have to write a footnote to your footnote, indicating that your allegations are wrong. You may then wish to do a footnote to my footnote, then I to yours, and so on. I suggest that we put a stop to such a piece of business before it gets started."[93]

This passage's implications of a less than collegial discourse are highlighted by the knowledge that, in 1961, a change was introduced to include the name of the official requesting the footnote in the footnote itself. As Berkowitz and Goodman dryly note: "This change may have been intended to increase the [personal and institutional] costs of dissenting."[94] In other words, footnotes in CIA documents are at least partly a mechanism of controlling and channeling dissent.

The somewhat arcane practice of controlling dissent through footnoting remained so pervasive that in their attempt to update Sherman Kent's 1949 classic *Strategic Intelligence for American World Policy*, Berkowitz and Goodman's 1989 *Strategic Intelligence for American National Security* has an extended discussion—ironically, mostly in a footnote—of what they call the Intelligence Community's "game of footnotes." To begin with, they record the obvious: "It was more difficult to develop [a dissenting] argument in a footnote than in the main text. Also, the implication of this format was that the main text was 'the authoritative view' and should be given more credence than the footnote, which was apparently 'the alternative view.'"

They further describe how the system was changed under DCI Turner (1977–1981), when dissenters were allowed to elaborate their disagreements in the main text, and footnotes were used "primarily for identifying which members of the Intelligence Community subscribed to a given portion of the text." As a result, "Upon receiving a new NIE, readers would often skim through it to see where the footnotes appeared . . . they knew that footnotes indicated which issues were more controversial. As a result, the footnoted sections of the NIEs—and possibly even the footnotes themselves—often received more attention than the rest of the estimate."[95] Apart from "elevated debate" or their usual functions in scholarship, at the CIA footnotes without a doubt have a role in channeling and controlling debate.

On the level of individual CIA analysts, though, the tension between opinions and "collegiality" seems much the same. To cite one example, in a landmark 1982 speech to analysts, soon after assuming the post of DCI, Robert Gates said that he wanted analytical "voices crying in the wilderness" and invited dissenting analysts' views to be sent to him. The ground rules for this practice would not encourage the errant analyst, however: Gates added that such views had to be sent through office directors (that is, the analysts' superiors) and should not be used for "trivial disputes." He further stipulated that there was "no excuse for breaching discipline and carrying complaints to outside audiences . . ."[96] Not surprisingly, instead of a warrant for analytical sedition and a clarion call for genuinely collegial dissension, Gates's speech was widely seen as muzzling analytical dissent.

Abundant evidence that this drive for consensus under cover of a "collegial" atmosphere is a perdurable problem at the CIA can also be found in the descriptions of the review process offered in the first section of this chapter. It is further indicated in the treatment the review process receives in one of the most widely cited volumes on improving intelligence analysis, the 1999 volume *The Psychology of Intelligence Analysis*:

> The realities of bureaucratic life produce strong pressures for conformity. Management needs to make a conscious effort to ensure that well-reasoned competing views have the opportunity to surface within the Intelligence Community. Analysts need to enjoy a sense of security, so that partially developed new ideas may be expressed and bounced off others as sounding boards with minimal fear of criticism for deviating from established orthodoxy.[97]

Moreover, in a 1991 resignation letter later made public, John A. Gentry, a twelve-year agency veteran, accused the CIA's Directorate of Intelligence of cooking the books to please superiors, in particular claiming that, at the CIA, "satisfaction of bureaucratic superiors is more important than superior analysis."[98] Gentry even claimed that "DI managers asked the psychiatrists of the OMS, and the Office of Security, to evaluate individuals who had differences with their managers over analytic substance or the slanting of analysis."[99]

In short, despite a veneer of collegiality, both structural and psychological factors have for decades combined to create a ferocious social mechanism to winnow out or marginalize dissent in intelligence analysis at the CIA. As one prescient 1957 article in *Studies* puts it, "Being in favor of coordination [that is, analytical consensus] in the US Intelligence Community has come to be like being against sin; everyone lines up on the right side of the question,"[100] but the end results do not accord with the stated description of a truly collegial environment (at least not insofar as it implies "shared power and authority vested among colleagues").

Analytical "Wisdom Literature" and an Academic Cargo Cult.   Despite the social mechanisms described thus far, there are superficial resemblances between the identity and culture a CIA analyst experiences and that of an academic community (despite the obvious fact that open dissent is an integral part of academic entrepreneurship above the undergraduate level). After all, DCI Allen Dulles moved the agency several miles outside Washington, D.C., to Langley, Virginia, to a sylvan facility that is still called the CIA's "campus." As we have seen, like any good academic community, the agency also has a journal, *Studies in Intelligence*. On closer inspection, one can argue that this journal is yet another social mechanism that perpetuates an identity and culture of the analytical arm of the CIA that is at odds with a real academic community. Instead—as is developed in the following discussion—these qualities contribute to the exact opposite: a culture in which empty academic forms encourage collective self-deception about the free flow of ideas.[101] We can see this first by returning to the inaugural issue in *Studies in Intelligence* and the essay called "The Need for an Intelligence Literature." Kent wrote:

> What [intelligence] lacks is a literature. From my point of view this is a matter of greatest importance. As long as this discipline lacks a literature, its method, its vocabulary, its body of doctrine, and even its fundamental theory run the risk of never reaching full maturity. I will not say that you cannot have a

discipline without a literature, but I will assert that you are unlikely to have a robust and growing discipline without one.[102]

So far, so good, with respect to advancing an epistemic community characterized by free inquiry. Indeed, in fairness to Kent (and to the hundreds of intelligence professionals who have contributed to *Studies* since), a large part of this foundation document is solid, liberal-tradition academic common sense. Since 1955, *Studies in Intelligence* has published more than 1,200 classified and unclassified articles by members of the Intelligence Community about a myriad of aspects of their craft.[103] The tone and form of most of these articles is as graceful as one could expect from any academic institution in the world.

But if one steps back and considers the whole of *Studies* rather than individual articles, the journal begins to reveal evidence—even at its genesis—that it is at least partly CIA "wisdom literature": a vehicle for a tightly bounded discussion rather than a forum for debate. There have been honorable exceptions to this generalization, but a stable pattern can still be discerned. As early as 1964, an article appeared that appeared to imply this: "Styles and Stereotypes in Intelligence Studies." It observed, "A uniform style adopted by all producing agencies and for almost all types of intelligence production has been perfected to a degree which may have reached the point of being self-defeating." The article speaks of the existence of an "invisible elite phrasebook," "editorial compulsion," and the favoring of "the elegant cliché" instead of attempt to take in a messy or indistinct reality.[104]

In the preceding discussion of collegiality, for example, we have Kent's exhortation for an "elevated debate" and for some members of the Community to "brood"; this was to lead to a "revitalized discussion among the people of the indicator business." What is revealing, however, is how that same paragraph continues:

> I hope that they now, more than ever before, discuss indicators *within the terms of a common conceptual frame and in a common vocabulary*. From the debate in the literature and from the oral discussion, I see another man coming forward to produce an original synthesis of all that has gone before. His summary findings will be a kind of intellectual platform upon which the new debate can start. *His platform will be a thing of orderly and functional construction* and it will stand above the bushes and trees that once obscured the view.

It will be solid enough to have much more built upon it and durable enough *so that no one need get back in the bushes and earth to examine its foundations.*[105]

In other words, Kent conceived of dissent within the CIA and this journal instrumentally, something that is necessary to lay the foundation for a *progressive science* or a *cumulative discipline.* An examination of hundreds of declassified articles—many fascinating, most earnest, and a few downright jocular (including even some doggerel)—from this journal both online and in a bound collection[106] produces little evidence that *Studies in Intelligence,* this "thing of orderly and functional construction," ever moved beyond this essentially positivist, instrumental approach to dissent. New methodologies are suggested, but positivism itself is not explicitly questioned or approached problematically. Throughout the scope of this book (and beyond), no articles in *Studies* get "back in the bushes and earth to examine" the epistemological and ontological assumptions underpinning of the "Sherman Kent School" of intelligence analysis (that is, 1950s positivism).[107] We see in numerous examples in the following paragraphs that the contrary is true—*Studies* is a vehicle to perpetuate Kent's approach. Moreover, in subtle ways, it discourages other approaches (for example, through the topics consider worthy of publication; the vocabulary employed to address issues). A single official journal, no matter how academic its form, will usually reinforce, not challenge, an intellectual monopoly.

Even worse, *Studies* may contribute to a "cargo cult" academic atmosphere on the CIA's "campus" in which the external form of academic convention masks a different reality.[108] Jeffrey Cooper certainly thinks so, saying baldly in his summary of the situation in 2005:

> The Intelligence Community presently lacks many of the scientific community's self-correcting features. Among the most significant of these features are the creative tension between "evidence-based" experimentalists and hypothesis-based theoreticians, a strong tradition of "investigator-initiated" research, real "horizontal" peer review, and "proof" by independent replication. Moreover, neither the community as a whole nor its individual analysts usually possess the ingrained habits of systematic self-examination, including conducting "after action reviews" as part of a continual lessons-learned process, necessary to appreciate the changes required to fix existing problems or to address new challenges.[109]

Nevertheless, each year, the CIA presents the Sherman Kent Award for "the most significant contribution to the literature of intelligence submitted to *Studies*." According to *Studies* itself, the award is "the Oscar of intelligence literature."[110]

Isolation, Compartmentalization, and Secrecy.   The inherent impossibility of peer review of *Studies in Intelligence* introduces another social mechanism at work at the CIA, the final one under the heading "socialization": the "compartmentalization" of information, the isolation of intelligence analysts from their social science peers (from other branches of government, and from each other), and the security mechanisms that surround intelligence work.

Johnston, in the previous subsection, defined intelligence analysis as "the application of individual and collective cognitive methods to weigh data and test hypotheses *within a secret socio-cultural context*." This section makes clear that this "secret socio-cultural context" introduces several powerful social mechanisms (overt ones like classification and compartmentalization but also an overarching culture pervaded by concern for secrecy) that can be tied to key features of the CIA's identity and culture. We discover that, as Thomas Powers says in his book on Richard Helms, "CIA people are cynical in most ways, but their belief in secrets is almost metaphysical."[111]

That the CIA has mechanisms for security is obvious—they are part of the tradecraft of intelligence work. As most people know, background checks and security investigations grant CIA employees access to "classified" information. Less well known is that there are subdistinctions beyond "classified," "secret," and "top secret," such as "cosmic," "NOFORN," and "SCI,"[112] each mandating how information must be handled. Many documents have different classifications within them (that is, they classify paragraph by paragraph; a "top secret" paragraph might be followed by a merely "confidential" one, and so on).[113] In the 9/11 case following, for example, we have access only to the executive summary of the agency's Inspector General's Report on CIA accountability for the attacks—the rest of the report remains classified.

In other words, because there is a perceived need for the vast majority of what the CIA does to remain opaque, information is not merely classified but compartmentalized[114] to protect "sources and methods" (that is, the specifics of how information is obtained such as the identity of agents or the exact capabilities of surveillance systems). Compartmentalization—the mandatory prohibition against information sharing on anything but a need to know basis—is one of the factors that make it difficult to connect the dots in intelligence work. An analyst working on economic growth in the Soviet Union, for example, could not expect to have routine access to information concerning the political leanings of the military officers of a particular country in South America, even if both analysts had a clearance of "top secret": The presumption is always against a need to know the details (or even the subject) of anyone else's work.

The informational costs of compartmentalization policies are obvious, and their role in specific strategic surprises is well recognized. What is less explored is the self-imposed social and psychological isolation that arguably go hand-in-hand with these security measures. It seems that because information cannot flow *out* of the CIA it also does not flow *in* as efficiently as it does in other environments.

Robert Gates recalls, for example, that Director Casey (an alumnus of the Research Institute of America, author of several books on tax law and one on the American Revolution, and an amateur historian) "was enormously impatient and frustrated with the career analysts' unwillingness to follow his lead in aggressively looking beyond the walls of CIA for new information and insights, in being willing to question their own assumptions and always challenging conventional wisdom."[115]

Casey's view is backed up by recent efforts to help the various information technology (IT) systems in the Intelligence Community work together and share data. John Grimes noted as late as 2006 that, although technological barriers to sharing intelligence were real, "cultural barriers" in and among the U.S. Intelligence Community "still remain the leading obstacle to communication between US Intelligence agencies."[116] CIA cultural barriers certainly appear in the 9/11 case study that follows. We see, for example, that in the 1990s DO officers assigned to work on terrorism requested additional safes and security procedures to keep their information away from the DI analysts working alongside them, despite the fact that these analysts had the same clearances that they did *and* despite the fact that their unit was started precisely to foster information sharing![117] Graham Allison and Philip Zelikow had phenomena like this in mind when they wrote, "Operational experiences in the field reinforce certain capacities and routines, even endow capacities and routines with a ceremonial power that provides legitimacy internally or in dealings with the outside world."[118]

Advocates of so-called open source Intelligence (OSINT) at the CIA make a similar point. To be sure, open source intelligence has long played a role in the analysis performed by the CIA.[119] Nevertheless, there is abundant anecdotal evidence that within the CIA there are social mechanisms that lead analysts to prefer secret information and to slight or ignore openly obtained information. As early as 1979, Daniel Graham essentially said that open literature was "too often regarded as soft data" and therefore "largely ignored" in assessments of the USSR.[120] The conflating of openly available data with "soft data" looms large in the four case studies that follow. A respected private intelligence service staffed by many former CIA personnel referred to the agency's open source efforts as historically "small and dysfunctional"[121] and contrasted it unfavorably with the Chinese approach. The operative assumption at the CIA is that "if information is worth knowing, why isn't it secret?"; arguably, such an attitude is fostered by an environment of pervasive secrecy and compartmentalization.[122]

This social mechanism even appears to separate the CIA from the highest levels of their intelligence "consumers" in Washington, and it fosters a sense of isolation. Former DCI Gates, speaking of the 1970s, relates:

> I realized quickly that CIA knew how foreign policy was made in every country in the world except one—our own. Analysts and their supervisors were oblivious to how information reached the President. They had no idea of the sequence of events preceding a visit by a foreign leader or a Presidential trip abroad, or even the agenda of issues the President and his senior advisers would be working on during a given week. In short, the distance from CIA's headquarters at Langley to the White House was vastly greater than the drive down the Washington Parkway.[123]

The final word on the social mechanism of compartmentalization, secrecy, and isolation, however, should go to Berkowitz and Goodman, both intelligence veterans. In a vivid passage in *Best Truth* (that also ties in to the mechanism of active selection, discussed earlier), they say:

> It is difficult for an outsider to appreciate just how thoroughly secrecy shapes the intelligence culture. For example, in the military, the first experience a new marine recruit enjoys is learning how to take orders, usually through the gentle prodding of a Drill Instructor. In contrast, the first experience a person has in an intelligence career is filling out a form for a security clearance—that

is, the process by which the Intelligence Community decides whether to share secrets with him or her. The clearance process is an experience all intelligence professionals share, just as all marines share the experience of boot camp. Once on the job, one of the first appointments a newly minted intelligence officer has on his or her schedule is to attend a briefing on security procedures—that is, to learn how to handle secrets. At each step in a career, moving to a new assignment usually means being "read into" a program, or learning new secrets . . . [a] culture of secrecy . . . defines an essential part of both how intelligence specialists see themselves and how the rest of society sees the Intelligence Community.[124]

Before closing this discussion, in the interests of fairness it is important to note here that the CIA's isolation and mechanisms of security we have discussed are relative. As individuals CIA analysts live in "normal" communities (unlike, for example, many of their Soviet counterparts during the Cold War, who lived in special compounds or apartment blocks reserved for those in intelligence work). In addition, there are efforts like the CIA "officer in residence" program, in which a small number of CIA employees openly spend two-year tours of U.S. university campuses teaching and speaking. This program, begun in 1985, continues and is deemed a success,[125] but it operates on a small scale (and does not appear to have had much direct impact on helping information flow into, as opposed to out of, the CIA. Although the officers in residence are specifically forbidden to recruit students during their tenure at these schools, great stress is laid on explaining the Intelligence Community to outsiders). Then there is the raw material on which this book is based: Although many articles in *Studies in Intelligence* were originally classified, many have since been declassified, and each quarter a few unclassified articles appear on the CIA's website. There is also scrutiny of CIA activities by Congress, even if the agency is not as open as many legislators and journalists would like.

Overall, despite a secret *internal* culture, in other respects it is clear that the CIA is probably the most open of the world's secret intelligence agencies. That the social mechanisms of security, compartmentalization, and even a degree of isolation are powerful at the CIA, however, is not difficult to document.

A Wilderness of Mirror Imaging

The fourth and final social mechanism that profoundly shapes the identity and culture of the CIA is "mirror imaging." In intelligence literature, mirror imaging is usually defined as either to become like one's targets or "to assume that the other country's leaders think like we do."[126] The phenomenon is widely acknowledged as a common source of analytical failure. In contrast, here mirror imaging refers to the related phenomenon in which the CIA's analysis inadvertently either assumes the characteristics of or makes assumptions about three exogenous groups: the *recipients* of its intelligence (in their parlance, intelligence "consumers" or "customers"), *other agencies* in the U.S. Intelligence Community, and the CIA's *targets*. What concerns us is not only the well-examined mental process of mirror imaging by individual analysts but also the social process of mirror imaging of these groups by the DI. What we want to bring to the foreground is the mechanism that links the "national" security culture[127] of the United States and the culture and identity of the CIA.

"The Customer Is Always Right" (Mirror Imaging the Customer).   Intelligence consumers have exercised direct editorial control over the content of intelligence estimates only in the most exceptional cases.[128] From early in their work, however, analysts are taught that, as individuals and as an organization, the CIA is "customer focused," that is, attuned to and responsive to the needs and desires of the recipients of their intelligence "products." The reasons for this focus are structural and historical. Gates, who served as DCI through five presidential administrations, says, "More than any other government department, the CIA's influence and role are determined by its relationship to the President and the National Security Adviser, a relationship that finds expression almost exclusively in the CIA director's personal relationship with those two individuals."[129] To win Washington's bureaucratic turf wars, the CIA must support and be seen to be trying to support executive branch power.

There is also the burden of consumer expectations: The Intelligence Community's huge budget and legendary technical capabilities feed into demands by consumers. Berkowitz and Goodman state flatly that "providing wisdom—crisp, unambiguous, to-the-point judgments—is part of the culture." But this wisdom spills into something more:

> Presidents expect that, for what they spend on intelligence, the product should be able to predict coups, upheavals, riots, intentions, military moves, and the like with accuracy . . . Presidents and their national security teams usually are ill-informed about intelligence capabilities; therefore, they have unrealistic expectations of what intelligence can do for them, especially when they hear about the genuinely extraordinary capabilities of U.S. intelligence for collecting and processing information.[130]

Obviously, however, allowing responsiveness to these customer demands and expectations to shape the CIA's work excessively is problematic because it assumes no unconscious ignorance on the part of intelligence consumers (despite the refreshing candor of one consumer—a former secretary of state—who reportedly admitted, "I don't know what kind of intelligence I need, but I know when I get it"[131]). Nevertheless, it does not seem that the CIA sets out systematically to disabuse consumers of the expectation that the CIA's intelligence products will cater to their policy interests, approaches, and expectations.

In fact, the reality is quite the opposite. A former director of analysis at the CIA wrote, "Anxious to impress each incoming [US] President with the sophistication of its product, the Intelligence Community [has been] understandably reluctant to emphasize its own limitations."[132] One scholar even contends:

> Intelligence professionals would probably never employ the term, but they often perceive their role as developing "wisdom." It is almost as much a part of the intelligence culture as secrecy. As with most cultural traits, *outsiders often reinforce this trait* by having the same perception . . . Access to secrets, people seem to believe, leads to better knowledge, and that can be interpreted as wisdom.[133]

This passage is interesting not only for the light it throws on mirror imaging of the intelligence customer but also for the linkage it points out between that phenomenon and the mechanisms of secrecy just discussed.

Unlike its traditional counterpart, mirror imaging of the customer by the DI is conscious. The CIA considers it so important that it begins even before the ultimate "consumer"—the president and his team—arrive in the White House. The volume *CIA Briefings of the Presidential Candidates, 1952–1992* (produced in cooperation with the CIA's Center for the Study of Intelligence) details such efforts. In the foreword to this volume, a revealing assertion occurs:

> The most important lesson of this book is that, if the CIA is to provide effective intelligence support to policymakers, there is no substitute for direct access to the President. There is the implied lesson also that, *if Presidents are to make the best use of the CIA, they need to make clear to the Agency at regular intervals what intelligence they do and do not want.*[134]

As we shall see, this tacit assumption of the omniscience by the CIA of intelligence consumers has serious consequences: If no consumer asks the CIA about Islamic fundamentalism in Iran, for example, the agency keeps watching the Soviets.

The mirror imaging of consumers starts early and starts at the top. In a CIA briefing that begins, "This paper is designed to give Governor [soon to be President] Carter an outline of our intelligence system and how it works," the CIA decided, "in light of his success in transforming the fortunes of his ailing family peanut producing and processing firm," to "appeal to Carter's business instincts."[135] To do so, they explained the work of the agency with reference to . . . a peanut factory. Carter had also been a naval officer and governor of a state; the point, however, is not to quibble with the metaphor the CIA employed to explain itself to a president-elect, but to highlight the pervasive "consumer focus" of CIA personnel and work practices.

The customer focus of the CIA continues once a president is installed in the White House. An incident in the early 1990s provides a semicomic example. During a briefing on developments in the highly unstable Soviet Union of the late Gorbachev era, President George H. W. Bush objected to the CIA analysts' "use of the word 'conservative' to describe Soviet hard-liners. He was, he complained, a conservative himself." In response, "the Directorate of Intelligence began to use the word 'traditionalist' instead. George Kolt, the director of SOVA (CIA Office of Soviet Analysis), preferred Leninist; Fritz Ermath . . . of the National Intelligence Council, suggested simply 'bad guys.'"[136] Did such a debate contribute to the quality of analysis of the fast-moving events in the USSR? More important, there is no evidence that these exchanges prompted any organizational introspection by the CIA about the nature of the different factions within Soviet leadership, much less how the USSR was perceived and analyzed by SOVA.

Some might charge that criticism of the CIA's top-level focus is misdirected. Perhaps the phenomenon described in the preceding paragraph is just the reality of sharp bureaucratic practice, the inevitable result of internal power politics, and an increasingly "imperial" presidency. To counter such criticism, what is also needed is evidence that mirror imaging of the customer permeates the agency's identity at all levels, as opposed to simply the presentational styles it uses for presidents. Fortunately, such evidence is abundant.

Take, for example, a section called "Addressing US Interests in DI Assessments," in a 1995 CIA document entitled "Notes on Analytic Tradecraft." The document's self-described purpose is: "This is the first of a series of Product Evaluation Staff notes to clarify the standards used for evaluating DI assessments and to provide tradecraft tips for putting the standards into practice."[137] The first section of this document, "Getting Started," provides five bullet points for CIA analysts to absorb. The first two points are what one would expect—laudable calls to "think of the analyst's role as that of the objective or tough-minded expert for a policymaking team" and to "recognize that research and reporting are inputs or means to an end." The next two bullet points, however, provide clear evidence of intentional mirror imaging of consumers' thinking in CIA analysis. They are worth quoting:

- *Put a face as well as a name on the five to 10 policy officials who are the core customers on a country or functional account.* Analysts should study what these officials have written or said on important substantive issues and debrief policy staffers who work for core consumers, as well as anyone on the intelligence side of the river who knows their professional habits. The goal is to learn how key officials absorb information and reach judgments, as well as their current priority interests.
- *Target the policymakers' specific interest in a substantive issue.* To identify lines of analysis that provide value added, analysts should think through what they would want to know if they were policymakers charged with leveraging an issue.

The final bullet point is also relevant:

- Be aware that consumers' needs may change as the policymaking process evolves.

This is also customer-focused, though difficult to argue with! Still, it is worth pointing out the foundational assumption that intelligence customers will always *know* that their needs have changed. The operative words seem to be the customer's "current priority interests."

Mirroring the customer even affected the choice of methodologies selected by CIA. In a passage that also highlights how the social mechanisms identified are mutually reinforcing, Richards Heuer admits, in *Quantitative Approaches to Political Intelligence: the CIA Experience*:

The ability to portray results of the analysis graphically was one of the strongest arguments for using a quantitative method like Bayes's [theorem used to recalculate probabilities when new information emerges], and the graphs in the publication have been well-received . . . It is just possible that much of the success of the reports is due more to this informative brevity than to the validity of the estimative technique.[138]

As one thirty-five-year British practitioner of intelligence put this view crisply: "Salesmanship is a part of the game,"[139] but the passage just quoted demonstrates that the CIA allows salesmanship to change the methodologies that analysts employ. Similarly, a 1964 *Studies* article about African statistics spends a page debunking Nigerian population statistics, only to conclude, "But we may be required to accept them by our customers."[140] Moreover, in the following USSR case, we will find that because elements of daily life were hard to quantify, the CIA did not meaningfully incorporate them in their analysis of the USSR's economy.

The final manner in which mirror imaging of intelligence consumers manifests itself at the CIA is in intelligence tasking, the first part of the so-called intelligence cycle. The bureaucratic process of formally tasking the CIA has changed over time, but the basic process has remained the same: It begins when CIA "issue coordinators meet with over a hundred . . . high-level consumers."[141]

The problem with such a customer-focused approach to tasking is that usually the biases, blind spots, and preconceptions of intelligence consumers divert collection and analysis resources from other, perhaps more important lines of inquiry. This is especially the case when those consumers are political appointees in an incoming administration. As Osama bin Ladin built his network during the Clinton administration, the CIA asked the National Security Council to rank threats in order to determine how to allocate resources and effort. Terrorism was merely part of Priority Three:[142] They should provide "intelligence about specific trans-national threats to our security, such as weapons proliferation, terrorism, drug trafficking, organized crime, illicit trade practices and environmental issues of great gravity."[143]

After the collapse of the Soviet Union, the Clinton administration was ideologically committed to a new and peaceful world order, so developed-world terrorism (largely enabled by the USSR and its allies) was a low priority. In addition, there was a concern not to offend Muslims (Madeleine Albright said that the administration stayed away from Samuel Huntington's "clash of civilizations" theory). One could therefore make the case that the CIA was mirror-imaging not just its customers, but the zeitgeist of the time. The argument that "we were surprised because everyone else was" is flawed, however. While it is not everyone's mandate to prevent strategic surprise, it is the CIA's. Escaping the zeitgeist of the time when it's needed to anticipate surprise is precisely what the CIA *should* do. The CIA should be the lizard part of America's brain—sensing danger before mere politicians do. It is the chief diplomat's job not to offend people, but it is the CIA's job to give warning.

When the NSC here groups al-Qa'ida alongside gangs illegally trading tropical hardwood, will a CIA analyst steeped in a culture that mirrors the intelligence customer push back? Any intellectual or epistemic problem created by mirror-imaging the consumers, moreover, is compounded by a vast scale and a huge—and presumably not always entirely rational—competition for resources.

Mirroring the Community: Technology and the 800-Pound Gorilla.   Another type of mirror imaging occurs when CIA analysis is shaped by a different exogenous factor: other agencies in the U.S. Intelligence Community. In some sense, the CIA's analysis must reflect the information provided by other U.S. intelligence agencies. That is their mandate, and it is the point of much of the "coordination" (as distinct from "review") discussed in the preceding pages. Like mirroring of the customer, this mechanism links the "national" security culture of the United States as a whole to that of the agency. Here, therefore, what we will underscore is the inadvertent ways that CIA analysis mirrors the rest of the Community. That mirror imaging occurs when the technical capabilities ("what is possible") drives what "should" be done at the CIA.

Despite the attention that Langley receives, the CIA is one of many agencies in the U.S. Intelligence Community. Measured by either number of personnel or budget, it is not the largest—the Pentagon is.[144] Collectively, the Pentagon agencies have been called the 800-pound gorilla of the Intelligence Community;[145] though their budgets are classified, in 1996 the U.S. House of Representatives estimated that the secretary of Defense controls about 85 percent of all U.S. intelligence spending,[146] much of it on technical collection systems. Indeed, since the 1950s the American Intelligence Community has been the most technically advanced in the world. This imbalance arose in part because under President Dwight Eisenhower the United States felt that it was losing the "secret war" against the Soviets, and a report recommended to him that the United States explore "every possible scientific and technical avenue of approach to the intelligence problem."[147] The military was deemed the best organization for this, despite the CIA's success managing the U-2 program.[148]

Political–military culture has been identified as a source of inertia in policy making across many cultures, and the DOD gorilla affects intelligence analysis in several important ways: Berkowitz and Goodman write that it "has greatly shaped the bureaucratic culture of the CIA."[149] Specifically, previous efforts to evaluate U.S. intelligence have found that it is generally overreliant on technical capabilities at the expense of human intelligence. Certainly, this was alleged after the Iranian Revolution. The previous section mentioned a reinforcing factor for this mechanism: The Community's technology has often dazzled consumers, thereby feeding demand for the technical "intelligence" generated, whether it supports better decision making or not.

Nevertheless, a simple "because of an excess of x (technology), then y (another form of intelligence) is neglected" conclusion misses the related social mechanism that has a larger effect in the end: the distortion of tasking (that is, the selection of what pieces of information the CIA *should* gather) that this advanced capability produces. One internal report on tasking, for example, was candid:

> After a year's working on intelligence requirements, we have come to realize that they are not the driving force behind the flow of information. Rather, the real push comes from the collectors themselves—particularly the operations of large, indiscriminating technical collection systems—who use national intelligence requirements to justify what they want to undertake for other reasons, e.g. military readiness, redundancy, technical continuity, and the like.[150]

The *type* of information such systems generate—frequently quantitative—is also shown to reinforce the CIA's "already powerful inclination to count rather than interpret"[151] and looms large in the Iran and USSR case studies.

In short, it is plain that mirror imaging of the Community reinforces the CIA's overreliance on technology, leads to a neglect of human sources for collection, and distorts tasking. We also see how such an overreliance reinforces a more insidious phenomenon: the mistaken belief that quantitative "hard data" obtained by secret technical means are more important than other forms of intelligence. Like the other social mechanisms discussed in this section, this view allows an understanding of how a key part of the CIA's identity and culture are created and maintained.

Mirroring the Target.   The final social mechanism we will examine shaping the identity and culture of the CIA is the mirror imaging of intelligence targets, especially the USSR. As a general phenomenon, mirror imaging of the target is discussed at length by Richards Heuer and in the *Studies in Intelligence* article "Fifteen Axioms for Intelligence Analysts." That article includes the unambiguous dictum: "Avoid mirror-imaging at all costs. Mirror-imaging—projecting your thought process or value system onto someone else—is one of the greatest threats to objective intelligence analysis."[152]

Still, it happened, sometimes at crucial junctures. One famous example occurred when Sherman Kent personally oversaw the agency's report on the likelihood that the Soviets would move missiles into Cuba. As we see in the case study in Chapter 5, even after massive increases in shipments of Soviet military equipment into Cuba were detected, Kent deemed any movement of missiles to be "too provocative" to be "a rational decision."[153] As we shall explore, "rational" depends partly on one's point of view. Nevertheless, Kent defended his analysis in 1964, writing in *Studies* that "no estimating process can be expected to divine exactly when the enemy is about to make a dramatically wrong [sic] decision."[154]

DCI Gates admitted that a similar process was at work when the CIA failed to predict the Soviet invasion of Afghanistan in 1979. He said analysts "simply could not accept that Brezhnev or the others might see the equation differently. The analysts thought that the Soviet leaders thought as they did. It was not the first or the last time that they would make this mistake."[155] At the same time, while he was DCI, Gates displayed on his desk the maxim, "As a general rule, the best way to achieve complete strategic surprise is to commit an act that makes no sense or is even self-destructive."[156] (Presumably the limits of this axiom were evident on September 12, 2001; as we see in the 9/11 case, the Dutch historian of culture Johan Huizinga had pointed in the 1930s that rationality is only one human value among many and that wars have been fought simply to "obtain a decision of holy validity" or as "a form of divination").[157]

What concerns us primarily here, however, is not the mental process of mirror imaging by individual analysts of the intelligence target, but the *social process* of mirror imaging by the analytical institution. This *social* mirror-imaging mechanism links to other social processes already described and like them feeds directly into creating the persistent traits of the CIA's identity and culture. CIA analysts might prize, for example, an intercepted cable not only because of the impressive technology used to intercept it but also because—no matter what its content—the cable was deemed "secret" by the Soviets. This approach presupposes that one's target's classification system is fully "rational," and such rationality is "bounded" by factors the same as one's own: Despite the Soviet penchant for utterly counterproductive secrecy,[158] once such "secret" information is obtained with difficulty, it is hard to believe that it is treated objectively.

Open source intelligence advocates frequently make the same charge, saying,

> There remains an ingrained Intelligence Community (IC) prejudice—sometimes no more than a subliminal one, but a prejudice nonetheless—against open sources. There will always be IC officials, and some of their policy customers, who believe that the greater the difficulty involved in collecting the intelligence, the better the intelligence has to be.[159]

Michael Handel, a national security and strategy scholar, agrees, pointing out that having worked to obtain secret information, intelligence services are psychologically predisposed to believe it.[160] One can imagine the cumulative effects of such an attitude when working against totalitarian regimes!

Where can one find such distortions? They can be detected most easily in the tasking and collection phase of the intelligence cycle. What many critics say ended up happening during the Cold War, for example, was that the CIA largely spied on itself (through counterintelligence) and its counterparts: the KGB and GRU, the Soviet military industrial complex, and the urban elites. One internal critic charged SOVA (the CIA's Office of Soviet Analysis): "You guys just take in each other's laundry" (that is, the CIA targeted the KGB and vice versa).[161] The KGB officer Victor Cherkashin, who "handled" the CIA traitor Aldrich Ames and FBI traitor Robert Hanssen, agreed.[162] Memoirs recently published by Markus Wolf, the former head of foreign intelligence for the German Democratic Republic, echo these sentiments, adding, "Most spying has actually made little difference . . . [the USSR's] problems were lying in plain sight."[163] Although on an institutional level this spy-on-their-spies approach made sense (especially viewed in light of the security mechanism already discussed), the cases in later chapters explore how it also lays the groundwork for surprises of which the KGB and others knew little or nothing. We even learned after the Cold War that the KGB, in order to foil fictitious reporting by party bosses, employed its own spy satellites to ascertain the size of the Uzbek cotton harvest;[164] in the 1980s, the KGB also used CIA estimates to forecast Soviet grain harvests[165] and to correct problems in their oil industry,[166] proving that economic forecasting about the USSR in the 1980s was at least partly an unacknowledged "wilderness of mirrors."

If organizational mirror imaging can be found during tasking and collection, the effects of overexposure to a totalitarian society in a secret environment can also be discerned in the analysis part of the intelligence cycle. Here is one scholar's evocative recollection in *Intelligence and the Mirror*:

> Soviet consensual reality was eventually translated into US forms or put into US boxes. Gradually, the process was standardized. A whole generation of scholars emerged in the late 1950s who engaged in Talmudic-like studies of the military texts and signs. For instance, Harriet Scott . . . discovered that there were hidden messages about disasters and upheavals in official obituaries. She taught generations of analysts the importance of ritual in intelligence analysis. Robert Herrick discovered, during his research into Soviet naval doctrine, its infernal Dantesque structure. He identified those who said the word "aircraft carrier" at the wrong time and died, and those who proposed it and lived, and those who suffered for lack of courage to say it at all . . . James McConnell, like a Shakespearean scholar meticulously comparing folios, deduced a new system of interpretation by observing which concepts and words in Soviet military texts were changed, which was missing, which ritual was intoned, which authority praised. *From these divinations he could conjecture how close we were to war, and his insights taught a generation of analysts the importance of signs and signals.*[167]

A glimpse of such activities is also found in the glossary provided for "Sherman Kent and the Board of National Estimates: Collected Essays." It defines the term *cratology* as "the study of the size and function of shipping crates seen on photographs (from various sources). The size and configuration of a shipping crate often will indicate what is inside."[168] We see cratology in action in the Cuban Missile Crisis case, but what these passages reveal is the social mechanism by which the nature of the USSR shaped and maintained the identity and culture of the CIA.

Based on evidence like this, one can hypothesize that the more abstruse analytical efforts at the CIA from its inception until 2001 result as much from the mirroring of their totalitarian targets as from the sometimes necessary secrecy of their other efforts. At the far end of such a hypothesis, one might even view the CIA's drive for consensus as a mirror-image of Leninist "democratic centralism," by which in theory Communist parties could combine free discussion prior to a decision with strict hierarchical discipline once a decision was reached; in practice, however, the former was always much subordinate to the latter.[169]

3 THE IRANIAN REVOLUTION

THIS CHAPTER INTRODUCES THE PATTERN that is used when considering all the cases of surprise to follow. First, it provides general evidence for the existence of a massive intelligence failure, a strategic surprise. Second, it employs the intelligence cycle to model that failure in depth and map it back to the key attributes of the CIA's identity and culture identified in Chapter 2: homogeneity, scientism, an excessive regard for secrets, and a drive for consensus.

That modeling process will also reveal evidence for the existence of Cassandras prior to strategic surprise. (As a reminder, Cassandras are defined as "individuals inside or outside the agency who anticipated the approximate course of events that comprised a strategic surprise based on reasoned threat assessments that differed sharply from those of the CIA.") Thus, Cassandras help demonstrate that the origin of strategic surprises is less the inherent unpredictability of external events than internal factors at the CIA creating the sufficient conditions for the surprise to occur.

EVIDENCE OF THE FAILURE

On December 31, 1977, President Carter and the shah of Iran welcomed the New Year together at a lavish party in the opulent Niavaran Palace in Tehran. "Iran," the president began his toast, "because of the great leadership of the Shah, is an island of stability in one of the more troubled areas of the world." As his toast went on, Carter called the shah "a man of wisdom" who was "loved by his people."[1] Carter had good reasons to flatter the shah in this way. As Secretary of State Henry Kissinger explained in his memoir *The White House Years*, Iran mattered a great deal to America:

Under the Shah's leadership, the land bridge between Asia and Europe, so often the hinge of world history, was pro-American and pro-West beyond any challenge. Alone among the countries of the region—Israel aside—Iran made friendship with the United States the starting point of its policy. That it was based on a cold-eyed assessment that a threat to Iran would most likely come from the Soviet Union, in combination with radical Arab states, is only another way of saying that the Shah's view of the realities of world politics paralleled our own.[2]

Indeed, Iran was a regional anchor for U.S. policy in the Gulf since 1953, when Kermit Roosevelt and his CIA compatriots overthrew Premier Mossadeq in Operation Ajax (November 1952–August 1953) cumulating in the installation of the shah.[3] While "there had always been someone somewhere predicting the fall of the Shah,"[4] the prevailing U.S. view of Iran in Langley and in Washington was summed up in Carter's New Year's Eve toast: The shah was secure.[5]

Perhaps this view prevailed because, as one scholar puts it, "The Shah's downfall had so often been predicted and his survival so often observed that warning about his imminent downfall had gradually lost credibility."[6] "The CIA considered the Shah to be a 'professional worrier' and an alarmist,"[7] but a *Foreign Affairs* article in 1978 called him "the most important of the five major absolute monarchs left in the world [and] undoubtedly one of the cleverest political leaders of this century."[8] "Mohammed Reza Shah Pahlavi" generally maintained a brave public face (even as events spun out of control at the end of his reign). In June 1978, for example, in an interview with *US News and World Report*, the shah said: "Nobody can overthrow me. I have the support of 700,000 troops, all the workers, and most of the people. Wherever I go, there are fantastic demonstrations of support. I have the power, and the opposition cannot be compared in strength with the government in any way."[9] Gary Sick, the NSC White House aide for Iran whom we have already met, agrees with the shah, saying that the Pahlavi monarch:

... had thirty-seven years' experience on the throne and had survived crises which, by appearance, were no less severe than the riots of 1978. [He had control over Iran's oil wealth, the army, and a prominent place on the world stage, and ranged against him were merely] "An aged cleric . . . congeries of aging Mossadeghists [supporters of the premier deposed in Operation Ajax] village ecclesiastics and disgruntled job seekers."[10]

Nevertheless, after a sequence of increasingly dramatic upheavals, on January 16, 1979, the shah left Iran to go "on vacation"[11] to Egypt, never to return; in so doing, he set firmly in train a series of events that culminated in the creation of an Islamic state led by the Ayatollah Khomeini and his fundamentalist Shiite supporters. As a former member of the NSC staff said at the time, "With the fall of the Pahlavi regime in Iran . . . a profound change in the regional balance took place."[12]

Since the shah's "vacation," the dramatic events in Iran routinely figure on lists of American strategic surprises. Indeed, a (still classified) 1983 CIA internal review of the intelligence that preceded the collapse of the regime was tasked, "To examine the quality of judgments preceding significant historical failures over the last twenty years or so," and it cites the Iranian revolution as a clear case of intelligence failure.[13] One intelligence insider said baldly:

> Everyone is aware that as the Shah of Iran was falling, a score of highly paid analysts at CIA was writing that Iran was not in a revolutionary situation or even a pre-revolutionary one. That kind of ignorance not only crippled our policies in the years prior to the revolution, years which could have been used to warn and bolster our friends, it also could have led us to think the foolish thoughts by which we advised our Iranian friends during December and January 1978–79 and which proved lethal to them.[14]

No less a figure than the DCI during these events, Stansfield Turner, acknowledged, "In my time as director of the CIA, our greatest failure was inadequately emphasizing the dangerous waters into which the Shah Reza Pahlavi of Iran was sailing in 1978."[15] He later elaborated:

> We had not appreciated how shaky the Shah's political foundation was; did not know that the Shah was terminally ill; did not understand who Khomeini was and the support his movement had; did not have a clue who the hostage-takers were or what their objective was; and could not pinpoint within the embassy where the hostages were being held and under what conditions.[16]

There is no doubt that with the fall of the shah, a profound, long-lasting, and—from America's point of view, adverse—change took place in the regional balance of power, and the CIA was as surprised as anyone in Washington.

If that is the general conclusion regarding the CIA's performance prior to this surprise, what are the specifics?

First, we see a fundamental lack of knowledge of Iranian society. Fewer than 10 percent of U.S. embassy personnel spoke Farsi, and when the CIA station chief in Tehran pleaded for more Persian speakers in December 1978, Langley refused.[17] The name of Ali Shariati—a revolutionary and sociologist who was the most influential opponent in Iran in the 1970s before Khomeini rose to prominence—was apparently largely unknown to embassy personnel in Tehran,[18] so we can assume the CIA wasn't monitoring such figures. Meanwhile, without any Muslim officers, U.S. embassy personnel could not even enter mosques to hear what was being preached on Fridays![19] DO veteran (and one of America's fifty-two Iranian hostages from 1979 to 1981) William J. Daugherty says that for years prior to 1978, the CIA was not tasked to collect information on the Iranian internal political situation, and at no time in the 1970s did American officials meet with any of the exiled opposition.[20] Instead, there was a myth of the shah's invincibility.[21]

Let us then turn the focus to the CIA's reporting on the man who would emerge as revolutionary Iran's de facto leader, the one-time exile Ayatollah Ruhollah Khomeini. A June 1963 study by the CIA highlighted Khomeini's rise to prominence and called him "the most outspoken critic of the government's reform programs" and "an extremely dangerous threat to the regime";[22] a 1978 CIA report, however, simply considered the cleric anti-Communist, but reasoned, without providing evidence, that his movement "may be susceptible to Communist and radical penetration."[23]

The intelligence provided by and to the U.S. embassy in Tehran was poor enough so that as late as November 9, 1978, in a dire telegram entitled "Thinking the Unthinkable," Ambassador William Sullivan[24]—in what must be one of the most ill-judged personality sketches ever—described Khomeini as a "Gandhi-like" figure who "would not get personally involved in politics."[25]

To compound matters, the agency reported innocuously on October 27, 1978—less than 100 days before the shah fled the country—that "the political situation is unlikely to be clarified at least until late next year [that is, autumn 1979] when the Shah, the cabinet, and the new parliament that is scheduled to be elected in June begin to interact on the political scene."[26]

The intelligence situation was no better in Washington. Samuel Huntington, who served on the NSC staff at the time, recalls that because of the "Jaleh Square massacre" (an event that Sick calls "the turning point from sporadic acts of popular rebellion to genuine revolution")[27], he asked the CIA for "an assessment of prospects for a post-Shah Iran." In response, he received "a discussion of the Iranian constitution and the chances of creating a regency council for a transition within the Pahlavi dynasty. There was no mention of potential successor regimes."[28]

Such an omission of potential successors is only natural: Just the year before, in August 1977, the CIA produced a sixty-page estimate that directly addressed the subject of "Religious and Intellectual Opposition to the Shah."[29] It concluded that "the Shah will be an active participant in Iranian political life well into the 1980s" and that there would "be no radical change in Iranian political behavior in the near future."[30]

In short, the fall of the shah of Iran was a massive intelligence failure. It also surely constitutes a strategic surprise by the definition set forth in Chapter 1: "the sudden realization that one has been operating on the basis of an erroneous threat assessment that results in a failure to anticipate a grave threat to 'vital' national interests." DCI Turner later said of this calamity, "We were just plain asleep";[31] the next section examines the factors that engendered this slumber.

REVEALING THE CASSANDRAS AND REFRAMING THE FAILURE

How did an intelligence failure of this scope and scale occur at CIA? What are its proximate and distal causes? The answers to those questions go to the heart of this book, and an examination of each phase of the intelligence cycle through the prism of the CIA's culture and identity points to some of them. We begin, therefore, with the CIA's tasking on Iran in the 1970s.

Tasking

First of all, the homogeneity of CIA personnel and their obsession with "objectivity," "science," and "reason" led to a consistent lack of curiosity about the religious opposition to the shah and to a corresponding neglect of less quantifiable questions of the legitimacy of the regime. While such opposition could have been introduced as a variable in positivist models of political change in Iran, it seems to have been almost wholly omitted from CIA calculations until the situation was irretrievable.

Intelligence expert Angelo Codevilla, for example, says that in this period there was at the CIA an "educated incapacity to take seriously reports dealing with religion from the Middle East."[32] Already in December of 1979, former DCI Richard Helms agreed that "the lack of coverage in depth of church [sic] activities during the '70s may well have prevented an adequate understanding of religious forces at work when trouble started in 1978."[33] The ethnocentric bias inherent in Helms's choice of words is itself telling of the lack of curiosity about or sensitivity to cultural differences that might influence "models." In fact, between 1975 and 1977 the CIA provided not a single report based on sources within the religious opposition,[34] and there is no evidence that they sought any such sources until too late. Ofira Seliktar observes:

> In the Iranian case, there was a strong partiality [at the CIA] for the study of empirical indices of performance, but little inclination to follow the more esoteric field of normative judgment, culture and spirituality. The diffuse notion of legitimacy that was at the heart of the crisis was beyond the pale of the intelligence purview.[35]

This failing was so widely recognized that a 1979 satirical article in the *Washington Post* entitled "A Primer for Spies" suggested—in a tragic precursor of criticism of the agency after 9/11—that the agency adopt the analytical heuristic, "Many people take God seriously."[36]

On some levels, it is easy to see why in the day-to-day press of reporting events in Iran such "squishy" matters were ignored. Seliktar cites an instance in which "the followers of the ayatollah had also made good use of the ubiquitous Iranian rumor mill. One notorious rumor . . . held that the face of Khomeini would appear on the face of the moon on November 27, and all but 'miscreants and bastards' would be able to see him." Had CIA analysts paid sustained attention to this seemingly absurd prediction, however, they would have noted that "on the appointed night *millions attested to seeing the apparition*, a line that was supported by *Novin* [the newspaper of the Iranian Communist Party, *Tudeh*, which was printed in the Soviet embassy in Tehran]."[37] The lack of anthropologists and sociologists on the CIA's staff is addressed later; here one can simply adduce that their absence is in keeping with a preference for hard data and that this absence had adverse effects on the CIA's tasking, collection, and analysis. Ironically, had CIA been inclined to pursue such matters, there would have been no shortage of outliers that would have inspired further review of the situation inside the country. These quantifiable indicators *could* have been tasked:

> More new mosques were built between 1968 and 1978 than in the previous two centuries and the number of pilgrims to Mecca reached some one hundred

thousand in 1977. The number of theology students quadrupled and private donations to clergy reached an estimated $200 million, a sevenfold increase from the previous decade.[38]

Other quantifiable elements would have set off alarm bells had the CIA been monitoring them: "It was estimated that between October 1 [1978] and January 1979, some 100,000 Iranians left and some $2.6 billion were transferred abroad."[39] Nobody, however, among the CIA's customers asked deep questions about Iran; as one insider observed in an unconscious summary of tasking (and an example of mirror imaging at work): "No ping [from an intelligence consumer], no priority; no priority, no warning. [Topics] slip between the cracks."[40] An analyst later testified to Congress: "Until recently you couldn't *give* away intelligence on Iran . . . Policymakers were not asking *whether* the Shah's autocracy would survive indefinitely; policy was premised on that assumption."[41]

Why were these, along with softer indicators (such as the perceived religious illegitimacy of the regime), not tasked? More than scientism was at work. Tasking was also distorted by a need to maintain the consensus about the shah's regime already noted. The CIA's generalized preference for consensus was amplified here by a more specific desire not to "rock the boat" of the special relationship between Iran and the United States generally and between the shah's entourage and the CIA particularly. This is one of the historically unique features of this strategic surprise.

As a postmortem from the *Washington Post* observed, "The Central Intelligence Agency's long and close ties to the Shah of Iran and his intelligence service effectively prevented Langley from giving the White House a clear warning that public unrest posed a major threat to the Shah and U.S. policy."[42] In fact, after the military agreement between President Nixon and the shah in 1972, the CIA "dismantled many of its own operations in Iran, and it thus became more and more reliant on SAVAK, the Shah's feared secret police, for information about internal events."[43]

Iran was, in the mind of intelligence consumers in Washington, as Secretary of State Henry Kissinger has already been quoted, "pro-American and pro-West beyond any challenge." Because of this mind-set, "American diplomats and politicians [that is, the CIA's consumers] tended to take what the Shah and his military and intelligence men told them on trust. They completely ignored the strength of religious opposition which ultimately revealed itself as the driving force of the revolution."[44]

To compound this tasking problem, in order "not to offend the Shah," the CIA was persuaded not to establish links with opposition figures.[45] As one exasperated analyst told the *Washington Post* (while events firmly took the saddle in 1978 and when the CIA began to be criticized on Iran): "We can't do much with opaque regimes headed by friendly authoritarian figures."[46] The *Post* went on:

> The political opposition and officer corps have been off limits for years to the 50 to 75 agents the CIA maintains in Iran. The agency's professional intelligence on domestic Iranian developments has had to come largely from the Shah's own secret police, SAVAK, which could hardly be expected to report that the Shah was in trouble. "If we had tried to penetrate the opposition, we would have been caught immediately by SAVAK," a CIA official said. "Iran is an ally. In England, we would not try to penetrate the opposition."[47]

There is also evidence that SAVAK, to whom tasking and collection were effectively "outsourced" by the CIA, was brutal but not especially competent. Apparently they were unable to distinguish between the various types of non-communist opposition groups and frequently confused them with communist groups or with each other.[48] SAVAK had poor success infiltrating subversive groups and performed little analysis; the information it gathered was mostly limited to what could be obtained through torture.

Finally, it is clear that the CIA's preference for secret information—in this case, about the USSR—distorted tasking priorities in Iran. A newspaper article of the period hypothesized that the CIA restricted their contacts with political opponents in Iran because they feared displeasing the shah, and had they done so they would have lost signals intelligence facilities in Northern Iran that were exceptionally important for monitoring the USSR. In short, the CIA viewed Iran mostly as a window on its main target, the USSR. Almost ten years later, one of President Carter's advisors revealed that this was indeed true:

> Our understanding was that the deal with the Shah was, "You rely on me for what goes on here, and I'll let you have all the telemetry and monitoring equipment [against the USSR] up north you want" . . . it was more important to

monitor Soviet missiles and so forth than have agents keeping tabs on the political situation inside Iran.[49]

Given the short-run priority of the Strategic Arms Limitation Talks II (SALT II) taking place at the time, it was difficult to argue with this logic. On the other hand, "Iran may have been something of an exception,"[50] as the CIA routinely has contact with the political opposition within countries even if it displeases their hosts. Clearly misplaced tasking priorities—rooted firmly in the CIA's identity and culture—played a critical part in this strategic surprise.

Collection

The preference for secrets about the USSR in tasking noted in the previous section overlaps with problems in the collection of intelligence on Iran. When we review the list of the CIA's identity and cultural features in Figure 2.1, we see that three—homogeneity, the reification of objectivity and reason, and a preference for secrets—also distorted the collection phase. Inasmuch as we have already mentioned the agency's focus on secret Soviet missile telemetry over other types of information, let us begin there. In his account of the Iranian Revolution, Barry Rubin points out that "a study of media coverage found that 'a full year before the revolution began, the best American newspapers were clearly telling a story of a country with a harsh dictatorial government, severe economic difficulties, and an unhealthy emphasis on importing weapons.'"[51]

We can conclude that these open sources had little effect on collection by the CIA because, as Walter Laqueur, a historian and terrorism expert, stated in 1985, the CIA may have been the victim of "the most transparently naïve . . . idea that something published in the 'open literature,' ranging from newspapers to scholarly journals, need not be taken into account when making intelligence assessments that have to be based on secret information." Tellingly, Laqueur goes on in a footnote to reveal, "A striking example was a series of important articles in the French newspaper *Le Monde* during the spring of 1978 on events in Iran. These were taken into account by the Intelligence Community *after an academic had called them to high-level White House attention in the fall of that year.*"[52] (Note that it is the White House not *tasking* the CIA after reviewing open sources but performing *collection*!) As Robert Gates would later observe in an interview: "There were scholars out there saying the Shah was in trouble, and somehow that never got incorporated into any official assessment."[53]

Eric Rouleau, the chief Middle East correspondent for *Le Monde*, observed in 1980, "From the very beginning of the Iranian Revolution [the United States] seems to have been struck by a peculiar sort of political blindness."[54] A 2004 study of intelligence failures prior to the shah's downfall also concluded that "it's a mentality out at the CIA that if you don't get the information from spying, it's not intelligence,"[55] and that factor played a part in analytical failures regarding Iran.

It would seem that academic open sources were not the only overt sources ignored at CIA. The business world, too, could have offered valuable information had the CIA been minded to collect it:

> Executives who did business in Iran were somewhat anxious during a briefing for [Ambassador] Sullivan in May. The ambassador was amazed to discover that few corporations made long-term investment in Iran, normally a sign of low business confidence. By mid-1977, there was a growing reluctance to engage in new ventures. Some businessmen noted that Iranians were sending out record amounts of money. Political risk analysis services picked up the social tremors in Iran. Business International, which used the Delphi technique, gave Iran a score of 10, a midpoint between "long term stability" and "active factionalism." Business Environment Risk Index rated Iran's stability at 43 out of a possible 100.[56]

Also ignored in Langley was well-informed, more generalized, open source analysis like that offered by Archibald Roosevelt, the political advisor to Chase Manhattan Bank, who warned about the danger to the shah. In fact, between October 1, 1978, and January 31, 1979, more than 100,000 well-heeled people fled Iran, taking some 10 percent of the country's foreign currency reserves with them.[57] In the right circles, such information isn't remotely secret.

There is also the issue of how the Ayatollah Khomeini communicated with his followers. Pilgrims returning to Iran from the holy Shia city of Najaf, Ayatollah Khomeini's place of exile in Iraq, brought back with them cassettes of his sermons lambasting the shah. These tapes were patently not secret: They "were played in mosques all over Iran almost immediately."[58] According to Mossad, by the end of 1978, there were over 600,000 such tapes circulating in the country.[59] Though this activity went on for over ten years, it would seem that because "it did not require a covert operation to obtain copies of Khomeini's tape-recorded sermons,"[60] the CIA ignored them.

Contrast also the CIA's singular focus on Soviet telemetry data with the fact that when—under pressure from Tehran—Khomeini was sent by Iraq into exile in France, he continued to direct events in Iran simply by using an international direct-dial telephone.[61] According to Ronen Bergman, an Israeli investigative journalist and author, Paris even agreed to install a number of special telephone and telex lines linked directly to Iran at the post office near Khomeini's home. In concert with the National Security Agency (NSA), the CIA could presumably have listened to these calls with ease. Khomeini also granted—over a four-month stay in Paris—over 400 interviews, and a local recording studio canceled all of its other contracts to produce thousands of cassettes of his daily broadcasts and interviews.[62] Though he and his entourage employed *taqieh* in this period (a particular form of dissimulation, fully defined later),[63] it was during this time that Khomeini "spelled out in some detail his program for establishing an Islamic republic."[64] The CIA's collection efforts ignored all of these factors.

DCI Turner later cast some light on this phenomenon and put it in the wider collection context (one that extends beyond a preference for secrets, encompassing also the homogeneity of the CIA's identity and culture):

> What we needed to know that Ayatollah Ruhollah Khomeini and his lieutenants were secretly scheming in Paris and employing such unorthodox techniques [sic] as sending taped cassettes of propaganda into Iran . . . American intelligence operatives were simply not in touch with the mullahs in the mosques, who were telling the peasants how the Shah was "profaning" Islam; nor with the merchants in the bazaars, who were grumbling about the stranglehold of the regime on the economy; or the politically educated, who were exasperated with the Shah's unwillingness to share political power. Not only were we not talking with a broad enough cross-section of people, we were not sampling attitudes widely enough across the country. In part that was because in the past few decades the State Department, and with it the CIA, have confined their operations only to the capitals and one or two cities in major countries.[65]

Such collection techniques were only unorthodox from the point of view of conventional planning of coups d'état,[66] not for religious figures.

As the 1970s unfolded in Iran, "Fundamentalism, once the preserve of illiterate peasants and urban poor, had spread to the middle class . . . pilgrimages to Mashad and Mecca became socially in," writes Ofira Seliktar. The CIA, both because of its preference for secrets and because (as Turner indicates in the preceding block quotation) a homogeneous identity that confined their collection operations to a narrow range of Iranian society, failed to detect the true nature of the changes happening in Iran. "Almost to the very end," Seliktar adds, "the Carter administration took 'the middle-class fellow travelers' [of the Iranian Revolution] as the 'real makers of history' and ignored the Imam [Khomeini] and his foreign policy vision."[67] Thus, it would seem that, in the collection phase the homogeneity of the CIA allowed it to maintain, in the face of mounting evidence to the contrary, the same operative assumptions as the end users of its intelligence.

The agency's perennial obsession with objectivity, reason (as narrowly defined), and science also effected collection in Iran. Their "infrequent forays into monitoring public opinion lacked depth and sophistication; *little attention was paid to cultural and theological issues.*"[68] Adda Bozeman, a scholar who has written about culture and foreign policy, confirms that this neglect stemmed from the CIA's "ahistorical and anticultural" bias, and from their "emphasis on materialism, economic determinism, and current events."[69]

Majid Tehranian models a situation in which Iran at that time was composed of two "epistemic nations" with two belief systems and two parallel communication systems.[70] "With only limited intercourse between them, it was easy for American observers, largely attuned to the epistemics of modernization, to overlook the growth of the fundamentalist movement."[71] Bill agrees: "The Intelligence Community . . . that supplied much of the daily evaluation focused for the most part on the analysis of the official power elite. There was little understanding of the *legitimacy discourse and its key players and efforts to study religious leaders were dismissed as 'sociology.'*"[72] This assertion is supported by the fact that, in January 1979, the Senate Foreign Relations Committee was told that because of "the Islamic revolt that helped drive the Shah of Iran from his country this week," the CIA was ordered by the White House to "survey Moslems worldwide."[73] In short, the Senate ordered the CIA to close the barn door.

A more commonly discussed malign influence on the CIA's collection prior to the revolution in Iran must also be raised. It ties back to the CIA's culture and identity, but only in a general sense. At the very least, knowledge of it reveals further the operation of some of the social mechanisms introduced in Chapter 2 that have such a deep impact on other traits of the agency. It is rooted in American political culture, in this particular era in U.S. politics, and especially in the *Weltanschauung* of the main intelligence "consumer" of the agency's "products" on Iran, President Carter, and the man whom he appointed to lead the CIA, Stansfield Turner.

Arriving in Washington condemning "the national disgraces" of "Watergate, Vietnam, and the CIA," Carter and his team were "skeptical and suspicious" of the agency.[74] According to British historian Christopher Andrew, Carter opted for a military man to lead the CIA to "hit the pacifism [charge] in the neck" and settled on his former Annapolis classmate, Admiral Stansfield Turner, whom the Senate duly approved. Both Carter and his new DCI considered the "traditional human spy" as largely outmoded and had an "exaggerated faith in advanced technology."[75] Andrew adds that the president's "view of intelligence collection [was] dominated by the high-tech wonders of IMINT and SIGINT." That positivistic mind-set resulted in a systematic effort to "hamstring or ignore" human intelligence sources.[76] Their mind-set is revealed perfectly in a gee-whiz passage in Turner's *Secrecy and Democracy*:

> Now that we have technical systems ranging from satellites travelling in space over the entire globe, to aircraft flying in free airspace, to miniature sensors surreptitiously positioned close to difficult targets, we are approaching a time when we will be able to survey almost any point on the earth's surface with some sensor, and probably with more than one. We can take detailed photographs from long distances, detect heat sources through infrared devices, pinpoint metal objects with magnetic detectors, distinguish barely moving and stationary objects through the use of Doppler radar, use radar to detect objects that are covered or hidden by darkness, eavesdrop on all manner of signals from the human voice to electronic radio waves, detect nuclear radiation with refined Geiger counters, and sense underground explosions at long distances with seismic devices. Most of the activities that we want to monitor give off several kinds of signals. Tanks in battle can be detected by the heat from their engines, the magnetism of their armor, or photographs. A nuclear weapons plant emits radiation, has a particular external physical shape, and receives certain types of supplies. One way or another, we should soon be able to keep track of most activities on the surface of the earth, day or night, in good weather or bad.[77]

Note well—Turner wrote this paean to high-technology intelligence collection over five years *after* the Iran fiasco! Imagine the effects on collection (and tasking, and analysis) at the CIA when such positivistic views are held by the man at the top, a DCI who was not only "interested in analysis" as opposed to covert methods, but who "spent a lot of time with analysts from every subject area and at all levels of seniority."[78] Even if they were so inclined, it would have been difficult for other CIA employees to be both "collegial" and to insist that phantasmagoria like Khomeini's face appearing on the moon should enter into the CIA's evaluations of Iran.

Alexander Wendt observes that "people act towards objects, including other actors, on the basis of the meanings that the objects have for them" and these meanings are intersubjectively constituted.[79] It seems clear that, on that basis, the CIA's culture and identity, with one of its central planks as a faith in "science," was woefully ill disposed to see that religious material was collected for analysis of the internal situation in Iran.

Along with an exaggerated faith in high technology, Carter, Turner, and those who followed in their train (that is, those Washington critics taking a so-called New View of intelligence in this era), felt that technical means of intelligence collection were somehow morally superior to human intelligence. They posited, according to Seliktar, "Human espionage corrupts the process of intelligence gathering"; they "wanted to replace it with 'clean' technical intelligence." As one Turner appointee describes, "HUMINT was likely to be suspect on moral grounds and do moral damage to the collector."[80] This moral factor, along with his faith in technology, led Turner to cut 820 positions from the DO, which handles HUMINT. While exact figures to put these cuts in perspective are not available, scholars agree that Turner's cut of the DO was substantial and was a "reduction both then-current and retired DO officers regarded as crippling and unwise."[81] In addition, critics at the time said that Turner's "preference for technology over people . . . [and other measures] have destroyed morale with the CIA, led hundreds of key CIA personnel to resign and prompted far more to 'retire in place.'"[82]

The effects of these New View changes (which, one can argue, partly reflect a mirroring of the customer and are partly in keeping with the trait of venerating "objectivity") on collection in Iran prior to the end of the Pahlavi dynasty are easy to surmise. "The complicated [new, moral] rules for recruiting agents adopted by the Agency—summed up in a 130-page manual—made it hard to draft foreign nationals." To make matters worse, "veteran chiefs of station who were associated with the old [CIA] regime were often replaced with people who had no knowledge of the language and culture of the country."[83] These New View changes, too, had come on the back of a "brutal" set of personnel cutbacks of CIA HUMINT personnel begun (at President Nixon's instigation) by DCI James Schlesinger in 1973 and that continued under DCI Colby. By the end of 1978, only 10 percent of the State Department's diplomats in the embassy (a figure that would encompass the vast majority of the CIA's case officers in the country, who are usually under "official cover" as U.S. government employees while collecting intelligence) spoke fluent Farsi.[84] In summary, as Seliktar says:

> The Carter–Turner restructuring affected the CIA's ability to discern the revolutionary dynamics in a number of ways. At the organizational level the "New View" reform dismantled much of the human intelligence operation that was considered "corrupt" and morally tainted . . . The "clean" technical intelligence on which Turner planned to rely was poorly equipped to deal with the complexities and chaos of an esoteric revolution.[85]

Over a decade later, Turner mused, "What we missed was the breadth and intensity of feeling against the Shah inside Iran . . . Those feelings against the Shah were shared by disparate groups that came together for the specific and temporary purpose of deposing him."[86] They missed registering these feelings about the shah despite the fact that, at least as early as 1977, a CIA employee sent to the U.S. Embassy in Iran was approached by academics and others who, he said, "would find 15 to 30 seconds to whisper in my ear that all was not well . . . that there was great unrest, that the Shah was not popular."[87] It is evident that key elements in the CIA's culture and identity—elements that both reflected and amplified specific properties of intelligence consumers—played a role in ensuring that the collection phase of the intelligence cycle missed numerous signals that might have raised in advance at least the possibility of instability in Iran.

Analysis

Given the warping of tasking and collection already discussed, a balanced and open-minded analysis of the situation in Iran in the late 1970s from a vantage point in Virginia would have presented a considerable predictive challenge. Instead, the factors previously related compounded problems in analysis and for the same deep-seated reasons. The fingers of critics of the agency's performance in this era usually point to the Carter/Turner reforms and their "attempt to castrate the CIA"[88] after Vietnam and Watergate. A closer inspection of this part of the intelligence cycle through a constructivist lens reveals that the real sources of these failures are the same enduring attributes of the CIA's identity and culture: homogeneity's unreflective regard for objectivity, reason, and science; a reflexive preference for secret information; and an impulse for consensus.

It is clear, in addition, that contra those defenders of the CIA already mentioned, like Adelman and Helms who might allege that the event was an inherently unpredictable mystery, the facts speak otherwise. Apart from the more diffuse warnings about the situation issued by Cassandras among academics, business, and the media already revealed, the historical record reflects that two rival foreign intelligence agencies were also deeply concerned about Iran. Around May of 1978:

> The American Embassy in Tehran became aware of two reports predicting that the Shah would be deposed within a year. A junior intelligence officer of the French Service de Documentation Extérieure et de Contre-Espionnage (SDECE) wrote one, and Uri Lubrani, the unofficial Israeli envoy in Tehran and Reuven Merhav, a Mossad operative, authored the other one.[89]

Indeed, Ambassador Sullivan was told by the Israelis in 1978 that the shah's regime would last no more than another three years, while the French embassy said the shah would be gone "within a year."[90]

It is an obvious point that if foreign intelligence analysts—clearly Cassandras—could draw these conclusions and issue warnings about Iran's stability, then CIA's analysts could have, too. What stopped them?

Before beginning a dissection of the core causes of the analytical failure, it is crucial to record that there was a key "uncollected" secret, a piece of the puzzle missing from the CIA's analysis of the Iran situation until it was too late: The shah had cancer. Though the shah's cancer was diagnosed in 1974 in Europe, and both the monarch's doctors were French, French intelligence was also ignorant of his condition. The shah took extreme measures to keep his condition a secret, and his wife and twin sister learned of it only after he had left Iran. Gary Sick later said: "The Shah's cancer was, without question, one of the best-kept state secrets of all time."[91] Sick's assertion, however, is flatly contradicted by some, who say that Tehran was "alive" with the rumor that the shah was dying of cancer.[92] Perhaps for that reason, in 1991 Turner admitted, "We [that is, the CIA] were remiss in not knowing how ill the Shah was."[93]

In 2005, just how remiss Langley was became (with rich irony) clear. In that year, an article from *Studies in Intelligence* entitled "Remote Medical Diagnosis: Monitoring the Health of Very Important Patients" was declassified. The article's case studies detail the CIA's efforts at long-range monitoring of the health of Georges Pompidou of France, Hourari Boumediene of Algeria, Leonid Brezhnev of the USSR, and Menachem Begin of Israel . . . and revealed that it was published and circulated in the CIA in the spring of 1979![94] This fact makes it probable that the shah's cancer was only "the best-kept secret of all time" due to the CIA's excessive deference to the shah's sensibilities regarding collection within Iran to preserve their right to pursue secrets about the USSR.

In any case, the shah's illness was important because, during the key events in the autumn of 1978, he was extraordinarily indecisive and frequently depressed, both characteristics that were likely the result of secret chemotherapy treatments. According to Seliktar, "By fall numerous reports about the Shah's unusual behavior reached Washington, including a Mossad message conveyed by the Israeli Foreign Minister, Moshe Dayan." An updated CIA psychiatric profile "included [a] reference to depression and impaired leadership but cancer was not considered."[95] In fact, that CIA assessment, issued on November 22, concluded (more truthfully than they knew) that the shah's "mood is not inappropriate to this situation"; unfortunately, they also concluded, "that he is not paralyzed by indecision."[96]

No matter what, the CIA can also be faulted for failing to take full account of the openly available fact that the shah had "painstakingly constructed the machinery of the state around his person"[97]—an inherently fragile arrangement.

Even if the shah's condition had been known, the analysis that the CIA conducted would still likely have been subsumed by other problems created by the culture and identity-driven factors previously discussed. First, because of Turner's recent reforms, reflecting his high-tech approach to intelligence, the CIA's analytical unit on Iran lacked Persian specialists. Experienced Iran operatives from the DO like Kermit Roosevelt also were largely ignored. We know, too, that the people who left because of Turner's reforms were not only "black operators" from DO but career professionals from the DI such as Ernest Oney, the agency's chief Iranian analyst.[98] Allison, writing in 1980, said, "The inadequacy of current analytic expertise [is the result of a lack of] a small, dedicated group of experts focused on Iran." He cites not only Turner's reforms for creating this problem: Allison also discusses the social mechanisms of self-selection and isolation described in Chapter 2, saying, "The deterioration [of the cadre of analysts at CIA] of recent years also reflects the estrangement between the Intelligence Community and the institutions that maintain our society's storehouses of knowledge, especially universities and corporations."[99]

In his memoirs, Turner acknowledged that in the late 1970s the CIA did not have the anthropologists and sociologists who could deal with the revolutionary situation in Iran. Magnifying this deficiency on CIA analytical teams was the fact that, according to Gates (who was a senior member of the DI at the time), managers at the CIA placed "little value on the idea that people of different cultures have different habits of thought, values and motivations."[100] Sharply questioned by Carter in November of 1978 over the CIA's failings, Turner mainly "blamed the mysterious aloofness of the Shiite clergy."[101] As one internal critic put it, "[We need] cultural intelligence, not just informants."[102]

These factors—lack of staff with Iranian experience, lack of anthropologists and sociologists on analytical teams, and managers with a low tolerance for consideration of cultural differences—are all entirely consistent with the portrait of the CIA's identity and culture presented in Chapter 2. They are an antecedent condition to a cultural blindness that tended to rule out certain directions of political and social change on the grounds that they are "irrational." More specifically, these factors combined to create the following analytical difficulty:

> It made it harder to decipher the deeply seated religious idioms and the ingrained mistrust and dissimulation that pervaded [Iranian] popular culture. In commenting on this failure, one observer described these beliefs as "centuries of tradition, superstition, magic and mythology, cocooned in a xenophobic and ritualistic Islam." Even if this depiction is too harsh, the inability to discern the discourse of the traditional "epistemic community"—the ulama, the bazaaris, and peasant migrants—was costly. Deep cultural knowledge was essential because 1979 represented the "first modern revolution whose idiom of discourse is exclusively derived from native sources and whose moral claims are advanced in confrontation with the ideological and political currents of the modern world."[103]

After the fact, many observers insisted on comparing the Iranian revolution of 1978–1979 with its French predecessor almost two centuries before, but—because it was entrenched in Shiism—"the Iranian revolution is like no other."[104] Certainly, the CIA's Western economic models would have been little help understanding what occurred in Iran. Soon after the revolution, Khomeini responded to complaints about the state of Iran's economy with the retort, "We did not make the Islamic Revolution so the Persian melon would be cheap."[105]

There was another feature of the Iranian revolution made to order (some might say, "heaven sent") to confound the CIA's analysis constructed under assumptions of objectivity, science, and Western notions of reasonable behavior: *taqieh*. *Taqieh* is a form of Machiavellian dissimulation "most closely associated with the Shia," who practice it "systematically and widely . . . to hide their beliefs," especially "where no useful purpose would be served by publicly affirming them."[106]

Unfortunately for Langley's analysts, "Iranian political culture, not to mention the tactics of the fundamentalists, was permeated by *taqieh* and other tools of dissimulation and deception."[107] This is part of the reason that experienced observers like Codevilla could write that "anyone who watched the Iranian revolution of 1978 unfold on television screens could not help but notice incongruities of which the crowds seemed unaware: Muslim mullahs led crowds brandishing Soviet-made AK-47 rifles and shouting un-Islamic slogans that sounded as if they had been written in Moscow, together with quotes from the Koran."[108]

The ultimate origin of this failure to cope with *taqieh*, however, arguably lies in Kent's analytical doctrine, an intelligence dogma at the CIA that

> . . . exuded a strong positivistic belief in a 'rational' political universe which experts could objectively analyze. It relied heavily on predictions that were considered 'objective' truths—derived from what was considered a detached parsing of political reality—and left little room for cultural difference.[109]

As Halliday says, Iran was "one of the most difficult Third World countries to deal with, not least because *the understanding of what constitutes 'reasonable behavior'* or 'good intentions' notoriously differ."[110] On the issue of *taqieh*, no matter what camouflage statements were made by Khomeini in Paris or actions were taken soon after his arrival in Iran, there is the awkward fact that:

> If there is a single constant in Khomeini's thinking—contained in sermons, statements and about 30 published books—it is a deep-seated sense of Iranian nationalism and suspicion of foreign powers seen as exploiting his country. "All the problems besetting Iran and other Islamic nations are the doings of the aliens of the United States," he said in a fiery sermon in 1964, climaxing several years of attacks on the Shah, which led to his exile.[111]

Behind each of these individual factors distorting the analysis phase of the intelligence cycle, however, is an antecedent condition, the overriding fact that CIA analysts, because of the workings of culture and identity already detailed, lacked a "conscious epistemology." Deeper epistemic and methodological self-awareness would have "helped analysts and their consumers understand the implications of developmentalism and dependency on forecasting political change"[112] during the analysis part of the intelligence cycle:

> The unprecedented nature of Iranian fundamentalism confounded accepted notions of rationality, linear progression and other time-honored tools for peering into the future . . . [CIA analysts] could not envision a country which would adopt a seemingly regressive collective belief system and proceed to institutionalize it amid breathtaking repression and violence . . . Expectations about Iran "were amplified through 'model fitting,' that is, the tendency of observers to corroborate their paradigmatic assumptions regardless of the political reality . . . [and] were often based more on the belief in the logic of the paradigm than on the detailed knowledge of the situation."[113]

In other words, the CIA ended up with what Milani describes as "a sort of theoretical glaucoma"[114] because they failed to be aware of the master theories (what Kuhn called paradigms) that dictated the standards of inquiry in their field. The strangeness of the revolutionaries' ideology—and its distance from Western preconceptions—was captured by a distinguished Iranian historian of Islam. When asked soon after the revolution if he was acquainted with Khomeini, he answered: "I've never actually met him, but I feel I have known him for nearly 1,300 years."[115] Sherman Kent's analytical progeny dwelt not simply in Virginia, but in another millennium.

Even in 1986, the confusion among some analysts and political scientists was palpable: "If the Shah's regime collapsed despite the fact that his army was intact, despite the fact that there was no defeat in war, and despite the fact that the state faced no financial crisis and no peasant insurrections, where does this leave the usual generalizations about revolutions? Mostly in the pits."[116]

We should note, however, that this does not mean that there were no relatively recent Western parallels to important aspects of Khomeini's movement that a different CIA culture might have detected. Said Arjomand finds such correspondences between Iran and European fascist movements like the Slovak Republic established by Father Hlinka's People's Party (run by Father Tiso), the Ustasha movement in Croatia, and especially the Romanian Iron Guards and the Legion of the Archangel Michael—all movements characterized by "extraordinary cults of suffering and martyrdom"[117] and prominently combined priests and university students. Ramazani, meanwhile, finds two historical precedents in Iran's past with which the revolution of 1979 shared four factors,[118] all of them "soft" rather than quantitative features and thus less likely to register with agency analysts.

Production and Dissemination

Before closing our discussion of the key qualities of the CIA's culture and identity that contributed to the massive failure to understand Iranian society during the Carter administration, it is worth noting the effect of the CIA's inclination for consensus on the last two phases of the intelligence cycle, production and dissemination. Recall the game of footnotes and associated social mechanisms described in Chapter 2. Then consider this chain of events surrounding the CIA's failure to produce and disseminate an NIE on Iran in the autumn of 1978, and consider whether the "bureaucratic infighting" this passage suggests is an adequate explanation:

> Bureaucratic infighting impeded the drafting of the National Intelligence Estimate "Iran: Prospects through 1985" ordered by Turner in March . . . the INR claimed that the CIA and the DIA were too optimistic about the Shah; in turn, the agencies accused the INR of being unduly pessimistic. Griffin [of the INR] issued a dissenting note when, in August, the CIA published an interim report which stated that "Iran was not in a revolutionary or even pre-revolutionary state" and that the "Shah will be an active participant in Iranian life well into the 1980s." On September 1, the INR responded that there is a "basic unresolvable [sic] conflict between the Shah's liberalization program and the need to limit violent opposition," and predicted that there are "some chances that the Shah will be forced to step down." In a September 28 report, the DIA argued that the "Shah is expected to remain actively in power over the next 10 years." *Failing to achieve consensus, Turner quietly abandoned the NIE.*[119]

As the *Washington Post* put it, "Turner kept 'honing' the 1978 NIE on Iran until it simply was overtaken by events, arriving on U.S. policymakers' desks on the edge of the Shah's downfall."[120] Similarly, Turner may have been disinclined to use probability estimates about the shah's chances of remaining on the throne because he was sensitive to past criticism of the CIA waffling in its analysis. If, as we have already quoted Herman saying, "Salesmanship is a part of the game,"[121] Turner's mirror imaging of the customer's desires for certainty *and* his unwillingness to upset the consensus regarding the shah probably contributed to the CIA's "single outcome forecast" of the shah's permanence. At the same time, it is important to note that, through the summer of 1978, the

CIA as a whole remained almost sanguine about the Iranian situation and did not view it as revolutionary.[122]

In a manner fully consonant with the mirror-imaging hypothesis proposed so far, Seliktar offers details of this process at work in the analysis phase in a manner that links it to the production and dissemination phases:

> Left to their own devises [sic], individual analysts could probably have produced more nuanced and intellectually sophisticated analysis. Many of them are trained academics whose natural inclination is to write in ways that reflect the ambiguity and complexity of political change. However, *busy bureaucrats and politicians see ambiguity and complexity as irritants and impediments to good decision-making. There is even less tolerance for theoretically laden concepts such as discourse, legitimacy or collective belief systems.* In the words of one observer, "policymaking elites and intelligence bureaucracies are not readily disposed toward dealing with theories in a conscious, rigorous or sustained manner."[123]

In other words, we again see mirroring of the customer at work in the CIA's culture, to the detriment of strategic warning—the "consensus" will always drive toward crisp and simple analysis, even if the underlying reality is more complex.

This chronicle of the disastrous surprise of the Iranian Revolution first offered clear evidence that the end of the Pahlavi dynasty *was* a strategic surprise about which the CIA failed to provide warning. It then detailed how, beginning in tasking—and following the intelligence cycle through collection, analysis, production, and dissemination—the key attributes of the CIA's identity and culture that were detailed in Chapter 2 contributed to this intelligence failure. Along the way, it revealed Cassandras outside the agency's culture who accurately foresaw how the process in Iran might end and tried to provide strategic warning. In so doing, it put paid to the suggestion of some of Langley's defenders that because the *outcome* of unrest in Iran was unforeseeable, the intelligence agency is "not to blame" in any sense for the failure to give warning.

In short, this case detailed why—if the outcome of Iranian revolution of the late 1970s was a true "mystery"—the origin of the CIA's failure to predict its general outline is not: It ultimately resides in perennial internal characteristics of the agency's identity and culture.

4 THE COLLAPSE OF THE USSR

THIS CHAPTER ADDRESSES THE COLLAPSE of the USSR.[1] In Chapter 1, we discussed the fundamental logical difference between mysteries and secrets. Before discussing the evidence for the CIA's failure to anticipate the mysterious implosion of the USSR, three caveats are in order.

First, there is the obvious fact that the CIA was by no means alone in not anticipating the "self-liquidating" nature of the Soviet Union. Second, we need to spend a minute on the so-called triumphalist hypothesis. Finally, there is in a few quarters an absolute denial that the collapse of the USSR was a surprise to the CIA.

The first item on our preliminary agenda is to acknowledge that the CIA was not alone in failing to predict the demise of the USSR: It caught the Soviets themselves by surprise. In the West, however, it was the failure of an entire *profession*, Sovietology.[2] No less a figure than John Kenneth Galbraith, on returning from a 1984 visit to the USSR, asserted that the Soviet economy had made "great material progress" and remarked on "the appearance of solid well-being of the people on the streets"; Galbraith ascribed these facts to the idea that "in contrast to Western industrial economy," the USSR "makes full use of its manpower."[3] Nobel laureate Paul Samuelson, whose economics textbook is standard fare at many of America's best universities and business schools, wrote in the 1989 edition: "Contrary to what many skeptics had earlier believed . . . the Soviet economy is proof that a socialist command economy can function and even thrive." It was only on the edge of the mainstream, mainly the right-wing edge—hard-line conservative academics like Richard

Pipes, who maintained that the Soviet Union was an "Upper Volta with missiles"[4] and by the mid-1980s was in the midst of a systemic crisis. Crucially, the Right also perceived before others that the Soviet regime was largely illegitimate in the eyes of its own citizens.

On the other hand, before the CIA is lumped among the many others who misjudged the USSR, it is important to recognize the CIA's central (if unintended) contribution to the failure of the Sovietological profession as a whole. In 1990, the political economist Nicholas Eberstadt made the point this way: "The CIA's figures on Soviet economic trends are widely regarded as the most authoritative currently available . . . Unclassified CIA publications serve as basic reference sources on the Soviet economy in our universities, in our newspapers, and for the interested public."[5] Through its uniquely authoritative voice, the agency enabled and reinforced Sovietology's central misjudgments. Its basic data on the USSR, moreover, were not perceived as ideologically tainted in academe. In 1981, for example, a scholar in *Slavic Review* wrote: "By the traditional measures of quality employed by scholars, the work done by CIA [on the Soviet economy] receives high marks. It exhibits methodological integrity, analytical rigor and thoroughness in research."[6]

There is another preliminary aspect of this surprise to consider: the triumphalist hypothesis. It is summed up in the title of Robert Gates's book *Victory: The Reagan Administration's Secret Strategy That Hastened the Collapse of the Soviet Union*. What is the hypothesis? The publication of various memoirs and selected CIA declassifications reveal that, under President Reagan (or even before, during the Ford and Carter years), the United States undertook a covert strategic offensive to attack "the very heart of the Soviet system."[7]

There *is* ample evidence that all of the policies that advocates of this hypothesis enumerate[8] were pursued, both by the CIA and by other government agencies. It is not clear, however, the degree to which these policies were pushing on an already opening door or the degree to which a list of policies like this do not represent ex post facto pattern finding (that is, hindsight bias) of the sort that Nassim Taleb explores.[9] The approach used by advocates of this understanding of the collapse of the USSR also ignores the larger historical and geopolitical factors that contributed to the collapse and brings tactical measures to the foreground. These were factors internal to the communist experiment itself and transcended the merely economic or political, such as those Stephen Kotkin explores.[10] In other words, this offensive did not, as some allege, create the various crises that ended the USSR. It did, however, amount to a "comprehensive policy to exacerbate"[11] many of the problems involved in this downfall, and thus these policies arguably hastened the events of 1989–1991. What's more, the triumphalist thesis discounts Josh Kerbel's common sense (but oft-neglected) observation:

> Emphasis on economic leverage and levers illustrates how the linear template (in this case one providing for proportionality and identifiable cause-and-effect), when erroneously applied to a nonlinear system, provides the illusion of calibrated influence. Economies, like the nation-states and international system in which they are intertwined, are nonlinear and notoriously resistant to precise manipulation.[12]

The evidence presented in the following discussion shows that, though the strategic offensive of the Reagan years was real, there were at the CIA intelligence failures that involve "a deeper intellectual misjudgment of a central historical reality"[13] about the USSR. As in the Iranian crisis, and for many of the same underlying reasons, U.S. policy makers were once again not offered "the best available materials of decision."[14] In other words, despite the triumphalist hypothesis, the next section substantiates the scale and scope of the surprise of the CIA and the U.S. government as a whole at the collapse of the USSR. These misjudgments, documented in the following pages, ultimately demolish the logic of the triumphalist hypothesis: Complexity aside, it is not credible that an entity as profoundly misunderstood by the CIA as the USSR could nevertheless be manipulated into a planned outcome—peaceful collapse—with such precision.

This point leads to a final, related argument: those defenders of the CIA who allege that there was no surprise at the cessation of the USSR. For example, intelligence scholar Jeffrey T. Richelson says: "I think they did a good job . . . If you had read the estimates and studies that I read from 1985 to May of 1991, I don't think anybody would have been surprised by the evolution of events in the Soviet Union, and that's all that anybody could ask." Richelson ascribes the perception that there was a strategic surprise to two factors: "Partly it comes from statements by [Senator Daniel] Moynihan and partly it comes from the assumption that, because we didn't announce all of this was going to happen, there was no understanding that it could."[15] This effort to understand the CIA's record on the USSR—and to counter criticism of it—began in 1991, when the House Permanent Select Committee on Intelligence commissioned a group of nongovernment economic experts to review CIA's analysis of the Soviet economy. They concluded:

> Most reports [from 1979] through 1988 on the course of the Soviet GNP and on general economic developments were equally satisfactory: accurate, illuminating, and timely. In fact, we find it hard to believe that anyone who has read the CIA's annual public reports on the state of the Soviet economy since 1975 could possibly interpret them as saying that the Soviet economy was booming. On the contrary, these reports regularly reported the steady decline in the Soviet growth rate and called attention to the deep and structural problems that pointed to continued decline and possibly to stagnation.[16]

Similarly, in a 1995 article in *The National Interest* entitled "The CIA Vindicated: The Soviet Collapse Was Predicted," for example, two intelligence scholars flatly avow: "The Intelligence Community did not fail to predict the Soviet collapse. Quite the contrary, throughout the 1980s the Intelligence Community warned of the weakening Soviet economy, and, later, of the impending fall of Gorbachev and the break-up of the Soviet Union." On the issue of the USSR's economy, these same scholars assert: "Far from ignoring the Soviet economic malaise, by the middle of the Reagan administration the Intelligence Community understood as a matter of course that the Soviet economy had been consistently slowing down, slipping to mediocre—and, in some years, negligible—growth rates."[17]

At times, these scholars seem to rely on slender reeds indeed, as demonstrated by the following: "It is notable that the five-year prediction of stability presented in the 1985 NIE stopped just short of the actual date of the Soviet collapse (1991)." Dumb luck and bureaucratic convention do not an accurate forecast make. Nevertheless, these experts ultimately conclude of the CIA's record on the "strategic problem" of "detecting Soviet decline" that:

> By attempting to estimate specific growth rates, the Intelligence Community diluted its main message, which was that the Soviet economy was stagnating and—even more important—that there were no apparent or available means for it to be reinvigorated. This basic message, which was accepted throughout the Intelligence Community and was repeated in official estimates over the course of several years, was right on the mark.[18]

When republishing a 1995 monograph entitled *Intelligence Fiasco or Reasoned Accounting? CIA estimates of Soviet GNP*,[19] the RAND Corporation calls the debate over the CIA estimates of the Soviet economy "heavily politicized." The abstract says demurely: "The author finds little evidence to support the common indictment that the CIA seriously misestimated the Soviet growth record. [But] the author finds *somewhat greater reason to believe that the Agency's comparative size ratios were overstated*."[20] (The central significance of drawing such a careful distinction between "growth record" and "comparative size ratios," common among the defenders of the CIA's record, is addressed in a moment.)

A 1997 article in *Studies in Intelligence* makes a similar argument: "The assertions that the CIA got it blatantly wrong are unfounded—that charges that the CIA did not see and report the economic decline, societal deterioration, and political destabilization that ultimately resulted in the break-up of the Soviet Union are contradicted by the record."[21] Robert Gates, who began his career as a Soviet analyst and was the first former analyst selected to be DCI, said in a 1992 speech to the Foreign Policy Association:

> Obviously there were deficiencies in the CIA's work on the Soviet Union—things we did not know and areas where we were wrong. But the body of information, analysis and warning provided to policymakers and to Congress was of extraordinarily high quality. To claim that US intelligence in general and the CIA in particular failed to recognize the systemic weakness of the Soviet system, failed to inform policymakers of the growing crisis, or failed to warn of impeding collapse of the old order is not consistent with the facts.[22]

The following year, the CIA's Center for the Study of Intelligence even sponsored a three-day conference at Texas A&M University's Bush School of Government and Public Service, entitled "U.S. Intelligence and the End of the Cold War," that was intended to lay to rest charges that the failure of the USSR was a surprise.[23]

The former US Ambassador in Moscow during this period, Jack Matlock, also defends the CIA record and does so in a somewhat novel manner (for intelligence literature, at any rate). He does so by highlighting the practical danger posed by issuing a warning that might become a "self-altering prediction."[24] He says, "If the analysis leaked, as it certainly would have, it could well have precipitated a crackdown in the Soviet Union that reversed Gorbachev's reforms, restored many Cold War practices, and preserved authoritarian controls in the Soviet Union for a generation or longer."[25]

On one level, the ambassador and those like him are correct: The CIA was not completely wrong about every aspect of the USSR. It is indeed easy to find CIA studies that document many of the problems that led to the demise of the USSR, and (contra Julian Assange et al.) leaks do pose dangers. Moreover, there is also substantial disagreement among both scholars and veteran CIA employees themselves about the exact nature and timings of their surprise at the shape and speed of the USSR's downfall. Without a doubt, "the predominant value of the CIA's economic research on the USSR is that the Soviet economy does not function very well,"[26] and thus the story of this surprise is certainly more nuanced than the fall of the shah or than the somewhat simplistic charges made in Senator Moynihan's newspaper articles.

Nevertheless, asserting that the CIA's view of the USSR was essentially correct in its assessment of the political, military, and economic state of the USSR, is (to put it at in its most polite form) a selective reading of the CIA's record regarding the last decade of Soviet power. There is overwhelming evidence of a sustained misjudgment of the central political, social, economic, and military conditions of the CIA's primary target for over four decades and that its sudden demise was a strategic surprise. The overarching fact is that, for the U.S. government, the fall of the USSR meant a "sudden realization that one has been operating on the basis of an erroneous threat assessment": a strategic surprise.

We will now review evidence demonstrating that, despite the protestations of its bureaucratic defenders, a record of honorable service, and occasional triumphs, the foundation of the agency's threat assessments about the USSR was gravely flawed.

EVIDENCE OF THE FAILURE

As already explored, there is evidence that the CIA successfully identified many strains that eventually contributed to the collapse of the USSR. Despite a huge generational investment of resources, however, their threat assessment was badly skewed. As we begin, we should recall that during the Cold War much of what could be learned about the United States from the Government Printing Office or a local library had to be pieced together painstakingly about the Soviet Union. At one point, even samovar production figures were a state secret.[27] Obviously, this information vacuum exacerbated many of the factors discussed in this chapter. If the Soviet Union was secretive about its economy, it was still more so about its military might. In a military context, virtually everything had to be pieced together from information that was collected either secretly or by unusual means (such as interpreting telemetry from Soviet missile tests). Thus, no one should underestimate the complexities of the task with which the CIA was charged. Undoubtedly, the CIA's "quest to describe the Soviet economy absorbed enormous resources and marshaled considerable analytical talent": With some justification, it was called "the largest single social science research project in the history of humanity."[28] The crucial term in that description, of course, is *social* science.

We can begin by polling the opinion of Stansfield Turner, whom we met as DCI during the Iran debacle. In 1991, he stated:

> We should not gloss over the enormity of this failure to forecast the magnitude of the Soviet crisis . . . Yet I never heard a suggestion from the CIA, or the intelligence arms of the departments of Defense or State, that numerous Soviets recognized a growing, systemic economic problem. Today we hear some revisionist rumblings that the CIA did in fact see the Soviet collapse emerging after all. If some individual CIA analysts were more prescient than the corporate view, their ideas were filtered out in the bureaucratic process; and it is the corporate view that counts because that is what reaches the President and his advisers. On this one, the corporate view missed by a mile. Why were so many of us so insensitive to the inevitable?[29]

In 1994, Turner repeated the charge, saying that CIA assessments of the USSR were not necessarily always inaccurate but were essentially "irrelevant."[30] The leading intelligence scholar Richard Betts concurs: "Before the end of the Cold War, intelligence did not give advance warning that the Soviet Union would collapse"—though he feels that the CIA did provide ample evidence of "intractable" problems facing Soviet leaders.[31] But intractable problems are the stuff of politics everywhere, not a forecast of breathtaking change.

Contra claims made by the CIA's defenders in the preceding paragraphs, a similar assessment is given by some lower-ranking but long-serving CIA analysts and important intelligence "customers." Melvin Goodman, who worked in SOVA from 1966 to 1986, maintains, "Probably the greatest failure in the history of the CIA is the error with regard to exaggerating the size and the strength and the capabilities and the intentions of the Soviet Union."[32] Admiral William J. Crowe Jr., chairman of the Joint Chiefs of Staff under George H. W. Bush, remembers that in 1989 the CIA "talked about the Soviet Union as if they weren't reading the newspapers, much less developed clandestine intelligence." Harold Ford, a forty-year veteran of the CIA, says simply that they had been "'dead wrong' on the facts of life inside the Soviet Union."[33]

Documentary evidence supports the idea that the CIA's record of assessment of the USSR is not as sterling as some maintain. Defenders of the CIA's record rarely cite the agency's 1984 report that "concluded the leadership could muddle along almost indefinitely"[34] and that "although there had been a marked 'slowdown' in Soviet growth since the 1970s, 'the Soviet economy' was 'not going to collapse.'" Instead, CIA expected "GNP to continue to grow, although slowly."[35]

The most egregious, sustained, and important errors in the CIA's assessments concern the total size of the Soviet economy. Nicholas Eberstadt, formerly of the Senate Committee on Foreign Relations, says: "With the benefit of hindsight—and post–Cold War revelations—it is now widely agreed, I think, that many of the Intelligence Community's key estimates of Soviet economic performance were seriously off the mark, perhaps for decades."[36] John Wilhelm, another scholar, says: "CIA figures implied a picture that did not correspond to the reality we found when the veil of secrecy was lifted by *glasnost* and the fall of communism."[37] Melvin Goodman—the CIA analytical veteran already cited—has the same opinion in an article in *Foreign Policy*: The CIA failed to see the magnitude of the crisis in the Soviet Union in the 1980s.[38]

It is noteworthy—and somewhat ironic given the preference at CIA, previously documented, for quantitative measures—that most partisans of the "no surprise" school avoid mentioning the CIA's basic numbers about the USSR. That is probably because, as Senator Patrick Moynihan pointed out, numbers undermine the CIA's case:

> At the outset of the '50s, the CIA estimates (secret at first, but later published) depicted the Soviets with a sizable economic base, about 350 billion 1980 U.S. dollars and a formidable rate of economic growth. This growth rate was consistently depicted as higher than that of the United States. Over three decades there is only one five-year interval in which the United States outstrips the USSR. For the entire period, the Soviet growth is shown at 4.8 percent, almost half again the American 3.4 percent. Investment rates were seen to soar, doubling in three decades to 32.5 percent, twice that of the United States and equal to Japan. In the mid-'70s, the size of the Soviet economy in relation to the United States was thought to have passed into the 60 percent range.[39]

Similarly, in 1988, a noted expert could observe: "Until recently, the CIA stated that the national income per capita was higher in the Soviet Union than in Italy."[40] These patently absurd high-level economic figures are crucial *because they were the denominator used to calculate the total burden on the Soviet economy of their military expenditure* and thus inputs into almost every feature of U.S. government economic thinking. Insofar as other parts of the Intelligence Community were complicit in this overestimate, this simply confirms mirror imaging of the Community and the drive for consensus that is part of the CIA's culture and identity.

From 1975 to 1980, for example, the CIA put Soviet military spending at 11 to 15 percent of GNP. As became evident after the break-up, this is *one-third as large as the actual figures.*[41] In fact, what the "no surprise" school never addresses is the persistent logical clash between the *qualitative* statements that they use in defense of the CIA's analytical record and the *quantitative* estimates that the CIA continuously supplied to policy makers and Sovietologists for decades. Collections of primary sources (that is, declassified NIEs like *Soviet Defense Spending: A History of CIA Estimates 1950–1990*)[42] miss this point because they remove these NIEs from their central context: *the CIA's estimate of the USSR's GNP.* If, as the CIA's defenders contend, "A key purpose of intelligence is to provide some key 'concrete facts'"[43] to policy makers, then by the absolutely central measure of GNP the CIA was wildly off target. Washington makes policy using numbers, and the central numbers provided by the CIA for decades about the USSR point firmly toward a surprise.

Eberstadt makes another important link: A profound misreading of an adversary's military burden also strongly suggests an acute misreading of an adversary's intentions. Soviet authorities had committed their economy to something like a full war mobilization that lasted for decades, and that decision was extraordinarily significant. Far from being "right on the mark"[44] the CIA's decades-long gross underestimates of the USSR's military burden suggest a profound misunderstanding of the intentions of Langley's main target.

According to Mikhail A. Alexseev, a scholar who was a Soviet citizen then living in the USSR, the declassified NIE 11-18-85 of the Gorbachev period, *Domestic Stresses on the Soviet System* "lucidly and incisively" portrays the mounting political and socioeconomic challenges facing Gorbachev. One of the authors of this book, who visited four Soviet republics in 1984 and was a language student at the Pushkin Institute in Leningrad in 1985, agrees: This NIE's *qualitative* statements regarding daily life in the USSR accurately portray the country's profound social problems. But that same NIE and others at the time used extensive *quantitative* data to portray a *still growing* Soviet economy (albeit at a slower rate than previously estimated). While "little of what later proved fatal to the Soviet system escaped the CIA's attention," the quantitative information that the agency provided from the 1970s right up to the downfall of the USSR "set up quite a few hedges against anyone concluding that the Soviet Union was on a course leading to a meltdown."[45] As scholars Stephen Brooks and William Wohlforth astutely note, the longer that Soviet stagnation and qualitative indicators pointing toward decline continued, the more these factors should have become *variables* rather than *constants* in the CIA's analysis because every year that they continued was "another piece of evidence that the problem [was] systemic rather than cyclical"[46] and that something "had to give."

Lest a customer of the CIA's intelligence attempt to resolve the paradox between the qualitative and quantitative facts in *Domestic Stresses on the Soviet System*, the NIE began with a special insert that was separate from the narrative text: "The Exceptional Sector: The Soviet Military-Industrial Complex." This insert *does* say that the defense sector was "not isolated from the problems of the surrounding society," but it then (using the CIA's building-block methodology[47]) states that the USSR had spent about US$640 billion on roughly 200 new or modernized military systems (this in the larger context of a grossly overstated total Soviet GNP). Alexseev remarks that it certainly gives no hint of near-term collapse when it says that the USSR "scored major military and technology advances in solid-propellant strategic missiles, surface-to-air and air-to-air missiles, long-range cruise missiles, fighters, bombers, transport aircraft, tanks, command-and-control systems, and re-entry vehicles" *but then ventures no quantitative projections of the impact of these procurement policies*! As Alexseev points out, "During 1987–1989, the CIA's Office of Soviet Analysis continued to draw attention to major political and socioeconomic pathologies obstructing Gorbachev's reforms; yet once again, estimates of the quantitative impact of these challenges on Soviet defense outlays were explicitly absent."[48]

That trend of reporting continued until very close to the end of the USSR. In the 1988 report *Soviet National Security Policy: Responses to the Changing Military and Economic Environment*, the CIA wrote: "All this [that is, the reasoning and data presented in the report] suggests that we will see a prolongation of the trend of the past decade-continued high but flat or slowly growing defense spending."[49] There is no whiff of Robert Gates's warnings about the "impeding collapse of the old order"[50] in such statements.

Former DCI Turner appears more clear sighted about the CIA's assessments of the USSR: "We were appreciating as early as '78 that the Soviet economy was in serious trouble, [but] we didn't make the leap that we should have made . . . that economic trouble would lead to political trouble. We thought they would tighten their belt under a Stalin-like regime and continue marching on."[51] The CIA also missed completely the significance of the 1975 Helsinki Accords, which led to a full court press on Soviet diplomats and negotiators and further undermined the USSR's legitimacy at home and abroad.

This in turn raises the question of whether the CIA's defenders are being consciously disingenuous regarding the agency's record vis-à-vis the USSR given the information-processing habits of the CIA's customers: American policy makers. In this NIE and others, "predictions of a possible slowdown and decline of the Soviet economy" were not only based on a wildly inaccurate GDP estimate but were accompanied by additional grossly misleading quantitative data. As the Cold War ended, a U.S. Senate report could observe with considerable irony "the latest CIA handbook of economic statistics . . . suggests that per capita output of milk is today higher in the USSR than in the United States, making the Soviet Union not only a nuclear power, but a dairy superpower."[52] As Senator Moynihan wrote:

> At the same hearing of the Senate Committee on Foreign Relations [that produced that report], Michael J. Boskin, then-Chairman of the Council of Economic Advisers, estimated that the Soviet economy was "about one-third" the size of the United States. At this time, the official *Handbook of Economic Statistics*, produced by the Intelligence Community, put the ratio at 52 percent . . . The United States GDP for 1990 was $4.8 trillion. The Intelligence Community put Soviet GDP at $2.5 trillion. The President's chief economist made it more like $1.6 trillion. The difference is $900 billion.[53]

The same CIA *Handbook of Economic Statistics* that was almost a trillion dollars off about the economy of their primary target for decades estimated that per capita meat production in the USSR was nearly a third higher at the end of the 1980s than it was at the start of the 1970s. This conclusion would have astounded both Soviet citizens and Western visitors to the country.

The agency's record on political and military reporting is also more mixed than its partisans allow. Without a doubt, it was easy to misread the political signals coming from the USSR in the late 1980s: It was Brezhnev, Andropov, and Chernenko who capped Soviet military spending in the early 1980s. Mikhail Gorbachev began his tenure in office by *reversing* the cap on military spending, approving an effort to try to settle the Afghan war by a military escalation and increasing arms transfers to Third World states to magnify Moscow's leverage on other issues.[54]

However, Gorbachev also surprised agency analysts when he publicly admitted in 1988 the large and sustained deficit in the USSR's state budget—another key fact missing from Langley's understanding of the Soviet economy! Soviet deficit figures were falsified and doctored for over thirty years—a fact detected by an émigré researcher, Igor Birman, using only open-source data[55] but missed by the CIA.

According to some important consumers—selective NIE quotations not withstanding—the CIA was also back-footed by events on noneconomic issues. Former Secretary of State Colin Powell wrote that in his view the CIA "didn't anticipate events much better than a layman watching television."[56] Former Secretary of State George Shultz is more specific, writing:

> When Gorbachev appeared at the helm, the CIA said he was "just talk," just another Soviet attempt to deceive us. As that line became increasingly untenable, the CIA changed its tune: Gorbachev was serious about change, but the Soviet Union had a powerfully entrenched and largely successful system that was incapable of being changed.[57]

He continues: "When it became evident that the Soviet Union was, in fact, changing, the CIA line was that the changes wouldn't really make a difference."[58] According to Shultz, as late as 1988, Robert Gates still believed that Gorbachev was merely a Leninist trying to gain "breathing space with the West."[59] At the end of this period the rise of Gorbachev's replacement, Boris Yeltsin, also took the CIA by surprise.[60] Tim Weiner's book, *Legacy of Ashes*, supports Shultz's memory on the CIA's Gorbachev reporting and offers concrete examples:

> The CIA did not know that Gorbachev had told the Warsaw Pact meeting in May 1987 that the Soviets would never invade Eastern Europe to shore up their empire. The CIA did not know that Gorbachev had told the leader of Afghanistan in July 1987 that the Soviets were going to start pulling their occupying troops out soon . . . the CIA did not grasp the concept [that Gorbachev was

trying to change the fundamental dynamic of the Cold War]. Bob Gates spent the next year asking his underlings why Gorbachev consistently surprised them.[61]

According to Weiner, it would seem that Gates and his team did not find the underlying cause of this difficulty. On December 1, 1988, for example, the CIA issued a NIE 11-3/8-88: "Soviet Forces and Capabilities for Strategic Nuclear Conflict through the Late 1990s." In it, the CIA stated with assurance that "the basic elements of Soviet defense policy and practice thus far have not been changed by Gorbachev's reform campaign." Less than a week later, Weiner continues, the Soviet leader stood at the podium of the United Nations in New York and offered to unilaterally cut half a million troops from the Soviet military. Recall the importance of arms control in this period and the idea from Chapter 1 that NIEs are considered the analytical profession's most prestigious products, and it is difficult not to conclude that the CIA's understanding of the USSR was missing many important elements.

Despite voluminous (but uncontextualized) quotations from NIEs of this period (offered in depth in the Center for the Study of Intelligence's book *CIA Assessments of the Soviet Union: The Record Versus the Charges*[62]), the fundamental judgment—one that swamps the details offered by the "no strategic surprise" school—is that for decades Langley profoundly misjudged the total size of the USSR's economy, the true burden of their military spending, and the long-term political consequences of the system's numerous economic and social problems relative to those in the West. The CIA's central economic figures were not just wrong; they were off by at least 100 percent and probably closer to 200 percent. The CIA's basic figures point not to an economy in crisis but to sustainability and continuity: They point to *slowdown* but not to *breakdown*.[63]

We will close this section with a Gates quotation that the "no surprise" partisans frequently omit. In hearings before the U.S. Senate on March 19, 1986, when Gates (then head of the Directorate of Intelligence) was asked "what kind of work the Intelligence Community was doing to prepare policymakers for the consequences of change in the Soviet Union," he responded: "Quite frankly, *without any hint that such fundamental change is going on*, my resources do not permit me the luxury of sort of *just idly speculating on what a different kind of Soviet Union might look like.*"[64] That statement was unexceptional coming from an organization that had consistently told U.S. policy makers and the world of Sovietology that the USSR's economy from 1981 to 1988 had grown faster than that of either France or West Germany!

In the 1990s, it was a bureaucratic imperative for the CIA to downplay their surprise at the collapse of the USSR. To do so now, however, does the agency a disservice. As Nietzsche has Zarathustra say: "If you have a suffering friend, be a resting place for his suffering, but a *hard bed* as it were, a field cot: thus will you profit him best."[65] A problem must be faced squarely before it can be solved. By intellectually rigorous measures, the agency's USSR record does not pass Allison's central test of a national intelligence service: "how well its analyzes and estimates inform policy-makers of *probable* developments abroad."[66] As Zbigniew Brzezinski reminded us with Iran, "Failure is not so much a matter of particular intelligence reports"; instead it is *"a deeper intellectual misjudgment of a central historical reality."*[67]

We can now turn to how the culture and identity of the CIA contributed to this surprise and make clear how such deep intellectual misjudgments about the USSR happened. As in the case of Iran, the origin of this strategic surprise is shown to be less the inherent unpredictability of external events than internal factors at the CIA that created the antecedent conditions for these events to become a strategic surprise.

REVEALING THE CASSANDRAS AND REFRAMING THE FAILURE

As with the overthrow of the shah of Iran, the four perennial features of the agency's identity and culture made the CIA insensitive to the possibility of Soviet collapse. Moreover, as in Iran a decade before, distortions in one part of the intelligence cycle operated synergistically with deformations in other parts of the cycle: omissions and oversights in tasking and collection, open gaps in analysis, and vice-versa. For this reason, as was the case for Iran, the discussion that follows is a pointillist portrait, in which individual pieces of evidence contribute to an overall picture of how deeply rooted and interlinked patterns in the intelligence cycle interacted with the key components of the CIA's identity and culture to make the collapse of the Soviet Union a strategic surprise. While direct causal links cannot be drawn, the important epistemological question of "How possible?" becomes much clearer.

Tasking

Tasking in the decades prior to the end of the USSR appears to have been adversely affected by all four of the key components of the CIA's identity and culture: homogeneity, the reification of objectivity and reason, a preference for secret information, and a drive for consensus. As before, it is somewhat artificial to disentangle these interwoven factors, but for the sake of organizational clarity, we do so in the following discussion.

The homogeneity of CIA personnel probably contributed to tasking missteps regarding ethnic tensions in the USSR. As Pipes points out, "Both Russians and Americans tended to think of the USSR as a vast melting pot, much like the United States, made up of numerous ethnic groups that voluntarily discarded their ethnic identity in favor of a new, 'Soviet' nationality." Pipes ascribes this propensity to a deeply rooted mirror-imaging phenomenon: Not only were the United States and the USSR *self-proclaimed melting pots*, but he also notes that "the few native-born Americans who could claim expertise on the Soviet Union had been trained by Russians and identified completely with Russia and her culture."[68] Russia expert Peter Rutland agrees, saying in general that American "Soviet" specialists were actually *Russian* specialists who "lacked a rigorous grounding in the languages and histories of the region—particularly the non-Russian peoples of the USSR."[69] Robert Conquest, a historian of the Soviet Union, offers an example:

> This is even true for as simple a distinction as between Ukrainian and Russian—long after the fact Ukrainian–Russian tension has been assigned as one of the causes of the man-made Stalinist Great Famine of the late 20s and early 30s, but lack of understanding of the distinct Ukrainian language and identity contributed to a misunderstanding of the event in the West.[70]

Sadly, even an expert like U.S. diplomat and historian George Kennan could write in the late 1950s that "the Ukraine was economically as fully integrated into the Soviet Union as Pennsylvania was integrated into the United States."[71] In truth, according to Nikolai Leonov, one-time chief analyst of the KGB, "The Soviet Union resembled a chocolate bar: it was creased with the furrowed lines of future division, as if for the convenience of its consumers."[72]

It is not a wild surmise, therefore, to suggest that this unconscious ignorance of deeper questions of nationality in the USSR, when reinforced by the homogeneous background of most CIA personnel, could lead to a sustained failure to task intelligence assets to explore issues of ethnic integration in the USSR. DCI Gates said as much in 1991: "Our efforts had long been focused on events in Moscow, and we were only beginning to realize how small and inadequate were collection capabilities and expertise on the non-Russian republics and ethnic groups."[73]

Two annotated maps that appear in NIE 11-18-89, *The Soviet System in Crisis: Prospect for the Next Two Years*, published by CIA in November of 1989 are entitled "Reported Incidents of *Economic* Unrest, January 1987–September 1989" and "Reported Incidents of *Nationalist* Unrest, January 1987–September 1989." As a thought experiment, consider whether it is likely that specialists who "lacked a rigorous grounding in the languages and histories of the region—particularly the non-Russian peoples of the USSR"[74] would be likely to have foreseen or expertly interpreted the various incidents of national unrest that took place in the late 1980s. Being a Russian expert was not the same as being a Soviet expert.

The reification of objectivity and reason also permeated much of the intelligence tasking concerning the Soviet Union. "This is revealed," Seliktar writes, "by the over-riding priority given to either economic data (however spurious) or the counting of military hardware." She goes on to make the connection between this tasking and the strategic surprise of the collapse of the USSR explicit: "The emphasis on quantified indices detracted from efforts to analyze the more qualitative aspects of Soviet life that could have alerted the Intelligence Community to the impending legitimacy crisis." As previously touched on, she adds that the CIA's "exactitude reflected the penchant for quantitative evidence in the American political culture."[75] Recall the CIA's advice to its analysts noted in the preceding discussion: "To identify lines of analysis that provide value added, *analysts should think through what they would want to know if they were policymakers charged with leveraging an issue.*"[76] The CIA was mirroring their intelligence customers, who a veteran agency analyst attested "generally prefer to focus on pragmatic as opposed to theoretical matters, on material rather than abstract values, on measurable, quantitative distinctions rather than qualitative factors."[77] A tendency to allow quantitative tasking, collection, and analysis vis-à-vis the USSR to submerge other forms of intelligence was implicitly raised in 1990 by national security expert George Carver in "Intelligence in the Age of Glasnost":

> America's Intelligence Community has been excellent in addressing many problems, such as keeping track of the Soviet Union's evolving strategic weapons capabilities [but] analysts should never forget that *the methods and approaches that work so well in tackling those problem are frequently inappropriate for assessing, let alone predicting, emotion-driven, political upheavals such as the events of 1989. Such situations do not lend themselves to quantification, and*

they become totally distorted if forced into a conceptual matrix better suited to assessing missile telemetry data. If American intelligence analysts or academics or citizens—want to understand and assess the historic political tide shifts in which the world is currently immersed, they must *ignore their itch for quantification, curb their fascination with models that bear minimal relation to reality and avoid the temptation to use bad data (such as Soviet economic statistics) simply because it exists and can be run through computers.*[78]

Ironically, Gorbachev's reforms only *reinforced* this deformation of tasking: When glasnost began in 1985, many items already being counted by CIA were suddenly easier to count! As Robert Bathurst, a former intelligence officer, says: "US intelligence about the Soviet Union existed in a state of cultural deprivation until *glasnost* opened doors and windows . . . [but ironically] that encouraged the *already powerful inclination to count rather than interpret.*"[79]

On the preference for secret information in tasking, we already noted the charge leveled against SOVA that the CIA spent lots of time targeting secrets about KGB rather than the USSR as a whole, and vice versa, and Victor Cherkashin's observation that "some of the best-known Cold War espionage cases were more about spy versus spy than real issues of national security."[80]

Even Joseph Nye, a scholar generally sympathetic to the CIA, says that while "the Intelligence Community accurately reported a slowdown in the Soviet economy . . . it did not adequately estimate the rapidity of the economic collapse" (note that Nye mentions estimates of "slowdown" rather than *size* of the Soviet economy). He continues by asserting, "The questions posed by policymakers were not about some abstract future, but about whether even a weakening Soviet economy could support a formidable military threat."[81] This is undoubtedly true, but had policy makers not been so misled by the CIA's baseline quantitative estimates, they might have tasked the CIA to probe more deeply the sustainability of the Soviet enterprise.

Collection

As might be expected, factors of culture and identity shaping tasking largely mirror those bearing on collection: the agency's homogeneity, obsession with "objective" quantitative factors, and a partiality for secrets. With respect to homogeneity and how it affected judgments about the USSR, take two of the most prominent features of Soviet life that one of the authors witnessed in the mid-1980s: the lines for consumer goods and the moderately well-attended church services.

In the former case, one source of the failure of imagination was that an overwhelmingly large percentage of CIA personnel were male (see Chapter 2). Arguably, this skewed gender profile contributed to an underestimate of the societal strains created by shortages of consumer goods because Soviet women *bore the brunt of the immense effort needed to obtain simple household items.* The often Herculean efforts of Soviet housewives and mothers would be as invisible to Langley as the efforts of housewives were to traditional men in U.S. society.[82] Here we witness the social mechanism of the mirror imaging of the target at work. As already discussed, much of the CIA's analytical effort nominally devoted to the USSR was actually devoted to the KGB, the USSR's most privileged caste. As Oleg Kalugin, the highest-ranking KGB officer to ever go public, points out:

> We at Yasenovo [an immense KGB complex outside Moscow] like all the Soviet elite, lived in a privileged cocoon that left us far removed from the travails of daily Soviet life. For us, Communism was indeed a good thing, for all our needs were cared for as we glided above the fray, impervious to the lines and the humiliation and the squalor that had become the hallmarks of Soviet existence.[83]

In its quest for secrets, the CIA became most focused on the least representative segment of Soviet society, the KGB.

Similarly, the fact that a sizable majority of congregants at churches that the Soviet authorities permitted to operate were older women probably also led to an overestimation of the Soviet regime's legitimacy in the eyes of its citizens (because they may also be inferred to have been less visible to the CIA's mostly male staff). Yet religion continued to matter in the USSR: The outside world later learned that there were seventeen attempts at self-immolation in Red Square in 1981 alone by seekers after religious freedom.[84] As in the Iran case, Sherman Kent's technocratic progeny did not sufficiently register that "many people take God seriously."

In like manner, Robert Bathurst stresses the gender-skewed secondary effects of the alcoholism rampant in Soviet society, which hit females harder than males.[85] Here again, the imagination required to task information related to these societal issues might not easily arise in an environment made up almost entirely of middle-class, socially conventional males. What is certain is that American specialists never took full account of the effect of unchecked alcoholism in the Soviet Union.[86]

Tellingly, the single article in *Studies* that the authors found raising questions about the *real* standard of living in the USSR is a 1968 piece by one of the few woman CIA officers stationed in Moscow. To better understand Soviet life, Gertrude Schroeder dressed up in her shabbiest clothes and tried to live for a week as an average Soviet citizen. She quickly concluded that life in the USSR was "hard and very, very frustrating,"[87] with uncertainty, absurdity, coarseness, and dullness permeating almost every aspect of daily life. As a result, Schroeder explicitly questions the CIA's GNP assumptions. She writes that in the CIA's *US and USSR: Comparisons of Size and Use of Gross National Product, 1955–64* (Estimate CIA/RR ER 66-6, published in March 1966), the agency "equated apples with apples and bread with bread,"[88] and for consumer durables they merely raised the ruble–dollar price ratios an arbitrary 20 percent to make some allowance for the superior quality and durability of U.S. products. In contrast, Schroeder's "undercover" observations as an average Soviet housewife trying to provide for a family led her to assert:

> I think our measurements of the position of Soviet consumers in relation to those of the United States (and Western Europe) favor the USSR to a much greater extent than I had thought. The ruble–dollar ratios are far too low for most consumer goods. Cabbages are *not* cabbages in both countries. The cotton dress worn by the average Soviet woman is *not* equivalent to the cheapest one in a Sears catalogue; the latter is of better quality and more stylish. The arbitrary 20 percent adjustment that was made in some of the ratios is clearly too little.[89]

Schroeder's article is titled *Soviet Reality Sans Potemkin*—and appears under the editor's note, "A logical but little used methodology for overt observation in the USSR"! The "logical but little used methodology" was simply relying on common sense and open source observation but was never embraced by the CIA. Indeed, a 1960 article in *Studies* had concluded that although official Soviet economic statistics were to be interpreted "with care," they "are not seriously fudged or fabricated"[90]—a statement arithmetically correct but exceptionally misleading. In short, one need not be a partisan of "identity politics" to postulate that many key features of life in the USSR that might have offered hints of its future were systematically neglected in the tasking and collection due to the homogenous nature of the CIA's personnel.

Similarly, an obsession with "factual" data amenable to "objective" analysis and the collection of secret information led to fundamental misunderstandings about the trajectory of the USSR. A leading non-CIA scholar—and émigré—in the field of Soviet economics noted that the best material about village life and agriculture in the USSR appeared in the *fiction* of Soviet literary monthlies, where "reality appear[ed] in fiction."[91] However, as Bathurst records, "Few analysts assigned to the Soviet desk had the time, background or prescience to understand that they required a complete Russian *tour d'horizon* to perform their job adequately. It is difficult to leap cultural barriers and not easy to understand why it is useful to read Gogol's *Dead Souls* and Dostoevsky's *Notes From the Underground*"[92] to understand the Soviet economy or society.

As a result, Ofira Seliktar concurs that softer questions concerning the legitimacy of the USSR in the eyes of its citizens were ignored at CIA: Corruption scandals in the late Brezhnev and Andropov years were noted but "not given much prominence" in agency reports. Overall, she writes: "Limited by its analytical parameters, the Agency was hardly in a position to capture the subterranean and often esoteric legitimacy discourse" that was then occurring in the USSR. Because of this biased pattern of tasking and collection, the CIA had "little inside knowledge about the crisis of confidence among the Soviet leadership," so they "stuck to the linear progression model of forecasting. This type of prognostication posited that the 'future Soviet system [will reflect] the present pattern of institutionalized power relationships . . . [and] . . . the basic social policies of welfare-authoritarianism.' Radical change was virtually ruled out."[93]

In fact, the legitimacy discourse then raging in the Kremlin was ignored while General Secretary Constantin Chernenko lay dying. Seliktar adds, "His state of health was the subject of intense speculation in Washington, eclipsed only by the interest in his potential successor and the projections of economic performance. True to its analytic character, the CIA focused most of its attention on the Soviet economy"[94] and ignored the nonquantifiable issues of *legitimacy* or *stability*.

What did it mean, asks Kotkin, for example, when General Secretary Brezhnev began drooling on himself during appearances on Soviet television (after awarding himself more state awards than all previous Soviet leaders combined, and more military awards than Marshall Zhukov, who captured Berlin in 1945)? How could one quantify that in 1984 Chernenko ordered a hidden escalator built so that he and other leaders could still ascend Lenin's tomb for holiday parades? Nikolai Leonov (a top intelligence analyst at the

KGB) recalls, "We were ashamed of our state, of its half-dead leaders, of the encroaching senility," but the assumption of the inherent system's durability went unquestioned at CIA until almost the very end of the USSR.[95]

Here a comparison with the academic community—subject to other factors distorting its understanding of the USSR but more diverse and less distracted by "secrets" than the CIA—is illuminating. During the same period, "the academic community utilized the Chernenko interlude to engage in a wide-ranging debate about the legitimacy, durability and changeability of the Soviet enterprise."[96] It seems that the CIA did not.

The agency later conceded in a limited way that too great an emphasis on "factual" data and secrets adversely affected its analysis of the USSR. An internal CIA review in 1976, the famous Team A–Team B experiment,[97] released in 1992, admitted that NIEs "substantially misperceived the motivations behind Soviet strategic programs" and then continued thus:

> This misperception has been due in considerable measure to concentration on the so-called hard data collected by technical means, and the resultant tendency to interpret these data in a manner reflecting basic U.S. concepts while slighting or misinterpreting the large body of "soft" data concerning Soviet strategic concepts.

It concluded, "The failure to take into account or accurately to assess such soft data sources has resulted in NIEs not addressing themselves systematically to the broader political purposes which underlie or explain Soviet strategic objectives."[98]

Analysis

When considering the role that analysis played in this surprise and how misanalysis of the USSR occurred, the usual suspects of our culture and identity line-up appear: homogeneity of personnel, reification of objectivity and reason (especially reflected in a preference for quantitative data), and a partiality for secret over openly obtained information. Frequently, evidence for these cultural characteristics appears related to specific analytical problems and also links back to the generative social mechanisms previously examined. Fortunately, evidence of homogeneity and insularity—even provincialism— in analytical staff (both senior and junior) and their linkage to analytical failings regarding the USSR is not far to seek. The Cold War and restrictions on CIA travel within the USSR made it almost inevitable, and we have already discussed that émigrés were generally excluded from the CIA's talent pool.[99] Robert Gates, for example—between 1982 and 1989 the chief of SOVA[100] and then DCI (and holder of a doctorate in Russian and Soviet history from Georgetown University)—had never actually visited the Soviet Union. Was Gates representative? A 1996 report to the House Permanent Select Committee on Intelligence (HPSCI) and the Senate Select Committee on Intelligence (SSCI) suggested that his background was not unusual: "More intelligence analysts should be given the opportunity to serve in, and travel to, the country or countries they are expected to cover. *An extended visit to the country or countries involved should be a minimal pre-requisite for any intelligence officer prior to undertaking analytical duties.*"[101] Nevertheless, even in 2007 the CIA's Office of Security preferred to approve individuals for the DI who had little or no foreign travel experience or contacts.[102]

Moreover, despite Gates's contention that CIA in the 1970s "was not a Cold War, bureaucratic monolith,"[103] there is little doubt that SOVA in the late 1980s was the home of true "Cold Warriors." Milton Bearden, for example, the man charged with overhauling the old Soviet division in 1990, recalled that on August 20, 1991, immediately after the hard-line coup attempt against Gorbachev, many people around him felt a "delicious sense of vindication . . . Some of [analysts] were pretty happy about it . . . Happy days were here again."[104] It seems that this lack of access to the subject at hand, the inescapably ideological nature of the work, and "isolation from the core social science disciplines"[105] made Soviet analysis at the CIA methodologically feeble.

In the sphere of political analysis, self-selection was also at work as the CIA was apparently drawing from a pool of political scientists who became Soviet specialists because they were attracted to intrigue: "Students of such systems were not required to engage in what may appear the somewhat arid activity of counting votes, adding up figures representing public opinion, observing parliamentary coalitions forming and disintegrating—what for many students of politics is their very bread and butter."[106]

The robustness of the CIA's economic estimates also suffered because of secrecy: According to Eberstadt, they were never properly challenged by outside economic views. These outside views need not have only been academic. One alternative source of challenge might have been the famous scenario planning group at the oil company Royal Dutch Shell.[107] As early as 1982, Shell scenario planners presented a credible and coherent case that the USSR could collapse in the decades ahead.

Did the homogeneity and methodological naiveté have an impact on the distance between Soviet reality and the views at Langley? The case of émigré economist and Cassandra Igor Birman is instructive. Birman was a Soviet-trained economist, who, when he moved to America, continued to monitor open source Soviet publications. Birman was a persistent critic of the CIA for overestimating the health and size of the Soviet economy. Seliktar records,

> In a series of detailed analyzes that echoed much of the internal discourse in Moscow, Birman claimed that the Soviet Union was plagued by extremely serious problems and that the budget writers had used statistical gimmicks to mask considerable inflation. He confirmed Gorbachev's then still secret allegations that the government had tapped into people's savings to balance the budget.[108]

Birman's efforts, however, to meet with Gates—then director of the analytical wing of the CIA—were rebuffed.

In fact, according to John Wilhelm, Birman was "one of the first to argue that the Soviet economy was in deep crisis, with important implications for the stability of the Soviet political system." Given his track record, it is "a particularly egregious misrepresentation of the situation"[109] to call his work—as did the author of the 1991 House committee's report assessing the CIA's performance evaluating the Soviet economy—a "hunch." The same applies, of course, to other émigré Cassandras like Naum Jasny[110] and Vadim Belotserkovsky, whom Wilhelm also cites at length.

That the CIA failed to anticipate the actual course of events between 1988 and 1990 as accurately as did Cassandras does not ipso facto make it a low-probability outcome (as the House's specialists argued). In response, one can return to the fact that the CIA was so dramatically mistaken regarding the size of Soviet GNP that their predictions of continuity made sense to them and others but that a more accurate picture of the size of USSR's economy would have made instability a serious possibility. To reinforce this assertion, consider that the émigré Cassandras' predictions extended to areas beyond the Soviet economy. In 1975, writing in the avowedly opinionated *Partisan Review*, the émigré Belotserkovsky said:

> The centrifugal forces in the national republics have reached—to borrow a metaphor from Solzhenitsyn—force 10 on the seismic scale. The absence of real national freedom coupled with the authorities' lip service to this freedom

causes enormous popular discontent. The "empire" is maintained only by inertia, military force, and the KGB. Any radical changes in Moscow are likely to burst the dam of national patience, and any attempt by Moscow to stop the tidal wave will merely replenish it with blood. For the most part the Russian people have never perceived any benefit in a "Great Russia," nor are the masses ready to give moral support to the ruthless suppression of the national movements in the republics.[111]

Clearly, Belotserkovsky's characterization of the USSR was prescient. Yet Professor Harry Rowen, chair of the National Intelligence Council (NIC) from 1981 through 1983 and former president of RAND Corporation, writes that the CIA slighted as "biased" "practically every émigré." He concluded that from the 1960s forward there were literally thousands of émigrés who "said the place was falling apart." He then asked rhetorically: "What effect did this have on the American specialists in the subject? None."[112] Even Robert Gates conceded memoirs that "the clearest American vision of the future of the Soviet Bloc in the spring of 1989 came not from the Bush administration, and probably not from its Intelligence Community, but rather from a *handful of experienced outside observers.*"[113]

Even in that concession, however, Gates omits to mention the most prescient group of all, Soviet émigrés. Homogeneity of staff reinforced an unhealthy focus on objectivity, reason, and quantification in CIA's analysis. We can examine this misplaced focus operating at three levels: Sovietology generally, SOVA at CIA, and in a specific analytical problem that the CIA addressed.

Reflecting on the collapse of the USSR, Michael Novak, a religion, philosophy, and public policy scholar, says: "Communism destroyed, or perhaps gravely injured, the 'social capital' on which all human progress depends . . . Most Western economists, alas, have little or no comprehension of how much they take this sphere for granted."[114] And if that was the case for economists generally, it was certainly the case for Sovietologists. Richard Pipes says, "Sovietologists treated societies as if they were mechanisms."[115] In this passage, he recalls much of what we already know about the CIA's culture and identity:

It seems likely that ultimately the reason for the failure of professionals to understand the Soviet predicament lay in their *indifference to the human factor*. In the desire to emulate the successes of the natural scientists, whose judgments are "value free," politology (sic) and sociology have been progressively dehumanized, constructing model and relying on statistics (many of them falsified) and, in the process, losing contact with the subject of their in-quiries—the messy, contradictory, unpredictable *homo sapiens*. Anyone who spent an hour walking the streets of Moscow, the Soviet Union's richest city, with open eyes, would have dismissed as preposterous CIA statistics show-ing the Soviet gross domestic product as well as living standards to be nearly half of the United States. Talking to Soviet citizens with an open mind would have revealed that the appearance of widespread support for the regime was fraudulent. Such evidence, however, was generally dismissed as "anecdotal" and hence unworthy of serious attention.[116]

In short, Pipes lays much of the surprise at the downfall of the USSR at the door of an objectivity-as-totem analytical approach. If indifference to the hu-man factor was the sin of Sovietology generally, what of analysis at CIA? One can already see that by their inability to travel to the USSR, combined with the exclusion of people who had actually lived there, CIA analysts would have trouble effectively understanding the USSR. Seliktar offers a picture similar to Pipes's but shows how unique factors at the CIA (that she labels "the Kent Doctrine") magnified these mistakes at the CIA. She maintains that, in spite of efforts "to modify the Kent doctrine,"

> Like their academic counterparts, SOVA analysts were most comfortable with things that could be formally defined, put into a Western context, and prefer-ably, counted. This type of empiricism, exacerbated by cultural parochialism, ethnocentric projection, mirror-imaging, and plain gullibility, made it hard to discern the more amorphous expressions of delegitimation [and exhaustion of the regime] . . . [Among] other things the CIA did not understand religious or ideological beliefs.[117]

Clearly, the CIA's identity and culture blinded the agency to elements that proved central to this strategic surprise.[118] Speaking at a conference in 2002, former DCI James Schlesinger is clear on the blinding role that scientism played in the CIA's analysis of the USSR's economy:

> The intelligence agency was working on a giant computer model of how the Soviet economy worked. And that giant computer model acquired a life of its own, so that instead of looking at what was actually going on, we tended to interpret everything through that model of the Soviet economy. Madame Roland (I heard a reference to the French Revolution earlier) said, "Oh, Lib-erty! What crimes are committed in thy name?" Well, here was "Oh, Comput-

ing! What crimes are committed in thy name?" Through this model we were grinding out detailed calculations about the Soviet Union, and we were failing to look at the realities.[119]

One can trace these general cultural tendencies to a truly acute incapacity to understand their target and to quite specific analytical failings. The volume *Intelligence Analysis: A Target-Centric Approach* provides a concrete example of how this misperception could occur. It points out that "U.S. intelligence frequently overestimated the capability of Soviet military research and development institutes based on the large number of engineers that they employed." This is because the tendency to count reinforced a bias caused by cultural and experiential ignorance: "It took some time [for analysts] to recognize how low the productivity of those engineers could be, but the reason had nothing to do with their capability. They often had to build their own oscilloscopes and voltmeters—items available in the United States at a nearby Radio Shack."[120]

Senator Moynihan was making a similar point when he asked rhetorically: "What American could imagine that 40 percent of the crops would rot in the distribution system? . . . You can count tanks, and mostly they don't spoil."[121] As already discussed, these analytical problems added up and ultimately contributed directly to the strategic surprise that arrived beginning in 1989. Ofira Seliktar attributed this aspect of the CIA's analytical culture and identity directly to what we have called the mirror imaging of the customer and then linked it to the CIA's misestimates parsing the Soviet economy: "Because of the 'culture of exactitude' in Washington, the CIA . . . continued to use GNP and other statistical measures even when it became clear that the Soviet economy bore little resemblance to a rational Western model."[122] Eberstadt agreed, writing that part of the reason that the CIA was so credulous about official Soviet statistics was because making such assumptions facilitated the use of the complex econometric models they had devised.[123]

Philip Hanson, a British economist who worked on the USSR, took a broader but complementary view, asserting that the CIA was simply the victim of American political culture: "The notion that, though you can generate a number, it might be wiser not to, is un-American and un-governmental."[124] Indeed, as head of SOVA Gates had wanted to do away with direct dollar-cost estimates of the Soviet economy. Mikhail Alexseev is blunt about the quixotic result: "The Department of Defense and Congress insisted that without quantitative data, however flawed, on the Soviet economy and military spending, the United States would have tremendous difficulty in passing its own budget,"[125] so the CIA continued to produce them. This is a clear example of social mechanisms (mirroring of the IC and the consumer) acting to maintain a feature of the CIA's identity and cultural (scientism).

Igor Birman also made the point repeatedly to the CIA that because of the USSR's quality issues the agency should not compare capital investments in the Soviet Union and the United States by cost: Costs in the Soviet Union were tremendous, but the results were miserable.[126] Nevertheless, it would appear that the utility of the USSR's investments was never properly quantified in agency models. David Kennedy and Richard Neustadt take the argument further:

> In its zest for academic correctness [the CIA] had buried what was perhaps the most crucial bit of economic intelligence of the cold war, the most *politically* significant aspect of the Soviet economy: its inability to satisfy the mass of the Soviet people. Shortages, queues, rotting potatoes and exploding TV sets were hard to quantify, but they mattered a good deal to the Soviet citizenry and arguably thus to Gorbachev and the Kremlin.[127]

In other words, they attribute CIA's analytical problems regarding the USSR to this quantitative penchant but ascribed to them not merely a misestimate of the *economy* of the USSR but to a fundamental misreading of Soviet *political* reality.

Interestingly, mirror imaging of the USSR may also have reinforced CIA's analytical problems centered on the reification of reason and illusory notions of objectivity. How did this synergy occur? It made Langley particularly susceptible to the "scientific" linguist prevarication to which the Soviets were addicted: "The use of value-neutral 'scientific' terminology, the reliance of official statistics, and the use of comparative functional-structural methodology to analyze Soviet Institutions" led social scientists at the CIA to the conclusion that the regime was considered quite legitimate, even by Western standards.[128] In reality, the CIA's focus on "reason" when analyzing the USSR was particularly ill suited to the task in a macro sense. Bathhurst makes the point with some drama:

> If, on the eve of a war for survival [in the 1930s], a government which has been warning of war, planning for war, having already adopted a militarized economy at least eight years before, arranges the execution of three out of five

marshals, fourteen out of sixteen army commanders, all eight of its admirals, and 60 out of 67 corps commanders, as well as thousands of other officers and men, then a self-destructive cultural process of such magnitude is operating that it obviously overrides what we [that is, Americans] think of as rational behavior.[129]

His central point was that it was actually illogical for the CIA to attempt to be fully "rational" in any positivist sense about the USSR. We will revisit this point in Chapter 5's consideration of the CIA's analysis of Khrushchev's—a Great Purge survivor—likely behavior prior to the Cuban Missile Crisis. This cornucopia of illogic was a matter of historical record, and that fact leads us to the final aspect of the CIA's identity and culture that exercised a malign influence on the CIA's analysis of the Soviet Union: its preference for secret over open source information. Three examples of widely known facts that would have helped the CIA avert this strategic surprise will suffice.

The first commonplace fact ignored in the CIA's analysis of the USSR was the quality issue in Soviet production and abundant anecdotal evidence regarding the hardship of Soviet daily life due to shortages of consumer goods. As already noted, the longer Soviet qualitative indicators pointed to decline, and the longer anecdotes of consumer privation piled up, the more these factors should have become *variables* rather than *constants* in CIA's analysis: Every year these factors persisted was "another piece of evidence that the problem [was] systemic rather than cyclical."[130]

The second salient open source body of information that was largely discounted in CIA's analysis—but that arguably contributed substantially to the USSR's collapse—was its attempt at economic autarky. Even scholars from "the Left" such as Immanuel Wallerstein argued for years before the USSR collapsed that the Soviet Union was engaged in "mercantilist withdrawal"[131] from the world economy. But the USSR's economic isolation, always relevant, became increasingly important because "'globalization' was not global: it took sides in the Cold War."[132] As John Stopford, Susan Strange, and John Henley richly explored, the structure of global production began to change rapidly in the 1970s and accelerated in the 1980s.[133] As this trend accelerated, it greatly increased the opportunity cost of the USSR's isolation from the world economy. As Brooks and Wohlforth cover in detail, it did so for three reasons: (1) an upswing in the number and importance of interfirm alliances; (2) an increased geographic dispersion of production; and (3) a growing opportunity cost of a deficiency in foreign direct investment (FDI).[134]

Obviously, the fact that the USSR was cut off from the world economy was no secret. What is argued here is that the CIA failed to understand the implications of these facts partly because of its focus on secrets when the signaling function of these facts changed. The increasing dire consequences of this isolation *were* noted in Gorbachev's speech to the Twenty-Seventh Party Congress in February 1986, and he and other Soviet leaders were lectured on these same points by George Shultz, James Baker, and other U.S. officials. Yet, although the CIA definitely acknowledged Soviet difficulty in keeping pace with Western technology, they signally failed to analyze the possible *implications and consequences* of these particular shifts in the global economy and their special consequences for the USSR.

In July 1977, for example, the agency published Economic Research (ER) 77-10436U, *Soviet Economic Problems and Prospects*. Its summary makes clear that "reduced growth, as is foreshadowed over the next decade, will make pursuit of [the USSR's] objectives much more difficult, and pose hard choices for the leadership." It then lists four "factors tending to slow the rate of growth [that] have been apparent for some time," one of which is "a limited capacity to earn hard currency to pay for needed technology imports and intermittent massive grain purchases."[135] Lest someone start to unravel the long-term implications regarding these Soviet sectors, however, the next sentence reads: "These problems are not new." The report continues: "Looking towards the next five to ten years, these long-standing problems are likely to intensify, and will be joined by two new constraints which will greatly aggravate the resource strain: a sharp decline in the growth of the working age population and an energy constraint."[136] In sum, the soon-to-be enormous implications of the trends covered earlier in this chapter went undiscussed.

Similarly, in December of that same year, in ER 77-10769, *Organization and Management in the Soviet Economy: The Ceaseless Search for Panaceas*, the agency concludes, in effect, that the system itself is also ceaseless: "As long as present organizational arrangements continue to yield modest, even if declining, rates of growth, the leadership will probably prefer to put up with the familiar deficiencies in the systems, rather than to launch major changes with unknown payoffs and political risks."[137]

Finally, over ten years later, the second sentence of the "Key Judgments" (that is, the consumer-friendly Executive Summary) section of NIE 11-23-88,

Gorbachev's Economic Programs: The Challenges Ahead, published in December 1988, offers no warning of a coming sharp change. It reads: "Soviet attempts to raise technology levels will not narrow the gap with the West in most sectors *during the remainder of this century.*"[138]

Alexseev points out that when Bill Gates was starting Microsoft, Soviet scientists were still forbidden free access to photocopy machines;[139] by the late 1980s, the United States had 600 times as many personal computers as did the USSR (approximately 30 million versus 50,000).[140] There is no evidence among declassified documents, however, that these overt global economic shifts and glaring societal disparities prompted a fundamental rethink among CIA analysts of the "cone of uncertainty"[141] regarding the long-term viability of the USSR or the ultimate consequences of this particular vulnerability.

The third and final example of the effect of a preference for secrets on analysis draws on the work of one of the representative Cassandras outside the CIA, the émigré with whom the CIA refused to work until after 1990, Igor Birman. It is instructive—especially to counter the "hunch" or "hindsight" skeptics of the Cassandras—to observe the type of analysis that they performed using open sources, firsthand experience, and a detailed knowledge of the language, culture, and mores of the USSR. In an article entitled "The Soviet Economy: Alternative Views" in the journal *Russia*, Birman wrote:

> Finally, let me submit another very simple consideration. American agriculture produces more than does Soviet. Though our population is smaller, we eat much better and export food, whereas the USSR imports it. Nevertheless, let's assume the two agriculture sizes are equal. American agriculture is something like 3% of GNP. In regard to Soviet agriculture, it is not so clear, estimates vary. According to the CIA, in 1976, Soviet agriculture produced 16.7% of GNP. From this you may easily conclude that the total Soviet GNP was at most five and a half times less than [that is, about 18% of] the American.[142]

Here, a Cassandra trumped billions of dollars of spies, secrets, "experts," and satellites photos not with "hunches" but with grade-school arithmetic and ruthlessly consistent logic. Wilhelm, in a clear echo of Thomas Kuhn, maintained that phenomena of this type happened because "the model, or paradigm, for analyzing the system [of the USSR became] more important than the facts."[143]

Ultimately, the argument of this book as a whole rests on the idea that using constructivism to parse the culture and identity of the CIA, one can expose the naively empirical foundations of these analytical paradigms—and thus the surprises that flow from them. Regarding the hunger for consensus in the analysis phase, a single instance, directly addressing surprise at the implosion of the USSR, meets our requirements. It reveals many of the specific social mechanisms that create the CIA's persistent properties of identity and culture discussed in Chapter 2 and foregrounds the pernicious effects of consensus seeking on analysis. Allen Thomson, who worked as an analyst in the Office of Scientific and Weapons Research and the Office of Strategic Research at CIA from 1972 to 1985, related the following anecdote to the authors in an e-mail:

> [I] can confirm that many people knew that the Soviets were in considerable economic and societal trouble. But, however, *nobody knew what it meant for the future* . . . An example: I was on the small drafting team that wrote the Interagency Intelligence Assessment, "Possible Soviet Responses to the US Strategic Defense Initiative," now declassified . . . Being a technical intelligence analyst in the Office of Scientific and Weapons Research, I was unqualified to have a professional opinion about the Soviet economy, but had certainly read enough "it's in trouble" reports. Accordingly, trying to get inputs to the assessment, I put in some placeholder no-brainer lines such as, "If they attempted to deploy new advanced systems not presently planned, while continuing their overall planned force modernization, significant additional levels of spending would be required. This would place substantial additional pressures on the Soviet economy and confront the leadership with difficult policy choices."
>
> Going around to the economic analysts to try to get them to provide more in-depth comments and projections, *it turned out that no-one was willing to do so.* So the placeholders remained in place as the best and coordinated judgment of the Intelligence Community . . . *I guarantee that if someone had gotten up in a National Intelligence Estimate coordination meeting in 1983 or 1985 and said that the Soviet Union had even a miniscule chance of collapse, they'd have been branded a kook . . . In other words, we didn't have a clue what was coming.*[144]

This anecdote provides clear evidence of two things: (1) that the potential end to the USSR *was* a surprise at CIA until well into the mid-1980s; and (2) that even as the possibility of the USSR's collapse began to dawn on some analysts, one of the key attributes of the CIA's identity and culture—a drive for consensus[145]—contributed to the ultimate strategic surprise for the United States by muzzling clearheaded analysis.

Production and Dissemination

As Thomson's words foreshadow, a need for consensus at CIA further contributed to the social construction of this particular strategic surprise during the production and dissemination phases of the intelligence cycle. Despite the fact that "Warning Does Not Flow from a Majority Consensus" is the subchapter heading in the CIA analytical manual entitled *Anticipating Surprise: Analysis for Strategic Warning*, a consensus-driven approach is precisely what the Intelligence Community followed to produce reports about the USSR. *Anticipating Surprise* specifically cautions: "Warning has failed more than once simply because what the analysts really thought, and were saying to one another, was never put into print. Or, if it was, it was so caveated in 'coordination' or by a series of editors that what the analyst meant to convey was lost."[146] This was exactly the situation that Thomson described in the passage quoted in the preceding section.

Fritz Ermarth, a National Intelligence Officer (NIO) who helped prepare the 1985 NIE *Domestic Stresses on the Soviet System* (which characterized the USSR as a "very stable country"), agrees. Instead of pressures from the consumer, however, he (like Thomson) identifies pressures from the rest of the Intelligence Community: "I'm not proud of some of the bottom lines, because we pulled our punches. Not because [Director] Casey said so or [President] Reagan said so, but because it would have been too hard to get coordinated in the bloody Intelligence Community."[147]

An anonymous retired intelligence officer who was deeply involved in this issue in the last five years of the USSR relates a similar tale, but with more detail:

> I was present at a briefing by then chief of the Soviet Economy Division in SOVA in 1984 wherein he stated quite forcefully that the Soviets faced a Hobson's choice with the coming 5-year plan. That is, they could not make the capital investments they would need to carry the plan to success while meeting the projected military plan and the requirement for consumer goods simultaneously. His best judgment was that they would spend dear hard currency to buy grain from the US (they did just that) and try to meet the military plan while fudging on the capital investment. They did just that and economic

collapse was the result—just what he predicted. The problem here was that in 1984 *the rest of the community—especially the DOD—was not willing to even entertain such an idea.*[148]

In short, consensus (or mirroring the needs of the Intelligence Community and Consumers) trumped analysts' best instincts.

In summary, the CIA's record regarding the strategic surprise of the implosion of the USSR is certainly more complicated and nuanced than its record regarding the fall of the shah of Iran. Nevertheless, it seems clear that the Soviet collapse *was* a strategic surprise, and one whose origins can be traced to the identity and culture of Langley.

5 THE CUBAN MISSILE CRISIS

NO EPISODE IN THE HISTORY of international relations has received such microscopic scrutiny from so many historians and political scientists[1] as the October 1962 events that are known in the United States as "the Cuban Missile Crisis." Indeed, Graham Allison's *Essence of Decision* considers nothing else.[2]

Much of Allison's work, however, relates to what happened *after* the missiles were discovered, not to the intelligence provided by the CIA to President Kennedy *prior* to their discovery. The same is true for the vast percentage of other works in political science: They begin where this discussion ends—with Khrushchev's secret gamble revealed.

At the CIA, the missiles' discovery is usually positioned as a triumph: At the in-house gift shop at Langley, there are Christmas ornaments for sale featuring a miniature U-2 dangling in a gold ring above tiny maps of Cuba and the USSR.[3] In contrast, we approach these events as a study in the CIA's fallibility, which is in turn traced back to the leitmotifs of identity and culture previously sketched.

Because the intelligence and the argument presented here is complex, the chapter proceeds as follows. The first part is a timeline of events leading up to the Crisis. Timelines are used so commonly in intelligence that there are special printers at the CIA that print them out on long rolls of thick white butcher paper.[4] Here, one is employed because few people have a feeling for events prior to the Crisis or for the CIA's analysis of those events, and such background is central to the case. Next, we review evidence confirming that the Crisis *was* a strategic surprise and explore the scope of the intelligence failure that it represented.

In the second part, we use the prism of intelligence cycle to scrutinize how qualities of the culture and identity of the CIA contributed to this strategic surprise. After reviewing tasking, however, we break from the cycle briefly to cover three items vital to appreciating the remaining elements in the cycle. These three areas are the USSR's security measures, the deception techniques they employed (that is, "*maskirovka*"), and the main collection methods that the CIA used to watch Cuba at the time. Like the timeline, these areas are necessary background for a full understanding of this surprise and its origins.

We then resume the usual thread of the cycle and consider the interaction of the four key characteristics of the CIA's identity and culture with pre-Crisis events during the collection, analysis, production, and dissemination phases. We again find that the origin of this strategic surprise is related not only to an adversary's skill at keeping secrets (an exogenous factor), but also to Langley's identity and culture (an endogenous factor) shaping the antecedent conditions to allow this surprise.

EVIDENCE OF THE FAILURE

Timeline of Events

Before saying something new about this strategic surprise, a brief recap of preliminary events offers a contextual skeleton for this chapter.[5] This timeline both constructs a chronology of events before the Crisis and looks at the conclusions of a key intelligence product, SNIE 85-3-62, "The Military Buildup in Cuba," issued by the CIA just before the Crisis.

On January 1, 1959, Cuban President Fulgencio Batista fled Cuba, and Fidel Castro took power. The Soviets began supplying covert assistance to the Castro government as early as the spring of 1959 and secretly arranged the first arms sales in the fall of 1959; this military buildup began "well before such aid was detected by a United States government that was still deciding whether Castro would be a friend or a foe."[6] Later that year, on October 28, Turkey (a member of NATO sharing a border with the USSR) and the United States agreed to deploy fifteen nuclear-tipped Jupiter missiles in that country starting in 1961.

In September, 1960, the first large Soviet-sponsored arms shipment arrived in Cuba. Soon afterward, Czech and Soviet technicians were reported assisting the Cuban military in assembling equipment and installing weapons such as antiaircraft batteries. Warsaw Pact personnel also began to be employed as military instructors, advisers, and technicians.

On April 17 and 18, 1961, U.S.-backed Cuban guerrillas staged an abortive landing at the Bay of Pigs. On the night of August 12–13, all eyes focused on Europe as the Berlin Wall was erected to stem the flow of immigrants from the German Democratic Republic to the Federal Republic of Germany.

On January 1, 1962, the New Year's Day parade in Cuba provided the U.S. Intelligence Community with the first reliable overview of Warsaw Pact arms delivered to Cuba. These included around sixty Soviet-built jet fighters. Small numbers of helicopters and light transport aircraft were probably also provided to Cuba by this time.

In April of that year, U.S. Jupiter missiles in Turkey became operational. On May 21, after a visit to Bulgaria,[7] General Secretary Nikita Khrushchev told the Defense Council of the USSR of his decision to deploy Soviet MRBMs and IRBMs in Cuba. His decision was ratified at a combined meeting of Defense Council and the Presidium on Thursday, May 24. *Maskirovka*—deception operations—began immediately. For the Soviet general staff, Khrushchev's suggestion was a surprise, "like a roll of thunder in a clear sky."[8] The General Staff began a "blur of work"[9] to make the operation possible.

In June, the Cubans exhibited increasing sensitivity to U.S. violations of their airspace and territorial waters. The Cuban press began referring to the buzzing of Soviet and Cuban merchant ships by U.S. reconnaissance planes to photograph their cargos as "piratical actions."[10]

On August 10, after examining CIA reports on the movement of cargo ships from the Black and Baltic seas to Cuba, DCI John McCone dictated a memorandum for President Kennedy expressing his belief that Soviet MRBMs were destined for Cuba. McCone's memorandum was sent "over the objections of subordinates," who were concerned that McCone had no direct evidence to back his suspicions.[11]

On August 22, a CIA "Current Intelligence Memorandum" noted: "The speed and magnitude of this influx of bloc personnel and equipment into a non-bloc country [that is, Cuba] is unprecedented in Soviet military aid activities; clearly something new and different is taking place."[12] The following day, President Kennedy called a meeting of the NSC to air John McCone's concerns that the Soviets were introducing missiles into Cuba. Dean Rusk and Robert McNamara argued against McCone's interpretation of the military build-up, but Kennedy concluded the meeting by saying that a contingency plan to deal with Soviet nuclear missiles in Cuba should be drawn up. Kennedy's instructions were formalized in National Security Action Memorandum (NSAM)

181, issued the same day. The president directed several additional actions and studies be undertaken "in light of the evidence of new bloc activity in Cuba."[13] Papers were to consider the pros and cons of a statement warning against the deployment of any nuclear weapons in Cuba; the psychological, political, and military effect of such a deployment; and the military options that might be exercised by the United States to eliminate such a threat.

On August 29, after several delays due to bad weather, the second regularly scheduled monthly overflight of Cuba by a U-2 reconnaissance aircraft was flown. Minutes after the film was placed on a light table at the National Photographic Interpretation Center (NPIC— the specialized facility where U-2 film was taken for analysis), a photo interpreter shouted: "I've got a SAM [surface-to-air missile] site."[14] Complete analysis of the film revealed that the entire western third of Cuba was now defended by the Soviet Union's most sophisticated air defense missiles, a huge change from the last U-2 mission on August 5. The same mission revealed "fragmentary evidence" suggesting that the Soviets were installing another sixteen SA-2 sites elsewhere in Cuba. Within days, U-2 flights over Cuba risked being shot down.[15] McCone was highly agitated by this development, but for virtually every other senior CIA official and analyst, the deployment "came not as a shock, but as a problem to be dealt with deliberately":[16] the same missiles had been sent previously to other Soviet client states in the Third World.

On August 31, Senator Kenneth Keating told the U.S. Senate that there was evidence of Soviet "rocket installations" in Cuba. "When news of Keating's statement was flashed on the various wire services, a scramble ensued in the lower echelons of the Intelligence Community, with analysts calling one another to see if any information existed confirming Keating's statements."[17]

In early September, the Cuban Ministry of Foreign Affairs began to restrict the movement of all foreigners in Cuba.[18] Ernesto "Che" Guevara was reported by one agent "to be promoting the thesis that the NATO nations constituted a belt of bases surrounding the Soviet Union" and that "Cuba was going to become the buckle in that belt."[19]

On September 15, the *Poltava*, a Soviet large-hatch cargo ship, docked at the port of Mariel, Cuba, carrying the first MRBMs to be deployed. U.S. intelligence sources in Cuba reported on what appeared to be the unloading of MRBMs at that port on September 15–17, and the movement of a convoy of at least eight MRBMs to San Cristóbal, where the first missile site was constructed.[20]

On September 17 or 18, recognizable missile equipment reached the vicinity of San Cristóbal; these dates were subsequently fixed as the earliest after which U-2 surveillance might have gathered "irrefutable" evidence[21] of surface-to-surface missiles in Cuba.[22] (Of course, the USSR's plans could have been discovered earlier by other means).

On September 19, the United States Intelligence Board (USIB) approved a report on the Soviet arms buildup in Cuba, SNIE 85-3-62. It stated in part: "We believe that the military buildup which began in July does not reflect a radically new Soviet policy towards Cuba, either in terms of military commitments or of the role of Cuba in overall Soviet strategy."[23] As Sherman Kent wrote in 1964,

> This estimate was undertaken when reporting from Cuba began to indicate a steep acceleration in Soviet deliveries of military supplies to Cuba. The tempo of its production was more rapid than "routine," but far less rapid than "crash." At the time it was completed, those of us engaged in it felt that its conclusions A and B represented a basic analysis of the situation.[24]

These two conclusions in the SNIE—a document that is central to the following analysis of this case—read thus:

> A. We believe that the USSR values its position in Cuba primarily for the political advantages to be derived from it, and consequently that the main purpose of the present military buildup in Cuba is to strengthen the Communist regime there against what the Cubans and the Soviets conceive to be a danger that the US may attempt by one means or another to overthrow it. The Soviets evidently hope to deter any such attempt by enhancing Castro's defensive capabilities and by threatening Soviet military retaliation. *At the same time, they evidently recognize that the development of an offensive military base in Cuba might provoke US military intervention and thus defeat their present purpose.*

> B. In terms of military significance, the current Soviet deliveries are substantially improving air defense and coastal defense capabilities in Cuba. Their political significance is that, in conjunction with the Soviet statement of 11 September, they are likely to be regarded as ensuring the continuation of the Castro regime in power, with consequent discouragement to the opposition at home and in exile. The threat inherent in these developments is that, to the extent that the Castro regime thereby gains a sense of security at home, it will be emboldened to become more aggressive in fomenting revolutionary activity in Latin America.

The SNIE contained other conclusions, however, and they too bear on our examination of the interaction of the CIA's culture and identity with this surprise. In these conclusions, labeled "C" and "D," the agency attempted to predict further developments on the island. They read:

C. As the buildup continues, the USSR may be tempted to establish in Cuba other weapons represented to be defensive in purpose, but of a more "offensive" character: for example, light bombers, submarines, and additional types of short-range surface-to-surface missiles (SSMs). A decision to provide such weapons will continue to depend heavily on the Soviet estimate as to whether they could be introduced without provoking a US military reaction.

D. The USSR could derive considerable military advantage from the establishment of Soviet medium and intermediate range ballistic missiles in Cuba, or from the establishment of a Soviet submarine base there. As between these two, the establishment of a submarine base would be the more likely. *Either development, however, would be incompatible with Soviet practice to date and with Soviet policy as we presently* estimate *it. It would indicate a far greater willingness to increase the level of risk in US–Soviet relations than the USSR has displayed thus far, and consequently would have important policy implications with respect to other areas and other problems in East–West relations.*[25]

Kent later summarized: "As is quite apparent, the thrust of these paragraphs was that the Soviets would be unlikely to introduce strategic offensive weapons into Cuba. There is no blinking the fact that we came down on the wrong side."[26]

In early October, Robert Kennedy, the attorney general and the president's brother, "actively" demanded that McCone send CIA agents into Cuba not only to mine the harbors but also "to kidnap soldiers for interrogation about Soviet intentions."[27] These demands were not acted on by the agency.

On October 4, the Soviet freighter *Indigirka* docked at Mariel with a lethal cargo: "36 warheads in the 200–700 kiloton range for the MRBMs that had already arrived; 80 cruise missiles warheads, each in the 5–10 kiloton range; 12 charges for short-range Luna rockets at 2 kilotons each; and six atomic bombs for IL-28 medium bombers [being supplied in other shipments]."[28] The first missiles, sans warheads, had arrived about three weeks before.

On October 8, the CIA's Board of National Estimates (BNE) restated that the Soviets would not put offensive missiles in Cuba. In the memorandum for the DCI entitled "Implications of an Announcement by the President That the US Would Conduct Overhead Reconnaissance of Cuba, and the Actual Reconnaissance Thereafter," the BNE stated: "We do not believe that the announcement, or succeeding overflights, would cause the USSR to alter its Cuban policy in a direction which increased the provocation offered to the US, *e.g. the provision of medium-range missile bases.*"[29]

On October 14, Air Force Major Richard Heyser flew the U-2 mission over Cuba whose photographs would reveal the USSR's missile sites.[30]

On October 15, missiles were detected by NPIC personnel. When an employee asked what code word he should apply to the Cuban material now, his supervisor replied: "This is all so confused, a good term might be 'Mass Confusion.'" All subsequent photo laboratory work done throughout the Crisis received priority treatment if it bore the title "Mass Confusion."[31] Soon after the photos were verified, McCone's executive assistant, Walter Elder, told the DCI of the event over an unsecured telephone line: "That which you and you alone said would happen, has happened."[32]

On October 16 at 8:45 a.m., McGeorge Bundy informed President Kennedy that "hard photographic evidence" had been obtained showing Soviet MRBMs in Cuba. Later that morning, Sherman Kent (whose analysts bore primary responsibility for the flawed Cuban assessment) came out of DCI McCone's office and remarked: "I've just been made a charter member of the bleeding asshole society."[33] John Gaddis, a historian of the Cold War, records that later that day, a shocked Kennedy mused that the USSR's placing missiles in Cuba was "just as if we suddenly began to put a major number of MRBMs in Turkey." "Well we *did*, Mr. President," someone had to remind him.[34]

On October 22, Kennedy revealed to the world that Soviet missiles were in Cuba. "Khrushchev," said Soviet diplomat Vassily Kuznetsov, "shit his pants." He then behaved, however, in "the chillingly 'realist' manner of Stalin: walking over the egos and bodies of those who had helped in the implementation of his grandiose designs, but just happened to be in the way of retreat."[35]

Evidence of the Failure

Following that overview of key events prior to the Crisis, we now examine the evidence for the scale and scope of this intelligence failure. According to a CIA historical article entitled *A Look Back . . . Remembering the Cuban Missile Crisis*, the Crisis was a "watershed" for the CIA because it "demonstrated that the technological collection capabilities so painstakingly constructed to monitor the Soviet Union had matured to give the IC an unmatched ability to provide policymakers with sophisticated warning and situational analysis."[36]

In this view, the astounding abilities of the U-2 (matched with, it was later revealed, the technical intelligence on Soviet missiles provided by a GRU officer working for British and American intelligence, Oleg Penkovsky) caught the Soviets red-handed before their missiles were ready for launch, allowing Kennedy to call Khrushchev's bluff. Kennedy's subsequent handling of the Russian missiles in Cuba is remembered as a textbook case of effective crisis management.

That perception of success, however, is not shared by those with even a passing knowledge of the intelligence provided by the CIA to the White House prior to October 14. This fact is significant because as Robert Kennedy would later say: "The fourteen people involved [in the Crisis meetings] were very significant—bright, able, dedicated people, all of whom had the greatest affection for the US . . . *If six of them had been President of the US, I think that the world might have been blown up.*"[37] The CIA's failure to discover the Russian secrets or to divine their intentions in Cuba earlier brought the world to a three-in-seven chance of destruction.

There are four clear reasons why despite the ultimate discovery of the Russian plan, the Cuban Missile Crisis represented an intelligence failure for the CIA.[38] Each lends support to the possibility of earlier detection of the USSR's plans and therefore legitimates the classification of the Crisis as a strategic surprise. First, there is the fact that Khrushchev's plan was a "discoverable" secret at least five months before Kennedy's speech.[39] Khrushchev's motives remain a mystery (and are still widely debated[40]), but as soon as he suggested to his staff: "Why not throw a hedgehog at Uncle Sam's pants?"[41] Soviet plans moved into the realm of discoverable fact. Unlike the mysteries explored in earlier chapters, this strategic surprise presented no epistemological problems: Logically speaking, it was a "pure" failure to learn knowable facts in a manner that would have prevented such a close call.

Second, this was not a credible case of a failure of imagination:[42] The possibility of such a secret action by the Kremlin was entertained as a theoretical possibility for several years before it occurred. Marc Trachtenberg recounts that President Eisenhower had considered such a scenario in 1959.[43] Walt Rostow, a major adviser on national security affairs under Kennedy and Johnson, made a similar prediction in a memo to the secretary of state, the secretary of defense, and the DCI of April 24, 1961, saying that there was a threat that Cuba "might join with the USSR in setting up an offensive air or missile base."[44] These were not predictions, but the threat was imagined.

Third, the Cassandra of this case, DCI John McCone, *did* predict these events to his staff on August 10 (while Soviet plans were well underway, but weeks in advance of the fateful SNIE, and a full sixty-six days before the missiles were discovered). "If I were Khrushchev," he said, "I'd put offensive missiles in Cuba. Then I'd bang my shoe on the desk and say to the United States, 'How do you like looking down the end of a gun barrel for a change? Now let's talk about Berlin and any other subject that I choose.'"[45] McCone's fears were discounted until U-2 photographs provided irrefutable proof.

Fourth, no consumers were looking the other way: Cuba was under heavy scrutiny by U.S. intelligence assets at the time. In the terminology of the previous chapters, Cuba was definitely being pinged. In contrast to other cases, intelligence consumers in both the executive and legislative branches took an active interest in Cuba. Moreover, during the Crisis and for the previous ten years, the CIA's Office of National Estimates was directed by "perhaps the foremost practitioner of the craft of analysis in American intelligence history," a man we have met before: Sherman Kent.[46]

In spite of these four factors in favor of earlier detection of Russian moves, the Soviets were able to achieve what Wohlstetter called "a logistical surprise comparable to the technological surprise at the time of Pearl Harbor."[47] The gravity of the CIA's Cuba failure in 1962 can be compared to Pearl Harbor for four reasons: First, it had grave national security consequence; second, the CIA, even after the discovery of the missiles, missed several significant factors that—if known—could have dramatically altered Kennedy's handling of the Crisis, possibly leading to inadvertent nuclear war; third, the failure involved a *sustained* misestimate of Soviet intentions and actions—it was more than simply an incorrect one-off prediction; and fourth, the CIA inadequately allowed for the possibility of deception by the Soviets in Cuba. We should briefly explore each of these four dimensions of the failure before proceeding.

It should be obvious that Khrushchev's plan to dispatch surreptitiously nuclear-capable SS-4 and SS-5 missiles to Cuba dramatically upset the strategic balance between the United States and the USSR. Had the missiles become operational, they would have doubled or tripled the total number of Soviet warheads capable of reaching the United States. As Arnold Horelick says in his account of the Crisis: "It is difficult to conceive of any other measure that promised to produce so large an improvement in the Soviet strategic position as quickly and cheaply."[48]

Time, moreover, was a key element in America's retaliatory nuclear capability, and missiles in Cuba would have had a substantially diminished flight time (ten to twenty minutes less than that of missiles launched from the Soviet Union). According to General William Y. Smith, that extra force and the diminished warning time could have severely, perhaps fatally, limited the U.S. ability to retaliate and thus would have made the idea of a first strike much more tempting for the Soviets.[49] Dramatic illustrations like that can obscure the operational scope of the surprise inflicted. In an operation that later estimates say cost the USSR about one billion 1962 U.S. dollars,[50] the Soviets transported a *wide variety* of nuclear weapons and delivery systems to the island. According to Gaddis:

> On 4 October, 1962, the Soviet freighter *Indigirka* docked at Mariel with a lethal cargo: 36 warheads in the 200–700 kiloton range for the MRBMs that had already arrived separately; 80 cruise missiles warheads, each in the 5–10 kiloton range; 12 charges for short-range Luna rockets at 2 kilotons each; and six atomic bombs for IL-28 medium bombers [being supplied in other shipments]. Another 24 warheads in the 200–800 kiloton range, for the IRBMs, reached the port of La Isabella on another freighter, the *Alexandrovsk*, but were never unloaded because the missiles for which they were intended never arrived. In sum, at the time of the crisis, there were at least 158 strategic and tactical nuclear weapons in Cuba, 42 of which (the MRBM warheads plus the IL-28 bombs) could have reached some part of the United States.[51]

Langley missed all of these: Throughout the Crisis, the CIA stated that they did not believe that there were any nuclear warheads on the island.[52] Instead, they thought that the warheads would be delivered *after* the missiles were operational. Likewise, the existence of tactical nuclear weapons on the island during the Crisis was not discovered by the CIA until years later.[53] This seemingly technical failure is crucial because, as Betts relates, with hindsight we know that it generated extra dangers after the missiles' discovery: "In the biggest crisis in the Cold War, over Soviet missiles in Cuba, the relevant national intelligence estimate was proved completely wrong . . . intelligence collection failed to detect facts that might have yielded catastrophic results if Moscow had not backed down immediately." He supports claims that the CIA was unaware of the nuclear warheads, bombs, tactical nuclear rockets, and the four Soviet diesel attack submarines nearby carrying nuclear torpedoes; he writes,

"These were facts that would have been crucial matters for the deliberations and risk calculations made by American leaders had they known about them."[54]

To round out this catalogue of failure, the CIA's estimates of Soviet military personnel throughout the Crisis were four to ten times too low:[55] Langley estimated the presence of some 10,000 Soviet troops on the island, while the truth was that 43,000 military personnel were present.[56] This fact alone could have had dramatic consequences had the Crisis played out differently.

The Pearl Harbor analogy is also justified because the intelligence failures prior to the Crisis, like those prior to December 7, 1941, transcended a single estimate. Nevertheless, the key SNIE 85-3-62 of September 19, 1962, "The Military Buildup in Cuba," exemplified many of the CIA misestimates and misconceptions about Soviet intentions prior to the Crisis. This failure to assess accurately the dynamics of the situation is the third dimension of the intelligence failure preceding the Cuban Missile Crisis.

What were these dynamics? Prior to the Crisis, the CIA sustained a blind spot regarding the USSR's intentions, capabilities, and actions in Cuba so great that the possibility of Khrushchev's plan was unequivocally rejected by CIA analysts even as it happened. As Aleksandr Fursenko and Timothy Naftali say: "The US Intelligence Community *repeatedly* assured the White House that Moscow did not consider Cuba a vital interest and would neither station a significant force on the island nor send a military force in a conflict to defend Cuba."[57] As far as the CIA analysts were concerned, for the Soviets to install missiles in Cuba would have been "aberrational"[58] and therefore unlikely. As late as October 8, the Board of National Estimates stated its belief that the Soviets would not move offensive missiles to Cuba:[59] "We do not believe that the announcement, or succeeding overflights, would cause the USSR to alter its Cuban policy in a direction which increased the provocation offered to the US, e.g. the provision of medium-range missile bases."[60]

There is further evidence that this failure was more than a single bad estimate. On February 4, 1963, the President's Foreign Intelligence Advisory Board (PFIAB) issued a major postmortem about the Crisis, the "Killian Report." As James Hansen says:

> The Killian Report described the introduction and deployment of Soviet strategic missiles in Cuba as a "near-total intelligence surprise." It concluded that the Intelligence Community's analysis of intelligence indicators and its production of current intelligence reports "failed to get across to key government

officials the most accurate possible picture of what the Soviets might be up to in Cuba" during the months preceding 14 October. The report took the Community to task for inadequate early warning of hostile intentions and capabilities; failure to provide senior policymakers with meaningful, cumulative assessments of the available intelligence indicators; and failure to produce a revision of the erroneous National Intelligence Estimate (NIE 85-3-62) of 19 September 1962. . . . It is likely that with a trained, well-staffed, and deception-aware analytic corps, the United States could have uncovered Khrushchev's great gamble long before Maj. Heyser's revealing U-2 mission.[61]

Other postmortems agreed. The Stennis Report isolated one "substantial" error in the CIA's evaluation of Soviet intentions toward Cuba: the Agency's predisposition to the "philosophical conviction"[62] that it would be incompatible with Soviet policy to introduce strategic missiles into Cuba. Because Nikita Khrushchev had never put nuclear-capable missiles in any Soviet satellite country before, the CIA reasoned, he certainly would not put them in a country thousands of miles away from the USSR, and only ninety miles away from America. The Report also said that the CIA had reasoned that the Soviets "would almost certainly estimate that [introducing missiles into Cuba] could not be done without provoking a dangerous US reaction." As Laqueur notes, however, at the CIA "no consideration seems to have been given to the possibility that the Soviet Union did indeed allow for a strong US reaction in its calculations"[63] but were prepared to risk such a reaction!

The Soviet gamble almost paid off: Even once the missiles got to Cuba, there was a gap of thirty-seven days from the first visual observation made by a Cuban exile—on September 8, reported to the CIA on September 9—to October 14, the day that photographic evidence was obtained. This thirty-seven day lag, during which no U-2 flights covered the San Cristobal area,[64] is alarming. Allison speculates that had the presence of the Soviet missiles only become known a few weeks later when they were fully operational, possible American responses would have been severely restricted.[65]

The final dimension of the CIA's failure prior to the Cuban Missile Crisis was also touched on in the Killian Report: the Agency's lack of a "deception-aware" analytic corps. Until the Crisis arose, the CIA was not alive to the possibility of deliberate Soviet deception on the island. The best case in point for this is that the crucial estimate—SNIE 85-3-62—nowhere considered the possibility of deception. Instead, the SNIE accepted with a minimum of skepticism Soviet statements about their intentions in Cuba and cited earlier private reassurances conveyed by Ambassador Anatoly Dobrynin.[66] Yet the agency knew that the USSR's nuclear weapons program was always considered the crown jewel of Soviet secrets[67] and that the USSR used *maskirovka* to cover *all* nuclear deployments,[68] *even those occurring within the Soviet Union.*[69] Open-minded logic would dictate, therefore, that the Soviets would employ *maskirovka* extensively if they were to attempt to put nuclear weapons in Cuba. In fact, the Soviets did use *maskirovka* during Operation Anadyr (as they called this operation), though as we shall see much of this effort was highly imperfect.

Eyewitnesses support that the Agency did not consider deception by the USSR. When the director of the NPIC, Arthur C. Lundahl, first displayed the crucial U-2 photographs taken on October 14, Sherman Kent, director of the Office of National Estimates, "was shaking his head from side to side, in total disbelief that the Soviets would do something so earthshaking."[70]

In short, what is remembered as a triumph of crisis management and diplomacy by President Kennedy was also a strategic surprise for the CIA and, as Wohlstetter noted, "a narrow escape"[71] for the United States. What we have demonstrated in this section is that while the outcome of the Crisis was a success for the United States, the *emergence* of the Crisis was an intelligence failure, a clear strategic surprise. The scale and scope of this failure extended beyond a single poor judgment by the CIA about Soviet intentions on the island (though a single SNIE does distil several misjudgments), and the consequences were almost colossal.

REVEALING THE CASSANDRAS AND
REFRAMING THE FAILURE

The first part of this chapter provided a basic chronology of the Crisis, an overview of the intelligence produced by the CIA, and evidence of the scale and scope of this strategic surprise. We then outlined the scope of the failure. We now use the prism of the intelligence cycle to understand how properties of the CIA's culture and identity contributed to this strategic surprise. We get behind the questions of the postmortem reports on intelligence prior to the Crisis and seek to identify not only what some of the known errors were in tasking, collection, analysis, production, and dissemination but how they were possible. More specifically, we ask what the role played by the aforementioned attributes of the CIA's identity and culture was. Why, in the words of the Stennis Report, was there a predisposition at the CIA to the conviction that it would be "incompatible with Soviet policy to introduce strategic missiles into Cuba"? Why were "indications to the contrary" of what the CIA expected not "given proper weight"? Why was there a tendency "to discredit and downgrade the reports of Cuban refugees and exiles"?[72] If, as the PFIAB Report on the Crisis stated, the president had been "ill served" by the CIA, which had "failed to get across to key government officials the most accurate possible picture" of Soviet activity,[73] we seek to discover how this was possible.

In answer to all these questions, we see how in tasking, collection, analysis, production, and dissemination, familiar features of the CIA's culture and identity played a key enabling role. Repeatedly, the CIA's homogeneity, concentration on narrowly defined reason and scientism, overemphasis on secret versus openly obtained information, and a drive for consensus obscured clues that might have allowed the agency to discern Soviet actions earlier. In so doing, essential elements of the USSR's secrecy and deception measures are looked at, along with the collection mechanisms that had the raw capability to have prevented the Crisis from developing. The perspective of the Cassandra of the case, John McCone, highlights our contention that Khrushchev's secret moves could have been discovered far earlier.

Tasking

For many, the Cuban Missile Crisis seems an extraordinary period. Until the missiles were found, however, it was not. According to Graham Allison—arguably the leading scholar on the Crisis—"the organizational routines and standard operating procedures by which the American Intelligence Community discovered Soviet missiles in Cuba were neither more nor less successful than they had been the previous month or were to be in the months to follow."[74] In other words, despite the hindsight bias that makes the intelligence cycle that follows appear extraordinary (either in a positive or in a negative way), it was not, and this ordinariness makes it an ideal surprise for our analysis.

In the introduction to this section, we learned that Cuba was under heavy surveillance, but we should remember that many nations had as high a priority as Cuba. Cuba had been heavily tasked ever since the Castro regime came to power (and especially after the Bay of Pigs disaster in April 1961[75]) but not to the exclusion of other intelligence targets. One aide to the chief of the Joint Chiefs of Staff (JCS) even recalled, "To us, the buildup on Cuba seemed largely a sideshow. Berlin was the main draw, and Southeast Asia a coming attraction."[76]

Much of the tasking throughout the Intelligence Community was attentive to Cuba but was routine. Soviet ships going to Cuba were systematically tracked and photographed if they were deemed to fit a seven-part "special interest" profile prepared by the Office of Naval Intelligence. Because of this surveillance, the CIA certainly noticed a change in the Soviet–Cuban relationship: In a Current Intelligence Memorandum of August, 22, 1962, for example, they said: "The speed and magnitude of this influx of Soviet personnel and equipment into a non-bloc country is unprecedented in Soviet military aid activities; clearly something new and different is taking place."[77] Because there was a clear consensus at the CIA that Cuba was not a vital interest for the USSR, however, the CIA's tasking process was not focused specifically on whether the Soviets would try to make strategic use of the island (beyond the largely rhetorical actions of Castro, and the possible knock-on subversion of other countries in the hemisphere).

Such tasking priorities mirrored intelligence consumers' concerns. Instead of focusing on what the *Russians* might be doing on Cuba, they were mostly focused on internal developments on the island. McGeorge Bundy, Kennedy's national security advisor, remembers the situation thus: "When we thought of Cuba during 1962, at least until September, most of us thought first of our own frustrations, second about Castro's ambitions, and only after that about how Cuba might look to the Russians."[78] (The frustrations to which Bundy refers involved the Bay of Pigs and the ongoing failure of Operation Mongoose, a CIA plan to foment internal revolt in Cuba.)

It is well established (among others, by Cynthia Grabo, an inside observer during the Crisis and author of the CIA manual *Anticipating Surprise: Analysis for Strategic Warning*)[79] that in the early 1960s it was *Soviet experts* at CIA who were highly unwilling to believe that the Soviet Union would attempt something as rash as putting missiles in Cuba. Based on, in the words of the famous SNIE, "indicators derivable from precedents in Soviet foreign policy,"[80] such a bold Russian move was considered by the agency to be too radical a departure from normal Soviet behavior and thus improbable.[81] In this view, CIA experts both set and reflected the prevailing mind-set in Washington, which was that anything so provocative would be incompatible with traditionally cautious Soviet behavior. It is perhaps for this reason that the September 19 SNIE postulated that the construction of an arguably less provocative submarine base on Cuba was more likely than the deployment of missiles:[82] Such a course fit better with the tenets of Soviet foreign policy in the perception of the CIA.

At the CIA, too, there was the overconfidence that arose from the apparent omniscience offered by U-2 flights—that could reveal Soviet capabilities, if not intentions. The capabilities of the U-2 led Sherman Kent, for example, to say of the 1962 NIE "Soviet capabilities for Long-Range Attack" (NIE 11-8-62): "Hell, this isn't an estimate, it's a fact book."[83] Dino Brugioni relates how on a different occasion Kent said: "My views of the intelligence taken from the U-2 was the view I would have of a holy miracle,"[84] which presumably indicates both strong confidence and a profound lack of appreciation for the possibility of deception.

The Cassandra of this case, John McCone, later said: "Let me make it unmistakably clear that there was no—I repeat no—hard evidence supporting my view in August that there were offensive missiles going into Cuba. *It was wholly a question of judgment.*"[85] Indeed, it *was* a question of judgment, and the first part of the intelligence cycle to reflect the CIA's misjudgment of the USSR's view of Cuba was tasking. Had tasking been informed by different assumptions and judgments, the evidence gathered might not have been as inchoate as it was. Stated another way, the attitudes at the CIA about the situation in Cuba—formed by the four factors of identity and culture already identified—altered tasking of intelligence assets in a way that allowed the Soviets get close to a strategic coup. In particular, these factors prevented the agency from seeing the world more as the USSR and Khrushchev did and thus aided the construction of this strategic surprise.

What were the misjudgments that, had they been corrected in the tasking, might have altered the balance of probability away from surprise? Though we are of necessity dealing in counterfactuals when we examine these failures, a case can be made that unnecessary tasking misjudgments occurred in several important areas. The first way that the CIA's erroneous assumptions adversely affected tasking was that they did not account sufficiently for the USSR's sense of encirclement and vulnerability. The CIA's obsession with secrets blinded it to the obvious fact that the United States, through the Western Alliance, controlled the key industrial areas of Europe and Japan. The CIA also knew that, despite the showy triumphs of *Sputnik*, Leninism was delivering less than expected in the USSR. Dramatic demonstrations of Soviet citizens' profound dissatisfaction with Leninist policies can be seen in food riots (like the one at Novocherkassk that resulted in a massacre less than a year before the Cuban initiative. In fact, it was the commander of the troops that fired on these protestors, Issa Pliyev, whom Khrushchev put in charge of the missile assignment in Cuba: He felt that he could trust Pliyev to "obey orders to the last").[86]

The CIA also might have better appreciated the Soviet sense of vulnerability had they considered the implications of the missile gap that the U-2 had revealed. According to Allison, prior to the development of the doctrine of mutually assured destruction, governments believed: "Size matters. Significant strategic nuclear advantages conveyed significant bargaining advantages, especially in a crisis."[87] For that reason, Allison continues, "The detached analyst could note the symbolic importance of strategic nuclear weapons in the politics of nations and states: international, domestic, and bureaucratic." Were they to do so, CIA analysts might have deduced the USSR would perceive itself as at an unacceptable nuclear disadvantage—both practical and symbolic— that could not be rapidly fixed in conventional ways. Had they done so, they might have been more open to the notion that the Soviets would be tempted to try what John Gaddis called the "strategic Potemkinism"[88] that Khrushchev's maneuver represented (that is, a bold stroke, involving sleight-of-hand, "that would alleviate pressures from several directions").[89] Therefore, without recourse to any secrets at all, and knowing nothing about the government of the Soviet Union or its leaders, Allison maintains that a neutral analyst:

> . . . could have gotten quite far by examining objective facts . . . Starting only with the presumption that the goals of each state included survival and the avoidance of extreme coercion by the other, and objective facts about current and projected strategic nuclear forces of each [an] analyst would have put higher odds on the Soviet players moving missiles to Cuba than did Sherman Kent's Office of National Estimates. Objectively, the Soviet Union faced a serious and widening "Window of vulnerability."[90]

Khrushchev said as much in his memoirs: "The Americans had surrounded our country with military bases and threatened us with nuclear weapons, and now they would learn just what it feels like to have enemy missiles pointing at you; we'd be doing nothing more than giving them a little taste of their own medicine."[91] Even if Gaddis is right in maintaining that Khrushchev understood more clearly than Kennedy and the CIA that the West was winning the Cold War,[92] had the CIA more broadly considered the visible big picture instead of focusing on secret information, tasking prior to the Crisis might have been enhanced.

Another open secret was also at work, one that with a different culture and identity might have shifted tasking by the CIA. According to Fursenko and Naftali, "It was no secret that Khrushchev stood in awe of nuclear weapons." At the Vienna Conference (June 1961) Khrushchev described them as

"The new 'Gods of War,'" publicly stating, "They were the finest weapons in any arsenal." Fursenko and Naftali also feel that Khrushchev's obvious jubilation after *Sputnik* showed that the Soviet leader "correlated a country's nuclear capabilities with its vitality and potential."[93] Even if there is some hindsight bias, the record clearly shows that Khrushchev obviously "focused on missiles obsessively as an index of his country's military power, and for years claimed to have more of them than he really had."[94] That, after all, was what the missile gap was all about, but the CIA's tasking failed to account fully for this fact as Cuba grew ever closer to the USSR after 1959.

In a similar vein, tasking did not account for Khrushchev's alleged personal insecurities and peculiarities. Here, the culprit is partly an obsession with secret information, but partly also the CIA's pervading cult of objectivity and reason, which precluded the agency from understanding just how *personally* Khrushchev perceived strategic issues. Khrushchev regarded U.S. Jupiter and Thor nuclear missiles in Turkey (exactly the ones that Kennedy, as already mentioned, had forgotten about), as a "personal affront." Associates later remembered that his complaints about American missiles "tended especially to surface when he vacationed, as he often did, on the Black Sea. 'What do you see?' he would ask visitors after handing them binoculars. 'Nothing' they would reply, puzzled. Their host would then seize the binoculars, survey the horizon, and make his point: '*I* see US missiles in Turkey, aimed at *my dacha*.'"[95] The general secretary's sentiments were a world away from CIA-style objective analysis or relevant variables concerning the nuclear balance. For that reason, we now drill down into the human factor as it relates to the science of intelligence work prior to the Crisis.

Perhaps the CIA cannot reasonably have been expected to know of these conversations. Had they been more open to the human dimension of Khrushchev, however, they might have noted that what SNIE 85-3-62 called "Precedents in Soviet foreign policy"[96] might have less bearing on the situation than the insecurities of the flesh and blood human being now running the Kremlin.[97] They knew, for example, that Khrushchev was a man who had admitted to a sense of inferiority over his smaller plane as he flew into Geneva for a summit with President Eisenhower in 1955.[98]

The human factor is germane because, as Willard Matthias, a scholar who has studied America's strategic blunders, points out, what was attempted in Cuba was a very Khrushchevian concept. Instead of a conscious new Soviet policy on risk taking, what occurred had "the same kind of boldness that had led to Khrushchev's denunciation of Stalin, to his missile-rattling during the Suez Crisis, to his initiation of the Berlin Crisis. It was revolutionary romanticism—something quite different from Stalinist pragmatism."[99] Khrushchev's decision, according to General Anatoli I. Gribkov (who literally had a ringside seat as Khrushchev's plans were announced and executed), "was an old Bolshevik's romantic response to Castro and to the Cuban revolution and an old soldier's stratagem for deploying Soviet force to defend an endangered outpost and ally."[100]

In contrast, because its culture downplayed emotion in strategic issues and stressed the science of intelligence work, the CIA was less likely to task assets to detect such a "Soviet" (actually, a single human's) strategic move in Cuba. In 1964, for example, in defending the agency's work prior to the Crisis, Sherman Kent wrote: "Like any solid conceptual construction, the National Intelligence Estimate is prepared in rough accordance with the procedures of the *scientific method*."[101] That is fine, until one reads on to where Kent wrote:

It has been murmured that a misjudgment such as occurred in the Cuba SNIE warrants a complete overhaul of our method of producing estimates. In one sense of the word "method," this cannot be done. As indicated earlier, the method in question is the one which students reared in the Western tradition have found to be best adapted to the search for truth. *It is the classical method of the natural sciences, retooled to serve the far less exact disciplines of the so-called science of human activity—strategy, politics, economics, sociology, etc. This is our method; we are stuck with it, unless we choose to forsake it for the "programmer" and his computer or go back to the medicine man and his mystical communion with the All-Wise.*[102]

Here, we must simply question whether a man who would contrast the "science of human activity" with "the medicine man and his mystical communion with the All-Wise" is likely to task intelligence assets in the manner most capable of detecting Khrushchev's "strategic Potemkinism." Kent's revulsion at the intrusion of any human factors on analysis is here starkly revealed, and the straw man that such a phrase sets up points toward a multitude of tasking errors.

We can note, too, that the centrality of human issues to understanding what the USSR might attempt in Cuba went beyond Khrushchev himself. Here, in addition to scientism, Langley's homogeneity also distorted tasking. According to Gaddis, Eisenhower wrote in 1960, "I have been told that

Mikoyan on returning to Moscow from Cuba was exuberantly rejuvenated, finding that what was going on in the youthful and disorganized Cuban revolution brought him back to the early days of the Russian Revolution." Instead of viewing Cuba in a purely bloodless, geostrategic way, senior Soviet visitors to Cuba found that "the place had the invigorating effect . . . of an ideological Fountain of Youth." Mikoyan subsequently explained to Dean Rusk: "You Americans must realize what Cuba means to us old Bolsheviks. We have been waiting all our lives for a country to go Communist without the Red Army. It has happened in Cuba, and it makes us feel like boys again!"[103] Arguably, the pervasive scientism at the CIA would have veiled such emotional factors, thus having an effect on intelligence tasking.

Future DCI Gates observed (with some understatement) in a 1973 *Studies* article: "There is a wide cultural gap between a college educated analyst in the West and the Soviet leadership."[104] One can assume that such people would have difficulty granting adequate weight to how emotional Cuba was for the Soviet leadership. Even if we grant the romantic, ill-judged nature of the Soviet effort, as Knorr says, "Even irrational behavior may not completely defy prediction"[105] if *the human factor is deemed relevant in the first place* and there is sufficient cognitive diversity among the predictors.[106]

This insensitivity to emotional factors perhaps also helped ensure that the CIA's tasking ignored possible precedents and analogies from the Soviet perspective.[107] In Soviet publications, for example, it is widely held that the relative success of Khrushchev's coarse and bullying style along with blustered nuclear threats (and the promise of the dispatch of "volunteers") in the Suez Crisis of 1956 helped inspire Khrushchev to try placing missiles in Cuba.[108]

What is certain is that in Soviet eyes the U.S. missiles in Turkey legitimated their missiles in Cuba.[109] Gaddis is adamant on this point. He says that Khrushchev got the idea for placing missiles in Cuba from Eisenhower and Dulles—from their decision to place Thor and Jupiter missiles among NATO allies to reassure them of the U.S. commitment to their defense. This perception of equivalence, moreover, was not only Soviet and certainly not secret.

This section has served to illustrate the ways in which certain aspects of the CIA's identity and culture contributed to tasking misjudgments prior to the Cuban Missile Crisis that helped bring the United States to the moment of maximum danger before achieving an understanding of what Khrushchev planned.

Excursus—Security, *Maskirovka*, and Collection
Methods-Fix

Secrets, unlike mysteries, are the work of human agency. Almost by definition, they are shielded by security measures and deception. Before examining how the CIA's identity and culture interacted with collection and the other phases of the intelligence cycle, a quick look at Soviet security and *maskirovka* is required. After doing so, we will explore briefly the collection mechanisms at CIA's disposal prior to this surprise. This break in the framework of the intelligence cycle provides enough background on these matters to concentrate more on the role of the CIA's culture and identity as we move through the rest of the case.

Soviet Security.   First, let us consider the security measures—extreme even by Soviet standards—under which Khrushchev's plan was conducted. From the moment that Khrushchev shared his plans with his colleagues in the Kremlin, Gribkov claims, "The order of the day—every day of operation Anadyr—was secrecy, secrecy and speed."[110] Throughout the early planning stage, no secretaries were used to prepare final texts: All planning documents were handwritten. A colonel with good penmanship wrote the proposal that the Soviet Defense Council formally adopted, and even as it grew into a full-fledged plan it remained handwritten; neither the operation approved by Defense Minister Malinovsky on July 4 nor the final version approved by Khrushchev on July 7 was typed. Similar secrecy surrounded the delegation that went to propose Khrushchev's plan to Fidel Castro: The officials arrived in Havana with no fanfare amid a delegation of agricultural experts.[111] Only later in July, when a legal agreement clarifying Soviet–Cuban relations had to be written in Spanish (and thus with Latin rather than Cyrillic characters), was a typist used.

As plans turned into reality in the USSR, the secrecy measures continued with equal intensity. Troops for the operation were moved by rail only at night; the trains' routes and destinations were secret, and mail and telegrams along the way were forbidden. Once the troops arrived, they were restricted to base until they embarked on the ships taking them to their (yet unknown) destination. Likewise, the crews of these ships were forbidden shore leave and were prevented from corresponding.

Shipping for Operation Anadyr originated in eight ports in the USSR. Some of these cities were already "closed" (for example, Sevastopol—meaning there were always special restrictions on their residents, and foreigners were completely barred), and others, like Feodosia, were not. In early September, those Baltic and Black Sea ports that were not closed had that restriction imposed. All messages between the ports and Moscow were carried by couriers rather than radio or telephone. Missiles were loaded aboard the ships in darkness and under the strictest security conditions. Once aboard, any crates containing distinctive military hardware on deck were shielded with metal sheets to render infrared photography useless.

Before casting off, each ship's captain received a large envelope that contained instructions to open the smaller envelope within only at specific coordinates in the Atlantic. This smaller envelope—which revealed the ship's true destination—had to be opened only in the presence of a KGB officer. Every ship also carried thick folders of material on locations all over the globe. According to Gribkov, "buried in these packets, so that not even the compilers would know the real focus of Operation Anadyr, were the study materials on Cuba" for the troops and their commanders to master while under way.[112] Every detail was apparently considered: For those ships originating in the Black Sea, baskets of "vodka, brandy, caviar, sausages and other delicacies" were provided to be lowered overboard to induce pilots not to come aboard as the ships passed through the Bosporus and the Dardanelles.[113]

As the ships arrived in Cuba, Cubans themselves were almost completely excluded from relevant port areas.[114] At Mariel, the Soviets even built a cinderblock wall around the unloading area so that none of the port activity could be observed by land-based agents, and local inhabitants within a mile of the waterfront were ordered to evacuate their homes.[115] Regular Cuban stevedores were dismissed, and the ships were unloaded by special stevedore groups.[116]

Finally, the Soviets were aware of overhead surveillance. They knew U-2 capabilities in detail from the Gary Powers downing in 1960,[117] and they thoroughly studied the optical and film qualities of a number of Genetrix surveillance balloon cameras that had fallen into their hands in 1956.[118] For that reason (in theory at least), Khrushchev made defense against the U-2 a priority in the operation: "The original plan had given priority to erecting the nuclear missiles in Cuba. Khrushchev's suggestion was that the antiaircraft missiles, the fabled SA-2s, go up first so that American spy planes could be shot out of the skies before they detected the early construction of the ballistic missile sites."[119] In sum, the Soviets appeared to take every security precaution that they could think of to prevent the CIA from discovering their plans.

Maskirovka.   An integral part of the security measures described in the preceding paragraphs was a comprehensive deception campaign designed to
camouflage each step the Soviets took: *maskirovka*. The deception plan operated on several levels, began at the inception of the operation, and extended
even to its code name, Anadyr, which was designed to mislead Soviets as well
as U.S. observers[120] (the Anadyr is a river in Russia's north).

To reinforce the Arctic cover story, the trains carrying troops for the operation included carloads of skis, sheepskin coats, felt boots, and fur hats right
up to the loading docks.[121] Once these winter supplies were loaded, the Soviets applied the usual *maskirovka* measures that they used to send weapons to
Cuba. Not only was special foil used in the crates to defeat infrared photography, but the CIA's "cratology" was also accounted for: Any telltale military
equipment on deck was boarded up with planks to make it look like the ship's
superstructure. Even on-deck field kitchens were disguised.[122]

Once underway, *maskirovka* measures continued. As a rule, NATO forces
maintained a close watch on ships bound for Cuba from the moment that they
left the USSR's waters. A representative ruse to mask the mass movement of
troops from NATO's efforts was that organized on the Soviet passenger ship
Khabarovsk. Arkady F. Shorokhov, a political commissar on board the ship,
recalls that on August 16, as they rounded the Danish peninsula, a NATO
surveillance plane was spotted. As instructed, the Soviet military men on the
Khabarovsk "tried to create the impression of a spontaneous deck party. They
put out tables and invited the female nurses below to come above deck and
dance."[123] As they passed the Azores, the ruse was repeated for the benefit of a
curious U.S. reconnaissance plane.

Once they arrived, some Soviet troops were required to wear Cuban military uniforms or were kept in civvies. Until the end of August, moreover, the
Russians used Cuban tractor-trailers and transport machinery to move their
heavy equipment. Conscious of the NSA's signals intelligence capabilities,
all commands along the convoy routes from the ports to the future missile
bases were issued in Spanish. Once the forces arrived at their destinations,
total radio silence was maintained (except for brief equipment checks), and
not even written communications were permitted: Messages to Havana were
delivered orally.[124]

Meanwhile, in parallel with these tactical deception measures, the Soviets
employed strategic deception methods. These involved the Soviet diplomatic

corps, the Soviet press, the Miami émigré community, and the enthusiastic participation of Khrushchev himself. To begin the diplomatic *maskirovka*, in July 1962 Khrushchev used a back channel to try to minimize the threat of overhead reconnaissance (not by U-2s, but by other, lower-flying aircraft, like those photographing the ships headed to Cuba). He did this by sending a proposal via the Soviet "journalist" (in fact a Soviet GRU officer) Georgi Bolshakov, to the president's brother, Robert Kennedy. In this proposal, Khrushchev suggested that the "harassment" of Soviet ships in international waters be stopped "for the sake of better relations."[125] Afterward, during the September–October cocktail circuit, Soviet diplomats were instructed to repeatedly buttonhole Western diplomats "to pressure the United States to refrain from its warlike attitude" and to be especially critical of the "Pentagon clique" that seemed to want to inflame tensions.[126] Also, on September 4 the Soviet ambassador to Washington, Dobrynin, told Robert Kennedy that "he had received instructions from Khrushchev to assure President Kennedy that there would be no ground-to-ground missiles or offensive weapons placed in Cuba. Dobrynin also added that Bobby [Kennedy] could assure the President that the military buildup was not of any significance."[127]

As time went on, the Soviet press agency TASS was enlisted to mock U.S. suspicion of increased Soviet shipping to Cuba and to assert Soviet nuclear parity with the United States. In early September, the Soviet press began dwelling on two themes: incidents in Berlin and the violation of Soviet airspace by a stray U-2 over Sakhalin Island in the Far East.[128] (Providentially for the Soviet deception plan, on August 30, the pilot of a U-2 on an air-sampling mission in the Far East briefly violated Soviet airspace because he navigated using the wrong star). TASS called the pilot's nine-minute error a "gross violation" of the Soviet frontier that was "obviously provocative in nature" and repeated previous threats to destroy the air bases in other nations used by the United States for these flights. The protest, however, was not made until five days after the incident and coincided with the eve of a meeting of the UN General Assembly: It was probably timed to distract attention from Cuba.[129]

On September 11, when Soviet missiles and warheads were actually en route, TASS issued a statement that said that the buildup in Cuba was "strictly for defensive purposes." It went on to say, "The explosive power of our nuclear weapons is so great and the Soviet Union has such powerful missiles for delivering these nuclear warheads that there is no need to seek sites for them somewhere beyond the borders of the Soviet Union." Interviews with "indignant" Soviet civilians and military officers at "Hands Off Cuba" rallies were also published.[130] TASS maintained that Soviet ships were carrying only "necessary foods and foodstuffs to the Cuban people." As for the increased shipping generally, TASS addressed Washington with a sneer: "Gentlemen, you are evidently so frightened you're afraid of your own shadow."[131] As if on cue, on September 13 full-page articles in Havana, Warsaw, Sofia, New Delhi, Berlin, and Paris voiced support for the TASS statement.[132]

Meanwhile, another component of the *maskirovka* campaign was underway around Cuba itself. This effort involved the release of a mix of accurate and inaccurate information by the Soviets and the Cubans about events on the island both to refugees and to the Miami émigré community. In parallel, Cuban and Soviet intelligence planted misleading reports among CIA agents on the island (many of whom they actually controlled; see the following discussion).

A member of the Soviet General Staff has since admitted that as a part of the *maskirovka* campaign, Kennedy was "not just misled but lied to"[133] by Khrushchev during some of this back-channel diplomacy. Khrushchev's effort to conceal, cozen, and mislead about the Cuban operation went much farther than a simple lie, however, and operated on many levels. In fact, the centerpiece of the *maskirovka* effort involved Khrushchev's actions, schedule, and speeches.

In July, in his final meeting with U.S. Ambassador Llewellyn E. Thompson (who was rotating out of Moscow), Khrushchev made a point of raising the subject of U-2 flights several times and referred to the plane as "that beast" over which he had spent a number of sleepless nights. He kept emphasizing, "And you're still flying it."[134]

Similarly, when U.S. Secretary of the Interior Stewart Udall was making a goodwill tour of Soviet hydroelectric facilities in early September, he was shocked to suddenly be told that Khrushchev wanted to meet him. Udall was promptly flown to Khrushchev's luxurious Black Sea villa at Pitsunda, where Khrushchev starting talking bombastically about Berlin. As the meeting went on, however, Khrushchev also couldn't resist gloating, saying to Udall: "It's been a long time since you could spank us like a little boy—now we can swat your ass." He added: "So let's not talk about force; we're equally strong." The fact is, though, *Udall had not said anything about force*. This Soviet mind-set also came up as the Soviet Premier told the U.S. secretary: "Just recently I was reading that you have placed atomic warheads on Japanese territory, and surely this is not something the Japanese need," adding, "You have surrounded us with military bases." After shocking Udall, Khrushchev then teased him (perhaps letting pride stand in the way of his *maskirovka* campaign), saying: "Out of respect for your President we won't do anything until November" and going on to say that Cuba was "an area that could really lead to some unexpected consequences."[135]

Effective misinformation campaigns are about more than what is hidden, however—they are also about what is said and done to *distract* opponents.[136] In that spirit, despite the lapses already noted, Khrushchev attempted to create an atmosphere of normality in Moscow, and the Soviet press avoided any bellicose remarks. First, over that summer the Soviet press devoted considerable space and editorial attention to the problems of Soviet agriculture. Then, on September 4, Khrushchev sent a comprehensive memorandum to the presidium of the Communist party entitled, "Urgent Questions for the Further Development of Agricultural Production." This was followed on September 10 by a note entitled, "On the Reorganization of Party Leadership of Industry and Agriculture." Then, as Dino Brugioni related, "Even as some of the MRBM missiles were being moved to their sites in Cuba, Khrushchev, with considerable publicity, left Moscow on September 27 for a barnstorming tour of agricultural enterprises in the Turkmen and Uzbek republics." During this tour, Khrushchev made enough speeches to fill an entire volume, but he offered no signs of aggression and issued no threats against the United States.[137] Finally (by coincidence, just as Air Force Major Richard Heyser was flying the mission on October 14 that discovered the missiles in Cuba), the Soviets announced a distraction on the other side of the world: They announced that the USSR would be conducting missile tests from October 16 to November 30 at their Tyura Tam missile test range in Kazakhstan, firing ICBMs from there into the Pacific Ocean.[138]

For some of the Soviets the *maskirovka* measures worked too well. Gribkov reports being greeted by Major General Pavel Petrenko, a top political officer at their headquarters in Cuba with an ironic smile and the reproach: "You know-it-alls in the General Staff! Why did you saddle us with all this winter gear? If you'd done your job right, you would have sent us shorts and bathing suits." Gribkov remembers responding: "Try to think like an adult. Remember the secrecy of this operation. It's called Anadyr for a reason. We could have given away the game if we had put tropical clothing in your kits."[139] This incident reveals something of why the Soviet operation—especially as it was conducted in Cuba—had a schizophrenic mix of extreme secrecy and flagrant openness: The need for deception was not pushed down to the level of the Soviet soldiers actually conducting the operation in Cuba.[140] We will now turn to the collection sources and methods against which *maskirovka* was vying.

U.S. Collection Sources and Methods. As we said in the introduction to this section, an overview of the collection methods used to gather information about events in Cuba make the exploration of the problems in the rest of the case smoother. These collection methods fell into three categories: human intelligence, signals intelligence, and aerial surveillance.

HUMINT, or human intelligence about Soviet intentions in Cuba during this period arrived at the CIA from a variety of sources. From within the USSR, human intelligence about the plans for Cuba was nonexistent. There is no indication that the United States had forewarning from Penkovsky or other human sources in the USSR,[141] although the Soviets were certainly alive to that possibility, particularly in the later stages of the operation. Even though military attachés of the American embassy enjoyed only what one called a "worm's eye view"[142] in Moscow at the best of times, early in October an assistant U.S. naval attaché was declared persona non grata and a second member of the embassy staff got the same news on October 12.[143] In retrospect, the assignment of a known high-ranking KGB agent, Aleksandr Ivanovich Alekseyev, as ambassador to Cuba in June 1962 offered a clue that something special was afoot, but it was not recognized at the time.

In Cuba itself, the first source of information was travelers to the island. These sources sometimes even mentioned missiles, but they were not always reliable. Richard Helms recalled, for example, the following scenario: "A merchant seaman gave us a detailed description of what he thought might be a rounded concrete dome covering missiles—complete with range and bearings from the pier where his ship was docked. A map of Havana and a recent city directory established that it was a relatively new movie theatre."[144]

Diplomats and newspapermen from friendly nations also reported on events on the island. Indeed, because some of the Soviet troops were from Central Asia, the CIA received reports of "Mongol" and Chinese troops[145] arriving to support the Castro regime. On the other hand, by early autumn Cuban agents began both to watch and to harass foreigners, especially British embassy officials, who were known to be helping U.S. intelligence.[146] (By that time, the United States did not have formal representation in Cuba).

Meanwhile, the CIA was running agents on the island. The Castro regime was a coconspirator of Khrushchev's, and many Cuban personnel were certainly aware of Russian intentions. In principle, therefore, a solid Cuban network would have forewarned the agency. Regrettably, however, the agency had never been very successful at establishing a comprehensive network of agents on the island, and many of their agent-led collection efforts on the ground went awry. Indeed, it was partly the inability of the CIA to establish a working underground on Cuba that prompted the overt Bay of Pigs invasion of April 1961. Richard Bissell, in charge of the operation, said after that debacle: "We never got to first base in Cuba in building an underground organization," and the few extant agents were wiped out in the mass arrests and executions— Castro's "war on traitors"—that followed it.[147]

Crucially, however, this somber assessment of the CIA's human assets on the island is *retrospective*. Only following the defection of Florentino Azpillago Lombard, a major in the Cuban intelligence service in Vienna in 1967, did it become clear that "almost all"[148] CIA assets had been under the control of Cuba's Dirección General de Inteligencia (DGI). Foreshadowing our analysis in the following pages, it is fair to wonder here whether the CIA's established preference for secret information, combined with this thoroughly penetrated network, led the CIA to discount accurate reporting from sources such as simple travelers or refugees.

Off the island itself, there were other human sources of intelligence. Following the Bay of Pigs, Cuban refugees were arriving in the United States at a rate of 1,700 per week.[149] This flood was large enough to necessitate the active involvement, besides the CIA, of thirteen other government agencies. Many of these refugees were interviewed about events on the island by CIA staff at a refugee debriefing center at Opa-Locka, Florida.[150] The information elicited from these interviews was filed on cards and placed in specific categories, including "Missile sightings, rumors of missile or rocket launching pads or bases." In other words, properly exploited, it is conceivable that Khrushchev's plan could have emerged from HUMINT alone. Brugioni records that sightings from each of these categories were checked against U-2 photography,[151] so it is to aerial collection efforts on the island that we now turn.

Aerial collection not only covers Cuba. Following the Crisis it was decided that, had there been regular U-2 flights over the USSR's Black Sea and Baltic ports, they would likely have revealed the missiles destined for Cuba as they were loaded onto ships.[152] Soviet air defenses, however, made such flights impossible. Once ships left the USSR, we have already noted how those travelling to Cuba (and elsewhere) were shadowed by NATO aircraft for most of their journey. Over sovereign Cuban territory, however, such low-level photography was impossible, so the high-altitude U-2 was employed. The U-2 program was created by the CIA during the Eisenhower administration and provided "revolutionary"[153] capabilities for overhead surveillance. While the resolution of the U-2 cameras has sometimes been exaggerated, it *was* amazing: It could capture objects of about 0.25 square meters from altitudes of between 20,000 and 22,000 meters.[154] Once the plane landed, all of its film was processed by the National Photographic Interpretation Center (NPIC) near Washington. This was no small task: On the morning of October 18, for example, John McCone mentioned to his colleagues that the six U-2 missions flown the previous day generated about 28,000 linear feet of film. "When this is enlarged," he said, "it means the [NPIC] has to examine a strip of film 100 miles long and 20 feet wide."[155]

Could these collection capabilities have found the Russian missiles earlier? The answer must be an emphatic "yes." Consider that the Soviet MRBMs measured just over eighteen meters long (without their four-meter nose cones) and were 1.65 meters in diameter. Some help in picturing the scale of these missiles is provided by the knowledge that they were transported to Cuba via the lumber ships *Omsk* and the *Poltava*, both which had been designed with extra-large hatches for huge logs.[156] More significantly, despite the security and *maskirovku* measures sketched previously, once in Cuba the construction of MRBM and IRBM sites proceeded with little attempt at camouflage. Moreover, the sites that the Soviets constructed in Cuba were built to conform to exactly the same pattern as those in the Soviet Union and so would appear as such in photographs.[157]

It appears that a Soviet reconnaissance team sent before the operation overestimated the ability of Cuban forests to shield the missiles from overhead observation.[158] In fact, Gribkov later wrote, "Only someone with absolutely no competence in such technical matters could have reached such a conclusion. [A missile installation in the forests of Cuba] could be hidden from ground-level view. From above, however, it could—and did—stick out like a sore thumb."[159] Because standard operating procedure in the USSR did not require overhead camouflage of missiles sites, however, it was not done.[160] At the time, however, the Soviet's lack of subtlety was a mystery. Once the missiles had been discovered, the head of NPIC himself wondered, "Why would the Soviets leave the missiles and all the support equipment exposed in an open field in such a manner that they would certainly draw a photo interpreter's attention?"[161] Even so, Graham Allison estimates that if the Soviets had restricted construction of the sites to nighttime and camouflaged the sites during the day, they might have escaped detection.[162] Nevertheless, the missiles were not picked up by U-2 photographs earlier because no collection was done over Cuba for thirty-eight days—from September 5 until October 14.[163] We explore the reasons for this "photo gap" in the following pages.

The third category is SIGINT, or signals intelligence. Compared with other sources of information about the Soviet buildup prior to the Crisis, information about the signals intelligence gathered is sparse. According to the NSA, "Signals intelligence did not provide any direct information about the Soviet introduction of offensive ballistic missiles into Cuba."[164] It is worth reviewing those scattered facts that are known, however. Beginning late in 1960 and extending through the Crisis, the NSA intercepted messages concerning Soviet ships headed for Havana. The cargo manifests were "suspiciously blank,"[165] and Soviet ships were making false port declarations (that is, listing less than their known cargo-carrying capacity) indicating that what they carried was more than just the "palm oil" or "farm equipment" claimed.[166] We also know that whenever Soviet personnel lists were intercepted, they contained an unusually large number of personnel with the surnames "Petrov" and "Ivanov"—the Russian equivalents to "Smith" and "Jones."[167]

Well prior to the Crisis, moreover, RB-47 "Strato-spy" SIGINT planes were flying along the Cuban coast three times a day. Because of their high speed, however, aircraft are poorer collection platforms than ships,[168] so as Kennedy's interest in Cuba increased the SIGINT ship *Oxford* was dispatched to hug the Cuban coast,[169] as was the USNS *Muller*. "From the ship we could look up and down the length of the island . . . The quality of the intercept was good," said Harold L. Parish, an NSA Soviet analyst. These operations led to a gush of SIGINT from the island. Because of these surveillance activities, the NSA issued a dramatic report on the Soviet buildup to the rest of the Intelligence Community, including the CIA, on August 31, 1962. It showed that in the last three months of 1961 total gross tonnage of ships headed for Cuba was 183,923; in July and August alone of 1962, gross tonnage had jumped to 518,196. The CIA also knew—though the NSA apparently had not broken Soviet codes of the period—that Soviet cargo ships headed for Cuba were sometimes receiving "high precedence" messages from the USSR, which indicated that they were, in the words of an NSA report, "engaged in other than routine activities."[170]

There is detailed evidence, too, that on August 17 an electronic intelligence (ELINT) operator on the *Oxford* heard "an unusual sound, like the song of a rare bird out of its normal habitat. It was the electronic call of a Soviet radar codenamed Whiff," which indicated that Russian antiaircraft weapons were now operational on the island. Then, on September 15, the ship detected another rara avis, "Spoon Rest" radar, which indicated that SA-2s—surface-to-air missiles capable of bringing down the U-2—were operational. The NSA's reaction was to employ both submarines and listening stations in Florida, on Puerto Rico, and "elsewhere"[171] to collect intelligence on Cuba.[172]

In summary, this excursus offered some appreciation for the practical aspects of the work of hiding and exposing secrets. We now resume our examination of events and their interaction with the CIA's culture and identity via the intelligence cycle, beginning with collection. We consider how intelligence tasking interacted synergistically with collection to hide further the very secrets the CIA could have uncovered to prevent a full-blown crisis.

Collection

What, then, were the misjudgments that—had they been corrected in collection—might have altered the balance of probability away from a dramatic strategic surprise, and what is their relationship to the agency's culture and identity? The argument here is that claims made by other theorists about insufficient data prior to the Crisis beg precisely this question. Obviously, had there been sufficient information, there would not have been a Crisis. The question thus is: *Why*, with such high stakes and such a priority target, was more of the information needed not collected better and faster?

Woodrow Kuhns, a former CIA analyst, writes, for example: "A fair judgment would be that there was insufficient intelligence available to the drafters [of the September 19, 1962, SNIE] at the time of publication, to permit them to reasonably conclude that the Soviets were placing offensive nuclear missiles in Cuba."[173] Even accepting that argument on its merits, when examining the entirety of the intelligence cycle, one is left asking: "Why not? *What were the factors prior to the analysis* phase that contributed to this insufficient intelligence?" What were the antecedent conditions to that analytical failure?

First, we should remind ourselves that the dramatic aspects of the missiles' discovery in Cuba sometimes overshadow the simple fact that the CIA collected no information about what was going on in the *Soviet Union* in the spring and summer of 1962 that hinted at the USSR's preparations for the deployment of missiles to Cuba.[174] What appreciation Langley had for the situation was almost entirely dependent on what U.S. and NATO forces collected on the high seas and in Cuba. The meat of the problem, however, is to highlight how four properties of the CIA's identity and culture made the collection phase prior to the missile's discovery less effective. Let us start with the agency's partiality for secret information.

We know, for example, that the CIA received reports from friendly nations and newspaper correspondents indicating that hundreds of Russian troops in fatigues had been seen both in Havana and in "seemingly endless convoys along Cuba's main highways."[175] Significantly, many of the convoys appeared to be going to Torrens, where the missiles were later spotted.[176] It is at least possible that the agency's disdain for open sources led them to discount this openly collected information. This same preference for secrets led the agency to discount information collected in June and July 1962, when the Soviets began chartering Western vessels to carry general cargo from the Soviet Union to Cuba, reserving their own ships for other—presumably military—cargo.[177] Charter agreements, after all, require no clandestine theatrics to obtain, merely the correct hypothesis to collect and verify.

There were other clues for all to see on the Cuba's streets. According to Fursenko and Naftali: "The missiles were moved to launch sites on 67-foot trailers . . . Not built to negotiate the tight turns of Cuban town streets, the trailers left a trail of downed telephone poles and mailboxes when used to move the missiles into the countryside."[178] Again, detecting such clues required no special training or exotic sources and methods, but it would have allowed an analyst to conclude that something very special was going on in Cuba.

Similarly, many of the *maskirovka* measures employed could not have withstood scrutiny by casual observers. As far as the 40,000 Soviets troops' dress and behavior were concerned, much of the *maskirovka* was otiose. They wore civilian clothes, but these young, trim, physically fit, suntanned "agricultural experts and technicians" debarked at Cuban docks and then formed into ranks of four before marching out to truck convoys. Even Gribkov was struck by the fact that these men almost all wore the same checked shirts. He remembers: "So much, I thought, for the sophisticated foresight of our camouflage experts. Even without uniforms, Soviet troops nonetheless stood out from the Cuban civilian population; their clothes gave them away." Soviet soldiers even joked that the operation should have been code-named "Checked Shirt."[179] According to one source, the Soviets even used their standout vari-colored shirts as unit designations!

Sophisticated collection skill and mastery of Soviet military arcana was certainly not required to know something outside the usual Soviet pattern was occurring on an island 150 kilometers from Florida. Once they arrived at their barracks, many Soviet units decorated the area in front of their quarters with standard Soviet ground force insignia representing infantry, armor forces, elite guard badges, or large Red Army Stars.[180] In the Current Intelligence Memorandum of August 22, 1962, however, the CIA reported: "There is no hard evidence that any of these people are in combat military units. There is strong evidence that their mission is related to unidentified military construction."[181] No one seems to have pursued the logical follow-up question: "What specifically might that military construction be? Is something unprecedented occurring?"

Brugioni writes: "The Russians and the Cubans stoutly maintained that only Soviet 'technicians' were being sent to Cuba. They were supposedly ex-perts in soil cultivation, irrigation, sugar-cane growing, rice harvesting and animal husbandry."[182] Nevertheless, Gribkov says that if any of these "techni-cians" had been questioned about their field of expertise, "they wouldn't have the faintest notions of the answers to give."[183] Brugioni also admits that Luis Botifoll, a prominent Cuban exile, told the American embassy in Mexico City that "among the thousands of Soviet technicians who recently arrived on the island, many appeared to be between eighteen and twenty years of age, too young to have had time to have acquired any technical experience to impart to the Cubans." Botifoll reported that these young Russians "dress in sports clothes but give the appearance of having only recently completed their mili-tary training."[184]

In short, what we glimpse through these anecdotes is the strong possibil-ity that if prosaic sources had been pursued with more vigor in the collection phase, the alarm level at Langley might have been higher. Such higher levels of alarm might have affected another aspect of collection, one that in the key period was captive not to the preference for secret sources but to the need for consensus: the crucial overflights of Cuba by U-2s. As already mentioned, there was a lacuna of thirty-eight days—from September 5 until October 14—when no aerial collection was made because the U-2s assigned to Cuba were grounded. Following the Crisis, Kennedy administration officials claimed that bad weather had delayed the U-2 overflights,[185] but this was only partly true. In fact, a key cause of this delay was the "consensus culture" at Langley and "negative synergy" with the CIA's own previous assessments affecting tasking (exactly as the intelligence cycle would leave one to expect).

How did this synergy operate? Though the U-2 is often the hero of the piece, it is important to remember that prior to the Crisis Soviet propaganda had successfully managed "to turn U-2 into a kind of dirty word,"[186] as one columnist later put it. International opinion regarded the overflights as "illegal and immoral," and even some of Washington's staunchest allies found them unpalatable. In this general climate, a series of mishaps created conditions that made the overflight of Cuba particularly controversial. First, as already mentioned, the official Soviet daily *Pravda* made the accidental nine-minute overflight of Sakhalin Island a front-page issue. In addition, a Taiwan-based CIA U-2, flown by a Chinese Nationalist pilot, had lately been shot down over mainland China.[187] Both of these incidents gave the CIA pause about increased U-2 flights *and* led to a sharp reaction from the State Department: At a meeting called for the purpose of deciding if the U-2 should be flown over Cuba, Secretary of State Rusk asked CIA Deputy Director Marshall Carter: "How do you expect me to negotiate on Berlin with all these incidents?"[188] The meeting broke up with no decision.

Second, it was clear that the Cuban air defense system was rapidly improving. As of August 29, there was certainty that Cuba had surface-to-air missiles. These created, according to McCone, "an understandable reluctance or timidity"[189] to authorize more U-2 flights. Once the NSA reported the first operation of the SA-2–associated radar on September 15, the danger was even clearer. By then, Cuban air defenses went beyond merely switching on a type of radar: The system as a whole matured in September, and these Cuban air defenses added to the general climate against risking more U-2 downings. They constituted, however, only the proximate trigger for the collection problem known as "the photo gap."[190] The drive for consensus explains more.

There *were* what a *Studies* article later called "diplomatic problems"[191] regarding U-2 flights. What is frequently glossed over is the relationship between State Department objections and the CIA's own view of events in Cuba. According to Max Holland, a journalist who wrote about the photo gap, CIA Deputy Director (and, in McCone's absence, Acting Director) Marshall Carter proved incapable of reversing the decision to delay U-2 missions largely because the September 19 Special National Intelligence Estimate *reaffirmed the conventional wisdom* that the Soviets would not place offensive missiles in Cuba. Specifically, Holland says: "The presumption was that even if the Soviets dared to introduce SSMs, against all estimates, that would only occur after the SA-2 defense system was complete, which still appeared some weeks away."[192] In other words, *there was a negative feedback loop between CIA's earlier misestimates of Soviet intentions and later suggestions to increase collection efforts.* Yet the crucial U-2 flight *was* made, and it was made right into the "defensive thicket,"[193] that Johnson describes. Why? DCI McCone—the Cassandra of this case—had spent a critical few weeks in France on his honeymoon but intervened directly soon after his return and ordered the resumption of flights. A Cassandra—not a break in the weather—saved the day.

To one unfamiliar with the details of CIA history (or the operations of any large bureaucracy),[194] it seems counterintuitive that the DCI himself could be a "Cassandra," a man dramatically at odds with his own analytical staff. John McCone, however, was not an agency insider. He was new, and when he was appointed DCI following the Bay of Pigs fiasco in September 1961, most senior officials at the CIA—who had been admirers of Allen Dulles—were decidedly skeptical about being led by a newcomer without previous intelligence experience. According to one *Studies* article, senior officials at the agency "reserved their judgment [of McCone], some of them quite pointedly."[195] Because McCone was a Republican—according to Holland, "the stereotype of the wealthy, conservative Republican businessmen"[196]—some Democrats within the Kennedy administration were appalled by his appointment. These fears were matched inside the CIA, if for different reasons. As Holland says: "McCone was virtually a novice with regard to the craft of intelligence, and inflicting [sic] an outsider on the CIA was considered an even graver punishment [for the Bay of Pigs] than saddling it with a dogmatic man known for his molten temper and 'slide-rule mind.'"[197] In short, though nominally in charge, DCI McCone faced numerous internal challenges to his authority.

It was not only McCone's lack of intelligence experience that made him a problematic fit within the agency's culture. Unlike Dulles, McCone was no East Coast patrician. Instead, he was a devout Catholic who came from a working-class San Francisco Irish family who "exhibited all the traits of the classic self-made man."[198] As already mentioned, these traits included an explosive temper and an acerbic leadership style. Soon after he became DCI, for example, McCone was invited to visit Langley's computer center to give a pep talk for "morale purposes." McCone "declined the invitation with the acid

comment that . . . if the computer center was dependent upon him for morale, there must be something wrong with the management."[199] There is also
evidence that McCone's devout Roman Catholicism (he went on to be U.S.
envoy to the Vatican after leaving the CIA) might have rubbed some people
the wrong way. We have no direct evidence for this, but we do have substantia-
tion that his religiosity affected his role as DCI in dealing with other members
of the administration. Allison reports that at a meeting on August 10, 1962,
that "McCone was shocked when [Secretary of Defense] McNamara alluded
to the possibility of assassinating Castro. Then and later, McCone quashed any
discussion of such schemes on moral as well as practical grounds. 'I could get
excommunicated,' he affirmed with a wink."[200] It is well within the bounds of
possibility, therefore, that McCone's moral stance created an additional bar-
rier to full acceptance in the culture of the agency, especially among those
personnel concerned with Cuba.

If one follows the trail of evidence back from McCone's intervention in
favor of renewed U-2 flights over Cuba through the events of the preceding
few months, there is ample evidence of his lone voice saying that "something
new and different was going on"[201] in Cuba. Ephraim Kam, an Israeli security
expert, says:

> McCone had argued as early as the spring of 1962 that the Soviets might install
> medium-range missiles in Cuba. From the French Riviera, where he had gone
> for a three-week honeymoon, McCone bombarded his deputy with telegrams
> emphasizing his speculations, but the deputy did not distribute them outside
> the CIA . . . *Apparently from the standpoint of the CIA McCone was considered
> a nonexpert because of his lack of political or intelligence experience and exper-
> tise in Soviet affairs.*[202]

Kam understates the case: McCone was actively mocked for what his
deputy director for intelligence, Ray Cline, facetiously called his "honeymoon
cables" expressing suspicion of Soviet intentions in Cuba. During the three
weeks McCone was away, agency people got so sick of his warnings that they
repeated with delight one wit's remark that "I have some doubts that the old
man knows what to do on a honeymoon."[203] Worthy of emphasis here is that
the substance of these cables and McCone's earlier warnings do not simply
serve to corroborate McCone's status as a Cassandra. When they are combined with aspects of his background and our knowledge of the CIA's culture
and identity, they offer clues about *why* McCone was a Cassandra and why

the rest of the CIA failed to consider other evidence pointing toward Soviet missiles in Cuba.

When he was first briefed on August 29 about the emplacement of SAMs, for example, McCone observed: "They're not putting them in to protect the cane cutters. They're putting them in to blind our reconnaissance eye." In other words, as an intelligence novice, unclouded by Soviet expertise, McCone's deductive instincts as a successful businessman were alerted by this deployment. For virtually every other senior CIA official and analyst, however, because the same missile had been sent previously to other Soviet client states in the Third World, the SAM deployment "came not as a shock, but as a problem to be dealt with deliberately."[204] Soon thereafter, McCone left on his honeymoon. From there, his background as a business executive and engineer became apparent, as he expanded on the disconnect between the costs and benefits of the air defense system that the Soviets were installing. His honeymoon cable of September 10 read in part:

> Difficult for me to rationalize extensive costly defenses being established in Cuba as such extremely costly measures to accomplish security and secrecy not consistent with other policies such as refugees, legal travel, etc. Appears to me quite possible measures now being taken are for purpose of ensuring secrecy of some offensive capability such as MRBMs to be installed by Soviets after present phase completed and country secured from overflights. Suggest BNE [Kent's Board of National Estimates] study motives behind these defensive measures which seem to exceed those provided most satellites.[205]

In other words, according to Walter Laqueur:

> For John McCone, the emplacement of SAMs at sites apparently unrelated to the defense of specific military installations was sufficient evidence of Soviet intentions to install offensive missiles . . . McCone could not believe that such an expensive weapons system would be installed unless it was intended to defend very important military targets.

Laqueur, however, does not ask why McCone, in the absence of evidence, had the correct intuition of Soviet intentions, only commenting: "In a word, he had the *imagination* indispensable to superior intelligence work."[206] *Constructing Cassandra* maintains that McCone's imagination was only exceptional in the narrow context of the CIA's unique culture and identity.

For reasons that we explore during our examination of analysis, however, senior analysts at the BNE replied to McCone's cable the next day: "[We] are still persuaded that costly crash operation to install SA-2s is reasonably explained by other than desire to hide later build-ups and the Soviets likely to regard advantage of major offensive build-up not equal to dangers of US intervention."[207] Again, on September 16 McCone cabled "extensive comments on the Cuban situation making the point that we must carefully study the prospects of MRBMs in Cuba."[208] The DDI's response stated, "An introduction of MRBMs was unlikely because of the risk of US intervention."[209] Similarly, when McCone received the text of the September 19 SNIE in France, he questioned its conclusions. "As an alternative," he cabled Acting Director Carter, "I can see that an offensive Soviet Cuban base will provide Cubans with the most important and effective trading position in connection with all other critical areas and hence they might take an unprecedented risk in order to establish such a position."[210] Meanwhile, on September 15, the *Poltava*, a Soviet cargo ship, docked in Cuba carrying the first of the MRBMs to be deployed.[211]

In the last of his honeymoon cables to headquarters on September 20, McCone urged his agency to think further about Soviet intentions in Cuba. In response, according to Weiner, "the analysts sighed."[212] Though he was DCI, McCone was in many senses an outsider by background and temperament at the CIA, and it was easy for analysts to dismiss his cogent speculation as the dabbling of an amateur. Another measure of the climate of skepticism that greeted McCone's warnings is revealed by that which infected the final part of collection we consider, human intelligence, that is, information from both refugees and agents.

In the following paragraphs, we first consider five of the conventional, relatively mechanistic explanations for HUMINT collection failures prior to the crisis. Next, we look at three more subtle approaches to collection failures. These offer less direct lines of cause and effect from collection problems to Crisis. Finally, however, we offer evidence that joins these previous proximate explanations for failure back to the distal explanation: qualities of the agency's identity and culture that enabled and at times magnified them. The full import of some of the phenomena and evidence described in the following discussion becomes apparent only in the next section, on analysis, but they are introduced here because they occurred in the collection phase. One of the conventional explanations for the general discounting of Cuban HUMINT in the period was that agent and refugee reports were frequently incorrect or contradictory.[213] Indeed, analysis after the Crisis showed that the CIA's files had 211 intelligence reports[214] from HUMINT on missiles and "missile associated activity" in Cuba before January 1962, all of which were either false or misinterpretations of other kinds of activity.[215]

A second explanation is that skepticism at Langley about Cuban human sources slowed the speed of the collection effort in Cuba and Florida. As Richard Betts has pointed out, because HUMINT coming from Cuba had previously been poor, it was given a low priority and processed slowly.[216]

A third, related explanation extended beyond the slow speed at which HUMINT from Cuba was processed. According to Brugioni, agency personnel charged with merely *gathering* refugee reports began placing "qualifying comments" on individual reports emanating from the interrogation center (see the following discussion). He says that these remarks "became increasingly evaluative, to the extent that they ultimately demeaned the substantive worth of the reporting system."[217] In fact, it is clear that blatant "analysis during collection" was widespread at the time. It was later discovered, for example, that the Soviet ship *Poltava* was observed by one collector riding "exceptionally high in the water," meaning that it carried a low-weight, high-volume cargo. The unnamed collection organization decided that the Soviets were sending such ships to Cuba to remove all the "unnecessary" military equipment that they had previously provided, and thus they chose not to pass the information along to the CIA.

After the Crisis McCone was furious about this incident, and "ordered that intelligence-collection organizations never analyze intelligence they had collected."[218] As we have seen, however, in some ways, analysis during collection is inevitable; as we discussed in the Introduction, central to Roberta Wohlstetter's theory of strategic surprise is that, unless collectors have a hypothesis to guide them, it is impossible to sift signal from noise in a flow of information.[219] In addition to the importance of an overarching hypothesis for effective collection, Wohlstetter adds a fourth point specific to our analysis of pre-Crisis HUMINT: that refugee reports were discredited without careful verification because refugee intelligence on anti-Castro feeling in Cuba had not been properly discounted before the Bay of Pigs landing. Following logically from this, she adds that it was in the refugees' self-interest to push the United States to greater involvement in Cuba, and this likely increased CIA skepticism of their reports.

Fifth, we know that the Cubans and the Soviets were aware of the dubious light in which refugee accounts were held by the CIA and exploited it. Domingo Amuchastegui, a former Cuban security official, describes how this was done:

> From June to September, Cuban intelligence intercepted some 17,000 letters [between Cubans and friends and relatives in the United States] that had something to say about the deployment of Soviet troops and missiles in Cuba. In late September, Cuban authorities permitted those letters to arrive in Miami as part of the deception campaign. Just as Havana expected, the CIA paid no attention to these letters.[220]

With no clear (or an incorrect) hypothesis, noise easily drowns the signal.

If these five factors are the simplest explanations of HUMINT collection failures prior to the Crisis, what are the other, more subtle dynamics to which authors have ascribed problems? Robert Clark offers the first of three possible explanations. He links much of the tendency to discount Cuban refugees as merely crying "wolf" back to the agency's established analytical point of view that the Soviets would not place such missiles in Cuba.[221] Again, this is an example of negative synergy. In 2004, he wrote that the assessments of Soviet nuclear missiles in Cuba would have been made sooner, "except for the difficulty of changing a conclusion once reached and the tendency to ignore the Cuban refugees who cry 'wolf' too often . . . [And] *once an intelligence agency makes a firm estimate, it has a propensity to ignore or explain away conflicting information in future estimates.*"[222] In short, Clark blames a species of institutional cognitive dissonance acting in concert with the more mechanistic explanations given previously.[223] Kam, however, favors a return to the idea expressed by Sherman Kent's "holy miracle" comment quoted earlier, saying that the capability of U-2 pictures to provide (seemingly) relatively firm evidence of military activity in Cuba made analysts less inclined to rely on agents' and refugees' reports for conclusions regarding Soviet activities and intentions.[224]

Ted Shackley, an active participant in the operation, offers a third and—similar to Kam's—higher-level view of collection failures. In his memoirs, he makes it clear that a high evidential bar was set by the ultimate consumer of intelligence, President Kennedy. He recounts a meeting in July 1962 in which "the agents were now describing the canvas-wrapped equipment as being more in the length category of a royal palm tree." The president then asked

Shackley "a few questions about agent reporting in which royal palm trees were being used as a unit of measure." Apparently, Kennedy "finished his inquiry into this matter with the comment he needed 'hard intelligence' on what the royal palm trees were." Crucially, Shackley goes on to say: "No one at the meeting had the wit to ask what the President would accept as having met the requirements of hard intelligence."[225] From this dialogue, one can infer that the CIA would have been extremely reluctant, given the problematic nature of HUMINT from Cuba already explored, combined with its "customer focus," described in Chapter 2, to give much weight to intelligence that, unlike a U-2 photo, was not concrete. Graham Allison sums the situation up perfectly: "What the President and the administration least wanted to hear, the CIA felt reluctant to say, at least without solid proof."[226] Further evidence of this fact is that an internal CIA report on briefing Kennedy on September 6 about the discovery of coastal defense missiles noted a "freezing atmosphere at the White House"[227] following the delivery of this news. As a result, at the insistence of the president (who was worried about the reactions of Republicans like Senator Keating), a special "compartment" for intelligence related to missiles in Cuba was created and given the code word "Psalm."[228]

All of these explanations for problems in the collection phase sound convincing and undoubtedly contributed to the CIA's failure to detect Soviet missiles in Cuba sooner. They can also be viewed, however, as having been enabled and even magnified by the attributes of Langley's identity and culture. Specifically, there is evidence that the CIA's homogeneity led it to underweight HUMINT in the collection of intelligence prior to the Crisis. For this assertion, we have three pieces of evidence. Two are highly revealing articles from *Studies in Intelligence* that were written within two years of the Crisis, and one is a concrete reflection during the collection phase of the attitudes that these articles reveal.

When considering collection of HUMINT from Cuban sources, the first article of note (previously classified "secret") appeared in *Studies* in 1963, "The Pitfall of a Latin Quirk." This article demonstrates clearly an innate CIA tendency to discount intelligence from "Latin nationals":

> A problem of interpretation recurs from time to time in current intelligence on Latin America. The set-piece situation is created by spot reports of statements from a Latin national "in a position to know" to the effect that events in his country have passed into a critical stage. Of unimpeachable authenticity and

alarming content, these reports are immediately disseminated in raw form at the cabinet or Presidential level. At the same time, fill-in and assessment are urgently demanded of the area specialist. The analyst whose expertise is primarily Latin America is thus brought into contact with the higher levels of current intelligence—men whose background tends to give them a particular familiarity with European and Sino-Soviet problems—and it is often extremely difficult for him to explain to them his grounds for recommending caution about accepting reports whose authenticity [that is, provenance] he does not question . . . *The Latin American tendency to express the most nebulous of ideas in extremely positive fashion and describe dreams as if they were reality makes it difficult for the analyst himself to assess an unexpected report. He can never be sure immediately whether he has in a particular instance an example of this tendency.*[229]

From this quotation, published in-house at the CIA less than a year *after* the Crisis, one can fairly infer that Cuban refugee and agent reports collected about Soviet actions on the island were unlikely to be given full weight by analysts unless they were sustained and received in massive quantities. It also seems clear that the attitudes the article reflects are in keeping with our portrait of the CIA's identity and culture as uniformly Anglo-Saxon and technocratic. The traits that the article describes would also tend to be anathema to a culture that reified "objectivity" and "reason" (as we have established the CIA's did). At the very least, the attitude that this article reveals links back to the speed with which HUMINT was processed, and the marginal notes that Brugioni described. It also fits well with the "crying wolf" explanation that Clark suggested and touches on Shackley's thesis that Kennedy wanted "hard" intelligence about Cuba.

A similar article by CIA analyst Andrew Wixson, also originally "secret," appeared in *Studies* the following year. "Portrait of a Cuban Refugee" provided a frame of reference[230] for handling Cuban refugees recruited as agents. The article opens by noting that the refugees, though they "range from illiterate peasants to highly educated members of professional groups" have a level of intelligence "which is comparable over-all with that found in the United States"—it "runs from the nearly deficient to superior."

With this condescending baseline established, the author then shares with his CIA colleagues Cubans' attitudes toward work. Here he maintains that the average Cuban male admires intellectual achievement in others and can himself learn facts and procedures fairly rapidly, but *these attributes only make him appear better informed and intellectually oriented than he is or he himself feels.* Since he can retain information with more ease than he can assimilate or understand it, he tends to be defensive when he meets with any form of testing or criticism.

As a result, the author warns patronizingly, "He can work without supervision if he knows exactly what he is supposed to do." In contrast, the Cuban female can, "somewhat more than the male . . . perform boring, tedious, and repetitive activities for long periods with little apparent fatigue or loss of efficiency." The article concludes with a warning: "The biggest problem appears to be that of long-term loyalty and control . . . In his relationship with a case officer [a Cuban male] will tend to view himself as a colleague rather than as a subordinate."[231] As in "The Pitfall of a Latin Quirk," this article provides evidence for deeply seated cultural attitudes at Langley that would contribute to discounting HUMINT coming from Cuba dramatically and thus links the agency's culture and identity to the surprise of this case.

While both of these articles are children of their time, undoubtedly reflecting deeper U.S. Anglo-Saxon attitudes to Latin America, that is not the issue here. The point is that the analytical disdain for Cubans that they reveal almost certainly provides a context for suboptimal collection of HUMINT prior to the Crisis, especially in light of Chapter 2's demonstration that the CIA was more homogeneous than the United States as a whole. Even if a tendency can be detected, can these attitudes be linked plausibly to specific collection problems? In at least one instance, the answer seems to be "yes." Indeed, beyond any given anecdote, it can be shown where these attitudes contributed to an obvious *structural* impediment to rapid and complete information flow from refugees back to the CIA. In this instance, homogeneity not only precluded the objective consideration of information from Latin sources but also introduced an additional impediment to collection.

For entirely practical reasons, women were not housed at the CIA's refugee reception center at Opa-Locka, Florida. They were housed at a separate facility nearby. This facility, however, had only a single Cuban-born female Army intelligence officer assigned to it to determine if female refugees possessed any knowledge of interest.[232] If Cuban refugees were arriving prior to the Crisis at anything remotely approaching the 1,700 per week number previously offered, and if more than a tiny fraction were female, a single interrogator would be inadequate to elicit information about events on the island from them. Considering the transparent nature of much of the Soviet *maskirovka* (remember the Soviet joke about Operation Checked Shirt?), it seems likely that Cuban women—out and about at least as much as men—would have noticed revealing anomalies.

In closing this examination of HUMINT (and collection generally) prior to the Crisis, it is worth recording that, according to Aleksandr Fursenko, the U-2 flights that ultimately found the Soviet missiles were guided by HUMINT. Apparently, a source in Cuba had reported that there appeared to be some "very secret and important work" on a farm southwest of San Diego de los Baños and that the area had been cleared of all civilians. Specifically, this source said that a 130-square-kilometer, "roughly trapezoidal" swath of territory was guarded by Soviet soldiers. Fursenko says that "while CIA analysts thought it improbable that an area that size could be cleared," the report caught the eye of the analysts at the Defense Intelligence Agency (DIA), and U-2s were directed to photograph the area[233] after McCone authorized U-2 flights to resume.

Analysis

We now turn to analysis. The report by the PFIAB following the Crisis unequivocally laid the blame for this surprise at the door of analysts at CIA: "The near total intelligence surprise experienced by the United States with respect to the introduction and deployment of Soviet strategic missiles in Cuba resulted in large part from *a malfunction of the analytic process* by which intelligence indicators are assessed and reported."[234] The purpose of this section is to examine the connection between these malfunctions (essentially, an erroneous threat assessment) and the central features of the agency's identity and culture, especially the reification of reason and objectivity.

We have already seen how the agency's pre–Cuban Missile Crisis tasking and collection were frequently driven either by the incorrect assumptions embedded in its analysis of Cuba and the USSR or by the CIA's actual intelligence output itself (that is, NIEs and SNIEs) in a clear negative feedback loop. Now we look at what the misjudgments and assumptions were that—had they been corrected in the analysis phase—might have altered the balance of probability toward the earlier discovery of Khrushchev's plans. Just as important, we examine what the relationship was between these misjudgments and assumptions and the four persistent attributes of Langley's identity and culture.

Finally, we ask what an examination of John McCone's dissent reveals about analysis.

We begin by looking at a specific example of a phenomenon already touched on, the wholesale dismissal as unreliable of reports by Cuban eyewitnesses. David Martin, a journalist specialized in defense and intelligence matters, describes an incident in which an analyst clearly demonstrated the attitude expressed in "The Pitfall of a Latin Quirk." After receiving an eyewitness report from a Cuban accountant of a missile matching a Soviet MRBM, the analyst noted in the margin of the report, "Doubt that this should be in meters, probably ought to be in feet."[235] And what is the import of that marginalia? Changing the unit of measure here instantly downgrades the missile from an MRBM to a SAM.[236] If you shrink a ballistic missile by 67 percent, you have a fair approximation of an antiaircraft missile, and your *Weltanschauung* as a CIA analyst in 1962 is untroubled.

Previous looks at analytical errors prior to the Crisis stressed the proximate causes of skepticism already noted (that is, the "cry wolf" syndrome born of frequent incorrect reports). One can argue, however, that the attitude embodied in "The Pitfall of a Latin Quirk" and "Portrait of a Cuban Refugee" (enabled in part by the agency's homogeneity) played the major supporting role. It is almost as if the analyst is ascribing childlike naiveté to the eyewitness, who in his "Latin tendency" to express "nebulous ideas in extremely positive fashion and describe dreams as if they were reality"[237] has confused metric and Imperial units of measure. It is fair to wonder if an eyewitness report by, say, a Connecticut accountant named Williams or Johnson would have received the same marginal note.

In Chapter 2, we discussed the social mechanism of mirror-imaging the consumer as one of the ways that the identity and culture of the CIA shape outcomes. For that reason, it is interesting to note here that similar skeptical or dismissive attitudes to Cubans—at least Cuban revolutionaries—prevailed among the *consumers* of the CIA's intelligence in this period. According to international relations scholar Jutta Weldes, for instance, part of the reason that George Ball warned the president on the first day of the Crisis that Castro was "obviously erratic and foolish"[238] was Castro's "beardedness." She says that the dictator's beard was among the features that rendered what George Ball, a senior figure in the Kennedy administration, called "Castro and his gang"[239] instinctively unpalatable to middle-class Americans in the early

1960s because (given the standards of acceptable physical appearance then prevalent) having a beard "connoted unkemptness which, in turn, indicated a desire to flout middle-class conventions. This lack of respect for conventional niceties, in turn, implied a lack of responsibility and an unwillingness to act in an accepted civilized fashion."[240] While we do not know precisely how CIA analysts in the early 1960s felt about Cuban grooming choices, a 1991 *Studies in Intelligence* article called "The In-Culture of the DO" says clearly "No DO officer would be seen wearing a beard."[241] Certainly, no member of the NPIC analysis team of Brugioni's *Eyeball to Eyeball* is anything except clean shaven, crew cut, and at work in a necktie, as are the members of the U.S. Intelligence Board shown.[242] Being clean cut in CIA culture was a visual synecdoche for trustworthiness generally. This observation is completely in keeping with Allison and Zelikow's point that professionals try to distinguish the nature of their work from nonprofessionals by establishing norms of appropriate behavior, even by their "style of dress and manner of speaking";[243] what is of interest here is the possibility that unconscious assumptions about the professionalism of others get layered onto intelligence analysis as a result of those norms.

In a similar vein (as was pointed out in Chapter 2) we know that at the CIA "modern architecture with its dramatic departures from conventional design often plagues (sic) [photo] interpreters in their attempt to make identification."[244] External adherence to "convention" in most realms was the norm at Langley and likely had an impact on analysis. (Keep this idea in mind in the next case, when Michael Scheuer says of bin Ladin: "They [that is, CIA analysts] could not believe that this tall Saudi with a beard, squatting around a camp fire, could be a threat to the United States of America."[245])

In short, several highly varied indicators point to the conclusion that a considerable cultural gap separated CIA analysts from both their Cuban revolutionary targets *and* from their Cuban informers (both agents and refugees). As before, we cannot say HUMINT was poorly analyzed *because* it was examined by a homogenously Anglo-Saxon population of analysts, but that factor is a clue pointing to the answer to "How is this possible?" It is another element that forms a link between the agency's identity and culture and several strategic surprises.

While the examples given in the preceding paragraphs are symptomatic rather than decisive, there is certainly further evidence of analytical disdain for Cuban-supplied HUMINT's contribution to this surprise. Recall that the

CIA's failures prior to the Crisis extended beyond merely the introduction of missiles and included a dramatic underestimation of the total number of Soviet personnel involved in Operation Anadyr. Until the 1990s, the CIA was adamant that the number of Soviet troops in Cuba did not exceed 15,000, when the actual number peaked at over 43,000.[246] Here again, we can find evidence in the analysis phase that this error is traceable to a disregard for Cuban HUMINT.

A case in point is a CIA source who was a department head at the Cuban Ministry of Defense. This agent processed and approved all food requests for the Soviet contingent. Ted Shackley says: "Within forty-eight hours of the time these requests landed on the official's desk, we [the CIA] had them in Miami."[247] This agent reported that the most pressing requirement for the Soviets was for fresh meat and fish. By the summer of 1962, the Soviets were requisitioning 14,000 kilograms daily; by the fall of that year, the figure rose to between 15,000 and 16,000 kilograms. While the Cuban source was never told the number of troops for whom the requisitions were intended, he told the CIA that the Soviets were probably using a target about 400 grams per day per man. If so, this would mean that the Soviets were requisitioning meat for more than 40,000 men.

What did Langley make of this? Shackley says: "The first reaction from headquarters was a cautious comment that there was no way of knowing how much flesh the Soviets fed their troops."[248] When Shackley's Miami station pushed back on the Langley analysts, the analysts never revised its estimate of a maximum of 15,000 Soviet troops, even after a 1947 Soviet Army manual was found that gave the recommended meat consumption of 350 to 400 grams per man per day. Based on this example, it is again fair to infer that Langley's homogeneity was a high-level, surprise-enabling factor: The intellectual climate that published "Portrait of a Cuban Refugee" and "The Pitfall of a Latin Quirk" was inclined to disbelieve a department head at the Cuban Ministry of Defense even in his exact area of expertise.

The pervasive discrediting of Cuban sources by analysts is only one cog in the wheel of understanding this strategic surprise. The main event was not necessarily what Cubans saw and reported but what the Soviets did. Here we find not only the influence of the CIA's homogeneity but also a role for the reification of reason and objectivity. (The two factors are obviously related: As Thomas Quiggin says, diversity is one clear answer to the problem of fixed views,[249] such as reifying a scientific viewpoint.)

We should remind ourselves that we are not criticizing CIA analysts for a single incorrect guess—a one-off judgment that the Soviets would not risk putting nuclear missiles in Cuba. Instead, we are trying to understand how it was possible that a "knowable but unknown action of an adversary" was not discovered sooner[250] and how a stream of fundamental misjudgments about the scale, scope, and intention of the USSR in Cuba occurred (that is, how a fundamentally erroneous threat assessment was made and sustained).

Walter Laqueur frames the problem using the Cassandra of the case as a touchstone: "If McCone was able to make the leap from capability to intention, what prevented the CIA estimators from doing likewise?" His answer? "The primary reason seems to be that the estimators were inclined to foist American constructs about nuclear strategy on Soviet policy and to attribute American conceptions of rationality in policy making to the Soviet leadership."[251]

What we argue is that the roots of *how* such "foisting" and "attribution" of U.S. "rationality" on the Soviets by U.S. analysts was possible can be found in the properties of culture and identity of the agency revealed in Chapter 2—specifically, the reification of reason that pervaded the CIA. Some of the best evidence for a contribution to this strategic surprise by the CIA's obsession with an extremely narrow definition of reason comes from the reaction of analysts once the missiles were discovered. One theory analysts quickly advanced was that Soviet intelligence had fallen prey to a bad intelligence system, telling the top leaders only what they wanted to hear.[252] In the preface to the 1966 edition of his *Strategic Intelligence for America World Policy*, Sherman Kent speculates, "Perhaps one reason why the Soviet leaders got themselves into the fix they did with the missiles in Cuba was because some Soviet secret operative stole some secret documents which turned out to be the wrong documents."[253]

At the time of the crisis, Kent used the more salty language for which he was famous: He said that for something like this to occur, at the Soviet embassy in Washington there must have been "a lot of people that had their heads up their asses to believe that the President and the nation would accept missiles in Cuba without doing something about it."[254]

A few years later Kent expanded less colorfully on this sentiment: "I would like to suggest that if we were to study . . . more deeply we might discover that many a Soviet *misestimate and wrong-headed policy* is traceable to the peculiar way in which the Soviets regard the mission of their ambassadors and the role they assign to their intelligence service."[255] Under this argument, the Soviet action only *appeared* irrational because Khrushchev would not have tried such a move if he had understood the "facts" from intelligence and diplomatic reports.

Quite the opposite was true. According to Laqueur, the official statements of Soviet foreign Minister Gromyko and Ambassador Dobrynin were specifically designed to reinforce the American assumption that the Soviet Union would act according to American canons of rationality; that approach would certainly have been in the best tradition of *maskirovka*.[256]

A companion to Kent's "flawed intelligence" theory (which embedded the assumption of a unitary Soviet actor), is the "aberrant faction" theory. In "A Crucial Estimate Relived," Kent wrote: "We relied as usual on our own Soviet experts. As normally, they did try to observe and reason like the Soviet leadership. *What they could not do was to work out the propositions of an aberrant faction of the leadership to the point of foreseeing that this faction's view would have its temporary victory and subsequent defeat.*"[257] In this view, CIA analysts understood the Kremlin (and presumably Khrushchev himself), but some "anomalous faction" had "temporary ascendancy," and that faction decided—irrationally—to put missiles in Cuba.[258]

In another part of this article (which as a whole is the opposite of a mea culpa), Kent employed language that reveals Chapter 2's scientism starkly. He wrote: "Like any solid conceptual construction, the National Intelligence Estimate [about Cuba was] prepared in rough accordance with the procedures of the scientific method."[259] Consider the language Kent employed as he continued:

> As long as all the discernible constants in the equation are operative, the estimator can be fairly confident of making a sound judgment. It is when these constants do not rule that the real trouble begins. It is when the other man zigs violently out of the track of "normal" behavior that you are likely to lose him. If you lack hard evidence of the prospective erratic tack and the zig is so far out of line as to seem to you to be suicidal, you will probably misestimate him every time. No estimating process can be expected to divine exactly when the enemy is about to make a dramatically wrong decision. We were not brought up to underestimate our enemies. We missed the Soviet decision to put the missiles into Cuba because we could not believe that Khrushchev could make a mistake.[260]

Considered through the lens of scientism, this passage largely speaks for itself. Kent was saying that this surprise arose not from the CIA's error but because Khrushchev failed to compute properly the "discernible constants" in the "equation" that were "operative" and thus made a "dramatically wrong decision," a "mistake" that CIA analysts could not possibly have anticipated. Here, the reification of reason blinded Kent and his analysts even after the fact to the basic point that the criteria used to determine the selection, categorization, and corroboration of a foreign leader's choices cannot ultimately be detached from what Handel calls "ethnocentric biases, preconceived ideas and concepts, and wishful thinking."[261] Intelligence analysts do not work with "discernible constants" that resemble those of physicists. Working with Graham Allison's Model One (the Rational Actor Model), they always run the risk of either deception or circularity: If analysts rely on what actors *say* their preferences and interests are, they run the risk of being taken in by intentional deception. If analysts rely on what actors *do* to reveal their preferences and interests, they run the risk of circularity in their argument because every action taken by an adversary, by definition, is in an actor's interests when interests are defined purely through actions. Kent here seems to have missed both of these points.

Khrushchev, for example, was aware that offensive missiles would gravely alarm the United States, but apparently he thought of his missiles as defensive because they were few in number, because they were intended to deter a U.S. invasion of Cuba, and because the U.S. missiles cited earlier were aimed at *his* dacha.[262] Kent used what psychology scholar Philip Tetlock calls "The 'I made the right mistake' defense,"[263] but our knowledge of scientism pervading the culture of the CIA gives deeper context both to the analytical mistake made and such ex post facto rationalizations.

The same article considered the possibility that the Soviets misunderstood U.S. resolve. Kent wrote,

> With hindsight one may speculate that during the winter and early spring of 1962, when the Soviets were making their big Cuba decisions, they examined the posture of the United States and thought they perceived a change in it. Is it possible that they viewed our acceptance of setbacks in Cuba (the Bay of Pigs), in Berlin (the Wall), and in Laos as evidence of a softening of US resolve?

Under this approach, the embedded assumption of CIA-style rationality in the Kremlin can be preserved, and the miscalculation can be assigned to Jervis-style misperception. With this fig leaf in place, Kent went on: "Their estimate of the US mood was wishfully nudged in this direction," and he thereby concluded: "Even in hindsight, it is extremely difficult for many of us to follow their inner logic or to blame ourselves for not having thought in parallel with them."[264]

Dino Brugioni supports this point of view, saying that the consensus at the analytical meetings prior to issuing the SNIE was that the Soviets would realize that the deployment of an "offensive capability in the Western Hemisphere" would provoke strong American intervention.[265] The contrary was the case, but an assumption by analysts that was never documented, challenged, or subjected to validation prior to the crisis was that the Soviets understood how angry Americans were over the Cuban revolution.[266]

Kent ended this article (a wonderful, if unintentional, illustration of what Tetlock calls "belief system defenses") on a revealing note. He wrote: "It is tempting to hope that some research and systematic re-interrogation of recent defectors, together with new requirements served on our own intelligence services [that is, better tasking and collection], might turn up new insights into the Soviet process of decision making." He laments, however, "The odds are pretty strongly against it; and yet the—to us—incredible wrongness of the Soviet decision to put the missiles into Cuba all but compels an attempt to find out."[267] The possibility that Khrushchev's move was anything but a massive logical error, a blunder, simply could not be contemplated in the analytical culture of the CIA. Perhaps for this reason, one of the CIA's after-action reports on the Crisis was called "Cuba 1962: Khrushchev's Miscalculated Risk."[268] In fact, as Michael Handel points out, "There is no *rational* connection between the degree of risk on the one hand and the choice of strategy on the other. The temptation to choose a high-risk-high-gain strategy is always present."[269]

We have documented that the Soviet's past behavior also weighed on the analytical process. The ultracautious Joseph Stalin had been dead less than ten years, and in many ways his foreign policy legacy seemed to continue. When CIA analysts examined how carefully the Soviet leadership had threaded its way through other passages of the Cold War, they found no parallel for such a daring move. As Kent says: "When we then asked ourselves would the Soviets undertake the great risks at the high odds—and in Cuba of all places—the indicator, the pattern of Soviet foreign policy, shouted out its negative."[270]

As national security expert Thomas Schelling dryly notes in the context of Pearl Harbor, however, "There is a tendency in our planning to confuse the unfamiliar with the improbable."[271] Khrushchev's move was certainly unfamiliar and also unprecedented; except for a few brigade or regiment-size amphibious assaults during World War II (tiny compared to the American and

British invasions of North Africa, Sicily, and Normandy), the Soviet military had never moved large numbers of troops except by land.[272] Perhaps more significantly, the Soviets had also never moved nuclear weapons to another nation. At the same time, instead of being minatory, aspects of the buildup were reassuringly familiar to analysts at the CIA. The SA-2, for example, had previously been supplied as part of the pattern of progressively advanced conventional weapons buildups in Egypt, Syria, and Indonesia.[273]

This reliance on precedent sheds light on other aspects of the intelligence failure, especially the judgment during the Crisis that no nuclear warheads were delivered. Shulsky relates how CIA photo interpreters used visual signatures of nuclear installations in the Soviet Union to look for the warheads. In the USSR, these included extensive and elaborate security measures. We now know that the warheads were stored in rather innocuous-looking vans, and CIA analysts, seeing no special security or activity around the vans, left them unidentified or categorized them generically as missile-support vehicles.[274] This example shows how even after evidence of a massive paradigm shift in Soviet behavior, vital assumptions went unquestioned by agency analysts. We return to Schelling's point, however: The unfamiliar is not the same as the irrational. As Smith points out, even after the fact Kent and his analysts were oblivious to the possibility that it was not the Soviet decision-making process that was opaque and misleading but the inability of CIA experts to recognize a radical change in their field.[275] This conclusion is reinforced by our knowledge that the nonexpert McCone was able to detect what was unprecedented about the Cuban situation. After the Crisis, he wrote:

> The majority opinion in the Intelligence Community, as well as at State and Defense, was that this would be so out of character with the Soviets that they would not do so. They had never placed an offensive missile in any satellite area. *I pointed out that Cuba was the only piece of real estate that they had indirect control of where a missile could reach Washington or New York and not reach Moscow. So the situation was somewhat different.*[276]

In other words, we have a classic case in which a Cassandra—somewhat in the mode of Thomas Kuhn's figure whose breakthrough is explained partly by being on the edge of a discipline[277]—used purely deductive logic,[278] rather than predigested views of Soviet behavior, along with reason unclouded by scientism, to arrive at an accurate view of Soviet intentions. Other of McCone's remarks reveal this interplay between his status as a heterodox outsider and his ability to transcend the CIA's reification of reason to divine possible Soviet intentions. According to one witness, on August 21 McCone said:

> I had to put myself in Khrushchev's shoes. And adopting Khrushchev's mental attitudes, I would have to believe that what my intelligence officers were telling me and what the leaders in the United States were saying about our relative military strengths was true. Khrushchev is no fool. He's a conniving but very pragmatic man. *Men who are born poor are always like that* . . . If I were Khrushchev, I would put MRBMs in Cuba and I would aim several at Washington and New York and then I would say, "Mr. President, *how would you like looking down the barrels of a shotgun for a while*. Now let's talk about Berlin. Later, we'll bargain about your overseas bases" . . . That's the kind of situation that we can be faced with in the future, and we had better do some planning for it.[279]

Note two things about this passage. First, one can detect the understanding of one self-made man for the thought processes of another when McCone refers to the consistent behavior of men who are "born poor" (Khrushchev was a coal miner and the son of a miner before the Revolution). Second, when McCone reveals empathy with Khrushchev's personal resentment[280] of U.S. missiles in Turkey, he hypothetically asks the president to imagine himself looking down the barrels of a shotgun. In other words, aspects of McCone's biography appear to have informed the successful thought experiment that allowed him to anticipate Khrushchev plan. In addition, Khrushchev was not necessarily "eccentric" in his view of Cuba as an opportunity: A few months before McCone's insight, Yuri Andropov (then an advisor to Khrushchev) told him that Cuba was a way to take missiles and "to sight them at the soft underbelly of the Americans."[281]

No matter what his early background, had McCone been long immersed in the culture and identity of the CIA, he may not have been as insightful. His apparent empathy with Khrushchev is in sharp contrast to Kent's terse dismissal of the idea that analysts failed to put themselves in Khrushchev shoes in their estimates of Soviet intentions in Cuba.[282]

From such evidence, it is easy to argue that the dual factors of the analytical staff's homogeneity and its reification of reason allowed the formation of mental blocks that substantially contributed to the strategic surprise known as the Cuban Missile Crisis. An analytical staff with a self-conscious commitment to the "scientific method" that speaks of "discernible constants in the equation" is unlikely to anticipate in a timely fashion the moves of an adversary whose members "feel like boys again"[283] as a result of the Cuban revolution or who sees U.S. missiles "aimed at *my* dacha."[284] They may abstractly assess the risks involved in an initiative to place missiles in Cuba, but they will be prone to underestimate their adversary's willingness to up the ante.[285]

We have clear evidence, on the other hand, that John McCone, familiar with exactly the same facts but a stranger to this culture, successfully made that analytical leap. As the French polymath Paul Valéry once remarked: "There is no theory that is not a fragment, carefully prepared, of some autobiography."[286]

There is one final piece of evidence that Langley's analytical staff—immersed as they were in American constructs about "rational" nuclear strategy[287] and in the thrall of scientism—inappropriately and unconsciously attributed American conceptions of rationality to the Soviet leadership. This evidence is found in analysts' failure to consider what Richard Betts calls "The Logic of Craziness." By this phrase, Betts means to underline that "rational" strategy does not mean "good" strategy but simply that means are logically consistent with ends: "If surprise suffices to unbalance the defender long enough for the attacker to grab the objective, then paradoxically high risk is actually low risk."[288] Another way of saying this is that CIA analysts failed to appreciate what strategy expert Edward Luttwak describes as "The Strategy Paradox,"[289] the fact that it is frequently advantageous in strategy, especially military and diplomatic strategy, for one's enemy to do consciously the unexpected, seemingly irrational, or more difficult thing.

Under this argument, analysts working in a homogenous atmosphere and with a powerful, narrow, and superficial obsession with reason failed to appreciate the intensity of Khrushchev's desire to find a quick way to escape the missile gap.[290] They developed an erroneous threat assessment that failed to predict the emplacement of missiles in Cuba in 1962. We have already seen, moreover, that failure to consider possibilities in the analysis phase fed into both tasking and collection efforts, in turn ensuring that the Soviet effort remained secret long after it was discoverable.

In "A Crucial Estimate Relived," Kent offers no evidence that "the logic of craziness" was considered by analysts. We know, however, that it figured in the thinking of the Soviets. Gaddis confirms that on October 18 (two days after Kennedy had learned of the presence of the missiles but before he had said anything publicly) Foreign Minister Andrei Gromyko assured Khrushchev that "the very unexpectedness—even irrationality—of Moscow's commitment [of missiles to Cuba] would make it work."[291] Note that "the logic of craziness" contains a time factor: The surprise has only "to unbalance the defender *long enough* for the attacker to grab the objective."[292] Allison provides more evidence of the restricted rationality of analytical staff in this regard. He says that the CIA analytical staff opposing McCone "just did not believe that a sensible Soviet government would accept the extraordinary risk such a venture entailed. Specifically, the initiative's success depended on effecting a *fait accompli* without discovery."[293]

We know, in fact, that Khrushchev *was counting on this time factor*: Fursenko and Naftali report that even after the jungle's presumptive failure to mask the missiles from the U-2 became known, Khrushchev "clung to the thesis that the U.S would not detect the missiles until it was too late to do anything about them."[294] In other words, Khrushchev saw a way around the possibility of provoking U.S. military intervention that was not considered by the analysts, namely, presenting the United States with a fait accompli. As Smith notes: "A key assumption of the drafters was off kilter."[295] They were assuming perfect information arriving at Langley in real time, which we know, from our earlier examination of collection, was a deeply flawed assumption.

Here, we find a connection with Chapter 1's discussion of the employment of chess as a frequent but an inappropriate metaphor for intelligence analysis. One of the primary architects of U.S. nuclear theory and a codeveloper of game theory, John von Neumann, focused his analysis of nuclear strategy on games of perfect information, chess among them. This is odd, because apparently in his private life he preferred *Kriegsspiel*, a nineteenth-century German version of chess in which neither player can see the other's pieces (and that requires a third party to act as a referee).[296] In effect, before the Cuban Missile Crisis, it seems as if as U-2 flights over the USSR made the CIA think it was playing chess (see Kent's previously discussed "holy miracle" comment), when it was actually still playing *Kriegsspiel*.[297] Another way of saying this is that while the CIA was playing chess Khrushchev was playing a game of strategy but not pure reason: poker.[298]

As before, we see that the culture and identity of the CIA (specifically their reification of a narrow form of reason) hindered the agency's understanding of the fact that there is no rational connection between the degree of risk on the one hand and the choice of strategy on the other.[299] In the CIA's culture and identity, we find a path to understand how the crucial SNIE and other CIA estimates came to state that "the Soviets would not do anything so uncharacteristic, provocative and unrewarding"[300] as placing nuclear weapons in Cuba.[301]

Close consideration of the analysis phase thus reveals that the main culprits of CIA culture and identity contributing to strategic surprise were a decided emphasis on scientism and/or the reification of reason and objectivity. During the production and dissemination phases, we can see contributions of a different component of CIA identity and culture: the drive for consensus. In concert with other factors, the drive for consensus further altered the balance of probability away from a likelihood of quick discovery of Khrushchev's plan.

Production and Dissemination

To see the phenomenon of the drive for consensus at work, let us briefly review how NIEs—including the crucial special NIE that distilled the fatal Cuba opinion—were created. Kent described the process thus:

> When time allows (and it did in the case of the Cuba estimate) the process is fairly complicated; it involves a lot of thought and planning at the outset, a lot of research and writing in the intelligence research organizations of the military and the State Department, a drafting by the ablest staff in the business, and a painstaking series of interagency meetings devoted to review and coordination. Before it gets the final USIB imprimatur a full-dress NIE goes down an assembly line of eight or more stations. At each it is supposed to receive (and almost always does) the attention of a highly knowledgeable group. The Cuba estimate passed through all these stations.

This quotation crisply reveals the CIA culture's passion for consensus is reinforced by a powerful series of processes that make compromise—a softening of judgments and opinions—almost inevitable. It highlights how unlikely it would be for any dissenting analyst's—or even a dissenting DCI's—views to become part of the CIA's intelligence "product." That is exactly what occurred. McCone read the finished SNIE on September 19 and immediately cabled back on September 20 suggesting a "most careful consideration of the conclusion that introduction of offensive missiles was unlikely." From the agency's review after the Crisis, we know that "this paragraph, paragraph one of [McCone's] cable, was immediately passed to the DD/I."[302] The report then reveals: "However, no change was made to the estimate. *It had already been endorsed by the Intelligence Community and released.*"[303] In other words, the logic of McCone's argument was overridden by Langley's culture and machinery of consensus. Once consensus was reached, it could not be contravened, even by the DCI.

Anyone who has worked in any large organization would find this conclusion unsurprising (especially after reading the earlier discussion of Kent's NIE creation process); here we can simply note another data point confirming that the drive for consensus contributed to strategic surprise, in this case by hobbling the arguments of a perspicacious Cassandra.

In the next chapter, we examine another eminently knowable plot that a profoundly erroneous threat assessment hid: al-Qa'ida's 9/11 attacks. Once again, a Cassandra inside the CIA brings out the fundamental contribution of the agency's identity and culture to this strategic surprise. As in the first three case studies, we again find that the origin of the strategic surprise of 9/11 can be traced to Langley's internal identity and culture.

6 THE TERRORIST ATTACKS OF SEPTEMBER 11, 2001

EVIDENCE OF THE FAILURE

The final case study of surprise addresses the greatest debacle in the history of the CIA: the suicide attacks carried out by al-Qa'ida on September 11, 2001, in the United States.[1] We will not explore in detail the tactical aspects of the attacks or their aftermath. Here, we simply remind ourselves of the consequences by noting that a leading authority on strategic surprise called 9/11 "a second Pearl Harbor for the United States."[2] Their human cost actually exceeded that of the Japanese attack by a factor of two, and their economic cost was a huge multiple of it.[3] To make matters worse, as CIA veteran Melvin Goodman pointed out, in 1941 the United States did not have a "Director of Central Intelligence" and a CIA charged to provide early warning of an enemy attack, thirteen other intelligence agencies, or a combined intelligence budget of more than $30 billion.[4] We should also recall that the damage would have been far worse had heroic airline passengers not stopped one of the planes—at the cost of their lives.

As in the three preceding chapters, we set out to establish the relationship between the strategic surprise of 9/11, specific malfunctions in each stage of the intelligence cycle prior to the attacks, and aspects of Langley's identity and culture. It links these aspects to an across-the-board failure in the analysis stage of the intelligence cycle. As we have seen in previous chapters, elements of the agency's identity and culture also feed into failures through the entire intelligence cycle and exert an especially powerful influence during the tasking and collection stages.

Two things must be noted for this chapter with regards to sources. First, much material related to the 9/11 attacks remains classified by the CIA and many other branches of the U.S. government. This case draws heavily on what is popularly known as *The 9/11 Commission Report*, but even for the ten commissioners the process of declassification was apparently neither complete nor (allegedly) balanced. The members of the commission, for example, were not permitted to interview any detainees in U.S. custody who may have participated in the attacks.[5] In addition, a large body of material related to the attacks was discovered by the NSA too late for the 9/11 Commission to consider, all of which remains classified.[6] The CIA's internal report by its inspector general—the June 2005 *OIG Report on CIA Accountability with Respect to the 9/11 Attacks*, totaling several hundred pages—also remains classified. Fortunately, at the insistence of Congress, its summary pages, lightly redacted, have been released.[7] The earliest official report on the attacks by the U.S. government—*The Joint Inquiry into Intelligence Community Activities before and after the Terrorist Attacks of September 11, 2001*[8]—was conducted by a bipartisan group of politicians and released in the run-up to the November 2002 midterm elections. It is a sprawling, 858-page, heavily redacted muddle, and it is drawn on only lightly here.

Even those most critical of the *9/11 Commission Report* concede that its preattack historical sections (as opposed to its recommendations) are "detailed, precise, and exceptionally well done."[9] The commission did, after all, have far more time than the joint inquiry, a $15 million budget, the power of subpoena, access to much classified information (with some de facto power of declassification), the chance to interview all senior policy makers (including Presidents Bill Clinton and George W. Bush), and more than eighty staff. Nevertheless, because there has been cogent and detailed criticism of both the process and the content of the *9/11 Commission Report*, wherever possible this case also draws on the CIA's internal critique, the *OIG Report*.

The second thing to note is that there are few memoirs and first-person accounts by participants in these events, especially by CIA personnel. There are notable exceptions to this generalization—in fact, the Cassandra of this case, the head of the CIA's bin Ladin unit, Michael Scheuer—but compared to the preceding cases such sources are scarce. Similarly, serious scholarship by political scientists and IR theorists about the attacks remains relatively limited, though much that exists is used here.

In the wider world, a veritable flood of instant books and articles have been released about 9/11, al-Qa'ida, and the CIA. As the former head of the bin Ladin unit of the CIA says, however, looking into this literature you find yourself "harrowingly ensnarled in material that is overwhelmingly secondary, translated with varying degrees of accuracy, and sensationalized or embellished by the need to sell copies or by the sloth of those doing insufficient research."[10] Huge amounts of finger-pointing journalism and some serious scholarship have also focused on tactical "missed chances"[11] to stop the al-Qa'ida hijackers prior to 9/11. These works have generated anecdotes that are interesting but that are not particularly useful for understanding the root causes of the debacle.

Then, there are the conspiracy theories. There *was* a conspiracy behind the 9/11 attacks: a conspiracy by Usama bin Ladin and al-Qa'ida members to attack the United States (in the same way that there was a "conspiracy" by the USSR to place missiles in Cuba in the previous case). There are also certainly unanswered questions about these attacks and about al-Qa'ida's previous activities. Thanks to a predilection for baroque conspiracy theories in both the United States and the Middle East, however, there is a rich seam of work spinning mind-numbingly elaborate alternative explanations for 9/11. Such "literature" ranges from books by self-appointed terrorism experts to sensationalist Pakistani tabloids. Occam's razor[12] was applied to all such speculation, however, and no such "sources" are used in this chapter.

In a departure from the three preceding chapters, here we proceed directly to the intelligence cycle and consider the interaction of the four key characteristics of the CIA's identity and culture with pre-9/11 tasking, collection, analysis, production, and dissemination. While doing so, we weave in many of the singular elements that make this surprise historically unique. As usual, we also see that the presence of a Cassandra throws into relief how the attributes of the CIA's culture and identity enabled this surprise.

A few final preliminary notes are in order. First, it should be said clearly that 9/11 was certainly not purely a CIA failure: More than the previous three surprises considered, 9/11 was truly a failure of the entire U.S. Intelligence Community, U.S. politicians and policy makers, and government employees across a myriad of agencies. Betts, a respected expert on surprise and intelligence, baldly says that the "FBI fell down the most."[13] The authors, however, agree with Steve Coll and others that the CIA stands at the center of the failure.[14] Prior to 9/11, the CIA was primus inter pares among the agencies of the

U.S. Intelligence Community, chartered specifically to coordinate the community's activities against threats—especially surprise attacks originating abroad.

Moreover, unlike the mystery-based surprises in Chapters 3 and 4, the 9/11 plot was a secret—that is, it was knowable. The broad outline of the 9/11 attacks was given the green light by Usama bin Ladin sometime "in late 1998 or early 1999"; the actual Planes Operation (as it was known within al-Qa'ida) was approved by him in March or April 1999.[15] In other words, the CIA had twenty-nine months to discover the attack's secrets (that is, approximately five times longer than the agency had to discover the USSR's plans in the preceding chapter). As we explore, Langley failed to do so for some of the same reasons that brought disaster so close in Cuba almost forty years before: the dynamic between features of the threat and elements of the CIA's identity and culture.

Finally, Arabic words and names are transliterated into English in many ways; in the following text, the CIA's in-house spellings are used: Usama bin Ladin, al-Qa'ida, and so on[16] are used (except within quotations).

REVEALING THE CASSANDRAS AND REFRAMING THE FAILURE

Tasking

Toward the end of its report, the 9/11 Commission wrote plaintively: "The methods for detecting and then warning of surprise attack that the US government had so painstakingly developed in the decades after Pearl Harbor did not fail; instead, they were not really tried." One of the central reasons that these mechanisms were "not really tried" is rooted in the CIA's failure to task intelligence assets effectively to gather information about al-Qa'ida. Of this failure, there can be little doubt. To anyone who studies 9/11, it is clear that the CIA failed, as organizational theory specialist Amy Zegart says, "ever [to] develop a comprehensive collection and analysis plan [that is, tasking] for the rest of the Intelligence Community." Specifically, Zegart says that the agency's tasking failed to ask the following basic questions about al-Qa'ida: "What al Qaeda information did US intelligence agencies already possess? What questions still needed to be answered, and in what priority? What kinds of intelligence could fill in the gaps? Which agencies and people were best suited to the job, and how could they work together most productively?"[17] As we see in the following discussion, this tasking failure is partly understood by failures during the analysis phase: If you do not recognize an entity as a threat, you do not seek additional information about it.

Before we examine the role played in this surprise by the agency's identity and culture during the tasking, we should examine both the context of policy making before 9/11 and competing explanations advanced to explain this lack of tasking. The first piece of context needed to understand these failures is the formal priorities assigned by the primary "consumers" of intelligence. During the Clinton administration, the CIA asked the NSC to rank threats to help it determine how to allocate resources and effort. China, Iran, and Iraq were ranked number one; terrorism was ranked number three[18] as part of a sprawling grab bag of a mandate: Clinton's officials said that the CIA should provide "intelligence about specific trans-national threats to our security, such as weapons proliferation, terrorism, drug trafficking, organized crime, illicit trade practices and environmental issues of great gravity."[19] In other words, this tasking guidance officially ranked intelligence about al-Qa'ida equal to that about gangs engaged in the illegal trade of tropical hardwood. As an organization forever mirroring the concerns of consumers, the CIA did not "push back."

After the election in 2000, President Bush's security policy was more focused; its centerpiece was the pursuit of ballistic missile defense. To the extent that the government as a whole concentrated on terrorism, it was focused mainly on terrorists acquiring WMD. Some of the attention bin Ladin received, in fact, was due to his pursuit of such weapons;[20] it is possible that those clues that were available would have received more attention had the 9/11 plot included them. Paul Pillar (head of the CIA's Counterterrorism Center—the CTC—until 1999) summarized the prevailing view in Washington when he said a few months before 9/11: "It would be a mistake to redefine counterterrorism as a task of dealing with 'catastrophic', 'grand' or 'super' terrorism, when in fact these labels do not represent most of the terrorism that the United States is likely to face or most of the costs that terrorism imposes on US Interests."[21]

The reason for this relative lack of concern (in effect, a consensus that al-Qa'ida was relatively unimportant), and another explanation for why tasking was not more focused on al-Qa'ida, is the transient nature of previous terrorist groups. Al-Qa'ida's longevity makes it an outlier. Only 50 percent of terrorist groups survive a year, and only 5 percent survive a decade.[22] After the fact, one can speculate that the group's persistence alone should have been a cause for concern and thus raised al-Qa'ida's tasking priority, but that is the wisdom of hindsight. As Avi Shlaim said in the context of the Yom Kippur War, one must be wary of "conclusions crystallized in the light of history and the chain of events as they occurred"[23] and not in accordance with the internal logic of the presurprise situation. Until 9/11, the CIA had dealt with terrorist organizations in what Richard Shultz calls "an *episodic, transitory,* and *ad hoc* manner,"[24] and such an approach had seemed adequate.

The annual surveys of terrorism that the CIA published prior to 9/11 reflect this less-than-systematic approach. The survey covered only international terrorism, so if an Egyptian group killed tourists, it made the next year's survey; if the same group's victims were all Egyptians, the attack did not make the survey. As a result, some countries with substantial domestic terrorist movements (for example, Columbia and Sri Lanka) appeared in the CIA survey only because their terrorists also engaged in international drug smuggling.

Al-Qa'ida was also an outlier with respect to its (apparently) relatively minimal ties to governments. Michael Scheuer said in 2006: "There is no persuasive reporting or analysis showing that al-Qa'ida was dependent on any state for essential material or logistical support."[25] (It should be noted that other sources make a case for relatively light but important support for the group from Iran.[26]) In the 1970s and 1980s terrorism experts' frame of reference was that the level of threat posed by a terrorist group was determined by the strength and audacity of its sponsoring state, not that of its members. Even if light support was there, al-Qa'ida's departure from the Cold War paradigm of heavy state support probably contributed to its relatively low tasking priority.[27]

It is also only fair to recall that despite a timeline after 9/11 that reveals repeated and escalating attacks on America overseas, before 9/11 al-Qa'ida had killed fewer than fifty Americans in toto.[28] It had not carried out any hijackings, and in 2001 it had been fourteen years since the last U.S. plane had been hijacked and thirteen years since the last U.S. plane had been bombed;[29] no domestic hijacking had occurred since 1968.[30] A President's Daily Brief of December 4, 1998, had the subject "Bin Ladin Preparing to Hijack US Aircraft And Other Attacks"—but it did not discuss the possibility of suicide attacks, instead suggesting a plot focused on trying to obtain the release of Abdul Basit (also known as Ramzi Yousef) and his colleagues.[31] (On the other hand, al-Qa'ida broke its religious taboo on suicide bombing as early as 1993,[32] and the systematic use of suicide missions for political purposes in the modern age dated back ten years earlier.[33] Al-Qa'ida had also merged with a known lethal terrorist group, Ayman al-Zawahiri's Egyptian Islamic Jihad, in 1998, and their operatives trained with Hezbollah—a group skilled in suicide tactics—as early as 1994.)

Finally, before the 9/11 attacks, the jury was still out for many people on bin Ladin himself. In April 1999, *The New York Times* even sought to debunk claims that he was a terrorist leader: It ran the headline "US Hard Put to Find Proof Bin Ladin Directed Attacks."[34] In retrospect there was a "discourse failure"[35] regarding terrorism in Western society. Prior to 9/11, much of the media avoided the term *terrorist* and substituted such terms as *militant* or *activist*. The BBC would not use the term *terrorist* in the Middle East but applied it in the rest of the world. Reuters avoided the term both because it might offend dangerous people and thus endanger their correspondents and also because it might lose them customers. *The Chicago Tribune* jettisoned the term *terrorism* in the 1990s because "it is tendentious and propagandistic, and because today's terrorist sometimes turns out [sic] tomorrow's statesman."[36] If such views tended toward the Left of the U.S. political spectrum, the Right made its own contribution to this problem through a state-centered terrorism discourse.[37] Essentially, nonstate actors did not register on Realist policy makers' radar. Insofar as CIA tasking was driven by general intelligence consumer demands (for example, from Congress), this discourse failure reinforced the primacy of other issues for the agency.

Meanwhile, and perhaps partly as a result, ambiguous messages were sent *within* the agency regarding the importance of al-Qa'ida relative to other issues. Almost all the defenders of the CIA's performance prior to 9/11 raise the December 4, 1998, memo in which DCI Tenet wrote to several CIA officials and his deputy for Intelligence Community management stating: "We are at war [with al-Qa'ida]. I want no resources or people spared in this effort, either inside CIA or the Community."[38] As the 9/11 Commission records, however, "The memorandum had little overall effect on mobilizing the CIA or the Intelligence Community." This may be because of the example the DCI set: Much of Tenet's effort prior to 9/11 was in fact devoted to Arab–Israeli peace negotiations.[39]

Apart from rhetoric and his own time, there is another way to measure DCI Tenet's actual commitment to bin Ladin as a target for intelligence effort: budgets and personnel assignments. While not a perfect proxy for tasking, the numbers certainly say something about institutional priorities. As a whole, intelligence budgets have always been classified.[40] We do, however, have some evidence about CIA budgetary decisions prior to 9/11, and what they reveal is that terrorism generally and al-Qa'ida specifically were extremely low priorities: Almost all of the CIA's activities against al-Qa'ida prior to 9/11 were paid for by "emergency supplementals." In other words, there were *almost no baseline agency funds going into the effort against bin Ladin.* As Richard Clarke, who was chief counterterrorism adviser on the National Security Council under President Clinton, reports:

> In 2000 and 2001 we [that is, the NSC] asked CIA to identify some funds, any money, earmarked for other activities that were less important than the fight against al Qaeda, so that those funds could be transferred to the higher priority of countering bin Laden. The formal, official CIA response was that there were none. *Another way to say that was that everything that they were doing was more important than fighting al Qaeda.*[41]

Clarke's allegation was confirmed by CIA inspector general's report on the pre-9/11 failures, which found that the agency had repeatedly diverted money *away* from counterterrorism to other purposes. More authoritatively, the CIA inspector general's report itself devastates any contention that DCI Tenet was (as some have claimed) powerless to move people and money into the high priority area of counterterrorism. The IG's report is worth quoting at length:

> In the five years prior to 9/11, the DCI on six occasions used [his] authorities [in the Intelligence Community] to move almost [amount redacted] in funds from other agencies to the CIA for a number of important purposes [text redacted]. One of these transfers helped fund a Middle East program that was terrorism-related, but none supported programs designed to counter UBL or al-Qa'ida. Nor were DCI authorities used to transfer any personnel into these programs in the five years prior to 9/11. [The IG's report also found that agency managers moved funds from the base budgets of the CTC to] to meet other corporate and Directorate of Operations needs. The Team found that from FY 1997 to FY 2001 (as of 9/11) [amount redacted] was redistributed from counterterrorism programs to other agency priorities . . . Conversely, no resources were reprogramed from other Agency programs to counterterrorism, even after the DCI's statement in December 1998 that he wanted no resources spared in the effort . . . Finally, CTC managers did not spend all of the funds in their base budget, even after it had been reduced by diversions of funds to other programs.[42]

In other words, *if money or personnel decisions are valid indicators of the CIA's tasking priorities, al-Qa'ida ranked very low.* George Tenet would later testify before Congress that "people use the word 'failure'—'failure' means no focus, no attention, no discipline—and those were not present in what either we or the FBI did here and around the world."[43] The budgetary and personnel choices of Langley that he directed, however, contradict Tenet's assertion. CIA effort—that is, tasking—was simply not heavily directed at al-Qa'ida.

More damning still for the CIA's tasking priorities is the fact that not all intelligence consumers were quiescent about al-Qa'ida. Richard Clarke insists that as early as 1993, he, Anthony Lake (then national security advisor), Samuel Berger (then deputy national security advisor), and Nancy Soderberg (Anthony Lake's staff director at the time) persisted

> . . . in asking the CIA to learn more about the man whose name kept appearing in CIA's raw reports as "terrorist financier Usama bin Laden." It just seemed unlikely to us that this man who had his hand in so many seemingly unconnected organizations was just a donor, a philanthropist of terror. There seemed to be some organizing force and maybe it was he. He was the one thing that we knew the various terrorist groups had in common. And we kept coming back to the incredible notion offered by CIA and FBI that the gang that bombed the World Trade Center had just come together as individual agents who happened upon one another and decided to go to America to blow things up.[44]

The CIA, however, persisted in holding this happenstance view of Islamic terrorism. In fact, Paul Pillar, head of the CTC until 1999, even coined the term *ad hoc terrorists* to describe the first World Trade Center bombers.[45] Furthermore, we know that Berger "upbraided DCI Tenet so sharply after the *Cole* attack—repeatedly demanding why the United States had to put up with such attacks—that Tenet walked out of the meeting."[46] Nevertheless, although bin Ladin's name surfaced with increasing frequency in raw intelligence in the mid-1990s, when bin Ladin came up in the CIA analysis, they only referred to him as "terrorist financier," characterizing him as "a radicalized rich kid, who was playing at terrorism by sending checks to terrorist groups."[47] The agency never tasked intelligence assets to collect information that might verify this view of al-Qa'ida's chief.

There is one final argument employed by the defenders of the CIA's pre-9/11 tasking, which constitutes a variation on Roberta Wohlstetter "signal-to-noise" problem. A former government counterterrorism chief characterized the problem for intelligence agencies before 9/11 as sorting "Red flags in a sea of Red flags."[48] This statement is untenable, however: Al-Qa'ida was a known, abiding, and self-declared enemy of America that had repeatedly struck U.S. interests over a period of years, in multiple locations, on an escalating scale of violence, and displaying increasing sophistication. No other individual, group, or state at this time comes close to fitting that description. Yes, there was a great deal of terrorist "chatter"[49] in the years before 9/11, but the real question is: Why did al-Qa'ida *stay* so low on the scale of CIA's tasking priorities? Why, as Amy Zegart asks, was the signal "found and then lost,"[50] subsumed beneath other CIA priorities? The answer to this deeper, macro question of the loss of signal can be traced to a tasking process that was captive to familiar attributes of the agency's culture and identity; the Cassandra of the case throws this process into stark relief.

In 1996, the CIA set up a special "virtual station"—"Alec Station"—focused on bin Ladin. To stress its experimental nature, Alec Station was not based at CIA Headquarter in Langley but located in an office complex elsewhere in northern Virginia. It was conceived of as an entity that would operate focused on a particular subject much as traditional CIA stations at embassies focus on countries. According to the 9/11 Commission, the station's choice of bin Ladin as its focus was "essentially happenstance: the original idea had been to focus the station on terrorist finance."[51] When veteran agency analyst Michael Scheuer was recruited to run Alec Station, however, he suggested that the unit focus on bin Ladin (with whom Scheuer was familiar because he had previously been running the Islamic Extremist Branch of the CTC).

As we will soon explore, Scheuer is the Cassandra of this case: His nickname among some 9/11 Commission staffers was "the Prophet." More than anyone else in the CIA (and much earlier), Scheuer understood the danger posed by bin Ladin and al-Qa'ida.[52] For this reason, we might quibble with the term *happenstance* in the context of Alec Station's remit; their point that the focus on bin Ladin was not a result of strategic insight by the DI, however, is well taken. Nevertheless, Scheuer's epithet within the commission contains a revealing irony, making his role a good point of departure to look at culture and identity's role in this surprise.

Scheuer remembers that, as early as December 1996, he had trouble convincing anyone outside of Alec Station of the menace of al-Qa'ida. The reason that Scheuer gives for this trouble is extremely revealing: "They could not believe that this tall Saudi with a beard, squatting around a camp fire, could be a threat to the United States of America."[53] As with Castro in the previous case, external features as trivial as a man's beardedness was a heuristic used in CIA culture to judge a lack of seriousness. What makes this dismissal even more disturbing, however, is that in the intervening years the CIA had experienced the shock of our first case—the Iranian Revolution—to heighten its sensitivity to the power of radical Islam. A bearded, devout, and apparently other-worldly Muslim leader in robes caused vast amounts of damage to U.S. national interests. Despite that potentially salutary lesson, according to Miller, the CIA "continued to overlook, or at least underestimate, the breadth and power of the fundamentalist Islamic reform movement sweeping the Middle East."[54] Therefore, when Scheuer prepared a fifty-paragraph memo about bin Ladin's efforts to obtain WMD and sent it over to Langley that year (that is, 1996), his superiors refused to circulate it throughout the agency, saying that it was "alarmist and wouldn't be taken seriously; they agreed to circulate only two paragraphs from the report and only if they were buried in a larger memo."[55]

Obviously, this anecdote is about more than bin Ladin's beard: It brings into focus Langley's perception of the Third World as a whole. According to Vince Cannistraro, a former top-ranking CIA official,

> The Third World was just theater in the Agency's eyes, a stage on which to play out their conflict with the Russians . . . In 1979, Afghanistan was an officially neutral, landlocked Asian nation without any significance to our vital interests. The CIA didn't give it much strategic importance before the Soviets invaded; and *once they'd departed, I think they gave it even less*.[56]

While bearded men around campfires might have added local color to this theater, they certainly did not justify tasking additional resources to collect intelligence about potential threats.

Homogeneity likely also played a role. We have no numbers on the religious orientation of CIA officials responsible for deciding the agency's tasking priorities, but we can assume based on what we know of Langley's homogeneity already demonstrated that there were few (if any) Muslims among them. This "beard and campfire" anecdote is evidence of a larger pattern, one that persisted even after 9/11, in which non-Muslim Americans—even experienced consumers of intelligence—underestimated al-Qa'ida for cultural reasons.[57] The diplomat Richard Holbrooke, for example, wondered, "How can a man in a cave out-communicate the world's leading communications society?"[58] The answer is that Usama bin Ladin had always framed his movement "by calling up images that were deeply meaningful to many Muslims and *practically invisible to those who were unfamiliar with the faith*."[59] This "practical invisibility" also explains the lack of tasking to investigate al-Qa'ida more deeply before the attacks and constitutes a clear indication of the consequences of the DI's homogeneous makeup. Like many highly devout Muslims, Usama bin Ladin consciously modeled himself on the Prophet Mohammed: He fasted on days that Mohammed fasted, wore clothes like the Prophet's, and even sat and ate in the postures that Islamic tradition ascribes to him. One can assume that these facts would diminish the likelihood that the homogeneous (and scientifically oriented) tasking process at CIA would take a person of bin Ladin's appearance seriously.

A detailed example of this inversion phenomenon (by which the very features that granted bin Ladin credibility to one audience diminished his credibility for CIA analysts) is unlocked by Holbrooke's "caveman" rhetoric. Reference to caves is frequently used in the United States even now to disparage bin Ladin. Ironically, after his return to Afghanistan in 1996, bin Ladin began to make statements and to receive visitors in caves quite intentionally. For bin Ladin, it would appear that his frequent appearance with caves was a personal version of the Prophet Mohammad's *hijrah* (or *hijira*), the incident in 622 CE when Mohammad and his closest friend, Abu Bakr, fled in advance of his persecutors from Mecca to Yathrib (later renamed Medina). As every Muslim knows, though Mohammad's enemies searched for him, he was safe in a cave on Mount Thawr (partly through three wondrous events: a miraculous acacia tree blocked the entrance, and both a miraculous spider's web and a miraculous dove's nest containing an egg all made the cave where Mohammad hid seem unoccupied).[60] Muslims also know that Mohammad's revelation of the Koran occurred in a mountaintop cave. Pious Muslims make an association between caves and holiness automatically: Even Islamic architecture and art (when they venture beyond geometric abstraction and calligraphy) are replete with images of stalactites, references both to the sanctuary that a cave provided the Prophet and to his original encounter with the divine. In short, a key part of the backdrop that made bin Ladin appear "primitive" to non-Muslims placed him for pious Muslims outside "time, history, modernity, corruption, and the smothering West." From a cave, bin Ladin simultaneously earned the disdain of a homogeneous, rationalist, science-oriented CIA analytical corps and in the eyes of his followers earned the right to "presume to speak for the true religion."[61]

In sum, some of the very sources of bin Ladin's strength in the Islamic world—features such as his beard, his dress, and dwelling in caves—are the first tier of explanation of how this strategic surprise occurred. The CIA's faith in "science" served to magnify the inbuilt tendency of American culture to underestimate people of the sort that composed al-Qa'ida; in concert, the agency's homogeneity was an enabler for its unconscious ignorance about Islam. Together, these attributes of identity and culture hindered better tasking regarding this threat.

This almost diametrically opposing perception of bin Ladin's public persona raises a final matter to address with respect to pre-9/11 tasking failures: Al-Qa'ida made no secret that it had "declared war" against the United States. As in previous cases, this allows us to conjecture whether the CIA's cultural predilection for secret information curbed tasking about al-Qa'ida. To be fair to the agency, prior to these attacks there was an entire class of Islamists who "had consistently forecast catastrophic doom for the United States in many unpleasant ways."[62] Nevertheless, given the agency's demonstrated preference for secret rather than open-source information, we can here note five representative facts about al-Qa'ida available to anyone seriously interested prior to 9/11.

First, bin Ladin did not hide: He began speaking to the Western press corps in December 1993.[63] Second, bin Ladin publicly declared war on the United States on September 2, 1996, in his "Declaration of Jihad against the United States," which was first published in the Movement for Islamic Reform in Arabia's *Al-Islah* newsletter; he declared jihad again in the media on February 23, 1998. Third, it was no secret that his message was resonating in the Islamic world: After the USS *Cole* attack, in the Arab world bin Ladin's name was "scrawled on walls and plastered on magazine covers," tapes of his speeches were sold in bazaars, and in Pakistan T-shirts bearing his photograph and the caption "The Great Mujahid of Islam" were sold alongside calendars labeled "Look Out America, Usama Is Coming."[64] Fourth, his message's resonance was noted among informed Westerners. If you read *Foreign Affairs*, for example, in 1998 you would have noted Bernard Lewis's article "License to Kill: Usama Bin Laden's Declaration of Jihad."[65] Had that article inspired you to do more digging, two book-length studies of bin Ladin were published in English before the attacks, one by Simon Reeve and the other by Yossef Bodansky, a controversial Israeli author.[66] Fifth, even relatively "actionable" intelligence reached the public (or at least the semipublic) domain: on March 7, 2001, the

Russian permanent mission to the United Nations submitted a report on al-Qa'ida, bin Ladin, and the Taliban to the Security Council's Committee on Afghanistan. The report, later leaked to the press, gave information on thirty-one senior Pakistani military officers actively supporting bin Ladin and described the location of fifty-five al-Qa'ida bases or offices in Afghanistan.[67] From a tasking point of view, there was no secret to steal: Al-Qa'ida was a self-declared enemy of the United States.

Given this flood of public information about bin Ladin and what we know about Langley's preference for secret information, it is not a significant intellectual leap to imagine that bin Ladin's very public stance as an enemy of the United States actually worked against efforts at the CIA to task assets to collect intelligence on al-Qa'ida. Meanwhile, one imagines CIA analysts putting preannounced terrorist attacks in the same categories that Sherman Kent put coups in his aphorism: "Any coup that I have heard of is not going to happen."[68] In tasking, therefore, we find numerous indications that the CIA's homogeneity, scientism, and predilection for secrets contributed to its misconceptions about al-Qa'ida and thus to the strategic surprise of 9/11.

Collection

It is close to tautology to assert that those terrorist groups that endure are skilled at minimizing their exposure to the collection efforts of intelligence agencies.[69] Without a doubt, beginning in the mid-1990s, al-Qa'ida fit this description. Since its genesis, it has had an excellent understanding of U.S. intelligence, applied security rigorously, and possessed an impressive cadre of highly disciplined and competent covert operators.[70]

Bin Ladin's brainchild, therefore, was a hard target as far as collection was concerned, but it was not small. Consider the scope of his achievement. In addition to running training camps that vetted thousands of potential terrorists during basic paramilitary training,[71] by 2001 bin Ladin had created a truly global jihad network,[72] enlisting groups in Saudi Arabia, Egypt, Jordan, Lebanon, Iraq, Oman, Sudan, Algeria, Libya, Tunisia, Morocco, Somalia, and Eritrea. He had also established cooperative agreements with like-minded Islamic extremist groups in these countries plus in Chad, Mali, Niger, Uganda, Burma, Thailand, Malaysia, Indonesia, and Bosnia.

In other words, it is a mistake to imagine that penetration opportunities against al-Qa'ida existed solely in Afghanistan, "one of the poorest, most remote, least industrialized countries on earth."[73] It was active in regions in which U.S. and other Western intelligence agencies took an active interest in the late 1990s, like the Balkans. According to Richard Clarke, in fact, "What we saw unfold in Bosnia was a guidebook to the bin Laden network," though it was not recognized as such at the time. In the Bosnian case, al-Qa'ida used mosques, Islamic cultural centers, and Islamic relief agencies in the United Kingdom, Italy, the United States, Austria, and Saudi Arabia to provide funds and logistical support to their efforts to send hardened Arab veterans to fight.[74] Collection of intelligence about al-Qa'ida, therefore, was not solely a matter of Third World skullduggery; the tactical leader of the 9/11 attacks, Mohamed Atta, famously spent extended periods in Germany, for example. It is simpleminded, therefore, to limit thinking about the pre-9/11 collection failure to Afghanistan.

The popular wisdom, moreover, is that the monetary resources behind the 9/11 attacks were "trivial."[75] The 9/11 Commission cited a figure of al-Qa'ida using only between $400,000 and $500,000 to finance the attacks. Such paltry sums are disingenuous and misleading: They represent only the *incremental* costs of this attack. Any one terrorist act by al-Qa'ida might cost such sums, but it took far more to finance all of al-Qa'ida's activities in the years prior to 9/11. Bin Ladin's personal fortune was useful when establishing al-Qa'ida, but the organization's financial network dealt in sums that were far beyond his personal means. In other words, the organization called al-Qa'ida included a vast, global fund-raising machine,[76] the scope of which was partly concealed through its extensive use of *hawala* (a trust-based system for transferring funds outside of normal banking channels that has been used in the Islamic world for centuries).[77] Therefore, it is deeply ironic that although the CIA's Alec Station had originally been inspired by the idea of studying terrorist financial links, few personnel assigned to the bin Ladin case had any experience in financial investigations. As far as collection of financial information about al-Qa'ida, the 9/11 Commission reported: "Any terrorist-financing intelligence appeared to have been collected collaterally, as a consequence of gathering other intelligence." Given the tasking already discussed, this neglect of al-Qa'ida's finances is not surprising, but we should note that the collection opportunities extended well beyond tracking the half-million dollars or so that were the tactical funding for the 9/11 attacks.

Historically unique features of the pre-9/11 environment protrude beyond the conventional boundaries of any given phase of the intelligence cycle. As al-Qa'ida coalesced and grew, the CIA was suffering what most observers agree was a human intelligence meltdown as a result of the end of the Cold War.[78] Budget cuts had badly affected the Clandestine Service, the mainstay of the CIA's human intelligence collection system.[79] In 1995, for example, only twenty-five trainees became new case officers. One consequence of this crisis in human collection assets is that beginning in the early 1990s the agency began to respond to crises around the globe (for example, in Africa or the Balkans) by "surging," or taking officers anywhere they could find them to respond to immediate problems. "In many cases," the 9/11 Commission noted, "The surge officers had little familiarity with the new issues. Inevitably, some parts of the world were not fully covered, or not covered at all."

By one account, the CIA's collection efforts in Somalia during the U.S. intervention in 1992–1993—where it might have gained early appreciation for the seriousness of al-Qa'ida—fit this pattern (along with displaying the risk-aversion documented in the following paragraphs): "They [that is, the CIA] had nobody in the country when the marines landed. Then they sent in a few guys who had never been there before. They swapped people out every few weeks and they stayed holed up in the US compound on the beach, in comfy trailer homes that they had flown in by the Air Force."[80] Evidence later emerged that bin Ladin sent advisers into Somalia to organize attacks against U.S. forces, and al-Qa'ida elements helped down U.S. helicopters. In the event, it took three years for the United States to recognize fully al-Qa'ida's participation in the death of the eighteen U.S. soldiers in those actions.[81]

Thus, most sources discussing CIA collection efforts against al-Qa'ida prior to 9/11 are content to rest on the (obvious) fact that the CIA had no human sources inside al-Qa'ida (or among the Taliban security that surrounded bin Ladin)[82] in the years prior to the attacks.[83] The CIA did have a few assets in Afghanistan left over from the jihad against the Soviets[84] of the 1980s, but these people had no inside knowledge of the bin Ladin organization. In fact, in addition to being near useless for intelligence collection, the doubtful reliability of these assets was allegedly one of the important obstacles to the CIA's halfhearted efforts to capture or kill bin Ladin before 9/11. Clarke reports that as the NSC attempted to plan such operations in 1998–1999, the "CIA's assets in Afghanistan could usually tell us where bin Ladin was a few days earlier. They did not know, except rarely, where he would be the next day. On a few occasions, they were able to tell us where they thought he was at the moment."[85] Pakistani intelligence could have provided better information, but they repeatedly rebuffed the CIA when they were asked.[86] Clearly, there was a range of problems with the CIA's HUMINT capabilities that contributed to the strategic surprise of 9/11.

The quantitative problems of HUMINT collection—too few case officers—were amplified by a recurrence of the sort of "moral qualms" about human intelligence that we saw flourish in the post-Watergate era (that is, prior to the Iranian Revolution). This likely led to qualitative problems, too. Previously, we heard one Turner appointee to the CIA say in the 1970s, "HUMINT was likely to be suspect on moral grounds," something that would do "moral damage" to the collector.[87] Similarly, in 1995, the agency was criticized for having a Guatemalan army officer on its payroll who was suspected of involvement in the murder of another Guatemalan married to an American woman. The case triggered congressional hearings. As a result, the CIA instituted "new rules that required case officers to vet shady informants through a series of special committees."[88] Most sources agree that these new procedures caused many case officers to simply stop trying to recruit.[89] One officer remembers: "Nobody actually said you can't do recruitments. What they said was, 'If you recruit someone and he goes out and does something—you know, whacks someone—you're responsible. Your career's over.' So of course no one did anything."[90] It does not seem to have occurred to anyone drafting these rules that to recruit someone within a terrorist group, by definition one has to put on the payroll someone who associates with killers. The inspector general's report coyly says: "While agreeing that the dirty asset rules may have created a climate that had the effect of inhibiting certain recruitment operations, the [investigating] Team is unable to confirm or determine the extent of the impact."[91] Absence of evidence is not evidence of absence: Ipso facto, these rules cannot have made it easier to penetrate al-Qa'ida.

This scrutiny apparently led to a much more risk-averse culture in the DO generally.[92] One agent remembers requesting permission to go into Northern Iraq to conduct routine surveillance of the fighting between the Kurds and the Iraqi army but being ordered not to cross the border. He says his station chief "wanted me to monitor the war from Ankara. If he'd had his way, I'd have spent my days in the local Sheraton eating peanuts, watching CNN and reading two-day-old newspaper reports from Reuters."[93] Clearly, such an environment lowered the odds of collecting useful information about al-Qa'ida. Similar risk aversion hindered technical collection efforts. When the Predator unmanned aerial vehicle (UAV) flew over Afghanistan for the first time on

September 7, 2000, it provided video of truly astonishing quality. The Preda-tor had a long "dwell time" and could offer detailed, real-time video feed from 10,000 miles away. On at least one occasion, however, the Taliban scrambled MiG fighters to try to shoot it down.[94] Had they done so, they would likely have not only publicly trumpeted this fact, but they would also likely have sold the surviving pieces of the drone to either Russian or Chinese intelligence. Apparently, by 1997 the attitude to risk at the DO was best articulated by a sign that hung over a case officer's desk in the agency's Rome station: "Big Ops, Big Problems. Small Ops, Small Problems. No Ops, No Problems."[95]

In short, in the years before 9/11, CIA human intelligence collection as-sets in close proximity to Usama bin Ladin were nonexistent, and Langley's human collection system generally was abysmal. The use of some promising technical collection assets was hindered by a culture of risk aversion. If one looks deeper, though, these assertions about human intelligence meltdown and risk aversion are valid but insufficient to provide a complete picture of the collection failure prior to the attacks. To understand collection problems against al-Qa'ida more deeply, we have to explore how the gaps in and strains on collection assets were exacerbated by a familiar quality of the CIA's identity and culture: homogeneity.

Bureaucracies adjust to change slowly, if at all. The CIA certainly did not adjust the composition of its human intelligence assets rapidly following the collapse of the USSR. Despite a sweeping post–Cold War mandate, they re-mained just as homogeneous as before. As the 9/11 *Commission Report* noted: "New hires in the Clandestine Service tended to have qualifications similar to those of serving officers: that is, they were suited for traditional agent recruit-ment or for exploiting liaison relationships with foreign services but were not equipped to seek or use assets inside the terrorist network."[96] In other words, they were mostly white, middle-class, third-generation Americans.

One former CIA officer was slightly more graphic soon after the attacks and highlighted the effect of this homogeneity on the intelligence collection against al-Qa'ida:

> The CIA probably doesn't have a single truly qualified Arabic-speaking officer of Middle Eastern background who can play a believable Muslim fundamen-talist who would volunteer to spend years of his life with shitty food and no women in the mountains of Afghanistan. For Christ's sake, most case officers live in the suburbs of Virginia.[97]

While we have no exact figures, language skills tell part of the story: In 2001, only 20 percent of the graduating class of clandestine case officers were fluent in a non-Romance language.[98] Even after al-Qa'ida's 1998 embassy bombings, the CIA did not employ a single case officer who spoke Pashto, the primary dialect of their hosts, the Taliban (it still had none as of 2002).[99] In a revealing turn of phrase, witnesses to the Joint Inquiry emphasized, "The linguistic expertise needed to identify, analyze, and disseminate intelligence relating to the al-Qa'ida threat includes an understanding of colloquial expression in [redacted] 'terrorist languages' and dialects."[100] The mere fact that the phrase *terrorist languages* was used by members of the U.S. Intelligence Community in testimony to Congress is an indication of the cultural blindness imposed by its homogeneity.

There is also evidence that when the CIA *was* in contact with people in the same region as al-Qa'ida, its people brought American mind-sets with them: The Northern Alliance leader Ahmed Shah Massoud's intelligence men were frustrated "that the CIA always seemed to think Massoud and his men were motivated by money."[101] How could such teams take in the mind-sets of the nineteen men who became the 9/11 hijackers?

In addition to the impetus from the Africa embassy bombings, the persistence of homogeneity among human collectors is surprising in light of two recent episodes in the CIA's history: their massive failure in Iran in the early 1980s and their much-acclaimed success in assisting Afghans in their struggle against the Soviets in the 1980s. Apparently, neither episode substantially changed the makeup of the CIA's operations officers. After the Revolution in Iran, John Miller, Michael Stone, and Chris Mitchell say, the agency "failed to upgrade the competence and suitability of the agents it sent" to the Middle East.[102] Likewise, according to Middle East specialist Reuel Gerecht, even *during* the Afghan war, the CIA never developed a team of true Afghan experts,[103] much less a diverse range of collectors. One former DO officer recalls that through the 1990s the CIA had a "white-as-rice" culture.[104] Another DO officer said that prior to 9/11 the CIA "just kept driving down that set of tracks, working through diplomatic receptions, and areas that we knew there were no terrorists."[105] The U.S. embassy in Kabul was shut in January 1989, so no one was going to get closer to bin Ladin via that route. The fact that the number of nonofficial cover (NOC) officers—those not working out of embassies—remained flat from 1990 to 2001 reinforces this assessment. The odds become even bleaker when one learns that the vast majority of NOC officers tended to be fake businessmen,[106] poorly suited to infiltrating al-Qa'ida. There is no evidence that any CIA asset posed as the sort of Western lost soul who turned up on al-Qa'ida's doorstep prior to 9/11 (though some managed to join the fringes of the group).

Bin Ladin likely knew all these facts about the CIA and more. An anecdote concerning the NSA supports this assertion. Like the CIA, language problems hindered the NSA, on whom the CIA relied to collect much of its signals intelligence about al-Qa'ida. On 9/11, the number of Afghan language specialists (that is, those speaking Pashtun or Dari) at NSA was, James Bamford writes, "almost nonexistent . . . they could be counted on one hand with fingers left over."[107] Equally disturbing from a counterintelligence viewpoint is the NSA's manner of coping with this linguistic shortfall: It sent its al-Qa'ida intercepts to . . . Pakistan's ISI (that is, its intelligence agency) for translation, an organization with a long history of involvement with the Taliban and bin Ladin.[108]

Al-Qa'ida had spent years studying U.S. intelligence and understood the operational space that this crippling homogeneity afforded. How can we be sure? On Sunday, September 9, 2001, bin Ladin had the chutzpah to call his mother in Syria and tell her, in effect: "In two days you're going to hear big news, and you're not going to hear from me for a while."[109] Bin Ladin understood that his call would be intercepted, but he also knew that even for a relatively high-priority target like himself, the NSA's "intercept-interpret-analyze" cycle for the region was running at about seventy-two hours: Bin Ladin knew that by the time the phone call was collected, listened to, and understood by the CIA, the attacks would already have taken place![110]

In sum, in addition to immense problems with HUMINT generally, including understaffing and risk aversion, the CIA's homogeneity appears to have compounded its pre-9/11 blindness to the peril of al-Qa'ida during the collection phase.

Analysis

A few voices maintain that there was no failure at the CIA during the analysis phase prior to 9/11. Daniel Byman, for example, says: "The Intelligence Community, particularly the CIA, did well in providing strategic warning of an al-Qa'ida threat. The identity of the foe, the scale of its ambitions, and its lethality were known and communicated in a timely manner."[111] Similarly, the former head of analysis at the CTC until 1999 alleges: "The [9/11] commission staff used such techniques as highly selective use of material, partial truths,

irrelevant references, plays on words, quotations out of context, and sugges-
tive language leading to false inferences to portray as weak what had been a
strong strategic analytical performance."[112] Even Richard Betts does not hold
analysts fully to account, saying that the CIA vaguely warned *whether* an attack was coming, though he acknowledges that CIA analysis did not provide
actionable warning about where, how, or exactly when it would come.[113]

In contrast, this book argues that analytical failure at the CIA lay at the
epicenter of this strategic surprise. The failure during the analysis phase was
not entirely the product of the CIA's identity and culture, but the fingerprints
of those features that have been explored in previous surprises are also found
on 9/11. Therefore, in this section we first demonstrate that there *was* a basic
analytical failure responsible for this surprise. Second, we explore some explanations offered by other scholars for this failure. Third, we explore this failure
through the perspective of both culture and identity and through the words,
actions, and fate of the Cassandra of this case, Michael Scheuer.

The facts of the CIA's failure during the analysis phase are stark and reveal
misjudgments that are both broad and deep. First, al-Qa'ida was formed in
1988, and the CIA did not describe this organization—at least in documents
shown to the 9/11 Commission—until a decade later, in 1999.[114] As Walter Laqueur notes, the only short profile of bin Ladin by the CIA (published in 1996)
was entitled "Islamic Extremist Financier": This was true, but it was "only the
less important part of the truth." As Laqueur also says, the word "terrorism is
notably absent in the 1996 profile, and it said nothing about the motivation,
aims, or activities of al-Qa'ida outside of the Middle East."[115] These facts stand
in stark contrast to any exculpatory statements about the agency's pre-9/11
analytical performance.

Second, the CIA did not write any analytical assessment of possible hijacking scenarios by al-Qa'ida. In the words of the 9/11 Commission:

> The CTC did not analyze how an aircraft, hijacked or explosives-laden, might
> be used as a weapon . . . [T]he CTC did not develop a set of telltale indicators
> for this method of attack . . . [T]he CTC did not propose, and the Intelligence
> Community collection management process did not set requirements to mon-
> itor such telltale indicators.

Third, there was at the CIA "limited analytic focus on the United States
as a target."[116] We learn from the 9/11 Commission that even as late as 2001,
when the CIA briefed Attorney General John Ashcroft on al-Qa'ida on

July 5, the agency simply warned, "that a significant terrorist attack was imminent." Though Ashcroft was told, "preparations for multiple attacks were in the late stages or already complete and that little additional warning could be expected . . . the briefing only addressed threats *outside the United States.*" When questioned over this failure, DCI Tenet employed a semantic fig leaf, emphasizing to investigators that the CIA's 1995 NIE was entitled "The Foreign Terrorist Threat *in* the United States."[117] Tenet told them: "The preposition in the NIE's title was not 'against' or 'to.' The preposition was 'in.'"[118] Such legalistic hair splitting is hardly the stuff of analytically tight threat assessment or high-quality strategic warning.

Fourth, as we have already quoted Betts, the CIA's warnings about al-Qa'ida were vague about where, how, or when an attack would come. The best example of this nebulous strategic warning is the famous presidential daily brief (PDB) entitled "Bin Ladin Determined to Strike US," which President Bush received on August 6, 2001.[119] This was the thirty-sixth PDB item of the year to mention bin Ladin or al-Qa'ida, but it was the first devoted to a possible attack *in* the United States. However, few who actually read this document—alleged by some because of its title to be a "smoking gun" that shifts culpability squarely from the CIA to the White House—would say that CIA analysts issued a clear strategic warning in this document. According to the 9/11 Commission, the PDB was, as President Bush later described it, "historical in nature." The following, for example, are the bold typed headlines of this PDB, the key "take-aways" for the president:

- Clandestine, foreign government, and media reports indicate Bin Ladin since 1997 has wanted to conduct terrorist attacks in the US;
- The millennium plotting in Canada in 1999 may have been part of Bin Ladin's first serious attempt to implement a terrorist strike in the US;
- Although Bin Ladin has not succeeded, his attacks against the US Embassies in Kenya and Tanzania in 1998 demonstrate that he prepares operations years in advance and is not deterred by setbacks;
- Al-Qa'ida members—including some who are US citizens—have resided in or traveled to the US for years, and the group apparently maintains a support structure that could aid attacks;
- We have not been able to corroborate some of the more sensational threat reporting, such as that from a [redacted] service in 1998 saying that Bin Ladin wanted to hijack a US aircraft to gain release of "Blind Shaykh" 'Umar 'Abd al-Rahman and other US-held extremists.

Except for the last three sentences of the PDB (which discuss ongoing FBI activities in response to the historical portrait just painted), this "strategic warning" is almost entirely historical background. It is disturbing, yes, but it is not a basis for action, especially in light of the thirty-five other snippets about bin Ladin and al-Qa'ida in the preceding seven months' PDBs. If anything, this PDB makes gaining an understanding of the CIA's failure to better task and collect information about bin Ladin even more pressing (or it makes these failures even more outrageous). The PDB of August 6, 2001, is certainly not evidence of a strong analytical performance by the CIA prior to 9/11, that is, it was not "actionable warning."[120] It amounts to what is called in Washington a "backgrounder" about an ongoing FBI investigation.

In fact, this PDB exemplifies the CIA's analytical failure regarding al-Qa'ida and not simply because it is overwhelmingly historical. It exemplifies the failure because it is representative of the stream of minor historical or tactical reports about al-Qa'ida that the CIA issued without preparing an NIE or SNIE about the threat. Despite numerous individual papers dealing with al-Qa'ida and bin Ladin,[121] prior to 9/11 the CIA provided no complete portrayals of his strategy or of the extent of al-Qa'ida's involvement in past terrorist attacks. As we have seen in the three previous cases, NIEs and SNIEs are "considered to be the DCI's most authoritative written judgments on national security issues,"[122] yet the last time an NIE focused on foreign terrorism prior to 9/11 was in 1997. That NIE was six pages long; it devoted three sentences to bin Ladin and did not mention al-Qa'ida at all.[123] The previous NIE on terrorism, issued in July 1995, did not mention bin Ladin or al-Qa'ida.[124]

Betts says, "The intelligence system can avert policy failure by presenting relevant and undisputed facts to non-expert principals who might otherwise make decisions in ignorance."[125] Those presentations must be made in the format and manner that principals can digest and act on. Because of this lack of an NIE, however, the 9/11 Commission reported:

> Policymakers knew that there was a dangerous individual, Usama Bin Ladin, whom they had been trying to capture and bring to trial. Documents at the time referred to Bin Ladin "and his associates" or Bin Ladin and his "network." They did not emphasize the existence of a structured worldwide organization gearing up to train thousands of potential terrorists.

In other words, not one of the hundreds of reports on al-Qa'ida produced by the CIA between 1998 and September 11, 2001, provided a broad overview of al-Qa'ida's involvement in past terrorist acts, a comprehensive overview of their strategy, a summary of their financial reach, or an in-depth discussion of the nature of their relationship with governments in the Middle East. As Amy Zegart says, "CIA assessments pointed out the trees but never provided a picture of the forest."[126]

We have seen this pattern in our previous cases. Zbigniew Brzezinski's comments about the Islamic Revolution in Iran are equally appropriate to 9/11: "Failure is not so much a matter of particular intelligence reports"; instead failure results from "a deeper intellectual misjudgment of a central historical reality."[127] An NIE is where the CIA would convey such a judgment to policy makers and to the rest of the Intelligence Community—in the language of strategic surprise, how it would have provided a "high-quality" warning. As a former member of the National Intelligence Council said: "The lack of an NIE is a strong piece of evidence that Director Tenet and the Intelligence Community failed to take a strategic view of the terrorism threat."[128] In this instance, the threat assessment prior to the strategic surprise was not so much distorted as inchoate.

The 9/11 Commission arrived at the same conclusion. Commission staff member Douglas McEachin—a veteran former CIA analyst himself—thought that it was "unforgivable" that no NIE on al-Qa'ida or terrorism of any sort was produced for four years before the attacks. McEachin was "shocked that no one at the senior levels of the CIA had attempted—for years—to catalog and give context to what was known about al-Qa'ida." Shenon reports that, to make this point to the 9/11 commissioners, McEachin even prepared—"as a piece of wise-ass theatre,"—a bogus intelligence report nominally written in 1997 that detailed everything that was then known by the different parts of the CIA about al-Qa'ida. It was filled with graphs, charts, and timelines. McEachin then summoned the ten commission members to a special briefing where he unveiled this concocted "pre-9/11 CIA report." In response, the members were outraged at the apparent lack of action by U.S. policy makers (for example, Commissioner Jamie Gorelick said: "I insist that we get a copy"; Commissioner Bob Kerrey responded more passionately: "What the *fuck*?"). After McEachin explained the actual origin of the report, the ex-CIA man's point was clear: Instead of providing analysis that gave context to a national security threat, the CIA had turned itself into a "headline service" that "fed small nuggets of intelligence about terrorist threats to policy makers but never made the larger context clearer."[129]

At least one current CIA supervisor, known to the 9/11 Commission as "John," agreed with McEachin's view; certainly an excessive preoccupation with current intelligence is identified in the literature on strategic surprise as a precipitating factor of surprises.[130] In its conclusions, the 9/11 Commission made plain their view that the failure of the CIA to produce an NIE about al-Qa'ida was a grave blunder, not least because "[NIEs] provoke widespread thought and debate, have a major impact on their recipients, often in a wider circle of Decisionmakers. The National Intelligence Estimate is noticed in Congress, for example." In other words, a potentially important tool to prompt better tasking and collection by both the CIA and the rest of the Intelligence Community was never employed.

The CIA–IG Report echoed the commission's conclusion, saying that the IG "team found that neither the DCI nor the DDCI followed up [their] warnings and admonitions by creating a documented, comprehensive plan to guide the counterterrorism effort at the Intelligence Community level."[131] As journalist John Diamond says, prior to 9/11: "What was missing was an analytical overview that could have given the harried operators [of collection platforms and tasks] a better idea of what they should be looking for, what kinds of intelligence should be deemed important."[132] An intelligence cycle is only as strong as its weakest link, and analysis prior to 9/11 was very weak indeed. The questions are, "How and why?" We now move to answer that question in the second part of our examination of the analysis phase.

Numerous indicators and informed judgments point to a massive failure in the analysis phase at the CIA prior to 9/11. Oddly, however, the reasons for this failure have not been fully explored. Soon after the attacks, those who chose to see bin Ladin as a "megalomaniacal hyperterrorist"[133]—a sort of lone gunman, a Lee Harvey Oswald writ large—contended that al-Qa'ida did not receive sufficient attention from analysts because it did not fit into the traditional classifications of terrorist groups "along organizational or ideological lines, with revolutionary left wing, conservative right wing, separatist-nationalist and religious terrorism as typical categories."[134]

Another approach was that of the *9/11 Commission Report*, which popularized the phrase *failure of imagination* to explain analytical failures at the CIA. As international affairs specialist Richard Falkenrath says, however, "The Commission's 'failure of imagination' is more of a slogan than an argument: it sounds good but is an almost indecipherable muddle."[135] This slogan did capture, however, the imagination of the media, and spawned some scholarly efforts that put the focus back on the individual psychological makeups of intelligence analysts,[136] on organizational theories of intelligence failure,[137] and on the various ways that imagination might be "institutionalized."

It has also been suggested that, in addition to a failure of imagination, the CIA's CTC focused too much on tactical issues and operations and collection problems, and not enough on analysis.[138] The CIA's Inspector General Report concluded that the CTC's operational focus "overshadowed collaborative strategic analysis."[139] Even Deputy DCI John McLaughlin (generally a supporter of Langley's pre-9/11 performance) has conceded that most of the work of the CTC's thirty- to forty-person analytic group (out of a unit of about 400)[140] dealt with collection issues. The 9/11 Commission reports that in late 2000 DCI Tenet himself had recognized this deficiency at the CTC and appointed a senior manager to create "a strategic assessment capability" there. The CTC established this strategic assessment branch in July 2001 but then labored to find analysts to staff it. It was too little, too late: The new analytical chief reported for duty at the CTC on September 10, 2001.

Another explanatory factor already touched upon deserves further exploration. When the Cold War ended, the culture of the Directorate of Intelligence moved away from "a patient, strategic approach to the long term accumulation of intellectual capital" to "the culture of the newsroom."[141] In the era of CNN, the so-called twenty-four-hour news cycle "eroded the CIA's strategic analysis capabilities."[142] Some have suggested that, as a result, "Current intelligence"—as opposed to strategic intelligence—was where analysts could "look good and occupy center stage."[143]

This change also impinged on the analytical talent pool. According to one insider, the DI's concentration on current intelligence led to a premium being put not on substantive expertise but on analysts who were generalists, who wrote well, and who met tight deadlines quickly.[144] Meanwhile, the post–Cold War resource problems plaguing the DO were also at work in the Directorate of Intelligence, where they were also solved by "surging." A 1997 *Studies* article titled "The Coming Intelligence Failure" says that "the analytic base is dangerously thin" and that there is an attitude that "analysts are fungible . . . [A] belief that we can meet crises by moving analysts between disciplines has distinct limitations."[145]

There is also the fact that bin Ladin used rumors and disinformation to keep the system on alert,[146] which naturally leads to analysts' warning fatigue.[147] For example, bin Ladin "routinely told important visitors to expect significant attacks against US interests soon, and [in the summer of 2001] during a speech at the al Faruq camp, exhorted trainees to pray for the success of an attack involving 20 martyrs."[148] Clearly, combined with other factors, this drumbeat of threats and invective by al-Qa'ida against the United States desensitized some analysts.

Soon after 9/11, a former CTC chief gave a different explanation. He told the Joint Inquiry that the CTC "have underinvested in the strategic only because we've had such near-term threats. The trend is always toward the tactical . . . The tactical is where lives are saved. And it is not necessarily commonly accepted, but strategic analysis does not . . . get you to saving lives."[149] In any case, the IG Report found that "the DCI Counterterrorism Center (CTC) was not used effectively as a strategic coordinator of the IC's counterterrorism efforts. Before 9/11 . . . the Center's focus was primarily operational and tactical."[150]

All of these assertions may contain elements of the truth. In the third part of our examination of pre-911 analysis, however, we advance a different explanation for the analytical breakdown. The four characteristics of the CIA's identity and culture—scientism, homogeneity, an obsession with secrets, and an impulse for consensus—are shown to have played a highly influential role in this surprise.

In Chapter 2, we the discussed the scientism that pervaded the analytical culture of the CIA. In doing so, we quoted a passage in which Sherman Kent poured scorn on his colleagues who resisted his attempts to create an "airtight vocabulary of estimative expressions" for CIA analysts to employ. Specifically, Kent alleged that his substantial efforts in this arena were opposed by "the 'poets'—as opposed to the 'mathematicians'—in my circle of associates." He added: "If the term [that is, *poet*] conveys a modicum of disapproval on my part, that is what I want it to do."[151] We have also seen how this narrow approach to reason endured in the CIA's analytical culture.

It is revealing, therefore, to realize that bin Ladin's first declaration of war against the United States included a poem addressed to then Secretary of Defense William Perry:

> O William, tomorrow you will be informed
> As to which young man will face your swaggering brother
> A youngster enters the midst of battle smiling, and
> Retreats with his spearhead stained with blood.[152]

In fact, bin Ladin was prone to expressing himself in poetry. In the following, he praises the attack on the USS *Cole* by writing that the U.S. ship:

> Sails into the waves flanked by arrogance, haughtiness, and false power.
> To her doom she moves slowly. A dinghy awaits her riding the waves.
> In Aden, the young men stood up for holy war and destroyed
> A destroyer feared by the powerful.

In the same poem, bin Ladin alluded to future attacks, saying:

> Your brothers in the East have readied their mounts . . . and the battle camels
> are prepared to go.[153]

We have returned to a situation akin to that of bin Ladin's use of caves: A medium perfectly attuned to appeal to his audience is also tailor made to be ignored in a CIA culture steeped in scientism. Bin Ladin's penchant for versifying and the poetry itself was not merely in the foreign language of Arabic; it derived from a conceptual universe light years from Langley. It is a revealing symptom of the profoundly differing worldviews of analytical subject and object (the fact that both the Taliban and much of Persian culture also routinely express themselves in poetry should give contemporary analysts pause). As in the Iranian case presented in Chapter 3, it is evidence of the difficulty that CIA analysts had entering the mind-set of an enemy for whom "the Crusades were a continual historical process," one who was "spiritually anchored in the seventh century."[154] Sherman Kent and his progeny found (as "students reared in the Western tradition") the scientific method "to be best adapted to the search for truth."[155] In bin Ladin, however, analysts confronted exactly that which Kent had disdained in the same article: "the medicine man and his mystical communion with the All-Wise." Far from embodying elements of science and progress (not to mention U.S. benevolence):

> Bin Ladin clearly believes that the twentieth century was characterized by a steady return to barbarism, and more precisely, barbarism refined, modernized and practiced by the Christian West, and especially the United States, against Muslims in a high-tech replay of the murderous practices used by Catholic armies during three-plus centuries of Crusades.[156]

Institutionally, the CIA's persistent analytical culture of reason was almost an exact opposite of al-Qa'ida's, which married the assumption that faith is stronger than weapons or nations with the idea that the ticket to enter a sacred zone where miracles occur is the willingness to die. Of course, bin Ladin and al-Qa'ida also embodied many qualities at odds with such caricatures, including a strong sense of personal responsibility, patience, and professionalism.[157] We begin to see here why Alec Station, composed of a group of analysts who had studied bin Ladin and his worldview enough to grasp his intent, encountered such problems selling a threat to the rest of the CIA.

Facing the CIA analysts was, after all, a self-proclaimed enemy who was hosted by the Taliban, a group not known for its commitment to Enlightenment ideals. After the fall of Kabul, one of its number jumped into a cage at the Kabul Zoo and cut the nose off a bear because the animal's "beard" was not long enough to satisfy Koranic injunctions.[158] Such heinous behavior was writ large when bin Ladin's hosts dynamited and shelled the "idols" at the UNESCO World Heritage site of Bamian in 2001. A sign posted on the wall of Kabul's (Saudi-trained) religious police would seem to say everything a CIA analyst needed to know about Afghanistan and the movement that it harbored: "Throw reason to the dogs: it stinks of corruption."[159]

When one's analytical background is "science based" and one's analytical mandate involves "weapons proliferation, terrorism, drug trafficking, organized crime, illicit trade practices and environmental issues of great gravity,"[160] a self-proclaimed enemy with such a *Weltanschauung* is difficult to credit as a top-priority threat.

A focus on reason and a worldview accustomed to framing its thinking entirely in post-Enlightenment terms would also find al-Qa'ida's grievances against America opaque. Without a doubt, deference to the supernatural is omnipresent in the United States, but bin Ladin's declarations that during the 1990 Gulf War the United States gravely insulted Islam by "entering a peninsula that no religion from among the non-Muslim states has entered for 14 centuries" and that "never has Islam suffered a greater disaster than this invasion"[161] would strike the non-Islamic specialists among U.S. analysts as eccentric. As Ofira Seliktar discusses in the context of the Iranian Revolution, Islamic fundamentalism confounded "accepted notions of rationality, linear progression and [therefore the] time-honored tools for peering into the future."[162] Once again, the CIA's culture and identity, especially its deference to Western reason, led to a "theoretical glaucoma"[163] much like that that blinded analysts to the threat posed to the shah by Islamic fundamentalism in our first case. Bin Ladin and U.S. analysts were operating in different Kuhnian paradigms. Despite the lesson of 1979, the CIA's culture and identity still could not credit the idea that "many people take God seriously."[164] This blindness was not limited to CIA analysts. Ralph Peters issued this warning to the Department of Defense in a 1999 essay in *Parameters* entitled "Our Old New Enemies":

> We maintain a *cordon sanitaire* around military operations, ignoring the frightening effect of our enemy's will and persistence. We accept the CNN reality of "mad mullahs" and intoxicated masses, yet we do not consider belief a noteworthy factor when assessing our combat operations . . . We shy away from manifestations of faith, suspecting them or ignoring them, or, at best, analyzing them in the dehydrated language of the sociologist. But if we want to understand the warriors of the world and the fury that drives them, we had better open our minds to the power of belief.[165]

What we argue here is that the CIA's pervasive privileging of reason—Peters's "dehydrated language of the sociologist"—amplified a general American cultural predisposition to underestimate danger from al-Qa'ida. The same analytical outlook that led to a misassessment of al-Qa'ida's sincerity of intent contributed to a blind spot about its likely aims and modus operandi. Michael Handel points out that in the Western tradition it is usually assumed that if it is impossible to win a war, then starting one is counterproductive and irrational. Handel says, however, that a crucial point repeatedly missed by Western analysts is that for many non-Western cultures (among them the Chinese, the Vietnamese, and the Arabs), Clausewitzian primacy is taken one step farther. He argues that, in these cultures, "it makes sense to resort to war even if victory is impossible, as long as one can win *politically*."[166] Johnston also underscored this point in the context of Islam: "As a result of the fundamental cultural rejection of war for religion by the West in the early modern period, it has been especially difficult for Western culture to accept and make sense of the ongoing presence of the phenomenon of war for the faith in modern Muslim societies."[167] How much more difficult for CIA analysts steeped in an internal culture of positivism? As Richard Betts reminded us in the context of Khrushchev's plans for Cuba, rational strategy was simply one in which means were logically consistent with ends and said nothing whatever about the nature of those ends. For that reason, we can say that bin Ladin's worldview—while definitely grounded in a form of reason—was pre-Clausewitzian. As scholars Kristen Monroe and Lina Kreidie say in "The Perspective of Islamic Fundamentalists and the Limits of Rational Choice Theory," rational choice requires "some sequential ordering of events, but *the events themselves need not be real.*"[168]

One might take this argument a step further and suggest that the most useful guide to bin Ladin's worldview might be the Dutch cultural theorist Johan Huizinga, who pointed out that prior to the notion of either total war or limited war, wars were sometimes fought to "obtain a decision of holy validity" or even as "a form of divination."[169] The CIA's analytical culture, exuding "a strong positivistic belief in a 'rational' political universe which experts could objectively analyze,"[170] simply could not register bin Ladin as a serious threat, except perhaps to characterize him as one of Peters's "mad mullahs."[171] It was an analytical culture singularly ill equipped to understand the nature of many—though not all[172]—of al-Qa'ida's grievances, many of its aims, and especially its "theory of victory."[173]

Such a "rationalistic" worldview likely also contributed to the failure by CIA analysts to explore al-Qa'ida's method of attack on 9/11: that aircraft, explosive laden or otherwise, might be used as part of a suicide operation. Contra the 9/11 Commission, more than a failure of imagination is required to understand this oversight. In 1994, an Algerian group hijacked a plane in Algiers and apparently intended to fly it into the Eiffel Tower;[174] in 1995, Manila police reported in detail about a suicide plot to crash a plane into CIA Headquarters;[175] since the 1996 Atlanta Olympic Games, the NSC actively considered the use of aircraft as suicide weapons. Tom Clancy also wrote a novel about such an attack. As the commission itself noted, the possibility of commercial planes as suicide weapons was both "imaginable and imagined,"[176] *just not at the CIA.* It is likely that the persistent cult of reason we have documented among CIA analysts played a role in this failure.

Another factor of CIA culture and identity that contributed to under- and misestimating al-Qa'ida in the analysis phase is the homogeneity of the agency. While this persistent attribute has already been heavily documented, the CIA became even more homogenized when the Cold War ended. Former DCI Gates speaks of the post–Cold War CIA as less and less willing to employ

> . . . people that are a little different, people who are eccentric, people who don't look good in a suit and tie, people who don't play well in the sandbox with others. The kinds of tests that we make people pass, psychological, and everything else, make it hard for somebody who may be brilliant or have extraordinary talents and unique capabilities to get into the Agency.[177]

Perhaps as a result, very few CIA analysts can read or speak Chinese, Korean, Arabic, Hindi, Urdu, or Farsi—which collectively comprise the languages spoken by nearly half the world's population. To this effect must be added the security requirements, which the 9/11 Commission underscored as a particular problem for recruiting counterterrorism analysts:

> Security concerns also increased the difficulty of recruiting officers qualified for counterterrorism. Very few American colleges or universities offered programs in Middle Eastern languages or Islamic studies. The total number of undergraduate degrees granted in Arabic in all US colleges and universities in 2002 was six. Many who had travelled outside the United States could expect a long wait for initial clearance. Anyone who was foreign born or had numerous relatives abroad was well-advised not even to apply [to work at the CIA].[178]

We have no direct evidence, but considering that al-Qa'ida was drawn from what Wright calls "a stateless, vagrant mob of religious mercenaries," who "as stateless persons . . . naturally revolted against the very idea of the state" and who "saw themselves as a borderless posse empowered by God to defend the entire Muslim people,"[179] the average CIA analyst (likely to be an "average American") would struggle to fathom al-Qa'ida's motives to anticipate its possible actions. Michael Scheuer himself—our Cassandra—highlights this problem, saying that most Americans are simply puzzled when America is vilified, so we assume our accusers must be "demented." Superficially crazy people, in a poor land, far away, rarely constitute a threat worth much serious analysis.

As already discussed, Scheuer also mentions the appearance of al-Qa'ida and its influence on the average American's analysis: "The West has been too often misled by the raggedy appearance of bin Ladin and his subordinates—squatting in the dirt, clothed in robes and turbans, holding AK-47s and sporting chest length beards—and automatically assumes they are antimodern, uneducated rabble."[180] Given the homogeneity of the CIA's analysts, what Scheuer calls a problem of the West was most surely an acute problem of the CIA. It was akin to that described in a 1969 article in *Studies* (originally classified both "secret" and "not for foreign distribution") that addressed the problem of unidentified objects in photographs. It read:

> An analyst who was born and raised in rural America immediately recognizes a barn, a silo, or a windmill on an Iowa farmstead . . . the same analyst, however, might spend hours trying to identify fishnets drying on poles in Thailand

because they resemble antenna arrays at certain electronic sites in the West, even though drying fishnets are as common in Thailand as windmills in Iowa . . . A domed building in a remote area of the western world is at once suspect as a radar site, but a domed building in an area inhabited by Moslems is usually a mosque.[181]

The CIA's culture and identity remained that of the hypothetical photo interpreter of this piece: Someone from an Iowa farmstead whose rearing and training predisposed him or her to watch for radar domes, not mosques, and almost certain to ignore what is said inside them.

In fact, the latest generation of analysts, insofar as they had encountered Islam, were probably like most American graduates in the social sciences produced by U.S. universities since the 1970s. As a result, Edward Said's 1979 thesis in *Orientalism*[182] had a central place in their theoretical baggage. We know that graduates from so-called post-Orientalist study centers and departments later joined many government agencies, and this very likely included the CIA. This is part of the discourse failure previously raised. Walter Laqueur writes: "The post-Orientalist mainstream views were perhaps most authoritatively expressed by Professor John L. Esposito of Georgetown University, not an extreme exponent of this school." Esposito's main text was *The Islamic Threat: Myth or Reality?* It voiced his belief that the threat was "largely or perhaps entirely a figment of imagination." Prior to September 11, Esposito called bin Ladin merely a "champion of popular causes";[183] others of his colleagues were even more skeptical of any danger from Islamic terrorism. It is therefore possible that chariness to accusations of Orientalism interacted with the CIA's cultural appetite for consensus to downplay the menace of al-Qa'ida.

As we begin the third and final section of our look at pre-9/11 analysis, we should remind ourselves that convincing colleagues of a new and somewhat radical threat scenario is difficult. Lempert relates, "In 1940, future General Matthew Ridgway wrote a war-game scenario about a surprise attack on the US fleet at Pearl Harbor. Ridgway's fellow officers refused to take part in the war game because they regarded it as a 'possibility so improbable that it did not constitute a proper basis for maneuver.'"[184] The experience of the Cassandra of the 9/11 case, Michael Scheuer—like DCI McCone a CIA employee—sheds light on how the demand for consensus played a part in the CIA's haphazard analysis of al-Qa'ida.

In 1998, simultaneous al-Qa'ida bomb attacks in Nairobi and Dar es Salaam killed about 220 people and wounded over 4,000. Within a few days, one of the bin Ladin Unit's female analysts confronted DCI Tenet "crying and sobbing" (or, according to Tenet, "quivering with emotion"). In "a very rough scene," she told him: "You are responsible for those deaths because you didn't act on the information we had, when you could have gotten him."[185] Tenet records: "I had some self-doubt . . . but given the emotion of the moment, I let the analyst vent and just walked away."[186]

Apart from its inherent drama and tragedy that this incident foreshadows, it raises a pertinent question: "How, after a confrontation like that, could even an analytical culture as poorly suited to al-Qa'ida as that we have already described fail to give proper strategic warning?" As the 9/11 Commission wrote: "Those government experts who saw Bin Ladin as an unprecedented new danger needed a way to win broad support for their views or at least spotlight the areas of dispute, and perhaps prompt action across government."[187] We have seen that Langley failed to do so, and the familiar features of the CIA's identity and culture, appearing in the experience of Michael Scheuer, offer clues as to why.

In the years before 9/11, there were two CIA analytical units working on al-Qa'ida. At Langley, there was the CTC, a unit of some 400 people that included approximately thirty analysts working on terrorism. Al Qa'ida was not these CTC analysts' primary responsibility; their remit included all sorts of terrorism around the world.[188] The CTC, however, was not housed either as a stand-alone unit (like Alec Station; see the following) or inside the Directorate of Intelligence—it was embedded in the DO. For this reason, the CTC was viewed as an "operations shop" and as a result "had difficulty attracting top-flight analysts":[189] a small minority of CTC analysts had PhDs, one former senior manager had a master's degree in English, and a former chief at the CTC had a bachelor's degree in forestry.[190] As already noted, when the attempt was made to give the CTC a more strategic focus in 2000, the DCI struggled to find analysts to staff it.

Amy Zegart holds that for strategic analysts, working in the DO was "akin to operating behind enemy lines: the DO was home to people who ran spies, stole secrets, and conducted clandestine operations, not for egghead analysts who sat behind desks piecing together information about future threats."[191] As a result, it has already been argued, the CTC's resulting operational focus overshadowed its strategic analysis. The DO's obsession with secrets[192] made for an exceptionally constrained analytical environment. Zegart writes that when the CTC was created in 1986:

> Nowhere was a culture of "need to know" more deeply rooted than in the DO: when the CTC was first created about fifteen years before 9/11, *DO personnel assigned to it requested additional safes and procedures to keep their information out of the hands of analysts working alongside them*, despite the fact that (1) the analysts all had the same clearances that they did, and (2) the CTC was started precisely to foster this kind of collaboration.[193]

Ironically, here DO personnel treated the secrets that they managed to collect about al-Qa'ida exactly as bin Ladin would have wished: They concealed them from CIA analysts! Even after 9/11, CTC analysts continued to complain of a lack of trust between DO and DI officers assigned there. Information at the CIA was compartmentalized to protect it against exposure to technologically sophisticated adversaries, not al-Qa'ida. Protection of sources and methods is important, but it is always a matter of degree. Here, they obviously affected the quality of analysis. One can also speculate that the DO obsession with secrets would also make one unusually prone to imagine as chimerical a foe who declares war in a newsletter and who announces future attacks to groups of trainees.

With this sketch of the CTC, we can already begin to see why no NIE on al-Qa'ida was produced by the CTC. The DO's operational concentration drove the culture of an unevenly staffed and poorly qualified CTC obsessed with secrecy, which took as an article of faith that "strategic analysis does not . . . get you to saving lives."[194]

What about the bin Ladin unit, Alec Station, the part of the CIA directly responsible for al-Qa'ida? In the cool prose of the 9/11 Commission, prior to the attacks analysts in the bin Ladin unit "felt that they were viewed as alarmists even within the CIA." This antiseptic statement masks a dramatic—even tragic—history of a Cassandra struggling to make a warning heard by his own agency. As already discussed, Alec Station was an experimental "virtual station" based in an office complex in Northern Virginia. It was conceived as an entity that would operate against bin Ladin much as a traditional CIA station at an embassy would operate in a foreign country. Veteran analyst Michael Scheuer was recruited to run it, having previously run the Islamic Extremist Branch of the CTC. The unit started with about twelve analysts, and on September 10, 2001, it was staffed by about forty people. Scheuer told 9/11 Commission investigators that he first came to see bin Ladin as a "truly dangerous man" the same year that the station was established, at his instigation, with a focus on bin Ladin:

> Scheuer remembered clearly sitting at his desk at Alec Station one morning in September 1996, reading through the twelve page translation of the fatwa and thinking My God, it sounds like Thomas Jefferson. This was not a "rant" by some crazed religious fanatic. Instead, the fatwa read like "our Declaration of Independence—it had that tone. It was a frighteningly reasoned argument." It contained none of the usual Islamic extremist rhetoric about the dangers of "women in the workplace or X-rated movies." Instead, it was a clear statement of how a generation of Muslims was outraged at the Western exploitation of Arab oil, at American support for Israel, and, most important, at the presence of infidel troops in the land of the prophet Muhammad. "There was no ranting in it," Scheuer said of the fatwa. "These were substantive, tangible issues."[195]

For the next four years, his concern grew, and Scheuer—known in the 9/11 Commission Report as "Mike"—would do little but think of ways to capture or kill bin Ladin and to stop al-Qa'ida. As we saw, as early as December 1996, Scheuer prepared a fifty-paragraph memo about bin Ladin's efforts to obtain WMD. As mentioned, his superiors refused to circulate the memo, saying that Scheuer's work was "alarmist and wouldn't be taken seriously"; it was cut to two paragraphs buried in a larger memo.

After that memo, Scheuer became increasingly alarmed about al-Qa'ida and, in a directorate that affected scholarly detachment and cool reason, his passion about the danger it posed became part of the problem communicating with the DI.[196] Like McCone, Scheuer's personality probably contributed to this problem. Shenon writes that his mannerisms betrayed that "his father was a marine"[197] and that he was educated by Jesuits, an upbringing that Shenon speculates made Scheuer "prickly." This view of Scheuer extended beyond the CIA. At the NSC, Clarke saw the chief of Alec Station as "dysfunctional," a "tantrum thrower," someone "whose difficult personality undermined his effectiveness."[198] Scheuer's increasing passion, however, was also part of the problem. According to Shenon, Scheuer was "committed to his mission to the point of what some of his colleagues saw as zealotry. It could be off-putting. His eyes almost glowed with passion; it had made many of his colleagues at the CIA uncomfortable."[199] In an interview with the investigative CBS television series 60 Minutes, Scheuer was confronted with the following: "My understanding is you had a reputation within the CIA as being fairly obsessive about this subject." "I dislike obsessive," replied Scheuer. "I think hard-headed about it."[200] As a result, in a DI that the 9/11 Commission said "still retained some of its original character of a university gone to war," Scheuer's bureaucratic position came to mirror his physical location: He became an outsider.

The other analysts of Alec Station were in no position to amplify Scheuer's warnings to the rest of the agency. We have already seen how Alec Station was deemed such an undesirable posting that no one from the DO wanted to run it.[201] Similarly, once Scheuer agreed to take it over, the analysts who ended up at Alec Station were extremely junior. The Joint Inquiry's report found that they averaged about three years of experience, in contrast to the overall DI average of eight years of experience for analysts.[202] The obvious inference is that anyone with seniority or savvy avoided assignment to the bin Ladin unit. One former DO officer remembers: "It's so smart to set up an Usama bin Ladin station, but then it gets stood up with a GS-13 [that is, a mid-level] analyst and a few others?! . . . The measure of true commitment is where your A+ people are. *We didn't put the right people in place.*"[203]

There was another factor at work, a direct result of the agency's homogeneity. The Near East Division had a very masculine culture, and most of Scheuer's team were women, which counted against them in the sense that their colleagues in the rest of the division patronized them.[204] The combination of this fact and Scheuer's passion meant that Alec Station came to be seen in the agency as a group of fanatics. The bin Ladin Unit was caustically dismissed by the rest of Langley as "The Manson Family"[205]—a nickname making reference to the mostly female followers of the murderous cult led by Charles Manson.

The Inspector General's Report confirms this characterization of Alec Station and points to additional problems between the unit and external CIA liaison partners (that is, other foreign and domestic intelligence agencies, either U.S. or foreign). In the section of the report called "Operations (Unilateral and Liaison)," the report states:

> The [investigating] Team also found, however, that UBL Station and [redacted] were hostile to each other and working at cross purposes over a period of years before 9/11. The Team cannot measure the specific impact of this counterproductive behavior. At minimum, however, the Team found that organizational tensions clearly complicated and delayed the preparation of Agency

approaches [redacted] thus negatively affecting the timely and effective functioning of the exchange with [redacted] on terrorism issues.[206]

In other words, by 1999, not merely Michael Scheuer but Alec Station as a whole was performing its role of tracking and analyzing bin Ladin in isolation, both physical and cultural, from the rest of the CIA and the Intelligence Community. Just as clearly, elements of the CIA's institutional culture and identity played a large role in this seclusion.

We can pinpoint 1999 as the latest possible year that Alec Station lost its institutional voice because it was in that year that Scheuer's frustration boiled over.[207] In a letter to the House and Senate Intelligence Committees in 2004, Scheuer explained that Alec Station had provided the CIA hierarchy with about ten opportunities to capture or kill bin Ladin and that all were rejected.[208] In response, Shenon says:

> [Scheuer] committed what amounted to professional suicide: he went outside his usual chain of command and sent an email directly to Tenet and most of Tenet's deputics on the seventh floor at CIA headquarters that listed the ten things that needed to change at the CIA if it was ever to succeed in ending the threat from al Qaeda. Within days, Scheuer found himself called into the office of Tenet's deputy, Jack Downing, and fired from Alec Station.[209]

Scheuer's e-mail was seen as "outrageous insubordination." Without mentioning Scheuer's e-mail, in his memoirs Tenet dismisses Scheucr as "an analyst not trained in conducting paramilitary operations," but he is careful to mention, "Six senior CIA officers stood in the chain of command between Mike and me."[210] What is indisputable is Scheuer's Kafkaesque fate. A few days after sending his e-mail, Scheuer was summoned to CIA headquarters and told by one of Tenet's assistants that he was "off balance" and "burned out." He was then banished to a cubicle in the library at Langley, where he said he was made a "junior librarian and given almost nothing to do."[211] Scheuer tried to telephone Tenet, but Tenet did not return his call. Scheuer's exile ended shortly after 9/11, when he was brought back to the bin Ladin unit as a "special adviser to the chief of station."[212]

In addition to insubordination, it seems clear that Scheuer and Alec Station were also guilty of working against one of the enduring four traits of the CIA's culture and identity: a thirst for consensus. What's more, for the other cultural reasons discussed, in an almost nightmarish spiral, the more that Alec Station's analysts understood about al-Qa'ida, the less convincing they seemed to the rest of the agency. A distinguished group of scholars and former intelligence analysts who examined the failure of warning prior to the al-Qa'ida bombings in East Africa (among other cases) hinted at this conclusion. Without offering specifics, in 2006 they wrote:

> The impulse to protect consensus revealed a systemic tendency to silence or even penalize professionals who tried to present new facts or judgments. Violating the implicit boundaries of accepted discourse proved damaging to professional credibility, in some cases causing lasting adverse consequences for individuals' careers. Professionals who were simply doing their jobs as analysts ran the risk of being cast as dissenters who had ceased to be "team players."[213]

In other words, Scheuer had not only been guilty of insubordination, but he and his analysts were also guilty of breaching the CIA's powerful mechanism for preserving consensus. This failure to be seen by the DI as "team players" also contributes to our understanding of why Alec Station failed to mobilize their fellow analysts even *after* Scheuer was replaced.

Following 9/11, a CIA analyst who was also a director of an interagency course to train analysts about warning concepts and techniques, Philip A. True, wrote: "Warning is difficult in a bureaucratic culture, where prudence and caution are more career-enhancing than raising alarms and challenging conventional wisdom."[214] Lest they forget, after 1999 the members of the DI had only to visit the agency's library for the salutary example of Michael Scheuer to remind them of the price of passionate dissent.

Scheuer himself ascribes the lack of action against bin Ladin to the CIA's (especially DCI Tenet's) risk aversion.[215] Here, we can see that its inaction transcended a single cause. The passionately committed analysts of Alec Station tried to raise warning in the context of an organization ideally evolved to be obtuse about al-Qa'ida: The CIA's scientism, homogeneity, preference for secrets, and drive for consensus all worked against the effective recognition of al-Qa'ida as a threat in the analysis phase.

Production and Dissemination

As in previous cases, the evidence for the operation of the culture and identity of the CIA in the production and dissemination phases of the intelligence cycle prior to 9/11 is not as massive as it is for tasking, collection, and analysis.

Still, we can find at least two pieces of strong evidence in this phase for a negative feedback loop between the agency's culture and identity and al-Qa'ida's plans.

We have overwhelming evidence above that the CIA is a consensus-driven organization. This trait derives in part from the fact that apart from their own peers, CIA analysts mostly look to policy makers for approval and guidance. Here is one example of the insidious effects of this fact for intelligence distribution prior to 9/11 and how it contributed indirectly to that strategic surprise. According to the 9/11 Commission, "Soon after the *Cole* attack and for the remainder of the Clinton administration, [CIA] analysts stopped distributing written reports about who was responsible." The reason given by the commission for this cessation is key: "The topic was obviously sensitive, and both Ambassador Barbara Bodine in Yemen and CIA analysts in Washington presumed that the government did not want reports circulating around the agencies that might become public, impeding law enforcement actions *or backing the President into a corner.*"

At the NSC, Clarke certainly appeared to believe that the CIA was equivocating in assigning responsibility to al-Qa'ida. He wrote Samuel Berger on November 7, 2000, that CIA analysts "had described their case by saying that 'it has web feet, flies, and quacks,'" but the analysts would not come out and call it a duck, that is, directly pin responsibility on bin Ladin. Clarke believed that for this reason the issue of going after bin Ladin more aggressively at this time "never came to a head."[216] He assigns, however, the reason for CIA analysts not distributing reports about who was responsible for the *Cole* attack purely to the fact that the CIA thought that the White House did not want to act against bin Ladin. He reported that he felt that both the FBI and the CIA were "holding back" because

> his impression was that Tenet and [Attorney General Janet] Reno possibly thought the White House "*didn't really want to know*" since the principal discussions by November suggested that there was not much White House interest in conducting further military operations against Afghanistan in the administration's last weeks.[217]

As with the Cuban Missile Crisis, "what the President least wanted to hear, the CIA was most hesitant to say plainly."[218] In other words, it was deemed better at the CIA to soft-pedal information about al-Qa'ida than to lose the approval of policy makers and to disturb the consensus for silence on the issue.

Who beside Tenet could have pressed the issue? Not the analysts: Less than a year before, Scheuer had gone from station chief to junior librarian for his stridency about al-Qa'ida. If there is one thing that the literature on strategic warning is clear about, however, it is that "one of the most difficult things for intelligence is to come to judgments which the policymaker does not want to hear"[219] (though at times this is also its raison d'être).

Another cultural factor, the DO's preference for secrets, also bears on the production and dissemination of pre-9/11 intelligence. Despite DCI Tenet's ringing memo proclaiming, "I want no resources or people spared in this effort, either inside CIA or the Community,"[220] the Joint Inquiry found that:

> In late 2000, according to FAA officials, FAA offered CTC Chief Cofer Black the support of its nearly two-dozen analysts regarding transportation security issues in exchange for broader information sharing, but *this offer was not accepted because of CTC concerns about protecting its sources and methods.* The Joint Inquiry was told that a similar offer of analytic support was made to CTC Chief Black by DIA in 2000, but with similar results.[221]

Said another way, the cultural impulse to privilege secrets at least partly for their own sake rather than due to the logic of the situation (along with the usual rivalry expected between bureaucracies[222]) apparently overrode DCI Tenet's melodramatic declaration that "we are at war." Amy Zegart flatly assigns this culture of excessive secrecy at the CIA a causal role in 9/11:

> Different CIA officials on more than one occasion neglected to watchlist two of the September 11 hijackers, share information, and distill vital pieces of intelligence scattered throughout the Community in large part because they were steeped in an organizational culture that regarded these activities as unnatural acts: embracing new tasks, thinking beyond the agency, and sharing secrets all ran against the grain of everything CIA officers had known, believed, and cherished for years. *The CIA was more than a job; it was a brotherhood, filled with lifelong members that shared a commitment to country, a willingness to sacrifice, and the knowledge that nearly everything they did would have to stay secret.*[223]

Though it did not speculate directly on the reasons for the CIA's failure to share information about Hazmi and Mihdhar, the Inspector General's Report confirms that the CIA knew for an extended period that both were at large somewhere in the United States and that they waited until just days before

9/11 to disseminate this information via the government's terrorist watchlist. In fact, according to the IG's Report, by 2000 "50 to 60" individuals at the CIA had known for eighteen months of intelligence reports indicating that two of the hijackers were in the United States, but none chose to notify the FBI.[224]

Thus, we find at least two instances where in the production and dissemination phases of the intelligence cycle features of the culture and identity of the CIA contributed to this strategic surprise. We saw first how the impulse for consensus on at least one occasion muffled clear attribution of responsibility for the *Cole* bombing by analysts. Second, we saw how secrecy and individual secrets were fetishized at the CTC to the detriment of building an adequate analytical capability and providing specific pieces of information with direct bearing on the strategic surprise that unfolded on 9/11.

The CIA's record regarding the strategic surprise of 9/11 is in most respects as straightforward as its failure prior to the fall of the shah. Mitigating facts exist, but the overall picture is clear. In no sense did the CIA develop an appropriate threat assessment about al-Qa'ida or provide effective warning prior to this strategic surprise. As a *Studies* article once said: "It is too often forgotten that the primary task of intelligence is to get a fact or judgment from the inside of a specialist's brain to the inside of a layman's, not simply to state it in words which a fellow specialist can certify as not irrelevant and not untrue."[225] Not only did the CIA fail to achieve this task prior to 9/11, but also it relieved of his duties the head of the very analytical team that attempted it! In each stage of the intelligence cycle prior to 9/11, and in the marginalizing of this Cassandra, the evidence for how this failure occurred points to the enduring elements of culture and identity that operated in other strategic surprises: the CIA's homogeneity, scientism, preference for secrets, and drive for consensus.

7 THE CIA AND THE FUTURE OF INTELLIGENCE

LESSONS LEARNED AND THEORETICAL IMPLICATIONS

This book set out to solve a puzzle: Since Pearl Harbor, the United States has repeatedly experienced strategic surprises. These include a politico-religious revolution in a key ally, the collapse of a long-time rival, a covert attempt to change the strategic balance, and the most dramatic terrorist attacks in history. We asked how a vast organization specifically dedicated to preventing such surprises allowed them to occur. Such an investigation also raised the question of how one reconciles the regular occurrence of such failures both with multiple competing theories of how or why strategic surprises occur, *and* with the presence of Cassandras (who seem to belie at least partly arguments about the inevitability of surprises). How, exactly, does Luttwak's idea of "strategic autism" occur in an agency explicitly created to prevent it?

In pursuing these issues, *Constructing Cassandra* addressed several questions implicit in previous attempts to understand or to explain intelligence failures and how they lead to strategic surprises. What is the origin of the hypotheses that Wohlstetter says are needed to sort signal from noise? Why are intelligence hypotheses sometimes so sticky in the face of contrary evidence? There seems limited utility in further resourcing collection platforms—either human or technical—until these questions are addressed. Proponents of technical fixes to intelligence problems (such as "total information awareness") are silent on this issue, but the record shows that better collection alone produces more chaff, and until the hypotheses generation part of the intelligence system is addressed, more wheat will not be found. In intelligence, good answers are easier to find than good questions.

Similarly, this question should be put to zealous reorganizers: Why do bureaucratic reforms—both those that alternately centralize and decentralize intelligence, and those that seek to minimize the politicization of intelligence—never evolve towards an optimal intelligence machine? To the psychologists: Are generic psychological factors of misperception and bias sufficient to understand what appears to be a sustained pattern of intelligence failures? If so, how can one explain the apparent insights and threat assessments of Cassandras? Clearly, culture and identity shape and bound all of these approaches to reform.

Recall the overture that opened this work. Does John McCone's hunch about SAMs not being shipped to Cuba "to protect cane cutters" have nothing to teach us? Were Israeli intelligence, French reporters, and Western businessmen all just lucky guessers before Iran convulsed? Were Soviet émigrés simply stopped clocks that were finally—and improbably—right about the fragility of the USSR? Was Michael Scheuer merely an obsessive station chief whom *all* reasonable intelligence analysts (or DCIs) would have ignored?

To address this puzzle, *Constructing Cassandra* set aside the easy explanation that such questions are answered by hindsight bias, by the ex post facto needs to develop a coherent narrative of how a surprise occurred. It rejected the idea that these surprises were pure examples of unforeseeable "black swans."[1] Instead, it developed a model of the CIA's identity and culture and then viewed surprises through it. This model included the personal and collective identities of the agency's corps of analysts (homogeneity), and elements particular to the organizational culture of Langley (scientism, a preference for secrets, and an overvaluation of consensus). This social constructivist approach afforded the theoretical breadth to explore both types of commonsense intelligence failures (mysteries and secrets), not just the surprise attacks examined by orthodox scholars of strategic surprise. It also allowed the exploration of the questions already posed about Cassandras and offered enough granularity in the case studies to see how each stage of the intelligence cycle, culture, and identity profoundly influenced hypothesis formation and information flow at Langley.

What has thereby been revealed about strategic surprises?

The Maze of Surprise and Ariadne's Thread of Culture and Identity

The first insight that *Constructing Cassandra* offers is self-evident by now: There are striking commonalities between strategic surprises rooted in mysteries and strategic surprises rooted in secrets. Langley's largest failures stem from erroneous threat assessments, and these mistaken assessments flow from distinct and lasting attributes of the agency's identity and culture. As the four cases demonstrated, these commonalities permeate the intelligence cycle prior to each surprise: The distinctive identity and culture of the CIA runs through the maze of its failures like Ariadne's thread. These commonalities are summarized in the chart found in Figure 7.1. Where a block is shaded in the chart, linkage between the features of the CIA's identity and culture in the x-axis and distortions in the intelligence cycle in the y-axis were demonstrated in each case study in that column.

While this insight about the role of identity and culture in strategic surprise in intelligence failure is by now clear, it should not be underestimated: Orthodox literature on strategic surprise, by excluding events stemming from factors beyond the plans of adversaries (that is, mysteries such as societal revolutions and the collapse of empires), did not unearth commonalities. In that approach, there were surprise attacks, and then there were other failures. This insight also has practical implications. Through this conclusion alone, *Constructing Cassandra* fulfills more than half of the nine objectives that the eminent American strategist Herman Kahn sketched for future-oriented policy research. Specifically: It improves our perspective on strategic surprises, clari-

Intelligence cycle phase	Homogeneity				Scientism				Secret				Consensus			
	IR	FSU	CMC	9/11	IR	FSU	CMC	9/11	IR	FSU	CMC	9/11	IR	FSU	CMC	9/11
Tasking	■	■	■	■	■	■	■	■	■	■	■	■	■	■	■	■
Collection	■	■	■	■	■	■			■	■	■	■	■	■	■	
Analysis		■	■	■	■	■	■	■		■	■	■	■	■	■	■
Production and dissemination													■	■	■	■

Figure 7.1. Summary of identity and culture's impact on surprises.

IR = the Iranian Revolution; FSU = fall of the Soviet Union; CMC = Cuban Missile Crisis; 9/11 = September 11, 2001, attacks.

fies major issues, generates new scenarios for intelligence failure, improves intellectual communication among disparate approaches to the topic, and increases our ability to identify new patterns and to understand their character and significance.[2] Treating strategic surprise as a social construction of a particular identity and culture brings new insights into the CIA's failures: its close call in Cuba in the 1960s, its obtuse evaluation of Iran in the 1970s, its decades-long failure to understand important aspects of the USSR, and its contribution to the worst surprise attack in U.S. history. This approach acknowledges some role for unpredictability in events but uses Cassandras to highlight the key distinction between events that are *foreseeable* and those that are simply *unforeseen* by certain people and organizations. For intelligence agencies (among other entities), this makes "hindsight bias" a far less convincing postdisaster retort.

The Puzzle of "the Wrong Puzzle"

The second source of theoretical leverage *Constructing Cassandra*'s approach offers is indicated by the observation that the only unbroken line in Figure 7.1 is tasking (that is, in 100 percent of the possible instances, the four aspects of the agency's identity and culture negatively affected tasking prior to the four surprises). That unbroken line in turn leads to another conclusion: The iterative nature of the intelligence cycle reinforces initial errors in tasking (that is, the CIA's hypotheses about what information was truly important), and then information filters imposed by identity and culture impede course correction in the rest of the cycle. These course corrections, naturally, are less likely to occur when the other phases of the intelligence cycle are influenced by the same characteristics of identity and culture that contributed to the initial tasking misjudgment.

Constructing Cassandra's approach thereby brings center stage what Cooper calls "the problem of the wrong puzzle" in intelligence analysis. He quotes an intelligence aphorism, "You rarely find what you're *not* looking for, and you usually do find what you *are* looking for."[3] An identity and culture-based analysis of strategic surprise reveals how the problem of the wrong puzzle arises and persists.[4] Ultimately, every foreign policy and strategic doctrine needs a plot.[5] If, as a result of a particular identity and culture that plot is too askew from reality—if the CIA has chosen the wrong puzzles—all the other parts of the intelligence cycle are working on irrelevant information. In that instance, elaborate intelligence machinery is for naught to improve strategic warning[6] (or worse: The irrelevant information that they provide wastes resources and results in false confidence).[7] Uniquely, the social constructivist model of strategic surprise developed in *Constructing Cassandra* helps understand how the wrong hypotheses (and thus the wrong puzzles) arise and persist and how they lead to failure.

Again, the implications of a better theoretical understanding of the problem of the wrong puzzle are substantial. Why? Consider Thomas Kuhn's comparison of the information value of failures in astronomy versus those in astrology:

> If an astronomer's prediction failed and his calculations checked, he could hope to set the situation right. Perhaps the data were at fault . . . perhaps theory needed adjustment . . . The astrologer, by contrast, had no such puzzles. The occurrence of failure could be explained, but particular failures did not give rise to research puzzles, for no man, however skilled, could make use of them in a constructive attempt to revise the astrological tradition. There were too many possible sources of difficulty, most of them beyond the astrologer's knowledge, control, or responsibility. Individual failures were correspondingly uninformative, and they did not reflect on the competence of the prognosticator in the eyes of his professional compeers.[8]

By addressing the root of the "problem of the wrong puzzle" in intelligence and then linking it to specific aspects of identity and culture in an intelligence producer, a constructivist approach *makes intelligence failures informative again* and opens new research puzzles. Identity and culture do not comprise a complete solution to preventing surprises, but considering them does forestall some of the intellectual shoulder shrugging sometimes provoked in those with a passing familiarity with the "inevitability" of surprise argument.

A Unified Model of Strategic Surprise

Previous work on the culture of national security found that abstract beliefs and values are more difficult to discard than simple instrumental beliefs;[9] here, some of the reasons for such persistence are detailed. When it incorporates the intelligence cycle, for example, an identity- and culture-based model of intelligence further reveals how the wrong puzzle, once chosen, is sustained (in some cases, for decades): It highlights the negative informational feedback loop[10] that begins in basic tasking decisions (that is, the hypotheses of intelligence producers) and how in the realm of social facts these problems endure.

This idea implies that understanding strategic surprises in light of identity and culture is logically prior to the orthodox school of strategic surprise's proximate and partial explanations (for example, signal-to-noise, bureaucratic politics or organizational behavior, and psychological). Thus, one can infer that even if surprises are "inevitable" because of the faults of intelligence consumers, a larger than necessary number of strategic surprises will continue if reform efforts in intelligence producers attend only to the proximate, positivist understandings of them. Another way of saying this is that, beyond a certain point, culture and identity appear to trump positivist reengineering of an intelligence bureaucracy. How is this so?

Roberta Wohlstetter correctly identified that "perception is an activity" and that the "job of lifting signals out of a confusion of noise is an activity that is very much aided by *hypotheses*." She and others, however, did not address in any depth how these hypotheses are formed and sustained. The hypotheses of intelligence analysts were largely unproblematic. Moreover, after a surprise, hypotheses in this approach functioned as dei ex machina, closing off further research. Social constructivism's identity and culture-based approach reopens the exploration of the linkage among intelligence failures, the origins of the hypotheses animating analysts, and the collection systems that serve them.

Graham Allison's Models II and III, on the other hand, approached political and bureaucratic culture in a largely positivist manner. The result is that these models cannot provide more than a proximate understanding of why particular political questions (and not others) are pursued time after time; they also cannot supply a fully convincing account of how specific bureaucratic idiosyncrasies repeatedly cooperate to metastasize into surprises. In contrast, *Constructing Cassandra*'s approach was to delve more deeply into the CIA's singular identity and culture, explore those factors' effects on the gathering and interpretation of social facts, and then relate these to the failure to prevent strategic surprises.

Similarly, merely saying that psychological factors lead analysts to "misperceive" certain signals begs two key questions: Why *these* misperceptions and not others, and how do patterns of misperception continue, sometimes for decades, in spite of supposed safeguards like "Review"? In Kuhnian terms, one would say that orthodox models of misperception work well explaining "normal" intelligence errors but break down when summoned to explain exactly the topic addressed here: massive "paradigm shifts" or strategic surprises that are often years in the making. *Constructing Cassandra*'s identity and culture model of surprise, rooted in an appreciation for social facts, squarely addresses failures involving the development and continuation of erroneous intelligence paradigms over time. Because intelligence analysts deal in social facts, their errors—like those of astrologers—cannot decisively disprove anything.

In so doing, *Constructing Cassandra* makes previous theories of strategic surprise more useful and old intelligence failures newly edifying. It does so by providing a coherent account of Figure 1.2's comparison of type I and type II errors as they relate to the social facts that are the bread-and-butter of intelligence. It also demonstrates that the notion of intelligence analysis as a "science" does severe injury to the term: At best, analysts practice alchemy, because their thinking can change the properties of the world that they study.[11]

This understanding of strategic surprises as a phenomenon embedded in intelligence producers' erroneous threat assessments, assessments that are the products of distinctive identities and cultures, shifts the burden of proof back to intelligence producers to demonstrate that their identity and culture were not responsible for strategic surprises. How? In the four cases, we saw Cassandras at odds with the CIA's particular identity and culture offer high-quality warnings that were ignored. By documenting the manner by which a consistent marginalization of some ideas occurred in an intelligence producer, the orthodox school's assertion that most strategic surprises have their origins among intelligence consumers becomes (to say the least) problematic.

A Choice between Cassandras and Socratic Agnostics?

Near the end of his seminal essay, "Analysis, War, and Decision: Why Intelligence Failures Are Inevitable," Richard Betts writes, "The intelligence officer may perform most usefully by *not* offering the *answers* sought by authorities, but by offering *questions*, acting as a Socratic agnostic, nagging decision makers into awareness of the full range of uncertainty, and making authorities calculations harder rather than easier."[12] This is certainly still true. The conclusion of this book, however, is that the CIA, as a result of specific and enduring attributes of its identity and culture, was often ill equipped to perform the role of "Socratic agnostic"—even to itself—on several occasions between 1947 and 2001. Evidence that this was so can be found among Cassandras, who were sidelined or ignored by the agency. From that conclusion flows the more hopeful idea that approaching strategic surprises as social constructions of intelligence producers is a fresh avenue for making intelligence failures informative again. In doing so, and while not a panacea, *Constructing Cassandra*'s approach to intelligence failure and strategic surprise may offer one way of bringing the CIA closer to fulfilling its original mandate of "preventing the next Pearl Harbor."

PRACTICAL IMPLICATIONS

A New Intelligence Cycle

As previously stated, while critical of the CIA, we do not underestimate the difficulty of their mandate, and we would like to make a constructive contribution to improving analytical performance at the agency. In part, we feel that the correct diagnosis of how strategic surprises arise help fulfill that task. But, beyond that understanding, there are also some practical actions that we feel flow logically from our analysis. If we were forced to choose a single change at the CIA, it would be simple and would involve a modest addition to the intelligence cycle. After hundreds of pages of text, that recommendation may sound anticlimactic, but it would be profound, so we will explain.

The intelligence cycle has been used here as a lens to focus further on specific problems in the CIA's intelligence processes created by identity and culture. As Berkowitz and Goodman write, the intelligence cycle is a durable concept that pervades the CIA's thinking about intelligence and it is prominent in agency publications and training materials.[13] The cycle has been criticized,[14] but we acknowledge that it is too deeply embedded to remove. We can live with it, but with one addition: Begin it with hypotheses.

Why add hypotheses as an explicit step in the intelligence cycle? For the CIA, such a change would accomplish three things. First, this change to the intelligence cycle would perpetually reinject intellect into a cycle that too easily becomes a bureaucratic process diagram. We have documented the effects of culture and identity on each stage of the intelligence cycle; making ideas the centerpiece of the intelligence cycle may allow greater sensitivity to these effects. Second, and related to that point, this change makes refreshing hypotheses and revising assumptions an explicit, inescapable, and ongoing part of intelligence work. This should have two salutatory effects: It may help prevent the sort of negative synergy between unquestioned hypotheses and the rest of the intelligence cycle that we have already discussed, and it may go some way toward remedying the "solving the wrong puzzle" problem, with all the wasted energy and resources that it entails. Third, hypotheses in the intelligence cycle might assist the agency when intelligence consumers demand only "answers." As we have documented, a mirror image of the customer and the

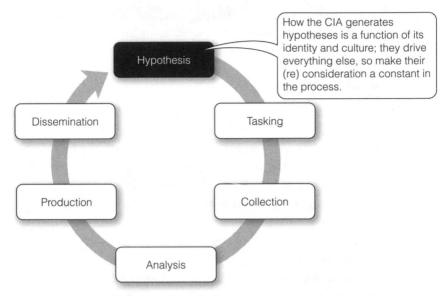

Figure 7.2. The intelligence cycle revised: Start with (and revisit) hypotheses.

rest of the intelligence community can make the same contribution to strategic surprise that mirror imaging of the enemy does. This change is no substitute for intellectual, bureaucratic, or political courage, but it may go some way toward helping the CIA to resist the impulse to simply serve up answers to policy makers' questions.

For policy makers, this change to the intelligence cycle would have two useful effects. It would perpetually remind them that hypotheses are the key mechanism by which analysts separate the signal of information from the background noise of data and events. When facing a sea of red flags, hypotheses are the sorting mechanism. This might help make policy makers more sympathetic to, or even collaborate with, the CIA in generating fresh hypotheses.

Second, the awareness of the ultimate importance of hypotheses in the agency's work that this change to the cycle might engender would reinforce the notion among policy makers that the work of the CIA is inherently ambiguous and uncertain. They cannot realistically equate the work of the agency with an exact science. (See Figure 7.2.) Policy makers can and should hold the CIA to a set of intellectual standards, but those standards must include the quality of the questions that the CIA asks itself, not merely the quality of the answers it provides to policy makers' questions.

Additional practical implications for the CIA
1. Enforce diversity at the CIA for practical, not just moral, reasons.
2. Recognize that tasking is a wicked problem for intellectual as well as bureaucratic reasons.
3. Educate—don't simply "train" analysts.
4. Drop the idea of intelligence "customers."
Practical implications for policy makers
1. Accept that the CIA delivers forecasts, not predictions.
2. Understand how to use analysts.
3. Cultivate and monitor your own Cassandras.

Figure 7.3. Recommendations for the CIA and for policy makers.

Several other practical recommendations for the CIA to prevent strategic surprises are related to this single, overarching change, however, and others for both the CIA and policy makers flow from the new understanding of strategic surprise as a social construction. (See Figure 7.3.)

Additional Practical Implications for the CIA

Enforce Diversity at the CIA for Practical, Not Moral, Reasons.   In the case studies in Chapters 3 through 6, we repeatedly saw that the homogeneity of the CIA personnel severely hobbles its central mission. Making a case for a diverse intelligence community is not new, but in the past this case has been made on the basis of notions of fairness, equity, or justice, that is, purely moral concerns, irrelevant to the CIA's mission. In contrast, *Constructing Cassandra* argues for diversity on the simple basis of long-term effectiveness: It make the catastrophic cost of the CIA's sustained homogeneity clear. With less than 5 percent of Earth's population, the United States needs intelligence agencies that offer the intellectual depth and cognitive diversity to protect it effectively from the tiny percentage of the rest of the world that would do it harm. Basic arithmetic sheds some light on the nature of the problem. If tomorrow an utterly brilliant U.S. public diplomacy campaign instantly convinced 99 percent of the one billion Muslims in the world that the United States was their best and greatest friend, that still leaves one million people in over fifty countries to host al-Qa'ida and its spawns. This diverse, educated, and dedicated population of opponents could do immense damage to the United States and its allies. Are the relatively provincial, Caucasian, liberal arts college graduates who have rarely lived abroad whom the CIA traditionally recruits best equipped to analyze their next move? How about the plans of the next bin Ladin, or the Chinese Politburo? In place of simple-minded vetting, properly targeted counterintelligence programs should replace blanket prohibitions on the recruitment of recent immigrants, people who have lived or traveled widely abroad, and those with family in other countries. The current approach puts the security cart before the analytical horse and without any good effect: Plenty of Caucasian, apparently conventional Americans have betrayed many of the deepest U.S. secrets—think John Walker of the Navy, Aldrich Ames of the CIA, and Robert Hanssen of the FBI. The downside of such blanket prohibitions is also obvious when one remembers the NSA's outsourcing of the translation of Taliban intercepts to Pakistan's ISI prior to 9/11.[15]

Quick wins are possible: Why (as one of the authors experienced) did the CIA seek to recruit his friends at the University of Chicago's MBA program while it ignored the American students at London Business School in the United Kingdom (which he attended), and the Instituto de Empresa in Spain (where he teaches)? Americans in these foreign MBA programs are required to speak foreign languages and are obviously attracted to working in an international milieu. Beyond the most technical or mundane matters, it is mystifying why anyone who has not traveled abroad extensively (but who purports to be passionately interested in international affairs) even makes it through the first screen to do *anything* at the CIA, much less become an analyst.

Needless to say, an increase in diversity inevitably poses the question of increased security risk. We have seen that émigrés were rejected because it was thought that they posed a security risk. We argue that security has been taken so far to hamper the work of the agency. Émigrés have also been rejected because they are thought not to be emotionally detached and would be unbalanced. But this is mistaking the level at which balance must exist: Balance should exist at the organization level, and for this to happen in a healthy way, it should be obtained by having a diversity of characters and profiles. It is valuable, and it doesn't harm, to have eccentric characters as long as their contribution can be assessed. This point is captured well by former DCI James Schlesinger. Reflecting on the lessons of the collapse of the USSR, he recommended: "Treasure your mavericks."[16] U.S. colleges achieve diversity not by admitting diverse students but by creating a diverse body of students. The Appendix of *The Human Factor*[17] by Ishmael Jones contains numerous other recommendations for reform of the clandestine service (and the Intelligence Community generally), along these lines, and is recommended.

Recognize That Tasking Is a Wicked Problem for Intellectual as Well as Bureaucratic Reasons. We propose a new intelligence cycle beginning with hypotheses instead of tasking partly because we believe that tasking is far more—or *should be far more*—intellectually complex than it has been credited with being. Tasking is never something that is handed to the CIA by intelligence "consumers" from across the policy divide: As a practical matter, it falls within the scope of the CIA's work. Step One of Sherman Kent's process of analysis (which reads, "The appearance of a problem requiring the attention of a strategic intelligence staff"[18]) is utterly naive and is a central part of the problem of strategic surprise. If it is ever to escape the problems of the 360-degree mirror imaging that the current tasking methodology creates, the agency must move beyond the idea that problems for analysis simply appear or that it must respond only to customer demands. The analyst, the agency, the Intelligence Community, and its customers participate in the definition and tasking processes, and the customer is not always right. We can hope that making problem definition more conscious would make it more subject to both revisiting and corrective action.

A recent book by three prominent intelligence scholars and practitioners stressed the importance of intelligence collection as opposed to analysis, saying,

> There is almost nothing written on designing a rational collection system, the interaction of collection with analysis, or the way that expanded collection systems made possible by modern IT have transformed the corporate culture and strategies of organizations ranging from global corporations to international organizations.[19]

This book partly accomplishes some of those tasks, but it also points to the faulty premise at the heart of such statements: More rational intelligence collection is predicated on better *tasking*, which is in turn driven by better hypothesis generation, which is ultimately dependent on culture and identity.

Our fresh approach to tasking is the logical, "actionable" corollary to Betts's assertion that "the intelligence officer may perform most usefully by *not* offering the *answers* sought by authorities, but by offering *questions*, acting as a Socratic agnostic, nagging decision makers into awareness of the full range of uncertainty, and making authorities' calculations harder rather than easier."[20] Until tasking is *less a mirror of policy makers' known unkowns* and more an exercise in exposing their unconscious ignorance, the CIA will remain in a wilderness of mirror imaging of itself, the IC, and the intelligence consumers.

A partial response to the problem of identity and culture's effects on task-ing might be to take a systemic operational design–style (SOD) approach to it, in effect to treat tasking as a wicked rather than a tame problem: systemic tasking design. As a pioneer of SOD says:

> Urban designers Horst Rittel and Melvin Weber coined the term [*wicked problem*] to refer to primarily social problems that are particularly difficult and confusing, though not necessarily irresolvable. Wicked problems stand in contrast to tame problems, which are by no means necessarily trivial or simple. Tame problems may be very challenging, but they are sufficiently un-derstood that they lend themselves to established methods and solutions.[21]

The key to wicked problems, however, is that frequently the entire question of problem definition becomes one of identity.

Our work implies a related solution to the problem of "getting fish to see the water" in tasking. This is not simply to draw outside experts in but to actively seek the views of dissidents—even those who disagree profoundly with the idea of working with the CIA. A logical (albeit wildly controversial) approach to achieving this end would be to run "false flag" analytical opera-tions: Some of the most valuable contributions may come exactly from those who would *never* self-select to work knowingly with the CIA. This approach to digging out dissent would go far beyond "Team A–Team B," "Red Teams," "Devil's Advocates," or scenarios (though increased use of all would be help-ful). Instead, it would resemble the analytical equivalent of "trust operations."

The trust operation was a fictitious opposition group set up by the Cheka and the GPU in the early 1920s.[22] It established ties with Russian émigré groups and thus was able simultaneously to monitor and to control them. Such an approach raises a thicket of ethical and legal issues that go beyond the scope of this volume, but it should be acknowledged as a logical possibility for improving analysis. A middle ground might be less overt versions of the web-based crowd-sourced analytical efforts like those recently funded by the ODNI's Intelligence Advanced Research Projects Activity.[23]

Educate—Don't Simply "Train"—Analysts.   It is difficult to imagine a quick fix for the lack of ontological, epistemological, and methodological self-awareness that *Constructing Cassandra* exposes (or for the persistent privileging of secret information and sources over open sources. It is hoped that the exposure of it is the first step toward a remedy). The implications of the key difference between social and natural facts have not been well digested by society at large (which is why people speak of "social science" at all; when your general field is named with a false metaphor, you're in for a rocky ride). One help might be to recognize explicitly the severe limitations of case study style of training (in international relations and political science generally and in intelligence specifically). Intelligence analysts should be educated as well as trained, and such set piece exercises work in the opposite direction: They are part of the discourse failure and contribute to the intellectual blinders that conventional education (focused on right answers and not good questions and perpetuating the false metaphor of social science) already imposes.

A good start would be a course similar to that which one of the authors took in Brussels in 2003, "The Philosophy and Methodology of International Relations," but most U.S. graduate schools are moving in the other direction, toward practical courses akin to trade-school classes and naïve "area studies" programs. Many students earn master's degrees in social science disciplines without being able to define or distinguish among ontological, epistemological, and methodological problems. Moreover, the fact that there are still numerous, sincere, and vocal intelligence practitioners who characterize their work as a "science" and crave simplistic quantification does not inspire hope.

Drop the Idea of Intelligence "Customers." Our cases have shown how the idea that the CIA is there to "serve" its "customers"—policy makers—is a straight and true path directly into a wilderness of mirror imaging. It also runs counter to the ideal of the mission of gadfly and agnostic question asker previously outlined. Being customer centric is a corrosive vocabulary and reinforces the idea that the CIA is there to provide quick answers rather than to ask tough questions. It led the CIA to wait passively until a question was asked and then to task narrowly on that basis. It also led the agency to rank the illegal trade in tropical hardwoods as of the same magnitude as al Qa'ida. A balance must of course be struck for the CIA to maintain access, relevance, and funding, but a part of the solution to that question is to explicitly educate the users of the CIA's information about its actual role. The agency must explicitly reject the role of "magic answer machine" and insist to policy makers that they are not a customer paying a bill for an intelligence product of their choosing—the American people are the customer paying a bill for the product called national security, and the CIA and policy makers both serve America by playing distinct roles.

In other words, while it is fine for the agency to respond to day-to-day customer needs, it is also the role of the CIA (and that of any business organization on which the agency is modeling itself) to anticipate such needs—just as businesses do not always show their future products until customers are ready for them, although they develop them nonetheless. And if the metaphor is sustained, the CIA should note that a finding of business innovation research is that firms that are *too* customer centric do well in the short term but often fall prey to disruptive innovation in the long run because customers sometimes don't know what they want until it is too late.[24]

Practical Implications for Policy Makers

Accept That the CIA Delivers Forecasts, Not Predictions.   As intelligence veteran Thomas Fingar writes, "Estimates always and intentionally push beyond what is known—or believed—to be true . . . they are not revealed truth or infallible prophecy."[25] Part of why we recommend the addition of hypotheses to begin the intelligence cycle is exactly to keep this fact before policy makers' eyes. Beyond that, policy makers should understand how the CIA works, what it can do, and what it can't. A NIE is not just a statement of current knowledge about an issue: It is also the product of a bureaucracy, requiring weeks or months of work by a large number of people among the different agencies that form the U.S. Intelligence Community. In that narrow sense, it is authoritative. At the same time, the policy maker should constantly bear in mind that all the collection, analysis, and synthesis in the world does not turn an indeterminate mystery into a predictable or "stealable" secret.

Moreover, policy makers (and the authors of NIEs) should appreciate that although not every NIE seems relevant to their work, they are a crucial part of how the U.S. intelligence community speaks to itself. As we saw in the 9/11 case, when an NIE is missing, the issue will never be a sustained priority of the intelligence bureaucracy.

An additional point is that, as we saw in the Cuba case, the very process of producing an NIE can weed out dissenting views, but dissenting views are what policy makers should expect. For that reason, to again use Fingar's expression, policy makers should not expect predictions from NIEs but possibilities. Prediction is a dangerous and ultimately doomed game, and attaching numerical probabilities only makes it worse; discussing possibilities based on current, necessarily imperfect knowledge and hypotheses is in the realm of what an intelligence agency can do well.

Understand How to Use Analysts.   In keeping with Betts's ideal of the intelligence officer acting as a Socratic agnostic, "nagging decision makers into awareness of the full range of uncertainty, and making authorities' calculations harder rather than easier," policy makers should understand how to use CIA analysts. Analysts are not there to be magic answer machines for policy makers; if anything, they are magic question machines. As a result, policy makers should especially guard against a phenomenon that we call "Gresham's Law of Advice,"[26] in which bad advice drives out good advice precisely because it offers certainty where reality holds none. They should expect analysts to provide forecasts, not predictions, and they should internalize the notion that CIA analysts' cautious statements laced with qualifiers are offered not for reasons of intellectual overfineness or bureaucratic hedging but are the result of intellectual integrity and professional self-awareness.

Cultivate and Monitor Your Own Cassandras.   There is no quick fix for the problem of strategic surprise. We hope that our diagnosis of the root cause of strategic surprise presented in the volume—that it flows from identity and culture—along with the practical suggestions previously given improve the CIA's batting average a little. At the same time, for any organization to be effective and cohesive, a strong culture and identity are inevitable. The unique nature and inevitable strains of the CIA's mission only magnify these needs. Policy makers should recognize this fact and its natural consequence: the creation of Cassandras on some issues. Even if all the recommendations we have already given were implemented in good faith, the very nature of the processes outlined will ensure that Cassandras will arise over time. For that reason, our final recommendation is that policy makers cultivate and monitor their own Cassandras—totally independent analytical voices and Socratic agnostics—in their areas of responsibility. The need for these people is not a reflection of failure by the CIA: It is a natural consequence of the social construction of strategic surprise. The doubts and conclusions of such people could then be fed into the CIA's process through robust, informed, and iconoclastic questioning of agency analysts and reports.

Chance and Necessity—The Future of Intelligence Studies

In the four case studies we have given, we have dealt with contingent events on the one hand (that is, the many particulars of each case of strategic surprise) and with a form of necessity, however diffuse, on the other: culture and identity. As Wendt points out, "Some causal mechanisms exist only on a macro-level, even though they depend on instantiations at the micro-level for their operation. Natural selection is one such case, temperature may be another, and 'collective memory' a third."[27] The case made here is that strategic surprise is such an instance: The internal identity and culture of the CIA act as a filter during each stage of the intelligence cycle, obscuring Langley's view of the possibility or likelihood of events. Together, they bound and shape the types and nature of strategic surprises that occur.

Using constructivism, we presented a loose form of cumulative causation (in which lines of direct cause and effect, however circuitous, cannot be drawn but a relationship is nevertheless deduced). Cassandras underlined that more than mere chance was at work in each case. Essentially, using constructivism to examine the agency's culture has tried to reconcile causation and contingency in the pattern of individual strategic surprises between 1947 and 2001.

A short historical excursus helps illuminate what we mean and will perhaps help refresh the research program of intelligence studies. Toward the end of his autobiography *My Life*, exiled Soviet leader Leon Trotsky undertakes a seemingly eccentric but ultimately revealing digression. In the chapter "The Conspiracy of the Epigones," devoted to the year 1923, at one moment Trotsky is discussing his escalating conflict with Stalin, Kamenev, and Zinoviev over leadership of the Bolshevik party; in the next moment he is deep in a lyrical description of autumn duck hunting in a locality near Moscow known as *Zabolotye* (literally, "Beyond the Swamps").[28] Trotsky, of course, has a purpose beyond the literary to this aside, which he finally reveals. It is to illuminate what he calls the "natural selection of accidents":

> From the canoe to the automobile I had to walk about a hundred steps, not more. But the moment I stepped onto the bog in my felt boots my feet were in cold water. By the time I leaped up to the automobile, my feet were quite cold . . . I took off my boots and tried to warm my feet by the heat of the motor. But the cold got the better of me . . . The doctors ordered me to stay in bed, and thus I spent the rest of the autumn and winter. This means that all through the discussion of "Trotskyism" in 1923, I was ill. One can foresee a revolution or a war, but it is impossible to foresee the consequences of an autumn shooting trip for wild ducks.[29]

Trotsky—as a Marxist, committed to understanding history as a process determined by necessity—here explores the role of chance in that same "determined" history. As he sits in exile, a master theoretician of historical necessity must account for how a simple chill caught from wet boots kept him ill the entire winter of 1923–1924 and absent from the leadership discussions of the Bolshevik Party. As he writes the words of the preceding quotation some ten years later, Stalin runs the USSR, and Trotsky says, "I cannot help noting how obligingly the accidental helps the historical law. Broadly speaking, the entire historical process is a refraction of the historical law through the accidental. In the language of biology, one might say that the historical law is realized through the natural selection of accidents."[30]

A short extension of the evolutionary analogy further illuminates this approach. There is a view of evolution that stresses the contingent. One of the best-known standard-bearers for this approach is Stephen Jay Gould. In his 1989 book *Wonderful Life*, Gould repeatedly employs a thought experiment called "replaying life's tape" to highlight the "staggeringly improbable series of events, sensible enough in retrospect and subject to rigorous explanation, but utterly unpredictable and quite unrepeatable" that led to life in its current forms. "Wind back the tape of life," Gould says, and "let it play again from an identical starting point, and the chance becomes vanishingly small that anything like human intelligence would grace the replay."[31] Many anecdotal accounts of strategic surprise take a similar view: Wind back the tape of tasking, collection, analysis, production, and dissemination, and the chance of a particular strategic surprise occurring becomes tiny.

In contrast to this stress on the contingent, however, there are biologists who stress convergence in evolution. As Conway Morris says in *The Crucible of Creation*, Gould's whole argument "is based on a basic confusion concerning the destiny of a given lineage . . . versus the likelihood that a particular biological property or feature will sooner or later manifest itself as part of the evolutionary process."[32] The system of natural selection, while on one level random, nevertheless has emergent properties. Some accidents, says Trotsky, "open the sluice gates of necessity."[33]

Similarly, given the somewhat fixed elements of the CIA's culture and identity, strategic surprises are just like certain convergent biological properties: They will eventually manifest themselves. In this regard, Betts's "inevitable" and seemingly accidental strategic surprises are a process akin to natural selection, but the biological metaphor is ultimately flawed. We have argued that intelligence work is social in nature. Unlike evolutionary biology, social problems are amenable to human action.[34] Unlike hard science problems, though, these problems are inherently complex and nonlinear, and "God gave physicists the easy problems." Because, however, intelligence is ultimately about *safeguarding the national welfare*, the CIA cannot be content with a fatalistic view of strategic surprise; the agency has a duty to learn from past failures, and we hope this work in a modest way advances that effort.

REFERENCE MATTER

NOTES

Introduction

1. National Security Act of 1947; retrieved on July 29, 2012, from: http://intelligence.senate.gov/nsaact1947.pdf.

2. Rhodri Jeffreys-Jones, "Why was the CIA established in 1947?" In R. Jeffreys-Jones and C. M. Andrew, eds., *Eternal Vigilance? 50 Years of the CIA* (London: Frank Cass, 1997), pp. 25–28.

3. The critical document usually cited is Special National Intelligence Estimate Number 85-3-62, "The Military Buildup in Cuba," dated September 19, 1962. The whole estimate has not been declassified, but the summary and conclusions are available in Mary S. McAuliffe, *CIA Documents on the Cuban Missile Crisis 1962.* (Washington, DC: History Staff of the Central Intelligence Agency, 1992), pp. 91–93.

4. *Richard L. Russell, Sharpening Strategic Intelligence: Why the CIA Gets It Wrong and What Needs to Be Done to Get It Right* (New York: Cambridge University Press, 2007), p. 34.

5. Gregory F. Treverton and James Klocke, "Iran, 1978–1979: Coping with the Unthinkable." In E. R. May and P. D. Zelikow, eds., *Dealing with Dictators: Dilemmas of US Diplomacy and Intelligence Analysis, 1945–1990.* (Cambridge, MA: MIT Press, 2006), p. 119.

6. *James A. Bill, The Eagle and the Lion: The Tragedy of American-Iranian Relations* (New Haven, CT: Yale University Press, 1988).

7. Stansfield Turner, "Intelligence for a New World Order." *Foreign Affairs* (Fall 1991), pp. 150–166.

8. For consistency with the economic debate as it was framed at the time, "GNP," or gross national product, rather than the now-preferred measure "GDP," or gross domestic product, is used throughout this book.

9. Mikhail A. Alexseev, *Without Warning: Threat Assessment, Intelligence and Global Struggle* (New York: St. Martin's Press, 1997), p. 193.

10. Quoted in Stephen Kotkin, *Armageddon Averted: The Soviet Collapse 1970–2000.* (Oxford, UK: Oxford University Press, 2001), p. 86.

11. For the sake of variety, sometimes the term "the agency" or "Langley" (the Virginia site of the CIA headquarters) will be used here to replace "the CIA": The choice is stylistic, and no distinction or difference is implied by this choice.

12. The spelling employed here of both al Qa'ida and its leader is that used by the CIA.

13. Commission, *The 9/11 Commission Report: Final Report of the National Commission on Terrorist Attacks upon the United States* (New York: W. W. Norton, 2004), p. 342. It cites "Bin Ladin Threatening to Attack US Aircraft [with antiaircraft missiles]" (June 1998); "Strains Surface between Taliban and Bin Ladin" (January 1999); "Terrorist Threat to US Interests in Caucasus" (June 1999); "Bin Ladin to Exploit Looser Security during Holidays" (December 1999); "Bin Ladin Evading Sanctions" (March 2000); "Bin Ladin's Interest in Biological, Radiological Weapons" (February 2001); "Taliban Holding Firm on Bin Ladin for Now" (March 2001); "Terrorist Groups Said to be Cooperating on US Hostage Plot" (May 2001); and "Bin Ladin Determined to Strike in the US" (August, 2001).

14. Ibid. The general failure of the CIA to provide strategic warning, however, is confirmed in the CIA inspector general's report on the pre-9/11 failures: CIA, "OIG Report on CIA Accountability with Respect to the 9/11 Attacks." Office of the Inspector General, editor. (Langley, VA: Central Intelligence Agency, 2005), p. xvii.

15. Amy B. Zegart, *Spying Blind: The CIA, the FBI, and the Origins of 9/11.* (Princeton, NJ: Princeton University Press, 2007), page 86.

16. Technically, this sentence should read *"Uncounted* billions of dollars": The budget of the CIA has been classified since 1947; for further information, see the Federation of American Scientists' website: www.fas.org. The best and most easily digestible summary of what information is available that the authors have found is in L. Britt Snider, *The Agency and the Hill: CIA's Relationship with Congress, 1946–2004.* (Washington, DC: The Center for the Study of Intelligence, Central Intelligence Agency, 2004), pp. 159–190.

17. The concept of rulers employing intelligence assets to achieve foreknowledge of future events, that is, to avoid strategic surprise, is probably as old as human society itself, as it is rooted in our species' instinct for survival. The Old Testament, for example, repeatedly refers to spies and recounts numerous intelligence operations. The title of this book refers to another ancient document that ponders the issue of strategic foreknowledge: Homer's *Iliad* (probably composed in roughly the eighth century BCE, though referring to events about 400 years earlier). Betts echoes a common complaint among U.S. intelligence consumers during the Cold War that, in many CIA assess-

ments of Soviet objectives, consumers "could substitute the name of any other great power in history—Imperial Rome, 16th century Spain, Napoleonic France—and [the assessments would] sound equally valid." See Richard K. Betts, "Analysis, War, and Decision: Why Intelligence Failures Are Inevitable." *World Politics*, 31: 1 (1978), 61–89, p. 71. A good collection of intelligence analysis cases from the distant and recent past is Timothy Walton, *Challenges in Intelligence Analysis: Lessons from 1300 BCE to the Present* (Cambridge, UK: Cambridge University Press, 2010).

18. In effect, the methodology used here argues that the term *social sciences* is a false metaphor, as the "facts" social science considers usually depend on the statements by observers that refer to them or define these "facts."

19. See Alexander Wendt, "On Constitution and Causation in International Relations." *Review of International Studies*, 24: 5 (1998), pp. 101–102. Another way of saying this is that, when people participate on some level in the events that they think about, they must acknowledge that their knowledge is incomplete, that their imperfect understanding and fallibility become part of reality and that such effects compound until "corrected" by reality. George Soros calls this idea "reflexivity," defining the concept in its simplest terms as follows:

> In situations that have thinking participants, there is a two way interaction between the participants' thinking and the situations in which they participate . . . When we act as outside observers we can make statements that do not correspond to the facts without altering the facts; when we act as participants, our actions alter the situation we seek to understand . . . We are confronted with a situation that is inherently unknowable in the sense that what needs to be a fact to make knowledge possible is, in fact, contingent on the participant's view of the situation.

See George Soros, *Alchemy of Finance: Reading the Mind of the Market* (New York: Touchstone Books, 1988), p. 2. For a full treatment of reflexivity, see chapters 1–3, pp. 49–92.

20. The distillation of intelligence work into these three areas is drawn from Thomas Powers, *The Man Who Kept the Secrets: Richard Helms and the CIA* (New York: Alfred A. Knopf, 1979), p. vi.

21. The various names by which the analytical activity has been called within the CIA (and the fact that the organization itself has been reorganized several times) are dealt with in the following pages. For simplicity's sake, the title DI is used throughout this manuscript, even when the term is technically ahistorical because of bureaucratic shuffling or renaming, especially after 2001.

22. This definition employs similar language to that used by Levite. See Ariel Levite, *Intelligence and Strategic Surprises* (New York: Columbia University Press, 1987), p. 1–3. Levite's definition, however, does not link erroneous threat assessment to predictive failures as directly. In addition, by speaking of "threat perception," Levite

(intentionally or not) calls to mind Jervis's cerebral processes (discussed later) rather than intelligence assessments that include far more than mental pictures. Levite also requires that strategic surprise possess seven distinct features, including a deliberately acting perpetrator of actions designed to catch a target by surprise, as in a surprise attack. As a consequence, surprises like the Iranian Revolution or the collapse of the USSR fall outside his definition.

23. Jack Davis, "Strategic Warning: If Surprise Is Inevitable, What Role for Analysis?" *Occasional Papers*, 2: 1 (2003), p. 2.

24. Sherman Kent, *Strategic Intelligence for American World Policy* (Princeton, NJ: Princeton University Press, 1949), p. vii. Emphasis added.

25. CIA, *A Consumer's Guide to Intelligence* (Washington, DC: Office of Public Affairs, Central Intelligence Agency, 1999), p. vii.

26. Davis, "Strategic Warning," p. 2.

27. In some cases, there were several possible Cassandras, but we limited our study to just one because, again, from a pure methodological perspective, identifying just one Cassandra is enough to prove that the surprise was not "a failure of imagination" but concerns instead the sociology of knowledge.

28. Michael Scheuer, *Through Our Enemies' Eyes: Osama bin Laden, Radical Islam, and the Future of America*, revised ed. (Washington, DC: Potomac Books, 2006), p. 307.

29. Philip Shenon, *The Commission: An Uncensored History of the 9/11 Investigation* (New York: The Hachette Book Group, 2008), p. 188.

30. Compare Stoppard's 1966 play, *Rosencrantz and Guildenstern Are Dead*, which tells the story of *Hamlet* from the point of view of these two minor characters.

31. Richard K. Betts, "Surprise, Scholasticism, and Strategy: A Review of Ariel Levite's Intelligence and Strategic Surprises." *International Studies Quarterly*, 33: 3 (1989), p. 330.

32. Graham T. Allison and Philip Zelikow, *Essence of Decision: Explaining the Cuban Missile Crisis*, 2nd ed. (New York: Longman, 1999).

33. Roberta Wohlstetter, *Pearl Harbor: Warning and Decision* (Stanford, CA: Stanford University Press, 1962).

34. Betts, op. cit. The "inevitable" aspect of surprises and hence the need to develop tools to anticipate radical changes are the subject of scenario planning. See Peter Schwartz, *Inevitable Surprises: Thinking Ahead in a Time of Turbulence* (New York: Gotham Books, 2004).

35. Ofira Seliktar, *Failing the Crystal Ball Test: The Carter Administration and the Fundamentalist Revolution in Iran* (Westport, CT: Praeger, 2000).

36. National Public Radio, "Difference between a Secret and a Mystery when It Comes to Intelligence Failures," in *All Things Considered* (September 18, 2002); available at http://www.npr.org/programs/atc/transcripts/2002/sep/020918.adelman.html.

Emphasis added. It is interesting to discover that one "secret" that was probably actually a mystery is the burden of Soviet Defense spending on the USSR. While certainly much greater than CIA estimates (see the following discussion), the true burden was probably not known to anyone, including Gorbachev. See Noel E. Firth and James H. Noren, *Soviet Defense Spending: A History of CIA Estimates 1950–1990*. (College Station: Texas A&M University, 1998), pp. 188–191.

37. See, for example, Willard C. Matthias, *America's Strategic Blunders* (University Park: Pennsylvania State University Press, 2001). See also P. T. Coogan, "America's Strategic Blunders: Intelligence Analysis and National Security Policy, 1936–1991." *Journal of Military History*, 66: 1 (2002), pp. 275–276.

38. Jeffery R. Cooper, *Curing Analytical Pathologies: Pathways to Improved Intelligence Analysis* (Langley, VA: Central Intelligence Agency, Center for the Study of Intelligence, 2005), p. 26.

39. Thomas Fingar, *Reducing Uncertainty: Intelligence Analysis and National Security* (Stanford, CA: Stanford University Press, 2011), p. 24.

40. Luttwak, Edward, *The Rise of China Versus the Logic of Strategy* (Cambridge, MA: Harvard University Press, 2012), pp. 13–23.

41. Avi Shlaim sums this argument up nicely in the context of surprise attacks, but his argument applies more generally: "Successes may be indistinguishable from failures" because successful prediction may lead an attacker to alter his or her plans because surprise has been lost. As Betts observes, in that case, successful analysis effectively discredits analysis. See Avi Shlaim, "Failures in National Intelligence Estimates: The Case of the Yom Kippur War." *World Politics*, 28: 3 (1976), p. 378. See also Betts, op. cit. p. 62n2.

42. For an extended discussion of its limits as an actual representation of the intelligence process, see Arthur S. Hulnick, "What's Wrong with the Intelligence Cycle." *Intelligence and National Security*, 21: 6 (2007), pp. 959–979.

43. Bruce D. Berkowitz and Allen E. Goodman, *Best Truth: Intelligence in the Information Age* (New Haven, CT: Yale University Press, 2000), p. 69.

44. The phrase a *wilderness of mirrors* was used by long-time CIA counterintelligence chief James Angleton to describe his job, but its origins are in T. S. Eliot's poem "Gerontion."

Chapter 1

1. For the CIA, see for example Rob Johnston, *Analytic Culture in the US Intelligence Community: An Ethnographic Study* (Washington, DC: Center for the Study of Intelligence, Central Intelligence Agency, 2005). For the Intelligence Community as a whole, see Cooper, *Curing Analytical Pathologies*. Even so, "Taylorist" studies of the analytical process are depressingly persistent, using twenty-first-century technology to capture data in pursuit of early twentieth-century "scientific management"

methodologies (see, for example, Tom Hewett, Emile Morse, and Jean Scholtz, *In Depth Observational Studies of Professional Intelligence Analysts* [The US National Institute of Standards and Technology, 2004]) or technologically driven attempts to apply data-mining and other "more-is-better" techniques to intelligence analysis. See, for example, John Hollywood et al., *Out of the Ordinary: Finding Hidden Threats by Analyzing Unusual Behavior* (Santa Monica, CA: The RAND Corporation, 2004). Many of these studies offer further evidence of the persistence of scientism at the CIA and the Intelligence Community as a whole.

2. Kent, *Strategic Intelligence,* p. 157.

3. Ibid., p. 155.

4. Abram N. Shulsky and Gary J. Schmitt, *Silent Warfare: Understanding the World of Intelligence* (Washington, D.C.: Brassey's, Inc., 2002), page 41.

5. Richards J. Heuer, *The Psychology of Intelligence Analysis* (Langley, VA: Center for the Study of Intelligence, CIA, 1999), p. 30. It is also worthy of note that the emblem of the Center for the Study of Intelligence (CSI) is a chessboard.

6. Ibid., pp. 180–181.

7. These collective elements are also ignored in Shulsky, who writes in the section "Intelligence Failure and Surprise":

> Speaking of intelligence failure is similar to speaking of "chess failure," defined as failure to win chess games. Obviously, to improve our chess-playing abilities, it makes sense to critique styles of play, as well as individual moves, as thoroughly as we can. *The result should be better individual chess play and if we share the insights we have gained, better play by others as well.*

Shulsky and Schmitt, *Silent Warfare,* p. 70; emphasis added. The chess metaphor is worse than useless when—as this work does—one is considering the "macro" factors lying behind strategic surprise; in fact, its repeated use highlights the problem that intelligence analysis is a social activity engaged in not by individual chess masters but by groups of individuals. George Elliot makes another important point about the limitations this metaphor—especially given the scientism of CIA culture:

> Fancy what a game of chess would be if all the chessmen had passions and intellects, more or less small and cunning; if you were not only uncertain about your adversary's men, but a little uncertain about your own; if your knight could shuffle himself on to a new square on the sly; if your bishop in disgust at your castling, could wheedle your pawns out of their places; and if your pawns hating you because they are pawns, could make away from their appointed posts that you might get checkmate on a sudden. You might be the longest-headed of all deductive reasoners, and yet you might be beaten by your own pawns. *You would be especially likely to be beaten, if you depend arrogantly on your mathematical imagination, and regard your passionate pieces with contempt.*

See George Eliot, *Felix Holt, The Radical* (New York: Harper & Brothers, 1866), p. 111. Emphasis added.

8. Cynthia M. Grabo, *Anticipating Surprise: Analysis for Strategic Warning* (Lanham, MD: University Press of America, 2004), pp. 133–134. She says,

> The collector in the field who elects to forward, or not forward, some fragment of information to his home office is making a judgement. The current analyst who decides to write up a given piece of information, or not do so, is making a judgment about it. The manner in which he writes it up, the emphasis he gives to this or that aspect of it, constitutes another judgement. The items that his immediate superior selects to include in a briefing for the senior officials of his agency or department are the result of another judgement . . . [Individual judgments are] an integral part of the process at all times.

9. Robert M. Clark, *Intelligence Analysis: A Target-Centric Approach* (Washington, DC: CQ Press, 2004), p. 3.

10. It is somewhat encouraging that although a psychological approach to analytical failure remains predominate, the social nature of analysis is at least implicit in this recent and quite comprehensive collection of analytic frameworks: Richards J. Heuer and Randolph H. Pherson, *Structured Analytic Techniques for Intelligence Analysis* (Washington, DC: CQ Press, 2011).

11. Johnston, *Analytic Culture in the US Intelligence Community*, p. 4.

12. Ibid., p. 5.

13. Martin Petersen. "Making the Analytic Review Process Work." *Studies in Intelligence*, 49 (2005): p. 1. Emphasis added.

14. Allen W. Dulles, *The Craft of Intelligence* (Guilford, CT: The Lyons Press, 2006), p. 75. Emphasis added.

15. Kent, *Strategic Intelligence*, p. 157.

16. Cooper, *Curing Analytical Pathologies*, p. 4.

17. Sherman Kent, "The Need for an Intelligence Literature." *Studies in Intelligence*, 1 (1955): p. 1. Emphasis added.

18. Peter M. Haas, "Introduction: Epistemic Communities and International Policy Coordination." *International Organization* 46: 1 (1992), p. 3.

19. Nicholas Onuf, "Review of The New Culture of Security Studies." *Mershon International Studies Review*, 42: 1 (1998), pp. 59–70.

20. Valerie M. Hudson, ed., *Culture & Foreign Policy* (Boulder, CO: Lynne Rienner Publishing, 1997), p. 28.

21. Jeffery S. Lantis, "Strategic Culture and National Security Strategy." *International Studies Review* 4: 3 (2002), pp. 104.

22. Michael N. Barnett and Martha Finnemore, "The Power, Politics and Pathologies of International Organizations." *International Organization*, 53: 4 (1999), pp. 706 and 711.

23. Nicholas Onuf, "Constructivism: A Users Manual." In V. Kubalkova, N. Onuf, and P. Kowert, eds., *International Relations in a Constructed World* (Armonk, NY: M. E. Sharpe, 1998), p. 61.

24. An agonizingly complete account of reforms is provided by Michael Warner and Kenneth J. McDonald, *US Intelligence Reform Studies since 1947* (Washington, DC: Strategic Management Issues Office and the Center for the Study of Intelligence of the CIA, 2005). The most ambitious of these reforms are the ones undertaken after 2001.

25. Hudson, *Culture & Foreign Policy*, pp. 28–29. Emphasis added.

26. Stephen Peter Rosen. "Net Assessment as an Analytic Concept." In A. W. Marshall and H. S. Rowen, eds., *On Not Fooling Ourselves* (Boulder, CO: Westview Press, 1991).

27. Peter Katzenstein. *The Culture of National Security* (New York: Columbia University Press, 1996), p. 56. Emphasis added.

28. Onuf, "Constructivism," p. 75.

29. In keeping with Haas, this phrase means "those knowledge-oriented work communities in which cultural standards and social arrangements interpenetrate around a primary commitment to epistemic criteria in knowledge production and application."

30. Jutta Weldes. "Bureaucratic Politics: A Critical Constructivist Assessment." *Mershon International Studies Review*, 42: 2 (1998), p. 224.

31. Onuf, "Constructivism," p. 61.

32. Barnett and Finnemore, "The Power, Politics and Pathologies of International Organizations," passim.

33. Jack Davis, "Combating Mind-Set." *Studies in Intelligence*, 36: 5 (1992), p. 34. The idea that strategic surprises are a species of normal accidents like those in nuclear plants as described by Perrow is addressed in the following discussion. See Charles Perrow, *Normal Accidents: Living with High Risk Technologies* (Princeton, NJ: Princeton University Press, 1999).

34. Weldes, "Bureaucratic Politics: A Critical Constructivist Assessment," p. 224.

35. See, for example: Robert Jervis, "Minimizing Misperception," in M. G. Bonham and M. J. Shapiro, eds., *Thought and Action in Foreign Policy* (Stanford, CA: Center for Advanced Studies in the Behavioral Sciences, 1973); *Perception and Misperception in International Politics* (Princeton, NJ: Princeton University Press, 1976); and "What's Wrong with the Intelligence Process?" *International Journal of Intelligence and Counterintelligence*, 1 (1986), pp. 28–43.

36. Berkowitz and Goodman, *Best Truth*, pp. 74–75. Emphasis added.

37. Gregory F. Treverton, "Risks and Riddles," *Smithsonian*, June 2007; available at www.smithsonianmag.com/people-places/presence_puzzle.html.

38. Stephen S. Rosenfeld, "Knowing the Outs as Well as the Ins," *The Washington Post*, December 7, 1979, p. A17. Emphasis added. The by-then pitiable shah, speaking

from his deathbed exile in Mexico, was equally convinced of the mystery of his end, calling the upheaval in Iran "unnatural and unpredictable." See Bill Gold, "The Shah Was Also Surprised," *The Washington Post*, November 19, 1979, p. B10.

39. National Public Radio, "Difference Between a Secret and a Mystery When it Comes to Intelligence Failures." Emphasis added.

40. Shulsky and Schmitt, *Silent Warfare*, p. 173.

41. Michael A. Turner, *Why Secret Intelligence Fails* (Dulles, VA: Potomac Books, 2005), p. 6.

42. Paul Saffo, "Six Rules for Effective Forecasting," *Harvard Business Review*, July–August 2007, p. 1.

43. Zbigniew K. Brzezinski, *Power and Principle: Memoirs of the National Security Adviser 1977–1981* (New York: Farrar, Straus, Giroux, 1983), p. 397.

44. Rosenfeld, "Knowing the Outs as Well as the Ins," p. A17.

45. George W. Allen, *None So Blind: A Personal Account of the Intelligence Failure in Vietnam* (Chicago: Ivan R. Dee, 2001), p. 161. Emphasis added.

46. Betts, "Surprise, Scholasticism, and Strategy," p. 331.

47. Treverton, "Risks and Riddles." Emphasis added.

48. Shulsky and Schmitt, *Silent Warfare*, p. 236, fn 9.

49. Gary Sick, *All Fall Down: America's Tragic Encounter with Iran* (New York: Random House, 1985), pp. 44–45.

50. Examples of prominence/use of the intelligence cycle can be found in CIA, *A Consumer's Guide to Intelligence* (Washington, DC: Office of Public Affairs, Central Intelligence Agency, 1994). See also CIA , *Factbook on Intelligence* (Washington, DC: Office of Public Affairs, Central Intelligence Agency, 1997), pp. 12–14.

51. The intelligence cycle is being used here only "conceptually," that is, as a lens to focus further on specific problems in the CIA's intelligence processes, not as a representation of the actual intelligence process. According to Berkowitz and Goodman,

> The intelligence cycle reflects the best thinking about how an information service should work from the late 1940s and 1950s, when people began to write about intelligence policy and develop concepts about how intelligence ought to operate. It has been a durable concept and it pervades our thinking about intelligence. CIA publications and training materials feature it prominently.

See Berkowitz and Goodman, *Best Truth*, p. 69. A recent book for intelligence analysts referred to it critically as "somewhat of a theological concept: no one questions its validity"; see Clark, *Intelligence Analysis*, p. 15. For an extended discussion of its limits as a representation of the intelligence process, see Hulnick, "What's Wrong with the Intelligence Cycle?"

52. The authors are grateful to Professor Kent Grayson of Northwestern University for this distinction as it applies to *Constructing Cassandra*.

53. The same process happens in the natural sciences and is by no means fool-proof. Each morning, the evidence of the senses persuasively verifies the hypothesis that the sun revolves around Earth if a limited subset of natural facts are considered.

54. Wohlstetter, *Pearl Harbor*, p. 70.

55. See B. Geddes, "How the Cases You Choose Affect the Answers You Get: Selection Bias in Comparative Politics, " in J. A. Stimson, ed., *Political Analysis: An Annual Publication of the Methodology Section of the American Political Science Association* (Ann Arbor: University of Michigan Press, 1990), passim.

56. See Soros, *Alchemy of Finance*, pp. 317–322. In the natural world, saying or thinking something doesn't make it so.

Chapter 2

1. Markus Wolf and Anne McElvoy, *Man without a Face: The Autobiography of Communism's Greatest Spymaster* (New York: PublicAffairs, 1997), p. 193.

2. Robert Callum, "The Case for Cultural Diversity in the Intelligence Community." *International Journal of Intelligence and Counterintelligence*, 14: 1 (2001), p. 28.

3. Dawn Ellison, "One Woman's Contribution to Social Change at CIA." *Studies in Intelligence*, 46: 3 (2002), p. 52. For a bit more background on this case and its aftermath see Snider, *The Agency and the Hill*. For an interesting commentary on this issue in the first few decades of the Cold War, see Kathryn S. Olmsted, "Blond Queens, Red Spiders, and Neurotic Old Maids: Gender and Espionage in the Early Cold War." *Intelligence and National Security*, 19: 1 (2004), pp. 78–94.

4. See Snider, *The Agency and the Hill*, p. 322. Snider says,

Taking note of these complaints, the HPSCI held open hearings in September 1994 to explore the Agency's personnel policies and practices with respect to the hiring and promotion of women and other minorities. While conceding that "minorities are still underrepresented in the Agency's workforce, and the advancement of women and minorities is still limited," DCI Woolsey said he was intent on breaking down any existing barriers. "The ability to understand a complex, diverse world," he stated, "a world which is far from being all white male—is central to our mission."

Amen.

5. Stansfield Turner, *Burn before Reading: Presidents, CIA Directors, and Secret Intelligence* (New York: Hyperion, 2005), p. 232.

6. Callum, "The Case for Cultural Diversity in the Intelligence Community."

7. Rhodri Jeffreys-Jones, "The Socio-Educational Composition of the CIA Elite: A Statistical Note." *Journal of American Studies*, 19: 1 (1985), passim.

8. Lawrence Wright, *The Looming Tower: Al-Qaeda and the Road to 9/11*. (New York: Random House, 2006), pp. 353–354. It is a reference to the cult comprised mostly

of women who blindly participated in the murderous cult formed by Charles Manson in 1960s California.

9. See CIA Press Release, February, 1, 1999, Statement of the Director of Central Intelligence, George J. Tenet, "On Diversity"; retrieved on July 29, 2012, from www .cia.gov/news-information/press-releases-statements/press-release-archive-1999/ ps020199.html. Tenet explains this connection thus:

> The consumers of our intelligence products will come from more diverse backgrounds as American society continues to shift demographically. Our customers will have a wider variety of perspectives and they will demand intelligence products that take a wide range of views into account. We are often asked by policymakers whether we have considered all factors and options in arriving at our assessments or in planning operations. Having a diverse workforce can deepen our insights and widen our frames of reference.

10. Kent, *Strategic Intelligence*, p. 156. Emphasis added.

11. Sherman Kent, "Words of Estimative Probability." *Studies in Intelligence* (Fall 1964).

12. See especially Chapters 1 to 3 in Ron Robin, *The Making of the Cold War Enemy: Culture and Politics in the Military-Intellectual Complex* (Princeton, NJ: Princeton University Press, 2001), pp. 19–71. Robin says:

> Having dismissed their humanist colleagues as captives of the vagaries of language, behavioralists of all persuasions endorsed a quantitative discourse. They believed that a positive reception of their disciplinary innovations hinged on the strict avoidance of the imprecision of conventional language . . . When forced to use words rather than mathematical representations, behavioralists resorted to technical jargon—the linguistic equivalent of numerical precision. Numbers, according to the behavioralists, offered transparent presentations of difficult problems. There was a symbiotic relationship among objectivity, openness and "trust in numbers" . . . "firm statistical rules" promoted a sense of order by suppressing the unruly, diverse forms of interpretation associated with ambiguous qualitative data . . . Numbers permitted comparison of people, places and problems that were otherwise different and ostensibly incomparable. Quantification enabled the codifying, unifying, and above all the simplification of large and diverse bodies of information.

13. Quoted in Shulsky and Schmitt, *Silent Warfare*, p. 162.

14. Rob Johnston, "Developing a Taxonomy of Intelligence Analysis Variables." *Studies in Intelligence*, 47: 3 (2004), p. 1.

15. Ibid., page 4. Also cited in Johnston, *Analytic Culture in the US Intelligence Community*, p. 37.

16. Cooper, *Curing Analytical Pathologies*, pp. 26–27.

17. Walter Laqueur, *A World of Secrets: Uses and Limits of Intelligence* (New York: Basic Books, 1985), p. 261.

18. See Ofira Seliktar, *Politics, Paradigms, and Intelligence Failures: Why So Few Predicted the Collapse of the Soviet Union* (Armonk, NY: M. E. Sharpe, 2004), pp. 214–116. This facet of Kent's approach was questioned almost immediately by a CIA colleague, Willmoore Kendall, in a 1949 review of Kent's book. See Willmoore Kendall, "The Function of Intelligence." *World Politics*, 1 (1949), pp. 540–552.

19. James E. Steiner, *Challenging the Red Line between Intelligence and Policy* (Washington, DC: Institute for the Study of Diplomacy, School of Foreign Service, Georgetown University, 2004), p. 1. On the intelligence–policy divide and the trade-off between influence and objectivity it entails, see Stephen Marrin, "Intelligence Analysis and Decisionmaking: Proximity Matters" (PhD dissertation, University of Virginia, 2009).

20. Seliktar, *Politics, Paradigms, and Intelligence Failures*, p. 214.

21. Barnett and Finnemore, "The Power, Politics and Pathologies of International Organizations," pp. 710–712.

22. Steve Coll, *Ghost Wars: The Secret History of the CIA, Afghanistan, and bin Laden, from the Soviet Invasion to September 10, 2001.* (New York: Penguin Books, 2005), p. 261.

23. Richard A Clarke, *Against All Enemies: Inside America's War on Terror* (New York: Free Press, 2004), p. 135. Note that that such quotations about bin Ladin appearing as a "mere" financier of terrorism in CIA documents is sharply disputed in Paul R. Pillar, "Good Literature and Bad History: The 9/11 Commission's Tale of Strategic Intelligence." *Intelligence and National Security*, 21: 6 (2006), pp. 1030–1031.

24. SNIE 85-3-62, "The Military Buildup in Cuba," cited in Laqueur, *A World of Secrets*, p. 81. The full text of this SNIE has still not been declassified; just the summary pages are available. These thoughts are certainly consistent with the message of the SNIE's summary, which also shares some of the same vocabulary, especially paragraph D of the summary, referring to still-classified SNIE paragraphs 29–33, available in McAuliffe, *CIA Documents on the Cuban Missile Crisis 1962*, pp. 91–93.

25. H. Bradford Westerfield, ed., *Inside CIA's Private World: Declassified Articles from the Agency's Internal Journal 1955–1992.* (New Haven, CT: Yale University Press, 1995), p. xii.

26. David Brooks, "The C.I.A: Method and Madness." *The New York Times*, February 3, 2004, page A4. Emphasis added.

27. Roger Z. George, "Fixing the Problem of Analytical Mindsets: Alternative Analysis." In R. Z. George and R. D. Kline, eds., *Intelligence and the National Security Strategist: Enduring Issues and Challenges* (Lantham, MD: Rowman & Littlefield Publishers, 2006), p. 320.

28. D. Cameron Watt, "The Historiography of Intelligence in International Review." In L. C. Jenssen and O. Riste, eds., *Intelligence in the Cold War: Organisation, Role and International Cooperation* (Oslo: Norwegian Institute for Defence Studies, 2001), p. 185. Note that although he is not describing U.S. strategic culture here, he captures the idea beautifully.

29. Christopher Felix, *A Short Course in the Secret War*, 4th ed. (Lanham, MD: Madison Books, 1963), pp. 32–46.

30. Dulles, *The Craft of Intelligence*, p. 177. The former director goes on to find an upside to this fact, noting that secrecy quickly ceases to be a burden for many CIA employees, as, after all, "Most wives, after the honeymoon is over, easily tire of hearing their husbands talk about the office and the intricacies of their business, or of the legal or governmental world in which they work."

31. Robert M. Gates, *From the Shadows: The Ultimate Insider's Story of Five Presidents and How They Won the Cold War* (New York: Simon and Schuster, 1996), p. 33.

32. Gregory F. Treverton, *Reshaping National Intelligence for an Age of Information* (Cambridge, UK: Cambridge University Press, 2003), p. 113. Emphasis added.

33. Johnston, *Analytic Culture in the US Intelligence Community*, p. 11. Emphasis added.

34. Stephen C. Mercado, "Reexamining the Distinction between Open Information and Secrets." *Studies in Intelligence*, 49: 2 (2005).

35. Jeffrey Richelson, Thomas Blanton, and William Burr, "Dubious Secrets." *The National Security Archive*: Electronic Briefing Book No. 90 (2003), available at www.gwu.edu/~nsarchiv/NSAEBB/NSAEBB90/index.htm. This issue is also addressed on a regular basis by the Federation of American Scientist's newsletter, "Secrecy News."

36. Mercado, "Reexamining the Distinction Between Open Information and Secrets."

37. Mark M. Lowenthal, "Open-Source Intelligence: New Myths, New Realities." In R. Z. George and R. D. Kline, eds., *Intelligence and the National Security Strategist: Enduring Issues and Challenges* (Lanham, MD: Rowman & Littlefield Publishers, 2006), p. 274.

38. Treverton, *Reshaping National Intelligence for an Age of Information*, p. 108.

39. CIA, *A Consumer's Guide to Intelligence* (1999), p. vii.

40. Petersen, "Making the Analytic Review Process Work." Emphasis added.

41. Johnston, *Analytic Culture in the US Intelligence Community*, p. 5. Emphasis added.

42. Cooper, *Curing Analytical Pathologies*, p. 33.

43. Thomas W. Shreeve, "The Intelligence Community Case Method Program: A National Intelligence Estimate on Yugoslavia." In R. Z. George and R. D. Kline, eds., *Intelligence and the National Security Strategist: Enduring Issues and Challenges* (Lanham, MD: Rowman & Littlefield Publishers, 2006), p. 333. Emphasis added.

44. George, "Fixing the Problem of Analytical Mindsets," p. 323.

45. John A. Gentry, "Intelligence Analyst/Manager Relations at the CIA." In D. A. Charters, S. Farson, and G. P. Hastedt, eds., *Intelligence Analysis and Assessment* (London: Frank Cass, 1996), pp. 140–141.

46. Personal e-mail correspondence between the authors and a retired CIA source who wished to remain anonymous, arranged by Allen Thomson on October 5, 2007.

47. For a wider treatment of this view of the collapse of the USSR, see Neil Robinson, *Ideology and the Collapse of the Soviet System: A Critical History of the Soviet Ideological Discourse* (Aldershot, UK: Elgar Publishers, 1995).

48. Catherine H. Tinsley, "Social Categorization and Intergroup Dynamics." In B. Fischhoff and C. Chauvin, eds., *Intelligence Analysis: Behavioral and Social Scientific Foundations* (Washington, DC: Committee on Behavioral and Social Science Research to Improve Intelligence Analysis for National Security, National Research Council, 2011), p. 202.

49. Throughout this chapter, references are made to social mechanisms. This approach draws mainly on the work of Peter Hedstrom and Richard Swedberg, "Social Mechanisms: An Introductory Essay." In P. Hedstrom and R. Swedberg, eds., *Social Mechanisms: An Analytical Approach to Social Theory* (Cambridge, UK: Cambridge University Press, 1998). These mechanisms form the operational "toolbox," or shorthand, to capture the rules, norms, institutions, and the like, with which the most fine-grained social constructivist approach deals.

50. Paul Kowert and Jeffrey Legro, "Norms, Identity and Their Limits, A Theoretical Reprise." In P. Katzenstein, ed., *The Culture of National Security: Norms and Identity in World Politics* (New York: Columbia University Press, 1996), p. 475.

51. Dulles, *The Craft of Intelligence*, pp. 170–171.

52. Stafford C. Thomas, "The CIA's Bureaucratic Dimensions." *International Journal of Intelligence and Counterintelligence*, 12: 4 (1999), p. 406.

53. For the Directorate of Operations, there have also been in some periods less utterly transparent methods of recruitment, such as placing "blind ads," or newspaper advertisements listing the skills wanted (for example, willingness to travel, foreign languages, and the like) without specifying the future employer, though at some point fairly early in the evaluation process, the future potential employer, the CIA, is unveiled. See Ishmael Jones, *The Human Factor: Inside the CIA's Dysfunctional Intelligence Culture* (New York: Encounter Books, 2008), p. 23.

54. For simplicity's sake, this acronym will be used throughout this book to refer to the Soviet and then Russian Federation intelligence organization headquartered at Lubyanka Square in Moscow and later (in the case of the First Chief Directorate, which dealt with foreign intelligence) in the suburb of Yasenovo, southwest of Moscow.

55. Vladimir Putin et al., *First Person: An Astonishingly Frank Self-Portrait by Russia's President Vladimir Putin*, trans. C. A. Fitzpatrick (New York: PublicAffairs,

2000), pp. 40–41. For a fascinating exploration of the degree to which the early conspiratorial tradition of underground communist movements shaped both intelligence tradecraft and the Cold War as a whole, see David McKnight, *Espionage and the Roots of the Cold War: The Conspiratorial Heritage* (New York: Frank Cass, 2002), passim.

56. The acronym GRU is a transliteration of the Russian "ГРУ," which is the abbreviation for the Main Intelligence Directorate of the (Soviet and now Russian Army's) General Staff: Главное Разведывательное Управление. It operates residencies and signals intelligence stations throughout the world.

57. Vladimir Rezun, a.k.a. Viktor Suvorov, *Aquarium* (London: Hamish Hamilton, 1985), p. 6. He precedes this assertion with its basis:

> The GRU is entirely secret. Since nobody knows about it, nobody can enter it on his own initiative. Even supposing that some volunteer were to come along, how would he set about finding the right door to knock at, to request admission? Would he be accepted? Not likely. Volunteers are not needed.

58. Berkowitz and Goodman, *Best Truth*, pp. 109–110. The same point might be made for other types of analysts (not purely financial), when offered careers at McKinsey, Accenture, or even private security firms.

59. As is discussed in Chapter 6, a great example of this was the CIA's Counterterrorism Center prior to 9/11. A small minority of CTC analysts had PhDs. Russell, *Sharpening Strategic Intelligence*, p. 124. One former senior manager had a master's degree in English, and a former chief at the CTC had a bachelor's degree in forestry. The same charge is made of the DI as a whole in the current era by Russell: He recalls,

> I remember sharing the news with my Middle East division chief that distinguished Harvard professor and political scientist Joseph Nye was named the chairman of the National Intelligence Council. My division chief looked at me curiously and asked "Who is Joseph Nye?" To which I had to reply, "Oh, he's just one of the most highly regarded political scientists of his generation." (p. 126)

60. Kowert and Legro, "Norms, Identity and Their Limits, A Theoretical Reprise," p. 475.

61. Johnston, *Analytic Culture in the US Intelligence Community*, p. 100. Emphasis added.

62. Mahl makes the point that the CIA's institutional lineage can be traced back to the OSS, but then beyond that to the Coordinator of Information, which in turn was begotten in the "image and likeness" of an entity known as British Security Coordination, which was both very effective in dampening isolationist sentiments in the United States and very tied to the WASP elite; see Thomas E. Mahl, *Desperate Deception: British Covert Operations in the United States, 1939–44.* (London: Brassey's, 1999), pp. 9–45.

63. David C. Martin, *Wilderness of Mirrors* (Guilford, CT: The Lyons Press, 2003), p. 37. The author of one privately printed memoir even referred to himself somewhat bitterly as a "plebe" compared to many of his counterparts. See Thomas Bell Smith, *The Essential CIA* (Privately printed, 1975), p. 9. Cited in Powers, *The Man Who Kept the Secrets*, p. 318n9.

64. Gates, *From the Shadows*, pp. 31–32. He says,

The late 1960s and early 1970s represented the last hurrah of those who had helped build the organisation and still ran it . . . Some, like Angleton, were mysterious, even weird—sitting in a darkened office with a single desk light, chain-smoking, a figure from another world. Others were very Ivy League, very establishment, very well connected. The people who ran the rest of the government at the highest levels were their personal friends and often their tennis partners.

65. Callum, "The Case for Cultural Diversity in the Intelligence Community," p. 29. Emphasis added.

66. Dino A. Brugioni, *Eyeball to Eyeball* (New York: Random House, 1991), p. 65.

67. Rupert Allison (writing as Nigel West), *Historical Dictionary of Cold War Counterintelligence* (Lanham, MD: Scarecrow Press, 2007), p. xxiv.

68. That émigrés are difficult to handle because they can be biased or self-serving is exemplified by the recent case of Ahmed Chalabi, a prominent émigré, or the German source "Curveball," both of whom misled the United States in the run-up to the Iraq war in 2002–2003. We would argue, however, that DOD estimates or indeed any estimate can also be biased or self-serving. It is the CIA's job to sort such conflicts of interest out rather than exclude and ignore émigrés a priori.

69. Kowert and Legro, "Norms, Identity and Their Limits, A Theoretical Reprise," p. 475.

70. Stephen Marrin, "Intelligence Analysis: Turning a Craft into a Profession." In *2005 International Conference of Intelligence Analysis* (McLean, VA: Mitre Corporation, 2005), p. 2.

71. Wilhelm Agrell, "When Everything Is Intelligence—Nothing Is Intelligence." *The Sherman Kent Center for Intelligence Analysis Occasional Papers*, 1: 4 (2002).

72. Cooper, *Curing Analytical Pathologies*, pp. 6 and 28.

73. Stephen Marrin, "CIA's Kent School: Improving Training for New Analysts." *International Journal of Intelligence and Counterintelligence*, 16: 4 (2003), p. 613.

74. Stephen Marrin, "CIA's Kent School: A Step in the Right Direction." *International Studies Association Conference* (New Orleans, LA: ISA Archive Online, 2002).

75. Tim Weiner, "Naiveté at the CIA: Every Nation's Just Another U.S.," *The New York Times*, June 7, 1998.

76. Frans Bax. Presentation at an Association of Former Intelligence Officers (AFIO) Luncheon. Fort Myer, Virginia, May 22, 2001. Cited in Marrin, "CIA's Kent School: A Step In the Right Direction."

77. Seliktar, *Failing the Crystal Ball Test: The Carter Administration and the Fundamentalist Revolution in Iran* (Westport, CT: Praeger, 2000), p. 192.

78. Steven R. Ward, "Evolution Beats Revolution in Analysis: Counterpoint to 'The Coming Revolution in Intelligence Analysis.'" *Studies in Intelligence*, 46: 3 (2002), p. 31.

79. Ernest R. May and Philip D. Zelikow, eds., *Dealing with Dictators: Dilemmas of US Diplomacy and Intelligence Analysis, 1945–1990.* (Cambridge, MA: MIT Press, 2006), p. 1.

80. Josh Kerbel, "Thinking Straight: Cognitive Bias in the US Debate about China." *Studies in Intelligence*, 48: 3 (2004), fn 5.

81. Ibid., fn 5.

82. Ibid., p. 6.

83. Katzenstein, *The Culture of National Security.*

84. Kent, "Words of Estimative Probability."

85. Ibid.

86. For a discussion on social categorization, see also Tinsley, "Social Categorization and Intergroup Dynamics."

87. Max Weber, *Economy and Society* (Berkeley: University of California Press, 1978), pp. 273–278.

88. These abbreviations are standard in intelligence literature: HUMINT = human intelligence; SIGINT = signal intelligence; MASINT = measurement and signature intelligence; IMINT = image intelligence.

89. Robert M. Gates, "Remarks to DDI Analysts and Managers on 7 January, 1982." Cited in J. A. Gentry, "Intelligence Analyst/Manager Relations at the CIA," in David A. Charters, Stuart Farson, and Glenn Hastedt (Eds.), *Intelligence Analysis and Assessment, 1996.* (London: Frank Cass, 1982), p. 207.

90. Kent, "The Need for an Intelligence Literature." Emphasis added.

91. Or even other intelligence organizations. One scholar, for example, unfavorably compares U.S. attempts at collegiality with those of British intelligence agencies and claims, "The history of US intelligence is littered with the remains of failed collegial bodies." He attributes this failure to "a traditional [US] emphasis on rugged individualism and standing by one's judgements and rights against all odds" and to structural/organizational features of the U.S. Intelligence Community's organization. He sums up the U.S. Intelligence Community as having "minimal collegiality." See Philip H. J. Davies, "Intelligence Culture and Intelligence Failure in Britain and the United States." *Cambridge Review of International Affairs*, 17: 3 (2004), pp. 498–503.

92. Petersen, "Making the Analytic Review Process Work." Emphasis added.

93. See "The Making of an NIE," March 19, 2007; retrieved on February 19, 2013, from the CIA website: www.cia.gov/library/center-for-the-study-of-intelligence/csi-publications/books-and-monographs/sherman-kent-and-the-board-of-national-estimates-collected-essays/making.html.

94. Bruce D. Berkowitz and Allen E. Goodman, *Strategic Intelligence for American National Security* (Princeton, NJ: Princeton University Press, 1989), p. 133. Emphasis added.

95. Ibid.

96. Gates, "Remarks to DDI Analysts and Managers on 7 January, 1982."

97. Heuer, *The Psychology of Intelligence Analysis*, pp. 180–181. Emphasis added.

98. Bill Gertz, "CIA Officials 'Cooked Books,' Ex-Analyst Says." *The Washington Times*, March 27, 1991, p. A3.

99. Gentry, "Intelligence Analyst/Manager Relations at the CIA," pp. 140–141.

100. Ray S. Cline, "Is Intelligence Over-Coordinated?" *Studies in Intelligence* (Fall 1957), p. 1.

101. One might observe (with Seliktar) that Thomas Kuhn's "paradigms" are instructive here. One of Kuhn's points is that there is dissent within a discipline, but only at the margins. There is actually an enforced conformity to what a discipline is, what questions it asks, and what methods are appropriate in answering them. Dissent normally comes about the methods and answers. Naturally, Kuhn's characterizations of the actual processes of science have been questioned, most prominently in Imré Lakatos and Alan Musgrave, *Criticism and the Growth of Knowledge* (Cambridge, UK: Cambridge University Press, 1970). See also, in a more general sense, Paul Feyerabend, *Against Method* (London: Verso, 1993).

102. Kent, "The Need for an Intelligence Literature."

103. Nicholas Dujmovic, "Fifty Years of Studies in Intelligence." *Studies in Intelligence*, 49: 4 (2005), p. 1.

104. Frank A. Knapp Jr., "Styles and Stereotypes in Intelligence Studies." *Studies in Intelligence*, 8: 2 (1964), pp. A2–A4.

105. Kent, "The Need for an Intelligence Literature." Emphasis added.

106. Westerfield, *Inside CIA's Private World*.

107. The closed nature of the CIA as a result of security concerns has already been discussed. Here we will simply record that one reason for this phenomenon might be that, for many years, the *Studies* articles "published" were classified. It is hard to see how it could ever achieve one of the key marks of a true scholarly journal: peer review, with free intellectual exchange with experts and scholars with a stake in overturning accepted wisdom, the intellectual status quo.

108. Soon after World War II, anthropologists in New Guinea noticed an unusual phenomenon: Tribes deep in the interior of the country were building full-sized ritual airfields and airplanes out of bamboo, grass, and so on. Anthropologists soon discovered that withdrawal of military forces had created a scarcity of modern technological goods, and the tribes, under the influence of so-called cargo cult prophets, were converting communities' desires for these possessions into the external forms that had

brought them in the past. The perfectly human hope that these prophets shared with their followers was that if the correct external forms were present, the actual goods associated with them would arrive. See Craig Calhoun, ed., "Cargo Cults." *Dictionary of the Social Sciences* (Oxford, UK: Oxford University Press, 2003).

109. Cooper, *Curing Analytical Pathologies*, pp. 5–6.

110. Dujmovic, "Fifty Years of Studies in Intelligence."

111. Powers, *The Man Who Kept the Secrets*, p. 297.

112. One of the authors' experience as an officer in the U.S. Marine Corps: NOFORN = no foreign distribution; SCI = special compartmented information.

113. Ibid.

114. Compartmentalization goes beyond mere secrecy or classification; it is the practice used in intelligence work in which analysts are given only classified information that is needed for the performance of their particular analytical task—on a need to know basis.

115. Gates, *From the Shadows*, p. 200.

116. "DNI Brings Private Firms into Intelligence Sharing Effort," *Intelligence Online*, August 25, 2006.

117. Zegart, *Spying Blind*, p. 91.

118. Allison and Zelikow, *Essence of Decision*, p. 155.

119. See, for example, Herman L. Croom, "The Exploitation of Foreign Open Sources." *Studies in Intelligence*, 13 (Summer 1969), pp. 129–136.

120. Roy Godson's discussion of the article written by Daniel O. Graham, "Analysis and Estimates," in R. Godson, ed., *Intelligence Requirements for the 1980's: Elements of Intelligence* (Washington, DC: National Strategy Information Center, 1979), p. 32.

121. "Bolstering Russia's Image—and Its Intel?," Stratfor, February 1, 2008; available at www.stratfor.com/geopolitical_diary/geopolitical_diary_bolstering_russias_image_and_its_intel. In keeping with the general thrust of this chapter, the report goes on to say,

> The Russian model of collecting intelligence has always been based on getting hold of tightly held secrets, usually in some elaborate or devious way. (The American model is based on the Russian model, but with more expensive gadgetry.) But the Chinese model is quite different. Beijing focuses on gathering open-source material from every part of the globe. The Chinese—using myriad tools, of which Xinhua is one—have put people in every nook and cranny of the world, no matter how insignificant or unpleasant. These agents send every piece of information they hear on the streets or observe in the media back to a massive central processing unit in China, where it is sifted in search of useful patterns and valuable nuggets. It is a colossal undertaking requiring enormous manpower—but China has plenty of that.

Nigel West maintains that "employing more than 400,000 personnel, including internal security troops and border guards, the KGB was the world's largest intelligence organisation, but lacked any independent analytical function." See Nigel West, "KGB." In N. West, ed., *Historical Dictionary of Cold War Counterintelligence* (Lanham, MD: The Scarecrow Press, 2007), p. 173.

122. The CIA's attitude toward open source is said to have evolved since 2001.

123. Gates, *From the Shadows*, p. 56.

124. Berkowitz and Goodman, *Best Truth*, pp. 150–151.

125. John Hollister Hedley, "Twenty Years of Officers in Residence." *Studies in Intelligence*, 49: 4 (2005), pp. 31–41, p. 31.

126. Heuer, *The Psychology of Intelligence Analysis*, p. 181.

127. As such, it draws generally on several of the essays in Katzenstein, *The Culture of National Security*.

128. In Allen, *None So Blind*. Allen narrates a few such incidents during the Vietnam War involving U.S. Ambassador Taylor. Drawing on thirty years of analytical experience, however, Allen says that he highlights these episodes because they are "unique in my professional experience."

129. Gates, *From the Shadows*, p. 31. Emphasis added.

130. Robert M. Gates, "An Opportunity Unfulfilled: The Use and Perception of Intelligence at the White House." *Washington Quarterly* (Winter 1989), pp. 38–39.

131. Laqueur, *A World of Secrets*, p. 21.

132. Christopher M. Andrew, "American Presidents and Their Intelligence Communities." In D. A. Charters, A. S. Farson, and G. P. Hastedt, eds., *Intelligence Analysis and Assessment* (London: Frank Cass, 1996), p. 104.

133. Laqueur, *A World of Secrets*, p. 307. Emphasis added.

134. John L. Helgerson, *CIA Briefings of the Presidential Candidates, 1952–1992.* (Laguna Hills, CA: Aegean Park Press, 2000), p. vi. Emphasis added.

135. Christopher M. Andrew, *For the President's Eyes Only: Secret Intelligence and the American Presidency from Washington to Bush* (New York: HarperCollins, 1995), p. 426.

136. Ibid., page 506. During fast-moving events such as the collapse of the Soviet Union or the Iranian Revolution, observers—including scholars—have a hard time with labels, especially if they do not fit the Western political vocabulary. We argue that this is made more difficult by the homogeneity of analysts and by efforts to sustain a preagreed "precise" vocabulary.

137. "A Compendium of Analytic Tradecraft Notes, Volume I" (Washington, DC: Product Evaluation Staff of the Directorate of Intelligence, Central Intelligence Agency, 1995), p. 1.

138. Richards J. Heuer, *Quantitative Approaches to Political Intelligence: The CIA Experience* (Boulder, CO: Westview Press, 1978), p. 11. Cited in Laqueur, *A World of Secrets*, p. 300. Emphasis added.

139. Michael Herman, *Intelligence Power in Peace and War* (Cambridge, UK: Royal Institute of International Affairs, 1996), p. 46.

140. Walter McDonald, "African Numbers Game." *Studies in Intelligence*, 8: 4 (1964), p. 18.

141. Berkowitz and Goodman, *Best Truth*, p. 46.

142. C. F. Parker and E. K. Stern, "Blindsided? September 11 and the Origins of Strategic Surprise." *Political Psychology*, 23: 3 (2002), p. 619.

143. Quoted in Coll, *Ghost Wars*, p. 362.

144. The National Security Agency (NSA) was founded in 1952 and performs cryptological intelligence and electronic interception; the Defense Intelligence Agency (DIA) was founded in 1961 and manages military intelligence for the Department of Defense (DOD); the National Reconnaissance Office (NRO) was established in 1960 and operates spy satellites; and the National Geospatial-Intelligence Agency (NGA) was started in 1996 and combined numerous previously independent agencies that had produced geographic information for the Community. The best one-volume source for understanding what all these agencies do and how they fit together is Jeffrey T. Richelson, *The US Intelligence Community* (Boulder, CO: Westview Press, 2008).

145. Loch K. Johnson, "The DCI and the Eight-Hundred-Pound Gorilla." In R. Z. George and R. D. Kline, eds., *Intelligence and the National Security Strategist: Enduring Issues and Challenges* (Lanham, MD: Rowman & Littlefield Publishers, 2006), p. 459.

146. Commission, "Commission on the Roles and Capabilities of the United States Intelligence Community" (Washington, DC: Permanent Select Committee on Intelligence, U.S. House of Representatives, U.S. Government Printing Office, 1996), p. 131.

147. David C. Martin, *Wilderness of Mirrors* (Guilford, CT: The Lyons Press, 2003), p. 62.

148. Chapter 4 in Turner, *Burn before Reading*.

149. Berkowitz and Goodman, *Best Truth*, p. 112.

150. Laqueur, *A World of Secrets*, p. 21.

151. Robert B. Bathurst, *Intelligence and the Mirror: On Creating an Enemy* (London: Sage, 1993), p. 89. Emphasis added.

152. Frank Watanabe, "Fifteen Axioms for Intelligence Analysis." *Studies in Intelligence*, Semiannual Edition: 1 (1997). Emphasis in original. Experimental psychology, by mostly using U.S. college students and other Western subjects to establish what constitutes "human nature," has long been biased and is only now being challenged.

This challenge is most recently discussed in "The Roar of the Crowd," *The Economist*, March 26, 2012.

153. George, "Fixing the Problem of Analytical Mindsets: Alternative Analysis," p. 314.

154. Sherman Kent, "A Crucial Estimate Relived." *Studies in Intelligence*, 8: 2 (1964), pp. 1–18.

155. Gates, *From the Shadows*, p. 134.

156. Andrew, *For the President's Eyes Only*, p. 538. Emphasis added.

157. Johan Huizinga, *Homo Ludens: A Study of the Play Element in Culture* (Boston, MA: Beacon Press, 1955), p. 91.

158. When one of the authors studied in the USSR in 1985, the only place where one could purchase an accurate street map of Moscow was at the U.S. Embassy: Soviet-produced maps of the city introduced intentional errors after German soldiers were found to be carrying Soviet maps in World War II. At the risk of mirror imaging, one can say that this was not a society that excelled at cost-benefit analysis!

159. Lowenthal, "Open-Source Intelligence," p. 274.

160. Michael I. Handel, "Intelligence and the Problem of Strategic Surprise." In R. K. Betts and T. G. Mahnken, eds., *Paradoxes of Strategic Intelligence* (London: Frank Cass, 2003), p. 9.

161. Milt Bearden and James Risen, *The Main Enemy: The Inside Story of the CIA's Final Showdown with the KGB* (New York: Random House, 2003), p. 459.

162. After the Cold War ended, he wrote:

> In the end, even the most valuable double agents were rarely worth the intensive efforts it took to run them. Taxpayers on both sides of the Atlantic paid huge sums for very little. More often than not, double agents were scarcely more than balls in the games played by intelligence agencies. Some of the best-known Cold War espionage cases were more about spy versus spy than real issues of national security. Aldrich Ames would arouse great emotion in the United States, not least because the information he gave us led to the deaths of ten U.S. agents. But with few exceptions, most of those executed were intelligence officers involved in the narrow game tasks assigned them, *with little knowledge about what was going on in the rest of the KGB, let alone the country . . . It was thieves stealing from thieves*, which again raises the question of whether all the years of work and hundreds of millions of dollars were worth it.

Victor Cherkashin and Gregory Feifer, *Spy Handler: Memoir of a KGB Officer* (New York: Basic Books, 2005), pp. 108–109.

163. Wolf and McElvoy, *Man without a Face*, p. 283.

164. Kotkin, *Armageddon Averted*, p. 67.

165. Sergo Mikoyan, "Eroding the Soviet 'Culture of Secrecy': Western Winds behind Kremlin Walls." *Studies in Intelligence*, 11 (Fall–Winter 2001), p. 7. There is also the amusing fact that, at the first SALT talks held in 1968, the senior Soviet military negotiators stopped discussions as soon as the American negotiators began to summarize the Soviet nuclear weapons programs and asked the Soviet civilian negotiators to leave the room. The Soviet military man stated that "they were not cleared for such information, even if it was considered unclassified in the West." See Robert W. Pringle, "Arms Control Intelligence." In J. Woronoff, ed., *Historical Dictionary of Russian & Soviet Intelligence* (Lanham, MD: The Scarecrow Press, 2006).

166. Turner, *Burn before Reading*, pp. 168–169.

167. Bathurst, *Intelligence and the Mirror*, p. 96. Emphasis added.

168. Sherman Kent, "Sherman Kent and the Board of National Estimates: Collected Essays" (Washington, DC: Center for the Study of Intelligence, Central Intelligence Agency, March 2007).

169. See Leopold Labedz, "Democratic Centralism." In A. Bullock and S. Trombley, eds., *The New Fontana Dictionary of Modern Thought* (London: HarperCollins, 1999), p. 209.

Chapter 3

1. Scott Armstrong, "Failing to Heed the Warning of Revolutionary Iran," *The Washington Post*, October 26, 1980, p. A1.

2. Henry Kissinger, *The White House Years* (Boston, MA: Little, Brown and Company, 1979), p. 1262.

3. Milo Jones is grateful to his stepmother Helen Roosevelt for reminding him of Kermit's central role in this affair. See, first and foremost, Donald N. Wilber, "Clandestine Service History: Overthrow of Premier Mossadeq of Iran (CS Historical Paper 208)" (Washington, DC: Central Intelligence Agency, 1954). Kermit Roosevelt also wrote a (rather ironically timed) history of the operation: Kermit Roosevelt, *Countercoup: The Struggle for the Control of Iran* (New York: McGraw-Hill, 1979).

4. Bill, *The Eagle and the Lion*, p. 424.

5. Berkowitz and Goodman, *Strategic Intelligence for American National Security*, p. 108.

6. B. Rubin, *Paved with Good Intentions: The American Experience in Iran* (New York: Oxford University Press, 1980), pp. 149–150.

7. Seliktar, *Failing the Crystal Ball Test*, p. 93.

8. James A. Bill, "Iran and the Crisis of '78." *Foreign Affairs*, 57: 2 (1978–1979), p. 324. Bill goes on to point out of the shah,

Since his accession in 1941 he has survived two public assassination attempts (1949, 1965), numerous plots against his dynasty, a popular political movement led by the charismatic Prime Minister Mossadeq (1951–53), and the machinations of dozens of other wily politicians who have sought to loosen his grip on the controls of powers. He has lost two prime ministers through assassination (Razmara in 1951, Mansur in 1963), and has thrice ordered his troops to turn their machine guns on demonstrators in the streets of his capital city (1952, 1963, 1978). He has had to overcome both Allied occupation of his country and Soviet-supported separatist movements in Azerbaijan and Kurdistan in the 1940s.

See Bill, "Iran and the Crisis of '78," pp. 324–325.

9. Dennis Mullin, "Nobody Can Overthrow Me—I Have the Power." *U.S. News & World Report*, June 26, 1978, p. 37.

10. Sick, *All Fall Down*, p. 41.

11. Jim Hoagland, "CIA Will Survey Moslems Worldwide." *The Washington Post*, January 20, 1979, p. A1.

12. William B. Quandt, "The Middle East Crises." *Foreign Affairs*, 58 (1980), p. 540.

13. Excerpts from this study appeared in Willis C. Armstrong et al., "The Hazards of Single Outcome Forecasting." *Studies in Intelligence*, 28: 3 (1984), pp. 57–74.

14. Roy Godson, *Intelligence Requirements for the 1980's: Elements of Intelligence* (Washington, DC: National Strategy Information Center, 1979), p. 24.

15. Turner, "Intelligence for a New World Order," pp. 154–155.

16. Turner, *Burn before Reading*, p. 180.

17. Charles Kurzman, *The Unthinkable Revolution in Iran* (Cambridge, MA: Harvard University Press, 2004), p. 145.

18. Seliktar, *Failing the Crystal Ball Test*, p. 93.

19. Penelope Kinch, "The Iranian Crisis and the Dynamics of Advice and Intelligence in the Carter Administration." *The Journal of Intelligence History* 6 (Winter 2006), p. 79.

20. William J. Daugherty, "Behind the Intelligence Failure in Iran." *International Journal of Intelligence and Counterintelligence*, 14: 4 (2005), p. 454.

21. Zachary Karabell, "Inside the US Espionage Den: The US Embassy and the Fall of the Shah." *Intelligence and National Security*, 8: 1 (1993), p. 48.

22. Douglas J. MacEachin, Janne Nolan, and Kristine Tockman, "Iran: Intelligence Failure or Policy Stalemate?" In *Discourse, Dissent and Strategic Surprise: Formulating American Security in an Age of Uncertainty* (Washington, DC: Institute for the Study of Diplomacy, Georgetown University, 2004), p. 5.

23. Treverton and Klocke, "Iran, 1978–1979," p. 124.

24. Equally damning is that the U.S. ambassador who preceded Sullivan was Richard Helms, who was DCI just prior to accepting the post in Tehran, where he served from 1973 to 1976. See Chapter 41 in Richard Helms and William Hood, *A*

Look over My Shoulder: A Life in the Central Intelligence Agency (New York: Ballantine, 2003). See also the account by his wife: Cynthia Helms, *An Ambassador's Wife in Iran* (New York: Dodd, Mead & Company, 1981).

25. Seliktar, *Failing the Crystal Ball Test*, p. 105.

26. Kurzman, *The Unthinkable Revolution in Iran*, p. 1.

27. Sick, *All Fall Down*, p. 59.

28. Treverton and Klocke, "Iran, 1978–1979," p. 119.

29. MacEachin et al., "Iran," p. 10.

30. Hoagland, "CIA Will Survey Moslems Worldwide," p. A1.

31. Tim Weiner, *Legacy of Ashes: The History of the CIA* (New York: Doubleday, 2007), p. 370.

32. Angelo M. Codevilla, *Informing Statecraft: Intelligence for a New Century* (New York: The Free Press, 1992), p. 17.

33. Rosenfeld, "Knowing the Outs as Well as the Ins," p. A17.

34. Treverton and Klocke, "Iran, 1978–1979," pp. 112–113.

35. Seliktar, *Failing the Crystal Ball Test*, p. 190.

36. Seth Lipsky, "A Primer for Spies," *The Washington Post*, March 12, 1979, p. A19.

37. Seliktar, *Failing the Crystal Ball Test*, pp. 97–98. Emphasis added. (One can deduce from this anecdote that *The Emperor's New Clothes* was not available in Farsi).

38. A. Taheri, *Nest of Spies: America's Journey to Disaster in Iran* (New York: Pantheon Books, 1988), p. 44. See also S. Arani, "Iran: From the Shah's Dictatorship to Khomeini's Demagogic Theocracy." *Dissent*, 27 (1980), pp. 9–27.

39. A. Taheri, *The Spirit of Allah: Khomeini and the Islamic Revolution* (Bethesda, MD: Adler & Adler, 1985), p. 233. See also Robin Wright, *In the Name of God* (New York: Simon & Schuster, 1989), p. 58.

40. Berkowitz and Goodman, *Best Truth*, page 60.

41. Congressional testimony quoted in Ephraim Kam, *Surprise Attack: The Victim's Perspective* (Cambridge, MA: Harvard University Press, 1988), pp. 209–210. Emphasis original.

42. Jim Hoagland, "CIA–Shah Ties Cloud Iran Data." *The Washington Post*, December 17, 1978, p. A21.

43. Gregory F. Treverton and James Klocke, *The Fall of the Shah of Iran*, Kennedy School of Government Case Program (Cambridge, MA: Harvard University, 1988), p. 2.

44. Andrew Gowers, "Review of *The Eagle and the Lion: The Tragedy of American-Iranian Relations*, by James A. Bill." *The Financial Times*, May 26, 1988, p. 26.

45. Andrew, *For the President's Eyes Only*, p. 440.

46. Hoagland, "CIA–Shah Ties Cloud Iran Data," p. A21. This problem also affects CIA reporting on Saudi Arabia; see Robert Baer, *Sleeping with the Devil: How*

Washington Sold Our Soul for Saudi Crude (New York: Crown Publishers, 2003), pp. 35–36.

47. Hoagland, "CIA–Shah Ties Cloud Iran Data," p. A21. In light of the activities of British Security Coordination in the United States prior to World War II, this is an absurdly naive analogy for a CIA employee to employ; see Mahl, *Desperate Deception*.

48. S. Armstrong, "U.S. Urged 'Crackdown on opposition,'" *The Washington Post*, October 28, 1980, p. A1.

49. John Ranelagh, *The Agency* (London: Weidenfeld and Nicholson, 1986), p. 649.

50. Rosenfeld, "Knowing the Outs as Well as the Ins," p. A17.

51. Rubin, *Paved with Good Intentions*, p. 348. Cited in Seliktar, *Failing the Crystal Ball Test*, p. 58.

52. Laqueur, *A World of Secrets*, p. 64. Emphasis added.

53. Stephen Engelberg, "CIA Says It Has Restored Link to Campuses to Get More Advice." *The New York Times*, January 19, 1986, p. 1.

54. Eric Rouleau, "Khomeini's Iran." *Foreign Affairs*, 59: 1 (1980), p. 1.

55. MacEachin, Nolan, and Tockman, "Iran," p. 9.

56. Seliktar, *Failing the Crystal Ball Test*, p. 69.

57. Ronen Bergman, *The Secret War With Iran*, trans. R. Hope (New York: Free Press, 2008), p. 21.

58. Treverton and Klocke, *The Fall of the Shah of Iran*, p. 7. This is not an unreasonable or especially exotic task: In a conversation between the authors and the U.S. Marine colonel in charge of the Iraqi city of Fallujah in Amman, Jordan, in May 2005, the colonel revealed that a large part of the Marines' anti-insurgency campaign involved monitoring every sermon in every mosque each Friday. The Egyptian and Turkish governments also listen closely to Friday sermons at major mosques around their countries.

59. Bergman, *The Secret War with Iran*, p. 11.

60. Andrew, *For the President's Eyes Only*, p. 440.

61. Treverton and Klocke, *The Fall of the Shah of Iran*, p. 7.

62. Bergman, *The Secret War with Iran*, p. 20.

63. Elaine Sciolino, "Iran's Durable Revolution." *Foreign Affairs*, 61: 4 (1983), pp. 894–895. See also Jonathan Randal, "Exile Leader Shifts View on U.S.–Iran Ties; Iranian Exile Leader Shifts Stance on U.S.," *The Washington Post*, January 1, 1979. Note that the interview took place the morning after Carter's New Year's toast, cited at the beginning of this chapter.

64. Jonathan Randal, "Khomeini: From Oblivion to the Brink of Power." *The Washington Post*, January 21, 1979, p. A23.

65. Turner, "Intelligence for a New World Order," p. 155.

66. See, for example, Edward N. Luttwak, *Coup d'État: A Practical Handbook* (Cambridge, MA: Harvard University Press, 1979), passim. See also Gregor Ferguson,

Coup d'État: A Practical Manual (Poole, Dorset, UK: Arms and Armour Press, 1987), passim.

67. Seliktar, *Failing the Crystal Ball Test*, p. 64.

68. Ibid., p. 189.

69. Adda B. Bozeman, "Political Intelligence in Non-Western Societies." In R. Godson, ed., *Comparing Foreign Intelligence: The US, the USSR and the Third World* (McLean, VA: Pergamon Brassey, 1988), p. 129.

70. M. Tehranian, "Communication and Revolution in Iran: The Passing of a Paradigm." *Iranian Studies*, 13 (1980), p. 13. Cited in Seliktar, *Failing the Crystal Ball Test*, pp. 60–61.

71. Seliktar, *Failing the Crystal Ball Test*, pp. 60–61.

72. Bill, *The Eagle and the Lion*, p. 414. Quoted in Seliktar, *Failing the Crystal Ball Test*, p. 189. Emphasis added.

73. Hoagland, "CIA Will Survey Moslems Worldwide."

74. Gates, *From the Shadows*, pp. 136–137.

75. Andrew, *For the President's Eyes Only*, p. 4.

76. Benjamin F. Schemmer, "The Intelligence Community's Case against Turner." *The Washington Post*, April 8, 1979, p. D1.

77. Stansfield Turner, *Secrets and Democracy: The CIA in Transition* (New York: Harper and Row, 1986), p. 92.

78. Gates, *From the Shadows*, p. 139.

79. Alexander Wendt, "Anarchy Is What States Make of It: The Social Construction of Power Politics." *International Organization*, 41: 3 (1992), pp. 396–397.

80. Seliktar, *Failing the Crystal Ball Test*, p. 52. For an exploration of whether this is indeed true, see Jan Goldman, ed., *The Ethics of Spying: A Reader for the Intelligence Professional* (Lanham, MD: Scarecrow Press, 2006). Part four, comparing espionage and intelligence work to other professions, is especially thought provoking.

81. Gates, *From the Shadows*, p. 138.

82. Schemmer, "The Intelligence Community's Case against Turner," p. D1.

83. Seliktar, *Failing the Crystal Ball Test*, p. 68.

84. Ibid.

85. Ibid., pp. 186–187.

86. Turner, "Intelligence for a New World Order," pp. 154–155.

87. Quoted in MacEachin, Nolan, and Tockman, "Iran," p. 9.

88. See letter from Richard Nixon to Richard Helms of October 24, 1983, reproduced in the photos in Helms and Hood, *A Look over My Shoulder*.

89. Seliktar, *Failing the Crystal Ball Test*, p. 84.

90. William Sullivan, *Mission to Iran* (New York & London: W. W. Norton & Company, 1981), p. 142.

91. Sick, *All Fall Down*, pp. 212–214.

92. S. Armstrong, "Carter Held Hope Even after Shah Had Lost His Way." *The Washington Post*, October 25, 1980, p. A1.

93. Stansfield Turner, "Purge the CIA of KGB Types." *The New York Times*, October 2, 1991, p. 25.

94. Myles Maxfield, Robert Proper, and Sharol Case, "Remote Medical Diagnosis: Monitoring the Health of Very Important Patients." *Studies in Intelligence*, 23: 1 (1979), pp. 9–14, passim.

95. Seliktar, *Failing the Crystal Ball Test*, p. 102.

96. Brzezinski, *Power and Principle*, p. 368.

97. Said Amir Arjomand, "Iran's Islamic Revolution in Comparative Perspective." *World Politics*, 38 (1986), p. 385.

98. Schemmer, "The Intelligence Community's Case against Turner," p. D1.

99. Graham Allison, "An Intelligence Agenda." *The New York Times*, December 21, 1980, p. 17.

100. Robert M. Gates, "Discussion." In R. Godson, ed., *Intelligence Requirements for the 1990s: Collection, Analysis, Counterintelligence and Covert Action* (Lexington, MA: Lexington Books, 1989), p. 114. Emphasis added.

101. Armstrong, "Failing to Heed the Warning of Revolutionary Iran," p. A1.

102. Quoted in MacEachin, Nolan, and Tockman, "Iran: Intelligence Failure or Policy Stalemate?" p. 9.

103. Seliktar, *Failing the Crystal Ball Test*, page 176.

104. Rouleau, "Khomeini's Iran," pp. 2–3.

105. Arjomand, "Iran's Islamic Revolution in Comparative Perspective," p. 405.

106. Cyril Glassé, *The Concise Encyclopedia of Islam* (New York: HarperCollins, 1991), p. 397. See also Adda B. Bozeman, "Iran: US Foreign Policy and the Tradition of Persian Statecraft." *Orbis*, 23 (1979), pp. 387–402.

107. Seliktar, *Failing the Crystal Ball Test*, p. 187.

108. Codevilla, *Informing Statecraft*, p. 382.

109. Seliktar, *Failing the Crystal Ball Test*, pp. 187–188.

110. Fred Halliday, "The Iranian Revolution and Great Power Politics: Components of the First Decade." In N. R. Keddie and M. J. Gasiorowski, eds., *Neither East nor West: Iran, the Soviet Union and the United States* (New Haven, CT: Yale University Press, 1990), p. 249. Emphasis added.

111. Jonathan Randal, "Views Differ on Islamic Role in Republic." *The Washington Post*, February 4, 1979, p. A23.

112. Seliktar, *Failing the Crystal Ball Test*, p. 192.

113. Ibid., p. 174.

114. M. M. Milani, *The Making of Iran's Islamic Revolution: From Monarchy to Islamic Republic* (Boulder, CO: Westview Press, 1988), p. 22.

115. Randal, "Khomeini," p. A23.

116. Arjomand, "Iran's Islamic Revolution in Comparative Perspective," p. 387.

117. Ibid., p. 412.

118. R. K. Ramazani, "Iran's Revolution: Patterns, Problems and Prospects." *International Affairs*, 56: 3 (1980), p. 444.

119. Seliktar, *Failing the Crystal Ball Test*, p. 92. Emphasis added.

120. Schemmer, "The Intelligence Community's Case against Turner," p. D1.

121. Robert G. Herman, "Identity, Norms and National Security: The Soviet Foreign Policy Revolution and the End of the Cold War." In P. Katzenstein, ed., *The Culture of National Security* (New York: Columbia University Press, 1996), p. 46.

122. Michael Donovan, "National Intelligence and the Iranian revolution." *Intelligence and National Security*, 12: 1 (1997), p. 147.

123. Seliktar, *Failing the Crystal Ball Test*, p 191. Emphasis added. She was here quoting "Intelligence and Crisis Forecasting." *Orbis*, 27: 4 (1989), p. 823.

Chapter 4

1. Note: Although it includes economic arguments, this case study is about the collapse of the USSR itself, that is, the state, not the economy of the USSR.

2. On the Soviet economy, see John Howard Wilhelm, "The Failure of the American Sovietological Economics Profession." *Europe-Asia Studies*, 55: 1 (2003), pp. 59–74. For a more complete coverage of the "Cold War consensus" and the failings of the profession, see Michael Cox, "Whatever Happened to the USSR? Critical Reflections on Soviet Studies." In. M. Cox, ed., *Rethinking the Soviet Collapse: Sovietology, the Death of Communism and the New Russia* (London: Pinter, 1998). See also the more recent Christopher I. Xenakis, *What Happened to the Soviet Union? How and Why American Sovietologists Were Caught by Surprise* (Westport, CT: Praeger Publishers 2002).

3. Seliktar, *Politics, Paradigms, and Intelligence Failures*, p. 118. This puts one in mind of George Orwell's observation that to believe certain absurdities it is necessary to have attended university. See Moynihan's introduction to Nicholas Eberstadt, *The Tyranny of Numbers: Mismeasurement and Misrule* (Washington, DC: American Enterprise Institute Press, 1995), p. xvii.

4. The famous phrase was first uttered by West German Chancellor Helmut Schmidt.

5. Eberstadt, *The Tyranny of Numbers: Mismeasurement and Misrule*, p. 137.

6. William Moskoff, "Review Essay: CIA Publications on the Soviet Economy." *Slavic Review*, 40: 2 (1981), p. 270.

7. These operations were apparently code-named "Famish," according to David Major, a former FBI agent and the first director of counterintelligence programs at the National Security Council during the Reagan administration; see "CI Centre Course 105: John Walker Case," in *Counter-Intelligence Centre Podcasts* (Great Falls, VA: The Counter-Intelligence Centre, 2007). See also Peter Schweitzer, *Victory: The Reagan*

Administration's Secret Strategy That Hastened the Collapse of the Soviet Union (New York: Atlantic Monthly Press, 1994), passim.

8. According to Schweitzer, *Victory*, pp. xviii–xix. These measures included:

(1) Covert financial, intelligence, and logistical support to the Solidarity movement in Poland that ensured the survival of an opposition movement in the heart of the Soviet Empire; (2) Substantial financial and military support to Afghan resistance, as well as supplying mujahedin personnel to take the war into the Soviet Union itself; (3) A campaign to reduce dramatically Soviet hard currency earnings by driving down the price of oil with Saudi cooperation and limiting natural gas exports to the West; (4) A sophisticated and detailed psychological operation to fuel indecision and fear among the Soviet leadership; (5) A comprehensive global campaign, including secret diplomacy, to reduce drastically Soviet access to Western high technology; (6) A widespread technological disinformation campaign, designed to disrupt the Soviet economy; and (7) An aggressive high-tech defence build-up that by Soviet accounts severely strained the economy and exacerbated the resource crisis.

9. Nassim Nicholas Taleb, *Fooled by Randomness: The Hidden Role of Chance in Life and in the Markets* (New York: Texere, 2004), pp. 1–69. Niall Ferguson also explores the issue of hindsight bias in a novel and empirical way. Most first-person narrative accounts and many historians describe the period before World War I as one of "mounting international tensions" and "escalating crises." Ferguson shows that none of these "tensions" and "crises" was reflected in contemporary imperial bond prices and thus this view is likely to be pure hindsight bias. See Niall Ferguson, "Political Risk and the International Bond Market between the 1848 Revolution and the Outbreak of the First World War." *Economic History Review*, 59: 1 (2006), pp. 70–112.

10. Kotkin, *Armageddon Averted*. Among other things, Kotkin points out the importance of the ultimate belief in "socialism with a human face" among Gorbachev and others.

11. Schweitzer, *Victory*, p. xv.

12. Kerbel, "Thinking Straight." Emphasis added.

13. Zbigniew K. Brzezinski, "Tragic Dilemmas of Soviet World Power: The Limits of a New-Type Empire." *Encounter*, 61 (1983), p. 397.

14. Rosenfeld, "Knowing the Outs as Well as the Ins," p. A17.

15. Vernon Loeb, "Back Channels: The Intelligence Community," *The Washington Post*, November 19, 1999, p. A43.

16. House Permanent Select Committee on Intelligence—Review Committee, *An Evaluation of CIA's Analysis of Soviet Economic Performance 1970–1990.* (Washington, DC: U.S. Government Printing Office, November 18, 1991.

17. Bruce D. Berkowitz and Jeffery T. Richelson, "CIA Vindicated: The Soviet Collapse Was Predicted." *The National Interest*, 41 (1995), p. 39.

18. Ibid., p. 41.

19. Abraham S Becker, "Intelligence Fiasco or Reasoned Accounting? CIA Estimates of Soviet GNP" *Post-Soviet Affairs* (Silver Spring, MD: V. H. Winston & Son, 1994).

20. See RAND Corporation, 1995; retrieved on February 18, 2013 from www .rand.org/pubs/reprints/RP414/, 1995. Retrieved 18 February 2013. Emphasis added.

21. Douglas J. MacEachin, *CIA Assessments of the Soviet Union: The Record Versus the Charges* (Washington, DC: Center for the Study of Intelligence, 1996), p. 1. A more recent attempt to defend the CIA's record is by Bruce D. Berkowitz, "US Intelligence Estimates of Soviet Collapse: Reality and Perception." In F. Fukuyama, ed., *Blindside: How to Anticipate Forcing Events and Wild Cards in Global Politics* (Washington, DC: Brookings Institution Press, 2007).

22. Cited in Kirsten Lundberg, "CIA and the Fall of the Soviet Empire: The Politics of 'Getting It Right,'" (Cambridge, MA: Kennedy School of Government, Harvard University, 1994), p. 2.

23. Loeb, "Back Channels," p. A43. Also described in *Studies* the next year: Henry R. Appelbaum and John Hollister Hedley, "US Intelligence and the End of the Cold War. *Studies in Intelligence*, 9 (2000), pp. 11–18.

24. For a general overview of the problem of self-altering predictions, see Richard L. Henshel, "The Boundary of the Self-Fulfilling Prophecy and the Dilemma of Social Prediction." *The British Journal of Sociology*, 33: 4 (1982), pp. 511–528. These issues are also dealt with extensively in the literature on "strategic warning" and "indicators analysis"; see, for example, Handel, "Intelligence and the Problem of Strategic Surprise," pp. 17–20.

25. See Jack F. Matlock, "Western Intelligence and the Collapse of the Soviet Union, 1980–1990: Ten Years That Did Not Shake the World (review)." *Journal of Cold War Studies*, 6 (Spring 2004), p. 100. The context of that remark is:

> In June 1990, when I was still the U.S. ambassador, I sent a top-secret message to the president and secretary of state advising them to make contingency plans for a possible break-up of the Soviet Union. The CIA circulated this message, without negative comment, in its briefing package to other senior officials. Why, then, did the CIA not predict the Soviet collapse, even when it was close at hand? There were very good reasons for avoiding a formal intelligence assessment with that prediction. If the analysis leaked, as it certainly would have, it could well have precipitated a crackdown in the Soviet Union that reversed Gorbachev's reforms, restored many Cold War practices, and preserved authoritarian controls in the Soviet Union for a generation or longer. Even if the collapse occurred as

predicted, many persons would draw the conclusion that it had been engineered by the United States. This would have greatly burdened future U.S. relations with a nuclear-armed successor state. That is why there was no formal CIA prediction. It was not needed, and it could have resulted in great damage to U.S. interests if it had been issued.

It would seem, under Ambassador Matlock's logic, that the CIA should never provide accurate forecasts of anything amenable to human agency, lest the prediction leak and trigger a self-cancelling response. In any case, if one considers his remarks in light of Figure 1.2, all pretence of intelligence as a science must go out the window: Self-canceling predictions do not occur in the real science. That is the essence of the deductive-nomological model.

26. Moskoff, "Review Essay," p. 270. Ironically, Moskoff goes on to characterize the CIA's analysis as "essentially negative" and therefore "unbalanced," citing such "facts" as that the USSR has "the second largest gross national product in the world" and "it has been a rare occurrence in the past twenty years when growth of real GNP (total or per capita) in the Soviet Union has been exceeded by that of the United States or the European community." Again—it wasn't just the CIA that got a lot wrong! As Wilhelm courageously says (in Wilhelm, "The Failure of the American Sovietological Economics Profession"), there was a failure of an entire *profession*.

27. Edward R. Allen, "The Validity of Soviet Economic Statistics." *Studies in Intelligence*, 4: 3 (1960), p. 1.

28. CNN, "Inside the CIA: An Interview with Former CIA Analyst Melvin Goodman." In *Cold War* (Cable News Network, January 10, 1998). Sakwa's point, however, is well taken:

The academic discipline of Sovietology was no more than a small, and by no means the most significant, part of the attempt by writers, émigrés, intellectuals and others to understand the origins not just of communism (in its various guises) but of Russia's ambiguous relationship with modernity and the West.

See Richard Sakwa, "Russian Political Evolution: a Structural Approach." In M. Cox, ed., *Rethinking the Soviet Collapse: Sovietology, the Death of Communism and the New Russia* (London: Pinter, 1998), p. 181.

29. Michael A. Turner, "Issues in Evaluating U.S. intelligence." *International Journal of Intelligence and Counterintelligence*, 5: 3 (1991), pp. 275–285. Emphasis added.

30. Matthias, *America's Strategic Blunders*, p. 313.

31. Richard K. Betts, *Enemies of Intelligence* (New York: Columbia University Press, 2007), p. 190.

32. CNN, "Inside the CIA."

33. Weiner, *Legacy of Ashes*, p. 432.

34. Cox, "Whatever Happened to the USSR?" p. 23.

35. Michael Cox, ed., *Rethinking the Soviet Collapse: Sovietology, the Death of Communism and the New Russia* (London: Pinter, 1998), p. 31n29.

36. House Committee on International Relations, *United States Policy toward North Korea: Testimony of Nicholas Eberstadt, American Enterprise Institute for Public Policy Research*, September 24, 1998. The thinking behind this claim is fully explored in Chapter 6, "CIA Assessment of the Soviet Economy," of Eberstadt, *The Tyranny of Numbers*.

37. Wilhelm, "The Failure of the American Sovietological Economics Profession," p. 68.

38. Melvin A. Goodman, "Ending the CIA's Cold War Legacy." *Foreign Policy*, 106: 106 (1997), p. 128. He also elaborates on the cost of this failure:

> The costs of this failure include the huge defense budgets of the Reagan–Bush years, with their damaging expansion of the deficit; a needlessly prolonged confrontation with Moscow that delayed arms control agreements and conflict resolution in the Third World; and a lost opportunity to influence developments in the Russian Federation.

39. Daniel Patrick Moynihan, "The Soviet Economy: Boy, Were We Wrong!" *The Washington Post*, July 11, 1990, p. A19. Emphasis added.

40. Anders Aslund, "The CIA vs. Soviet Reality." *The Washington Post*, May 19 1988, p. A25. Their 1987 *World Fact Book* also listed GNP per capita in West Germany as *lower* than that in East Germany!

41. Alexseev, *Without Warning*, p. 193.

42. Firth and Noren, *Soviet Defense Spending*.

43. Appelbaum and Hedley, "US Intelligence and the End of the Cold War," p. 16.

44. Berkowitz and Richelson, "CIA Vindicated," p. 41.

45. Alexseev, *Without Warning*, p. 218. We should also here note that the CIA has had at various times formal programs to evaluate the accuracy of intelligence estimates.

46. Stephen G. Brooks and William C. Wohlforth, "Power, Globalization and the End of the Cold War: Re-evaluating a Landmark Case for Ideas." *International Security*, 25: 3 (2000), p. 18.

47. Essentially the CIA used purchasing power parity (PPP), explained by one intelligence professional as follows:

> In the 1950s basic data either didn't exist or were suspect; moreover, because prices were determined by administrative fiat and the ruble wasn't convertible into any other currency, there was no way to calculate Soviet Gross National Product (GNP). The CIA's response was to examine Soviet goods and price them by Western standards . . . The CIA reconstructed the Soviet economy from the ground up."

See Treverton, *Reshaping National Intelligence for an Age of Information*, pp. 8–9. We refer any economists outraged by the suggestion that PPP lay at the root of CIA's analytical problems with respect to the Soviet economy (especially those who advocate its utility regarding the Chinese economy today) to A. Edward Gottesman, "Two Myths of Globalization." *World Policy Journal*, XXIII: 1 (2006), pp. 37–45. For evidence that the CIA accepted many of the USSR's official figures at face value as they were beginning the Sovietological enterprise, see Allen, "The Validity of Soviet Economic Statistics," passim. Allen concludes, "We can be reasonably sure that economic data presented by the Soviet Union will continue to have both meaning and significance"; see p. 8.

48. Alexseev, *Without Warning*, pp. 220–221. He goes on to give clear examples:

A February 1987 report suggested that "there will be a time in the next year or two, we think, when the question of cutting tools for the next generation of weapons systems will be a serious issue, and when debates begin on the next Five Year Plan. It is clear that the military is going to have to be dealt with insofar as its share of investments is concerned." In July, another CIA paper saw no signs of slackening in what was perceived as Gorbachev's military modernization program. In April 1988, while reporting troubles for Gorbachev with "too few investments chasing too many needs," the CIA testified to Congress that "military expenditures remained at the generally low rate of growth but they remained at an extremely high absolute level," a conclusion that generally fits the quantitative pattern outlined in the declassified NIEs for 1983–1984 and in Robert Gates' briefing of the Joint Economic Committee in 1983.

49. "Soviet National Security Policy: Responses to the Changing Military and Economic Environment, SOV 88-10040CX" (Washington, DC: Directorate of Intelligence, Office of Soviet Analysis, Central Intelligence Agency, 1988). To quote the preceding sentences:

Even if growth is constrained, the present high level of military spending ensures a continuing large input of new weapons that should keep the defense constituency mollified, as long as the military does not sense a serious deterioration of the Soviet side of the military balance. Because so much of the USSR's superpower status rests on military power, however, resistance to any efforts to slacken appreciably the defense effort will not be confined to the military. Indeed, what Soviet military writers tout as the Western thrust into high-technology hardware will continue to be a basis for arguing to increase defense resources.

50. Cited in Lundberg, "CIA and the Fall of the Soviet Empire," p. 2.

51. Weiner, *Legacy of Ashes*, p. 361.

52. Senate Committee on Foreign Relations, *Estimating the Size and Growth of the Soviet Economy: Hearing before the Committee on Foreign Relations*, 101st Congress,

2d session, 1990, p. 49. The Senate is referring to CIA, *Handbook of Economic Statistics* (Washington, DC: The Central Intelligence Agency, 1989).

53. Daniel Patrick Moynihan, "Report of the Commission on Protecting and Reducing Government Secrecy." U.S. Senate, ed. (Washington, DC: U.S. Government Printing Office, 1997), Appendix A.

54. Brooks and Wohlforth, "Power, Globalization and the End of the Cold War," p. 30.

55. Igor Birman, *Secret Incomes of the Soviet State Budget* (The Hague: Martinus Nijhoff, 1981).

56. Quoted in Turner, *Burn before Reading*, p. 218.

57. George P. Shultz, *Turmoil and Triumph: My Years as Secretary of State* (New York: Charles Scribner's & Sons, 1993), pp. 864–865.

58. Ibid., pp. 1002–1003.

59. Seliktar, *Politics, Paradigms, and Intelligence Failures*, p. 158.

60. Turner, *Burn before Reading*, p. 219.

61. Weiner, *Legacy of Ashes*, pp. 417–418.

62. MacEachin, *CIA Assessments of the Soviet Union*.

63. Eberstadt, *The Tyranny of Numbers*, p. 149.

64. Quoted in Lundberg, "CIA and the Fall of the Soviet Empire," p. 18. Emphasis added.

65. Walter Kaufmann, *The Portable Nietzsche* (New York: Penguin Books, 1982), p. 202.

66. Allison, "An Intelligence Agenda," p. 17. Emphasis added.

67. Brzezinski, *Power and Principle,* p. 397.

68. Richard Pipes, *Vixi: Memories of a Non-Belonger* (New Haven, CT: Yale University Press, 2003), p. 72.

69. Peter Rutland, "Who Got It Right and Who Got It Wrong? And Why?" In M. Cox, ed., *Rethinking the Soviet Collapse: Sovietology, the Death of Communism and the New Russia* (London: Pinter, 1998), p. 37.

70. Robert Conquest, *Harvest of Sorrow: Soviet Collectivisation and the Terror-Famine* (London: Pimlico, 1986), p. 5 and passim.

71. Pipes, *Vixi*, p. 72.

72. Quoted in Kotkin, *Armageddon Averted*, p. 86.

73. Quoted in Turner, *Burn before Reading*, p. 220.

74. Pipes, *Vixi*, p. 72.

75. Seliktar, *Politics, Paradigms, and Intelligence Failures*, p. 215.

76. "A Compendium of Analytic Tradecraft Notes, Volume I," pp. 2–3. Emphasis added.

77. Allen, *None So Blind*, p. 35.

78. George A. Carver Jr., "Intelligence in the Age of Glasnost." *Foreign Affairs*, 69: 3 (1990), p. 160. Emphasis added.

79. Bathurst, *Intelligence and the Mirror*, p. 89. Emphasis added.

80. Cherkashin and Feifer, *Spy Handler*, pp. 108–109.

81. J. S. Nye, "Peering into the Future." *Foreign Affairs*, 77 (1994), p. 85.

82. On the other hand, one of the "deans of American national income measurement, Edward Denison" said in 1990 in this context:

> I have been in a lot of countries and I have looked into a lot of stores, but I am convinced you cannot get a clue about relative consumption levels by casual observation. You can tell that one country is richer or poorer, or a lot richer or a lot poorer, but whether it is 3 times or 10 times as high is virtually impossible to say. I do not think that kind of casual observation is evidence one way or another.

Cited in Becker, "Intelligence Fiasco or Reasoned Accounting? CIA Estimates of Soviet GNP." *Post-Soviet Affairs* (1994), p. 321.

83. Oleg Kalugin and Fen Montaigne, *The First Directorate* (New York: St. Martin's Press, 1994), pp. 236–237.

84. Kotkin, *Armageddon Averted*, p. 46.

85. Bathurst, *Intelligence and the Mirror*, p. 73.

86. Seliktar, *Politics, Paradigms, and Intelligence Failures*, p. 216.

87. Gertrude Schroeder, "Soviet Reality Sans Potemkin." *Studies in Intelligence*, 12: 2 (1968), p. 46. A similar argument was made a few years before in *Studies* under an obvious nom de plume in Amerikanskiy Turist, "A Note on Casual Intelligence Acquisition." *Studies in Intelligence*, 2: 3 (1958), pp. 71–74.

88. Schroeder, "Soviet Reality Sans Potemkin," p. 43.

89. Ibid., p. 51. Emphasis in original.

90. Allen, "The Validity of Soviet Economic Statistics," p. 1.

91. Conquest, *Harvest of Sorrow*, p. 8.

92. Bathurst, *Intelligence and the Mirror*, p. 121.

93. Seliktar, *Politics, Paradigms, and Intelligence Failures*, p. 101.

94. Ibid., p. 117.

95. Kotkin, *Armageddon Averted*, p. 53. As Kotkin further observes on p. 59, the mere fact that Gorbachev showed up at his office rather than worked out of a hospital signaled a profound change.

96. Seliktar, *Politics, Paradigms, and Intelligence Failures*, p. 117.

97. Three independent groups looked at Soviet air defenses, missile accuracies, and strategic objectives. They arrived at very different conclusions from those of the CIA. The reports of both teams remain classified, but for a first-hand account of these experiments, and the controversy that they generated, see Pipes, *Vixi*, pp. 134–143.

98. Quoted in Matthias, *America's Strategic Blunders*, p. 309. Also quoted in Pipes, *Vixi*, p. 136.

99. There is some evidence that within the Directorate of Operations this bias against émigrés has been relaxed in certain periods. See, for example, Jones, *The Human Factor*, p. 105.

100. Alexseev, *Without Warning*, page 91.

101. Commission, "Preparing for the 21st Century: An Appraisal of U.S. Intelligence: Report of the Commission on the Roles and Capabilities of the United States Intelligence Community." In *Commission on the Roles and Capabilities of the United States Intelligence Community* (Washington, DC: U.S. Government Printing Office, 1996), chapter 8. Emphasis added.

102. Russell, *Sharpening Strategic Intelligence*, p. 131. The top secret clearance of one of the authors for the USMC took considerably longer than those of most of his peers because of numerous trips abroad, including both tourism and a language course in the USSR.

103. Gates, *From the Shadows*, p. 28.

104. Bearden and Risen, *The Main Enemy*, p. 484.

105. Rutland, "Who Got It Right and Who Got It Wrong? And Why?" p. 37.

106. Ron Hill, "Social Science, 'Slavistics' and Post-Soviet Studies." In M. Cox, ed., *Rethinking the Soviet Collapse: Sovietology, the Death of Communism and the New Russia* (London: Pinter, 1998), p. 216.

107. Scenario planning came out of Herman Kahn and Arnold Wiener's futurology (a term that they originated) done at the Hudson Institute in the mid-1960s. For general background on Shell's scenario planning unit, see Peter Cornelius, Alexander Van de Putte, and Matti Romani, "Three Decades of Scenario Planning in Shell." *California Management Review*, 48: 1 (2005), pp. 92–109.

108. Seliktar, *Politics, Paradigms, and Intelligence Failures*, p. 109. She is referring to Birman, *Secret Incomes of the Soviet State Budget*, passim.

109. Wilhelm, "The Failure of the American Sovietological Economics Profession," p. 69. Supported in Eberstadt, *The Tyranny of Numbers: Mismeasurement and Misrule*, p. 141.

110. An émigré figure from the 1950s and 1960s; see Naum Jasny, *Essays on the Soviet Economy* (New York: F. A. Praeger, 1962).

111. Vadim Belotserkovsky, "Letter to the Future Leaders of the Soviet Union." *Partisan Review*, 2 (1975), p. 269. Cited in Wilhelm, "The Failure of the American Sovietological Economics Profession," page 70.

112. Lundberg, "CIA and the Fall of the Soviet Empire," p. 65.

113. Gates, *From the Shadows*, p. 509.

114. Michael Novak, "The Silent Artillery of Communism." In L. Edwards, ed., *The Collapse of Communism* (Stanford, CA: Hoover Institution Press, 2000), pp. 112–113. Emphasis added.

115. Pipes, *Vixi*, p. 128.

116. Richard Pipes, "The Fall of the Soviet Union." In L. Edwards, ed., *The Collapse of Communism* (Stanford, CA: Hoover Institution Press, 2000), pp. 47–48. Emphasis added.

117. Seliktar, *Politics, Paradigms, and Intelligence Failures*, p. 214. These efforts were part of an effort made in the Reagan administration known by the shorthand "Team B" to incorporate the views of "an intellectual rival" of Sherman Kent, Wilmore Kendall, into analysis. According to Seliktar, Kendall "disputed the epistemic assumption that predictive 'truths' can be separated from the values and outlooks of analysis"; see Kendall, "The Function of Intelligence."

118. As Birman noted at a conference in 2002, "It is important to be scientific, but it is also important not to be wrong." Quoted in Blair A. Ruble, "Occasional Paper #283, U.S. Assessments of the Soviet and Post-Soviet Russian Economy: Lessons Learned and Not Learned" (Washington, DC: Kennan Institute of the Woodrow Wilson International Center for Scholars, 2002), p. 43.

119. Ibid.

120. Clark, *Intelligence Analysis*, p. 235.

121. Moynihan, "The Soviet Economy," p. A19.

122. Seliktar, *Politics, Paradigms, and Intelligence Failures*, p. 215.

123. Eberstadt, *The Tyranny of Numbers*, p. 139. For an example of this credulity, see Allen, "The Validity of Soviet Economic Statistics." See also William Terechow, "The Soviet Atlas as a Source." *Studies in Intelligence*, 10: 2 (1966), pp. 37–42. This is a longstanding problem. Kenneth Arrow, a Nobel laureate in economics, worked as a statistician during World War II. When he discovered that the Army's month-long weather forecasts were worthless, he tried to warn his superiors. In response, he was told, "The Commanding General is well aware the forecasts are no good. However, he needs them for planning purposes."

124. Quoted in Becker, "Intelligence Fiasco or Reasoned Accounting?" p. 317.

125. Alexseev, *Without Warning*, p. 91.

126. See Ruble, "Occasional Paper #283," pp. 44–45.

127. David M. Kennedy, "Sunshine and Shadow: The CIA and the Soviet Economy, Case C16-91-1096.0" (Cambridge, MA: Kennedy School of Government, Harvard University, 1991), p. 27. Emphasis in original.

128. Seliktar, *Politics, Paradigms, and Intelligence Failures*, p. 207.

129. Bathurst, *Intelligence and the Mirror*, p. 41. For a fascinating theory that employs a secret (that is, that papers had been discovered proving Stalin was an *Okhrana* informant), to make sense of Stalin's mysterious behavior see Appendix II of Alexander Orlov, *The March of Time* (London: St. Ermin's Press, 2004).

130. Brooks and Wohlforth, "Power, Globalization and the End of the Cold War," p. 18.

131. Immanuel Wallerstein, *Unthinking Social Science: The Limits of Nineteenth-Century Paradigms* (Philadelphia: Temple University Press, 2001), p. viii.

132. Brooks and Wohlforth, "Power, Globalization and the End of the Cold War," p. 35. See also Alexseev, *Without Warning*.

133. John M. Stopford, Susan Strange, and John S. Henley, *Rival States, Rival Firms: Competition for World Market Shares*, Cambridge Studies in International Relations (Cambridge, UK: Cambridge University Press, 1991), passim.

134. Brooks and Wohlforth, "Power, Globalization and the End of the Cold War," pp. 36–37. Emphasis added. They say:

> [The handicaps of economic isolation of the USSR] greatly increased in relative importance as the cost, complexity, and difficulty of technological development spiraled upward in the late 1970s and 1980s and as the globalization of production concomitantly accelerated. It is easy to see how isolation from the globalization of production increased the difficulty of keeping up with the West in terms of general economic and technological productivity . . . Less obvious is the fact that Soviet isolation from these global production changes simultaneously made it much more difficult to remain technologically competitive in the arms race . . . Interfirm alliances in the 1980s were concentrated in those sectors with rapidly changing technologies and high entry costs, such as microelectronics, computers, aerospace, telecommunications, transportation, new materials, biotechnology, and chemicals. At the same time, production appears to have been most geographically dispersed in those sectors of manufacturing with high levels of R&D costs and significant economies of scale, such as machinery, computers, electronic components, and transportation. These sectors read like a Who's Who of dual-use industries. Thus the very sectors that were becoming most internationalized in the 1980s were those that provide much of the foundation for military power in the modern era. For this reason, Soviet isolation from on-going global production changes became a tremendous handicap relative to the West in the 1980s in the military realm.

135. CIA, Economic Research (ER) 77-10436U, *Soviet Economic Problems and Prospects* (Langley, VA: CIA, July 1977). The other three provide no succor to the agency's defenders: "(1) The drying up of rural sources of urban labor force growth; (2) A slowdown in the growth of capital productivity; and (3) An inefficient and undependable agriculture which may be hit by a return of the harsher—but probably more normal—climatic patterns that prevailed in the 1960s."

136. Gerald K. Haines and Robert E. Leggett, eds., *CIA's Analysis of the Soviet Union 1947–1991: A Documentary Collection* (Washington, DC: Center for the Study of Intelligence, 2001), pp. 207–208.

137. Ibid., p. 218.

138. Benjamin B. Fischer, *At Cold War's End: US Intelligence on the Soviet Union and Eastern Europe* (Washington, DC: History Staff, Center for the Study of Intelligence, 1999), p. 3. Emphasis added.

139. Those copiers that were in the USSR were extremely primitive. When one of the authors was applying for Soviet visas, there was only one place in Washington, D.C., that took acceptable photos for these visas, because all photos submitted to the embassy had to be in black and white and with a particular matte finish to accommodate primitive Soviet copy machines both at the embassy and back in the USSR.

140. Brooks and Wohlforth, "Power, Globalization and the End of the Cold War," p. 115.

141. Saffo, "Six Rules for Effective Forecasting," p. 1.

142. Igor Birman, "The Soviet Economy: Alternative Views." *Russia*, 12 (1986), p. 66. Cited in Wilhelm, "The Failure of the American Sovietological Economics Profession," p. 71.

143. Wilhelm, "The Failure of the American Sovietological Economics Profession," p. 72.

144. Allen Thomson was also a consultant to the National Intelligence Council as an assistant to Larry Gershwin from 1988 through 1996. This account was originally posted in June of 2000 on Norman Yarvin's website, http://yarchive.net/space/politics/soviet_collapse_predictions.html; it was then confirmed—as were the edits of it—on October 4, 2007, though personal e-mail correspondence with Mr. Allen. Emphasis added.

145. It also confirms the operation of several of the social mechanisms that Chapter 2 posits create the agency's identity and culture.

146. Grabo, *Anticipating Surprise*, p. 15.

147. Lundberg, "CIA and the Fall of the Soviet Empire," p. 13.

148. Personal e-mail correspondence arranged by Allen Thomson on October, 5, 2007. Emphasis added. The anonymous official goes on to concede some points to Thomson and the "it was a surprise" thesis. He also—interestingly—echoes the remarks of Ambassador Matlock previously cited regarding the possible effects of leaks; overall, however, he convincingly supports the idea that a drive for consensus distorted analysis regarding the collapse of the USSR:

> In 1988 the last NIE-11-14 on Warsaw Pact Theatre Forces (which has subsequently been declassified) included a KJ [Key Judgement] that stated that the Warsaw Pact was still a formidable fighting force. In terms of equipment and numbers that was true—although it was not believed by any one on the Review Committee except the DIA Rep. That KJ was forced into the NIE by LtGen Lenny Peroots DDIA when the NIE was brought to the NFIB [the National Foreign Intelligence Board]. And the Agency leadership accepted it in order to placate Peroots—after all, it was not

wrong. But the same NIE stated that the Warsaw Pact was declining in size, quality of equipment and capability, and would continue to do so for the period of the estimate. I fought a 12 month battle to get that KJ [included]. I would also note . . . that this estimate made a strong case that one of the possible futures facing the Warsaw Pact was its demise. DIA went ballistic over that, but we kept it in the Estimate, though it did not make the KJs.

Chapter 5

1. John Lewis Gaddis, *We Now Know: Rethinking Cold War History* (New York: Oxford University Press, 1997), p. 260.

2. See Allison and Zelikow, *Essence of Decision*, passim. For a broad look at what can and what cannot be "learned" from the Crisis, see Richard Ned Lebow, "The Cuban Missile Crisis: Reading the Lessons Correctly." *Political Science Quarterly*, 98: 3 (1983), pp. 431–458.

3. John Diamond, *The CIA and the Culture of Failure: US Intelligence from the End of the Cold War to the Invasion of Iraq* (Stanford, CA: Stanford University Press, 2008), p. 3.

4. Shenon, *The Commission*, p. 137. Interestingly, Shenon notes that the day-by-day, hour-by-hour chronology used by the 9/11 Commission to look at the agency's knowledge of Al-Qa'ida measured "at least 150 feet."

5. Unless otherwise indicated, all dates and events are drawn from the site NuclearFiles.org, available at http://nuclearfiles.org/menu/key-issues/nuclear-weapons/history/cold-war/cuban-missile-crisis/timeline.htm. Note: The task of distilling such a complex event into a skeletal timeline is fraught with peril; many will argue that their pet explanatory variable of Soviet behavior (Operation Mongoose and other pre-Crisis CIA activities in Cuba are always popular candidates) is missing from the timeline but was *the* key variable.

6. Allison and Zelikow, *Essence of Decision*, p. 83.

7. Brugioni, *Eyeball to Eyeball*, p. 84.

8. Allison and Zelikow, *Essence of Decision*, p. 88.

9. Anatoli I. Gribkov and William Y. Smith, *Operation Anadyr: US and Soviet Generals Recount the Cuban Missile Crisis* (Chicago: Edition Q, 1994), p. 17.

10. Brugioni, *Eyeball to Eyeball*, p. 91.

11. Chronology of John McCone's Suspicions on the Military Build-up in Cuba Prior to Kennedy's October 22 Speech, 11/30/62; Recollection of Intelligence Prior to the Discovery of Soviet Missiles and of Penkovsky Affair, n.d. Available in Laurence Chang and Peter Kornbluh, eds., *The Cuban Missile Crisis 1962: A National Security Archive Reader* (New York: The New Press, 1998).

12. Available in ibid., p. 67.

13. Site NuclearFiles.org, available at http://nuclearfiles.org/menu/key-issues/nuclear-weapons/history/cold-war/cuban-missile-crisis/timeline.htm

14. Brugioni, *Eyeball to Eyeball*, p. 104.

15. Aleksandr Fursenko and Timothy Naftali, *One Hell of a Gamble: Khrushchev, Castro and Kennedy, 1958–1964. (New York: W. W. Norton, 1997), p. 204.*

16. Max Holland, "The 'Photo Gap' That Delayed Discovery of Missiles." *Studies in Intelligence*, 49: 4 (2005), p. 19.

17. Brugioni, *Eyeball to Eyeball*, p. 169.

18. Ibid., p. 148.

19. Ibid., p. 164.

20. The Soviet Bloc Armed Forces and the Cuban Crisis: A Chronology July–November 1962, 6/18/63, p. 152. Available in Chang and Kornbluh, eds., *The Cuban Missile Crisis 1962.*

21. The question of what constitutes "irrefutable" evidence in this case is dealt with in the following discussion.

22. Holland, "The 'Photo Gap' That Delayed Discovery of Missiles," p. 22.

23. Quoted in Brugioni, *Eyeball to Eyeball*, p. 143.

24. Kent, "A Crucial Estimate Relived," p. 1.

25. Original document reproduced in Chang and Kornbluh, *The Cuban Missile Crisis 1962*, pp. 73–74.

26. Kent, "A Crucial Estimate Relived," p. 1. Emphasis added.

27. Weiner, *Legacy of Ashes*, p. 196.

28. Gaddis, *We Now Know*, pp. 274–275.

29. Original quoted in McAuliffe, *CIA Documents on the Cuban Missile Crisis 1962*, p. 121. Emphasis added.

30. Allison and Zelikow, *Essence of Decision*, p. 219.

31. Brugioni, *Eyeball to Eyeball*, p. 212.

32. CIA, "A Look Back . . . Remembering the Cuban Missile Crisis." *CIA Featured Story Archive* (Langley, VA: CIA, 2007), available at www.cia.gov/news-information/featured-story-archive/2007-featured-story-archive/a-look-back-remembering-the-cuban-missile-crisis.html.

33. Martin, *Wilderness of Mirrors*, p. 144.

34. Gaddis, *We Now Know*, p. 264.

35. Vladislav Zubok and Constantine Pleshakov, *Inside the Kremlin's Cold War: From Stalin to Khrushchev* (Cambridge, MA: Harvard University Press, 1996), p. 268.

36. CIA, "A Look Back . . . Remembering the Cuban Missile Crisis."

37. Allison and Zelikow, *Essence of Decision*, p. 325.

38. There are a few dissenting perspectives to viewing the CIA's record prior to the missiles discovery as an intelligence failure; these again rely on counterfactuals. As Holland notes in a 2005 *Studies* article:

It has been argued, therefore, that the system basically worked. . . . Yet some students of the missile crisis have gone too far, raising a counterfactual argument to claim that the CIA's misestimates were the most significant shortcoming, and that the photo gap, in essence, did not even matter. "Discovery [of the missiles] a week or two earlier in October . . . would not have changed the situation faced by the president and his advisers," Raymond Garthoff, one of the most esteemed scholars of the crisis, has written. This is probably not the most appropriate counterfactual argument to pose, given that the missiles were found none too soon.

39. Gribkov and Smith, *Operation Anadyr*, p. 3.

40. Insofar as they touch on CIA analysis of Soviet motives, possibilities for Khrushchev's actions will be considered later in the discussion. Here, one may note, however, that speculation about Khrushchev's medley of motives is so varied that Fursenko compares it to Agatha Christie's popular thriller, *Murder on the Orient Express*:

The detective Hercule Poirot encounters a train full of individuals who had motive and opportunity to kill the wealthy American found dead in his luxury compartment. Students of the Cuban Missile Crisis have suggested a series of plausible explanations for Khrushchev's decision in May 1962 to break with Soviet tradition and station nuclear weapons outside of Eurasia. Some people have claimed that Khrushchev did this to paper over the USSR's strategic inferiority by doubling at a stroke the number of Soviet missiles that could hit the United States. Another explanation, especially popular in the 1980s, was that Khrushchev was genuinely concerned about the likelihood of an American invasion and thought that a battery of medium- and intermediate-range missiles could deter Kennedy. It has also been suggested that anger at the American decision to station Jupiter missiles in Turkey provoked the impulsive Khrushchev. Finally, there are those who interpreted Khrushchev's decision as an attempt to guarantee the status quo in Cuba and to prevent any attempt by the Chinese to dislodge him from the leadership of international communism. Like the all-star cast in this Christie mystery, all of these factors are responsible for the act. Each played a part in pushing Khrushchev to take the very serious step [of deciding to station missiles in Cuba].

See Fursenko and Naftali, *One Hell of a Gamble*, pp. 182–183. According to Lebow, new evidence from former Soviet officials suggests that Khrushchev wanted "to deter an anticipated American invasion, to compensate partially for American strategic superiority, and to establish an atmosphere of psychological equality." He may also have had strong domestic incentives that grew out of the failure of his economic and political reforms. See Richard Ned Lebow and Janice Gross Stein, "Back to the Past: Counterfactuals and the Cuban Missile Crisis." In P. E. Tetlock and A. Belkin, eds., *Counterfactual Thought Experiments in World Politics* (Princeton, NJ: Princeton University Press, 1996), p. 134. In his autobiography, Khrushchev himself says:

We had to think up some way of confronting America with more than words. We had to establish a tangible and effective deterrent to American interference in the Caribbean. But what exactly? The logical answer was missiles. The United States already surrounded the Soviet Union with its own bombers and missiles. We knew the American missiles were aimed at us in Turkey and Italy, to say nothing of West Germany. Our vital industrial centers were directly threatened by planes armed with atomic bombs and guided missiles tipped with nuclear warheads.

See Nikita Sergeevich Khrushchev, *Khrushchev Remembers*. S. Talbott, trans. (New York: Little Brown & Company 1970), p. 493.

41. Fursenko and Naftali, *One Hell of a Gamble*, p. 171.

42. See *The 9/11 Commission Report*, pp. 339–347.

43. Marc Trachtenberg, *History & Strategy*. Princeton Studies in International History and Politics (Princeton, NJ: Princeton University Press, 1991), p. 203. He says that in a meeting with his defense secretary, Eisenhower

. . . could see reasons for putting IRBMs into such areas as Britain, Germany and France. However, when it comes to "flank" or advanced areas such as Greece, the matter seems very questionable. He reverted to his analogy—if Cuba or Mexico were to become Communist inclined, and the Soviets were to send arms and equipment—what would we feel we had to do then.

44. Available in Chang and Kornbluh, eds., *The Cuban Missile Crisis 1962*, p. 16.

45. Weiner, *Legacy of Ashes*, p. 191.

46. Allison and Zelikow, *Essence of Decision*, p. 80.

47. Roberta Wohlstetter, "Cuba and Pearl Harbor." *Foreign Affairs*, 43: 4 (1965), p. 698.

48. Arnold L. Horelick, "The Cuban Missile Crisis: An Analysis of Soviet Calculations and Behavior." *World Politics*, 16: 3 (1964), p. 376.

49. Gribkov and Smith, *Operation Anadyr*, p. 104.

50. Zubok and Pleshakov, *Inside the Kremlin's Cold War*, p. 359.

51. Gaddis, *We Now Know*, pp. 274–275.

52. Chang and Kornbluh, *The Cuban Missile Crisis 1962*, p. xii.

53. Russell, *Sharpening Strategic Intelligence*, p. 34. See also Allison and Zelikow, *Essence of Decision*, p. 216. Here it is fair to note that, despite the information supplied by the spy in the USSR, Oleg Penkovsky, very little information was available on Soviet practices transporting and storing strategic nuclear weapons, and even less was known about the field deployment of tactical nuclear weapons (Brugioni, *Eyeball to Eyeball*, p. 541). This is understandable. "Security measures [for the USSR's nuclear weapons] included denial of access to production centres (including the establishment of ten "closed" nuclear cities), and the isolation of personnel employed in them" (at least fifteen of 114 Gulag camps supported these cities). In short, there was a spe-

cial cocoon of secrecy—extreme even by Soviet standards—around any information "even remotely associated with nuclear weapons" and extensive counterintelligence and technical countermeasures operations.

54. Betts, *Enemies of Intelligence*, p. 190. Emphasis added.

55. Gaddis, *We Now Know*, p. 248.

56. Chang and Kornbluh, *The Cuban Missile Crisis 1962*, p. xi.

57. Fursenko and Naftali, *One Hell of a Gamble*, p. 205. Emphasis added.

58. Laqueur, *A World of Secrets*, p. 367 fn 116.

59. In a memorandum for the director entitled "Implications of an Announcement by the President That the US Would Conduct Overhead Reconnaissance of Cuba, and the Actual Reconnaissance Thereafter."

60. McAuliffe, *CIA Documents on the Cuban Missile Crisis 1962*, p. 121.

61. James H. Hansen, "Soviet Deception in the Cuban Missile Crisis." *Studies in Intelligence*, 46: 1 (2002), p. 56. Emphasis added.

62. John Stennis et al., "Investigation of the Preparedness Program, Interim Report on the Cuban Military Buildup by the Preparedness Investigating Subcommittee" (Washington, DC: Committee on Armed Services, U.S. Senate, 88th Congress, 1st Session, 1963), p. 2.

63. Laqueur, *A World of Secrets*, p. 367 fn 115.

64. For the reasons for this poor coverage, see Holland, "The 'Photo Gap' That Delayed Discovery of Missiles," passim. See also Snider, *The Agency and the Hill*, p. 231.

65. Allison and Zelikow, *Essence of Decision*, p. 219.

66. Laqueur, *A World of Secrets*, p. 367 fn 114.

67. Oleg A. Bukharin, "The Cold War Atomic Intelligence Game, 1945–70." *Studies in Intelligence*, 48: 2 (2004), p. 2.

68. The central tenet of *maskirovka* is

to prevent an adversary from discovering Russian intentions by deceiving him about the nature, scope, and timing of an operation. *Maskirovka* covers a broad range of concepts, from deception at the strategic planning level to camouflage at the troop level. Russian military texts indicate that *maskirovka* is treated as an operational art to be polished by professors of military science and officers who specialize in this area.

See Hansen, "Soviet Deception in the Cuban Missile Crisis," p. 49. For more on *maskirovka*, see Henry S. Marsh and Jennie A. Stevens, "Surprise and Deception in Soviet Military Thought, Part I." *Military Review*: June (1982), pp. 1–11. For a wider history of *maskirovka* in the context of deception and operational mass see Shimon Naveh, *In Pursuit of Military Excellence: The Evolution of Operational Theory*, The Cummings Center Series (London: Frank Cass, 2004), pp. 30–69. For more on strategic deception generally, see Ronald G. Sherwin and Barton Whaley, "Understanding

Strategic Deception: An Analysis of 93 Cases." In D. C. Daniel and K. L. Herbig, eds., *Strategic Military Deception* (New York: Pergamon Press, 1982).

69. Fursenko and Naftali, *One Hell of a Gamble*, p. 190.

70. Brugioni, *Eyeball to Eyeball*, p. 219.

71. Wohlstetter, "Cuba and Pearl Harbor," p. 691.

72. Stennis, "Investigation of the Preparedness Program, Interim Report on the Cuban Military Buildup by the Preparedness Investigating Subcommittee," pp. 5 and 10.

73. Quoted in Weiner, *Legacy of Ashes*, p. 196.

74. Allison and Zelikow, *Essence of Decision*, p. 219.

75. Matthias, *America's Strategic Blunders*, p. 177.

76. Gribkov and Smith, *Operation Anadyr*, p. 97.

77. Quoted in Brugioni, *Eyeball to Eyeball*, p. 99.

78. McGeorge Bundy, *Danger and Survival: Choices about the Bomb in the First Fifty Years* (New York: Random House, 1988), p. 415.

79. Grabo, *Anticipating Surprise*.

80. Betts, *Enemies of Intelligence*, p. 56.

81. Klaus Knorr, "Failures in National Intelligence Estimates: The Case of the Cuban Missiles." *World Politics*, 16 (1964), p. 461.

82. Brugioni, *Eyeball to Eyeball*, p. 156.

83. Ibid., p. 93.

84. Ibid., p. 538.

85. Thomas L. Hughes, *The Fate of Facts in a World of Men: Foreign Policy and Intelligence-Making*, Headline Series (New York: The Foreign Policy Association, 1976), p. 44. Emphasis added.

86. Zubok and Pleshakov, *Inside the Kremlin's Cold War*, p. 264. See also Gaddis, *We Now Know*, pp. 276–277.

87. Allison and Zelikow, *Essence of Decision*, p. 94.

88. Gaddis, *We Now Know*, p. 262.

89. Adapted from James Richter, *Khrushchev's Double-Bind: International Pressures and Domestic Coalition Politics* (Baltimore, MD: The Johns Hopkins University Press, 1994), p. 194. Quoted in Zubok and Pleshakov, *Inside the Kremlin's Cold War*, p. 259.

90. Allison and Zelikow, *Essence of Decision*, pp. 91–92.

91. Khrushchev, *Khrushchev Remembers*, p. 547.

92. Gaddis, *We Now Know*, pp. 260–261.

93. Fursenko and Naftali, *One Hell of a Gamble*, p. 178.

94. Allison and Zelikow, *Essence of Decision*, p. 95.

95. Gaddis, *We Now Know*, p. 264. Emphasis in original.

96. Betts, *Enemies of Intelligence*, p. 56.

97. By relying on precedent, the CIA faced what philosophers call the "problem of inductive knowledge": How could they logically go from specific past instances of Soviet behavior to reach a general (and accurate) knowledge of future Soviet actions? Here we argue that the agency's culture and identity—its focus on secrets, its homogeneity, and the atmosphere of scientism permeating the CIA—formed barriers to such inductive knowledge. As a result, the CIA almost fell into the trap to which all inductive reasoning is prey, a problem that Taleb illustrates with a turkey (this is Bertrand Russell's famous example of the chicken modified for a North American audience): Every single feeding firms up the bird's belief that it is the general rule of life to be fed every day by friendly humans. On the Wednesday before Thanksgiving, after hundreds of consistent observations (and following each of which, its confidence grows) the turkey has reached, unaware, the moment of maximum danger. "What," Taleb asks, "can a turkey learn about what is in store for it tomorrow from the events of yesterday? Certainly less than it thinks." Nassim Nicholas Taleb, *The Black Swan: The Impact of the Highly Improbable* (New York: Random House, 2007), pp. 40–41.

98. Robert M. Gates, "The Prediction of Soviet Intentions." *Studies in Intelligence*, 17: 1 (1973), p. 40.

99. Matthias, *America's Strategic Blunders*, p. 181.

100. Gribkov and Smith, *Operation Anadyr*, p. 28.

101. Kent, "A Crucial Estimate Relived," p. 5. Emphasis added. Kent goes on to describe the scientific method thus:

> In very general and, I fear, over-simplified terms, the process goes like this. After a confrontation of the problem and some decisions as to how it should be handled, there is a ransacking of files and minds for all information relating to the problem; and an evaluation, analysis, and digestion of this information. There are emergent hypotheses as to the possible aggregate meaning of the information; some emerged before, some after its absorption. No one can say whence came these essential yeasts of fruitful thought. Surely they grow best in a medium of knowledge, experience, and intuitive understanding. When they unfold, they are checked back against the facts, weighed in the light of the specific circumstances and the analysts' general knowledge and understanding of the world scene. Those that cannot stand up fall; those that do stand up are ordered in varying degrees of likelihood.

102. Ibid., p. 7. Emphasis added.

103. Gaddis, *We Now Know*, p. 248.

104. Gates, "The Prediction of Soviet Intentions," p. 39. As he goes on to note, Czech Communist leaders returning from Moscow in 1968 remarked that they had expected "narrow dogmatists" but not the "vulgar thugs" that they found!

105. Knorr, "Failures in National Intelligence Estimates," p. 460.

106. Rebecca Mitchell and Stephen Nicholas, "Knowledge Creation in Groups: The Value of Cognitive Diversity, Transactive Memory and Open-Mindedness Norms." *Electronic Journal of Knowledge Management,* 4: 1 (2006), p. 68. Contemporary collaborative intelligence efforts may go some way towards addressing this problem. These include "Wikistrat" and the teaching of strategic intelligence through games with diverse players; see http://www.wikistrat.com/ and Kristan J. Wheaton, *Teaching Strategic Intelligence through Games,* available at http://sourcesandmethods.blogspot .com/2010/07/teaching-strategic-intelligence-through.html.

107. Unexamined analogical reasoning, of course, can be exceptionally misleading. See, for example, Yuen Foong Khong, *Analogies at War: Korea, Munich, Dien Bien Phu, and the Vietnam Decisions of 1965.* (Princeton, NJ: Princeton University Press, 1992); loose analogies are frequently crudely applied by the media. Consider, for example, the variety of conflicts considered "Vietnam-style quagmires" in the press: The list includes Nicaragua, Haiti, Bosnia, Colombia, Afghanistan and Iraq (all new American Vietnams), Afghanistan (the Soviet Union's Vietnam), Chechnya (Russia's Vietnam), Kashmir (India's Vietnam), Lebanon (Israel's Vietnam), Angola (Cuba's Vietnam), the Basque territory (Spain's Vietnam), Eritrea (Ethiopia's Vietnam), Northern Ireland (Britain's Vietnam) and Kampuchea (Vietnam's Vietnam). See Philip E. Tetlock, *Expert Political Judgment: How Good Is It? How Can We Know?* (Princeton, NJ: Princeton University Press, 2005), p. 38.

108. Isabella Ginor and Gideon Remez, *Foxbats over Dimona: The Soviets' Nuclear Gamble in the Six-Day War* (New Haven, CT: Yale University Press, 2007), pp. 20–21 and 31–32.

109. Fursenko and Naftali, *One Hell of a Gamble,* p. 196.

110. Gribkov and Smith, *Operation Anadyr,* p. 23.

111. Hansen, "Soviet Deception in the Cuban Missile Crisis," p. 50.

112. Gribkov and Smith, *Operation Anadyr,* p. 31.

113. Facts in this section taken from ibid. There is also at least one source that indicates that shipments through the Turkish or Danish Straits could have been monitored for radioactivity but apparently were not, as the Soviets did not use more northerly routes. See Dwayne Anderson, "On the Trail of the Alexandrovsk." *Studies in Intelligence,* 10: 1 (1966), p. 39.

114. Allison and Zelikow, *Essence of Decision,* p. 211.

115. Hansen, "Soviet Deception in the Cuban Missile Crisis," p. 53.

116. Justin F. Gleichauf, "A Listening Post in Miami." *Studies in Intelligence,* 46: 10 (2001), p. 52.

117. Brugioni, *Eyeball to Eyeball,* p. 94.

118. Ibid., pp. 204–205. For more on what the Soviets knew about the U-2 program, see Alexander Orlov, "The U-2 Program: A Russian Officer Remembers." *Studies in Intelligence* (Winter 1998–1999), pp. 5–14.

119. Fursenko and Naftali, *One Hell of a Gamble*, p. 192.

120. As Hansen relates:

The General Staff's code name for the operation—Anadyr—was designed to mis-lead Soviets as well as foreigners about the destination of the equipment. Anadyr is the name of a river flowing into the Bering Sea, the capital of the Chukotsky Au-tonomous District, and a bomber base in that desolate region. Operation Anadyr was designed to suggest to lower-level Soviet commanders—and Western spies—that the action was a strategic exercise in the far north of the USSR. Promoting the illusion, the troops that were called up for the Cuban expedition were told only that they were going to a cold region.

Hansen, "Soviet Deception in the Cuban Missile Crisis," p. 50.

121. Fursenko and Naftali, *One Hell of a Gamble*, p. 191.

122. Hansen, "Soviet Deception in the Cuban Missile Crisis," p. 52.

123. Fursenko and Naftali, *One Hell of a Gamble*, p. 198.

124. Gribkov and Smith, *Operation Anadyr*, p. 39.

125. Fursenko and Naftali, *One Hell of a Gamble*, pp. 193–194.

126. Brugioni, *Eyeball to Eyeball*, p. 132.

127. Ibid., p. 115.

128. Fursenko and Naftali, *One Hell of a Gamble*, pp. 207–208. At the height of the Crisis a U.S. plane again blundered into Soviet airspace. Kennedy—undoubtedly thinking back to his days in the Navy—is reported to have remarked, "There is always some poor son-of-a-bitch who doesn't get the word." See Allison and Zelikow, *Essence of Decision*, p. 143.

129. Brugioni, *Eyeball to Eyeball*, p. 109.

130. Quoted in ibid., p. 140.

131. "A U.S. attack on Cuba would mean nuclear war": Text of Soviet statement in *The New York Times*, September 12, 1962, p. 1.

132. Brugioni, *Eyeball to Eyeball*, p. 140.

133. Gribkov and Smith, *Operation Anadyr*, p. 3.

134. Brugioni, *Eyeball to Eyeball*, p. 93.

135. The incident and all quotations are from Fursenko and Naftali, *One Hell of a Gamble*, pp. 207–209. The American poet Robert Frost, also visiting the USSR, got a similar surprise invitation a few days later, where he pressed Khrushchev to forswear "blackguarding." After the visit, Frost was "exhilarated" and said of Khrushchev: "He's a great man; he knows what power is and isn't afraid to take hold of it." Events in coming months would prove the poet a prophet. See Fursenko and Naftali, *One Hell of a Gamble*, pp. 210–211.

136. Joint Chiefs of Staff, "Military Deception: Joint Publication 3-13.4" (Washington, DC: Joint Chiefs of Staff of United States Department of Defense, 2006), pp. 1–2.

137. Brugioni, *Eyeball to Eyeball*, pp. 157–158.

138. Ibid., p. 189.

139. Gribkov and Smith, *Operation Anadyr*, p. 15.

140. Specifically, according to Allison, this difference in behavior can partly be explained by the fact that the loading in the USSR, shipping, and unloading of the missiles was planned by the Soviet General Staff, working closely with Soviet intelligence agencies. Once the missiles were unloaded, however, operational command passed to the Group for Soviet Forces in Cuba, and their SOPs took over. For that specific fact, see Allison and Zelikow, *Essence of Decision*, p. 211.

141. Laqueur, *A World of Secrets*, p. 164.

142. Less than 1 percent of the total Soviet land area was open to their inspection. See William F. Scott, "The Face of Moscow in the Missile Crisis." *Studies in Intelligence*, 37: 5 (1966), p. 105.

143. Ibid.

144. Brugioni, *Eyeball to Eyeball*, p. 88.

145. Ibid., p. 101.

146. Hansen, "Soviet Deception in the Cuban Missile Crisis," p. 53n42.

147. Martin, *Wilderness of Mirrors*, p. 120.

148. Allison, *Historical Dictionary of Cold War Counterintelligence*, p. 74.

149. Gleichauf, "A Listening Post in Miami," p. 51.

150. Note that the man that the CIA sent to run the center apparently did not speak Spanish: He later recounted that in response to threatening phone calls that he was receiving at home, "I memorized Spanish insults, which I directed at Fidel via the open line. The calls eventually dwindled." Ibid., p. 50.

151. Brugioni, *Eyeball to Eyeball*, pp. 86–87.

152. Ibid., p. 117.

153. Allison and Zelikow, *Essence of Decision*, p. 222.

154. Brugioni, *Eyeball to Eyeball*, p. 185.

155. Allison and Zelikow, *Essence of Decision*, p. 222. McCone added laconically: "Quite a job." At the height of the Crisis, the analysts nevertheless completed the entire job in about a single day. This achievement is put in perspective by a quotation from the founder of the U.K. Air Ministry's Photographic Interpretation Unit: "Looking through magnifying glasses at minute objects in a photograph required the patience of Job and the skill of a good darner of socks." Andrew, *For the President's Eyes Only*, p. 200.

156. Allison and Zelikow, *Essence of Decision*, p. 203.

157. Ibid., p. 208.

158. Gribkov and Smith, *Operation Anadyr*, p. 16. Soviet General Staff officers quickly realized this fact while the operation was underway:

A detailed inspection of the area convinced me that even with the commanders' best efforts, total concealment was next to impossible . . . With some bitterness, I recalled Sharaf Rashidov's report that palm trees would make the missiles undetectable. Only someone with no military background, and no understanding of the paraphernalia that accompanied the rockets themselves, could have reached such a conclusion. But the Politburo had accepted it uncritically.

159. Ibid., p. 40.

160. Allison and Zelikow, *Essence of Decision*, p. 213.

161. Ibid., p. 207.

162. Ibid., p. 208. Allison notes here too that they "did use lights for night-time construction in the frantic days after the missiles were discovered."

163. Brugioni, *Eyeball to Eyeball*, p. 163.

164. Thomas R. Johnson and David A. Hatch, *NSA and the Cuban Missile Crisis* (Fort Meade, MD: U.S. National Security Agency, 1998), p. 1. On the other hand, Admiral Thomas H. Moorer, one-time chief of Naval Operations and subsequently chairman of the Joint Chiefs of Staff, told the U.S. Congress that "*electronic intelligence led to the photographic intelligence* that gave indisputable evidence of the Soviet missiles in Cuba." Quoted in James Bamford, *Body of Secrets: Anatomy of the Ultra-Secret National Security Agency* (New York: Anchor Books, 2002), p. 109. Emphasis added. Thus, one must agree with Laqueur that SIGINT might have played a role, but that "in the Cuban missile crisis, it had to appear that human intelligence and aerial photography provided the decisive intelligence information." Laqueur, *A World of Secrets*, p. 165.

165. Johnson and Hatch, *NSA and the Cuban Missile Crisis*, pp. 3–4.

166. Ibid., p. 2.

167. Brugioni, *Eyeball to Eyeball*, pp. 79–80. These were not the only pseudonyms used, but false names in general caused the Soviets problems. Indeed, the Soviet commander on the ground, Pliyev, even protested when he was issued a passport in the name of "Ivan Aleksandrovich Pavlov," that he "did not intend to take on a strange name, much less leave his real identification papers at the General Staff. He did not want to part with them for anything, and Ivanov and I had a hard time convincing him to live and work under a pseudonym from then on." With some understatement, Gribkov continues, "We should have taken that episode as an early warning of Pliyev's lack of subtlety and the difficulties it would spawn." See Gribkov and Smith, *Operation Anadyr*, p. 25.

168. Bamford, *Body of Secrets*, p. 102.

169. Hansen, "Soviet Deception in the Cuban Missile Crisis," p. 54 and fn 55, citing Johnson and Hatch, *NSA and the Cuban Missile Crisis*, pp. 2–3.

170. Bamford, *Body of Secrets*, p. 676 fn 109. Through electronic intercepts, the CIA also established that by fall of 1962 there were at least seven separate Soviet tactical radio networks in Cuba (which allowed them, incidentally, "to dispense with the existing American-built telephone and microwave systems" on the island). Laqueur, *A World of Secrets*, p. 166. While the Cubans never tried to scramble voice communications, the Soviets made a concerted effort to speak only Spanish on unencrypted networks. They would nevertheless revert to their native tongue when dealing with complex subjects. Bamford, *Body of Secrets*, pp. 99–101. One of the authors had similar experiences in the USMC that indicated that even exceptionally well-disciplined and trained troops with clear procedures had trouble maintaining "radio discipline" when faced with novel problems.

171. Bamford, *Body of Secrets*, p. 107. The NSA itself sums up the information it gained in this pre-Crisis period in this way:

> Cuban air defenses improved at an accelerating pace. In May, SIGINT reports had the first indication of airborne fire control radar on MIG-17 and MIG-19 planes. Ground radar activity became heavier all over the island. By early summer, NSA analysts concluded that the Cubans were putting together an air defense system copied from the Soviet model. Equipment, training, and procedures were the same. In fact, by early fall NSA was listening to Russian ground controllers speaking in heavily accented Spanish to Cuban pilots.

Johnson and Hatch, *NSA and the Cuban Missile Crisis*, p. 4.

172. Bamford, *Body of Secrets*, p. 104. How quickly SIGINT was passed from the NSA to the CIA is not known; what *is* known is that there was a shortage of Spanish-speaking linguists at NSA. This is a grim foreshadowing of the 9/11 case, where the NSA was farming most Taliban intercepts prior to 9/11 out to Pakistan's ISI for translation.

173. Woodrow J. Kuhns, "Intelligence Failures: Forecasting and the Lessons of Epistemology." In R. K. Betts and T. G. Mahnken, eds., *Paradoxes of Strategic Intelligence* (London: Frank Cass, 2003), p. 84.

174. Robert Gates, as a junior analyst in the early 1970s, makes this point exactly. He writes that a CIA analyst "must somehow perceive a change in policy between the time the decision is made in Moscow and the time when it is manifested in action—such as the building of the Berlin Wall or the dispatch of missiles to Cuba." Gates, "The Prediction of Soviet Intentions," p. 44. Khrushchev's plan was obviously "manifested in action" in the USSR long before anything changed in Cuba.

175. Hansen, "Soviet Deception in the Cuban Missile Crisis," p. 54. Citing Johnson and Hatch, *NSA and the Cuban Missile Crisis*, pp. 2–3.

176. Brugioni, *Eyeball to Eyeball*, p. 101.

177. Ibid., p. 92.

178. Fursenko and Naftali, *One Hell of a Gamble*, p. 216.

179. Gribkov and Smith, *Operation Anadyr*, p. 57.

180. Allison and Zelikow, *Essence of Decision*, p. 210.

181. Available in Chang and Kornbluh, *The Cuban Missile Crisis 1962*, p. 68.

182. Brugioni, *Eyeball to Eyeball*, p. 103.

183. Gribkov and Smith, *Operation Anadyr*, p. 38.

184. Brugioni, *Eyeball to Eyeball*, p. 103.

185. Allison and Zelikow, *Essence of Decision*, p. 337.

186. Holland, "The 'Photo Gap' that Delayed Discovery of Missiles," p. 21.

187. Bamford, *Body of Secrets*, p. 108.

188. Ibid.

189. Weiner, *Legacy of Ashes*, p. 194.

190. Holland, "The 'Photo Gap' That Delayed Discovery of Missiles."

191. CIA, "A Look Back . . . Remembering the Cuban Missile Crisis."

192. Holland, "The 'Photo Gap' That Delayed Discovery of Missiles," p. 23.

193. Johnson and Hatch, *NSA and the Cuban Missile Crisis*, pp. 5–6.

194. There is a large body of theory surrounding the working of bureaucracies, some of which Allison ably explores in his Model II. See Allison and Zelikow, *Essence of Decision*, pp. 143–196. After completing an MBA, serving in the U.S. military, working inside several large banks, and viewing from inside numerous large organizations as a management consultants, the authors favor two works to plumb the depths of bureaucracies: C. Northcote Parkinson, *Parkinson's Law, or The Pursuit of Progress* (London: Penguin, 1957) and also Lawrence J. Peter and Raymond Hull, *The Peter Principle: Why Things Always Go Wrong* (London: Souvenir Press, 1969). They distil and illustrate without management or sociological jargon the actual operation of large organizations.

195. Laqueur, *A World of Secrets*, p. 80.

196. Holland, "The 'Photo Gap' That Delayed Discovery of Missiles," p. 23.

197. Ibid., p. 16.

198. Brugioni, *Eyeball to Eyeball*, p. 63.

199. Ibid., pp. 64–65.

200. Allison and Zelikow, *Essence of Decision*, p. 333. Ironically, this was the first meeting at which McCone raised the possibility of Soviet missiles in Cuba. Equally ironically, on the matter of assassination, McCone was then bypassed, and the necessary authority and supervision of efforts to kill Castro apparently came directly from now often beatified Robert Kennedy.

201. Laqueur, *A World of Secrets*, p. 81.

202. Kam, *Surprise Attack*, p. 162. Emphasis added.

203. Brugioni, *Eyeball to Eyeball*, p. 97.

204. Holland, "The 'Photo Gap' That Delayed Discovery of Missiles," p. 19.

205. This cable of September 10, 1962, is quoted in a declassified top secret memorandum of October 31, 1962, "Soviet MRBMs in Cuba," reproduced in McAuliffe, *CIA
Documents on the Cuban Missile Crisis 1962*, p. 13.

206. Laqueur, *A World of Secrets*, p. 168. Emphasis in original.

207. McAuliffe, *CIA Documents on the Cuban Missile Crisis 1962*, p. 41.

208. Ibid.

209. Ibid., p. 42.

210. Quoted in James Kenneth McDonald, "CIA and Warning Failures." In L. C.
Jenssen and O. Riste, eds., *Intelligence in the Cold War: Organisation, Role, International Cooperation* (Oslo: Norwegian Institute for Defence Studies, 2001), p. 49.

211. Chang and Kornbluh, *The Cuban Missile Crisis 1962*, p. xi.

212. Weiner, *Legacy of Ashes*, p. 195.

213. Richard K. Betts, *Surprise Attack: Lessons for Defense Planning* (Washington,
DC: Brookings Institution, 1982), p. 94.

214. There is some disagreement in the sources about the exact number and type
of pre-Crisis missile sightings. According to "Excerpt from Memorandum for Director of Central Intelligence, 'CIA handling of the Soviet Buildup in Cuba' 14 November,
1962," there were 138 missile sightings in Cuba from May to August and nearly 900
in September, but almost all seemed connected to SAM or cruise missile installations;
the three that could not be traced back to those categories were "negated" by U-2
photos. See McAuliffe, *CIA Documents on the Cuban Missile Crisis 1962*, pp. 99–102.

215. McDonald, "CIA and Warning Failures," p. 48.

216. Betts explains this linkage:

A human source in Cuba reported sighting a missile on September 12, but the
report did not arrive at the CIA until September 21, two days after the meeting of
the U.S. Intelligence Board. *The time required to process reports could have been
shortened, but previously there had been no reason to invest the resources and take
the necessary risks (endangering agents and communication networks), because the
value of these sources had usually been minimal.*

Betts, *Surprise Attack*, p. 88. Emphasis added.

217. Brugioni, *Eyeball to Eyeball*, p. 87.

218. Ibid., p. 149. The imperfections of the intelligence cycle as a representation of
reality are here evident.

219. Wohlstetter, *Pearl Harbor*, pp. 386–396. In this specific instance regarding
the clue offered by the amount of water the ships were drawing, Wohlstetter certainly
agrees, writing:

[The] ships, in transit, had been noted to be riding high in the water. If intelligence
analysts in the American community had been more ready to suspect the intro-

duction of strategic missiles, would this information have led them to surmise, before as well as after October 14, that these ships carried "space-consuming [that is, large-volume, low-density] cargo such as an MRBM" rather than a bulk cargo?

220. Hansen, "Soviet Deception in the Cuban Missile Crisis," p. 54, citing Domingo Amuchastegui, "Cuban Intelligence and the October Crisis." *Intelligence and National Security*, 13: 3 (1998), p. 54.

221. For a discussion of "crying wolf" and so-called warning fatigue, see Mark M. Lowenthal, *Intelligence: From Secrets to Policy* (Washington, DC: CQ Press, 2002), p. 87.

222. Clark, *Intelligence Analysis*, p. 117.

223. The same defense was made in *Studies* by DI officers to DO critics soon after the Crisis. See Harlow T. Munson and W. P. Southard, "Two Witnesses for the Defense." *Studies in Intelligence*, 8: 4 (1964), pp. 93–98. They say on p. 97 that "we agree with Mr. Kent that Khrushchev made a serious mistake in judgment."

224. Kam, *Surprise Attack*, p. 136.

225. Theodore Shackley, *Spymaster: My Life in the CIA* (Dulles, VA: Potomac Books, 2006), pp. 62–63.

226. Allison and Zelikow, *Essence of Decision*, p. 335. Note that this is a prime example of mirror imaging of the customer, discussed in Chapter 2.

227. Ibid.

228. Ariel Levite, "Intelligence and Strategic Surprises" (PhD dissertation, Cornell, 1983), p. 139.

229. M. E. O. Gravalos, "Pitfall of a Latin Quirk." *Studies in Intelligence*, 7: 4 (1963), pp. 31–32. Emphasis added.

230. Andrew Wixson, "Portrait of a Cuban Refugee." *Studies in Intelligence* (Summer 1964), p. 36.

231. Ibid., p. 41.

232. Gleichauf, "A Listening Post in Miami," p. 52.

233. Fursenko and Naftali, *One Hell of a Gamble*, p. 221. Weiner also attributes the key insight to HUMINT, but in a different version:

> They took another look at a message received at least eight days earlier from a road watcher, a Cuban agent at the lowest rung in the intelligence hierarchy. He had reported that a convoy of seventy-foot Soviet tractor-trailers was moving mysterious canvas-covered cargo the size of thick telephone poles around the Cuban countryside near the town of San Cristóbal. "I never knew his name," the CIA's Sam Halpern said. "This one agent, the only decent result out of [Operation] Mongoose, this agent told us there's something funny going on . . . And after ten days of arguing in front of the Committee on Overhead Reconnaissance, it was finally approved to have an overflight.

See Weiner, *Legacy of Ashes*, p. 195. Laqueur, meanwhile, maintains that French intelligence apparently provided the CIA with at least one credible eyewitness report of missiles under transport and that that drove the overflight.

234. Quoted in Weiner, *Legacy of Ashes*, p. 196. Emphasis added.

235. Martin, *Wilderness of Mirrors*, p. 141. The incident is worth reporting in detail. Martin says,

> On September 12, three days after the *Omsk* unloaded her mysterious cargo under cover of darkness, a forty-four-year-old Cuban accountant in a small town southwest of Havana looked up from his desk to see a large missile being towed through the streets. By coincidence, the accountant was wrestling with a problem that hinged on the dimensions of the property across the street. As the missile passed by, he was able to gauge its precise length. The accountant packed his bags and headed for Florida . . . On September 20, eight days after he had spotted the oversized missile outside his office window, the Cuban accountant reached the CIA's refugee-debriefing center at Opa-Locka, Florida. The dimensions that he gave his interrogators exactly matched those of a Soviet medium range ballistic missile (MRBM). The interrogators, who had been listening to exiles tell of Soviet missiles in Cuba for more than a year, were doubtful. The accountant was shown photographs and drawings of all types of missiles from around the world. The pictures had all been reduced in size so that he would have to rely on characteristics other than length in attempting to identify the missile he had seen. Without hesitation, he pointed to a picture of the Soviet MRBM. The report was forwarded to Washington, where it was greeted with the same weary skepticism born of a thousand false missile sightings. "Doubt that this should be in meters, probably ought to be in feet," one analyst noted on the margin of the report.

Martin, *Wilderness of Mirrors*, pp. 140–141.

236. Ibid., page 141. A recent outstanding article on evaluating human sources objectively is David A. Schum and Jon R. Morris, "Assessing the Competence and Credibility of Human Sources of Intelligence Evidence: Contributions from Law and Probability." *Law, Probability and Risk,* 6: 1–4 (2007), pp. 247–274. Had many of the twenty-five questions that it poses of a theoretical source been asked in this case (under the rubric of methodology called MACE, or "method for assessing the credibility of evidence"), the outcome would have been very different.

237. Gravalos, "Pitfall of a Latin Quirk," pp. 31–32.

238. In the RAND study prepared for the Kennedy administration at about the same time, Albert and Roberta Wohlstetter concluded that "Castro was an unstable—which is to say, irrational—personality full of guile who could not be trusted." See Alex Abella, *Soldiers of Reason: The RAND Corporation and the Rise of the American Empire* (New York: Harcourt, 2008), p. 172.

239. See ibid.

240. Jutta Weldes, *Constructing National Interests: The United States and the Cuban Missile Crisis* (Minneapolis: University of Minnesota Press, 1999), p. 183. On page 185, ironically, Castro is on record agreeing with Ball on this point, saying to a colleague who made light of shaving off his beard, "You can't do it. It's a symbol of the revolution. It doesn't belong to you. It belongs to the revolution."

241. Charles G. Cogan, "The In-Culture of the DO." *Intelligence and National Security*, 8: 1 (1993), p. 81.

242. See Brugioni, *Eyeball to Eyeball*. Both pictures are in the forty-seven-photo insert between pages 368 and 369.

243. Allison and Zelikow, *Essence of Decision*, p. 155.

244. The article continues with a Cuban example:

A case in point occurred in Cuba when four odd structures were constructed atop the highest elevations of the Sierra Maestra mountains . . . these structures resembled large parabolic dish antennas. A missile or space satellite tracking role was postulated, but the necessary power plant and electrical transmission lines for such an installation could not be detected, and this facility was carried as unidentified for more than a year. Suspicion that it might be a military installation was heightened when a helicopter was observed at the site. Great was the surprise, therefore, when the Cubans, in a September 1963 issue of the periodical *Bohemia*, unveiled the installation as Castro's Museum of the Revolution. Because of a lack of water at the hilltop location, the roofs of the buildings had been designed by the "revolutionary" architect to trap rainwater and channel it to storage tanks.

Dino A. Brugioni, "The Unidentifieds." In H. B. Westerfield, ed., *Inside CIA's Private World: Declassified Articles from the Agency's Internal Journal 1955–1992.* (New Haven, CT: Yale University Press, 1995), p. 15.

245. Quoted in Shenon, *The Commission*, p. 190.

246. Chang and Kornbluh, *The Cuban Missile Crisis 1962*, p. xi.

247. Shackley, *Spymaster*, p. 61.

248. Ibid., p. 62.

249. Thomas Quiggin, *Seeing the Invisible: National Security Intelligence in an Uncertain Age* (Singapore: World Scientific Publishing, 2007), p. 128.

250. Abbott Smith, in 1969 article in *Studies* called "On the Accuracy of National Intelligence Estimates," says, "I think that a reader [of SNIE 85-3-62] might well have understood that it showed the Intelligence Community to be beset by the gravest doubts and concerns" because "The text of that paper was obviously labored, difficult, and inconclusive." In fairness, as Smith notes, "Nowhere does the estimate declare even that the Soviets would 'probably' not" put missiles in Cuba. Nevertheless—as Smith finally concedes—in that estimate and others leading up to the Crisis,

the agency "conveyed an unmistakable impression that the Soviets would probably not do what they did." He goes on "Sophisticated estimating indeed ought almost always to be something more than bald prediction ... A good paper on a complicated subject should describe the trends and forces at work, identify the contingent factors or variables which might affect developments, and present a few alternative possibilities for the future, usually with some judgment as to the relative likelihood of one or another outcome." By these standards, the CIA's work leading up to the Cuban Missile Crisis shows that it fundamentally misjudged "the trends and forces at work" in Cuba. See Abbot E. Smith, "On the Accuracy of National Intelligence Estimates." *Studies in Intelligence*, 13: 4 (1969), pp. 29–30.

251. Laqueur, *A World of Secrets*, pp. 168–169.

252. Brugioni, *Eyeball to Eyeball*, p. 147.

253. Sherman Kent, "Preface—1966." In *Strategic Intelligence for American World Policy* (Princeton, NJ: Princeton University Press, 1966), p. xxiii.

254. Brugioni, *Eyeball to Eyeball*, p. 247.

255. Kent, "A Crucial Estimate Relived," p. 18. Emphasis added.

256. Laqueur, *A World of Secrets*, p. 169.

257. Kent, "A Crucial Estimate Relived," p. 16. Emphasis added.

258. In effect, this is Allison's Model III, that of governmental politics.

259. Kent, "A Crucial Estimate Relived," p. 5.

260. Ibid., pp. 17–18. Emphasis added.

261. Handel, "Intelligence and the Problem of Strategic Surprise," p. 9.

262. Gaddis, *We Now Know*, p. 264.

263. Tetlock, *Expert Political Judgment*, p. 135.

264. Kent, "A Crucial Estimate Relived," p. 11.

265. Brugioni, *Eyeball to Eyeball*, p. 146.

266. Michael Douglas Smith, "The Perils of Analysis: Revisiting Sherman Kent's Defense of SNIE 85-3-62." *Studies in Intelligence*, 51: 3 (2007), p. 31.

267. Kent, "A Crucial Estimate Relived," p. 20.

268. CIA Office of Research and Reports, "Cuba 1962: Khrushchev's Miscalculated Risk." EP SC 64-5, February 13, 1964. Mentioned in footnote 2 of Munson and Southard, "Two Witnesses for the Defense." Smith, in a 2007 article in *Studies* entitled "The Perils of Analysis: Revisiting Sherman Kent's Defense of SNIE 85-3-62," agrees: "Kent and his colleagues do not appear to have examined their model of a Soviet decision maker, which was essentially a Russian-speaking Western rational actor who made choices with an understanding of US public opinion and pressures on our policymakers." Smith, "The Perils of Analysis," p. 31. Here we should note that Smith is continuing in a *Studies* article the best tradition of what Kent intended, which is a thoughtful reexamination of errors in the interests of improving analysis—just as this

book as a whole attempts to be, despite the bruising of Kent's reputation that must inevitably occur.

269. Handel, "Intelligence and the Problem of Strategic Surprise," p. 17. Emphasis in original.

270. Kent, "A Crucial Estimate Relived," p. 11.

271. Wohlstetter, *Pearl Harbor*. Foreword by Thomas C. Schelling, p. vii.

272. Gribkov and Smith, *Operation Anadyr*, p. 9.

273. Brugioni, *Eyeball to Eyeball*, p. 99.

274. Shulsky and Schmitt, *Silent Warfare*, p. 51. This is an interesting departure by the Soviets from Allison's Model II, organizational behavior, which in other ways so tripped up the USSR's effort. On the other hand, Allison says ultimately:

> The missiles sites were constructed in the configuration that was standard in the Soviet Union . . . At a White House meeting on the evening of October 16, the intelligence briefer explained that they could spot the launchers, in part, because "they have a four-in-line deployment pattern . . . which is identical to . . . representative of the deployments that we note in the Soviet Union for similar missiles.

See Allison and Zelikow, *Essence of Decision*, p. 109. In short, reliance on some precedents of Soviet behavior sometimes contributed to the ultimate detection of the missiles and at other times helped prevent it.

275. Smith, "The Perils of Analysis," p. 31.

276. Quoted in Brugioni, *Eyeball to Eyeball*, p. 146. Emphasis added.

277. For an outstanding general introduction to a Kuhnian view of intelligence analysis, see Seliktar, *Failing the Crystal Ball Test*. See also Seliktar, *Politics, Paradigms, and Intelligence Failures*. These two volumes, because they deal with the two mysteries of the previous two cases, are extensively cited in our earlier discussion, though Seliktar does not deal with strategic surprise per se and does not deal with intelligence failures or surprises rooted in secrets but rather mysteries like the Iranian Revolution and the collapse of the USSR. But note that Kuhn makes the point that *anomalies appear "only against the background provided by the paradigm" and this is clearly not the case with McCone's insight—the conventional view of likely Soviet behavior is why we notice his observation, but it is not why McCone made it. Thus, the Kuhnian paradigm is illuminating but not definitive in this instance.*

278. Fursenko and Naftali, *One Hell of a Gamble*, p. 199.

279. Brugioni, *Eyeball to Eyeball*, pp. 96–97. Emphasis added.

280. Gaddis, *We Now Know*, p. 268.

281. Allison and Zelikow, *Essence of Decision*, p. 98.

282. An obviously stung Kent said:

> Some of our critics have suggested that we could have avoided the error if we had done a better job of putting ourselves in the place of the Soviet leadership—that

if we had only looked out on the world scene with their eyes and though about it the way they did we would not have misread indicators and all would have been clear. . . . As such statements are made, I must confess to a quickening of pulse and a rise in temperature. I have wondered if such people appear before pastry cooks to tell them how useful they will find something called "wheat flour" in their trade.

Kent, "A Crucial Estimate Relived," p. 15. Kent also describes a so-called Red Team exercise (in which a group of people are set apart from the rest of the analytical effort and tried to simulate enemy thinking) as "a new high in human fatuity," concluding: "Of course we did not go in for this sort of thing [prior to the Crisis]." Ibid., p. 16. Any departure from a reified version of reason seems anathema to Kent.

283. Gaddis, *We Now Know*, p. 181.

284. Ibid., p. 264. Emphasis original.

285. James J. Wirtz, "Miscalculation, Surprise, and U.S. Intelligence." *Studies in Intelligence*: Special November 2002 Issue, pp. 85–93, p. 85.

286. Cited in Susan A. Crane, "(Not) Writing History: Rethinking the Intersections of Personal History and Collective Memory with Hans Von Aufsess." *History and Memory*, 8 (1996), pp. 5–29, p. 5.

287. Laqueur, *A World of Secrets*, pp. 168–169. It is also interesting to note here the connection with Chapter 1's discussion of the employment of chess as an inappropriate metaphor for intelligence analysis. One of the primary architects of U.S. nuclear theory and a codeveloper of game theory, John von Neumann, focused his analysis of nuclear strategy on *games of perfect information*, chess among them. This is odd, because apparently in his private life he preferred *Kriegsspiel*, a nineteenth-century German version of chess in which neither player can see the other's pieces (and that requires a third party to act as a referee). See Daniel Johnson, *White King and Red Queen: How the Cold War Was Fought on the Chessboard* (New York: Houghton Mifflin Company, 2008), p. 210. See also the Chess Variant Pages website, available at www.chessvariants.com/incinf.dir/kriegspiel.html. It would appear as if as soon as the U-2 began flying, the CIA thought it was playing chess when it was still playing *Kriegsspiel*.

288. Betts, *Surprise Attack*, p. 129.

289. Examined extensively in Edward N. Luttwak, *Strategy: The Logic of War and Peace*, 2nd ed. (Cambridge, MA: Harvard University Press, 2002).

290. Betts, *Surprise Attack*, p. 129.

291. Gaddis, *We Now Know*, p. 263.

292. Betts, *Surprise Attack*, p. 129. Emphasis added.

293. Allison and Zelikow, *Essence of Decision*, pp. 95–96.

294. Fursenko and Naftali, *One Hell of a Gamble*, pp. 191–192. The Soviet's chief military representative in Cuba, Major General A. A. Dementyev, raised the issue of detection by U-2s with Rodion Malinovsky, the Soviet defense minister, before the

Presidium conditionally approved the plan. "It will be impossible to hide these missiles from American U-2s," he warned. The comment not only provoked an angry verbal response from the minister, but according to Alekseev, who was sitting nearby, the defense minister actually kicked Dementyev under the table to register his disapproval.

295. Smith, "The Perils of Analysis," p. 30.

296. See Johnson, *White King and Red Queen*, p. 210..

297. This analogy also highlights the difference between a secret and the previous chapter's mysteries. As Sick says about the overthrow of the shah:

> In its inchoate appeal to social destruction and its incalculable effects, the revolution was no nicely plotted move on the international chessboard. On the contrary, it was the fury of the player who smashes his fist into the board and showers the pieces about the room in an emotional demand for a fresh board, new players and a radically restructured rulebook.

See Sick, *All Fall Down*, p. 45.

298. For more on poker as a game of imperfect information and its relation to strategy in business and military matters, see John McDonald, *Strategy in Poker, Business & War* (New York: W. W. Norton & Company, 1996).

299. Handel, "Intelligence and the Problem of Strategic Surprise," p. 17.

300. SNIE 85-3-62 "The Military Buildup in Cuba," cited in Laqueur, *A World of Secrets*, p. 81. The full text of this SNIE has still not been declassified; just the summary pages are available. These thoughts are certainly consistent with the message of the SNIE's summary, which also shares some of the same vocabulary, especially paragraph D of the summary, referring to still-classified SNIE paragraphs 29–33, available in McAuliffe, *CIA Documents on the Cuban Missile Crisis 1962*, pp. 91–93.

301. Just how enduring the reification of reason is at the CIA can be judged by the fact that, as late as 1989, some senior CIA analysts maintained that it was the Kremlin, not the CIA, who had "erred" by "ignoring the dangers of such a risky undertaking." Brugioni makes that assumption in 1991, writing, "Intelligence officers were confident that the Soviets would not be that irrational" (Brugioni, *Eyeball to Eyeball*, p. 127; emphasis added). Even after 9/11, the lesson has not been learned: A CIA analyst present during the Crisis writes in a 2002 handbook, *Anticipating Surprise: Analysis for Strategic Warning*, the sensible cautions that "before we conclude that some other nation is acting 'irrationally' . . . we should carefully examine our own attitudes and make sure we are not rejecting such action as illogical because we do not fully appreciate how strongly the other country feels about it." Amazingly, however, the analyst-author then goes on to say: "But there still remain those cases, like Cuba in 1962, that are not logical and do not meet objective criteria for rational action" (Grabo, *Anticipating Surprise*, p. 102; emphasis added). Clearly, even recently, the CIA's culture did not easily digest the notion that there is no absolute yardstick for judging what constitutes a

"rational" strategic move or even Handel's more basic warning above: "That which is considered a high risk in one culture may be acceptable in another" (Handel, "Intelligence and the Problem of Strategic Surprise", p. 15). Even faced with 9/11, the CIA continued to extol scientism and a reified brand of reason.

302. Declassified CIA memo, no date, by Lyman B. Kirkpatrick, "Memorandum for the Director, Action Generated by DCI Cables Concerning Cuban Low-Level Photography and Offensive Weapons," page 6; found in McAuliffe, *CIA Documents on the Cuban Missile Crisis 1962*, p. 44.

303. Ibid. Emphasis added.

Chapter 6

1. Russell, *Sharpening Strategic Intelligence*, p. 71.

2. Betts, *Enemies of Intelligence*, p. 104.

3. Scheuer, *Through Our Enemies' Eyes*, p. xv.

4. Melvin A. Goodman, "9/11: The Failure of Strategic Intelligence." *Intelligence and National Security*, 18: 4 (2003), p. 59.

5. Robert Windrem and Victor Limjoco, "9/11 Commission Controversy." *Deep Background: NBC News Investigates*, January 30, 2008, available at http://deepbackground .msnbc.msn.com/archive/2008/01/30/624314.aspx.

6. Shenon, *The Commission*, pp. 370–373.

7. Mark Mazzetti, "CIA Lays out Errors It Made before Sept. 11." *The New York Times*, August 22, 2007, p. A1.

8. U.S. Congress, ed., "Joint Inquiry into Intelligence Community Activities before and after the Terrorist Attacks of September 11, 2001" (Washington, DC: U.S. Senate Select Committee on Intelligence and U.S. House Permanent Select Committee on Intelligence Together with Additional Views, 2002).

9. Richard A. Falkenrath, "The 9/11 Commission Report: A Review Essay." *International Security*, 29: 3 (2004–2005), pp. 174–175.

10. Scheuer, *Through Our Enemies' Eyes*, p. 315.

11. Zegart does a wonderful job cataloguing tactical missed opportunities for the CIA and the FBI. See Zegart, *Spying Blind*, pp. 115–119.

12. Otherwise known as the "Law of Parsimony," it states that assumptions introduced to explain a phenomenon should not be multiplied unnecessarily, and therefore, all other things being equal, the simplest of competing explanations is the one most likely to be true.

13. Betts, *Enemies of Intelligence*, p. 108. In a somewhat involuntary recognition that strategic surprises are socially constructed, Louis J. Freeh, director of the FBI between 1993 and early 2001, admits that, until 9/11 altered the equation entirely, "We dealt with terrorist attacks against U.S. targets as if the assaults were a law-enforcement issue like organized crime or white-collar crime." He adds: "Al Qaeda is not the Cosa

Nostra." It is unfortunate that it took 9/11 for such recognition to take place. Louis J. Freeh, *My FBI: Bringing Down the Mafia, Investigating Bill Clinton, and Fighting the War on Terror* (New York: St. Martin Griffin, 2005), p. 290.

14. Coll, *Ghost Wars*, p. 16.

15. Commission, *The 9/11 Commission Report*, p. 154.

16. For a discussion of how the spelling, transliteration and translation of Arabic, Persian, Chinese, and so on names into English has proved an immense challenge for intelligence agencies and databases, and how they are using special software to circumvent this issue, see "What's in a Name? (Technology Quarterly)." *The Economist*, March 10, 2007.

17. Zegart, *Spying Blind*, p. 119.

18. Parker and Stern, "Blindsided?" p. 619.

19. Quoted in Coll, *Ghost Wars*, p. 362.

20. Shenon, *The Commission*, p. 190.

21. It must be noted, however, that by "catastrophic" or "grand," Pillar meant nuclear, bacteriological, or chemical attacks. What he failed to appreciate was the possibility that "grand" terrorism could be achieved with conventional approaches, the signature of 9/11. See Paul R. Pillar, *Terrorism and U.S. Foreign Policy* (Washington, DC: The Brookings Institution, 2001).

22. Bruce Hoffman, "The Modern Terrorist Mindset." In R. D. Howard and R. L. Sawyer, eds., *Terrorism and Counterterrorism: Understanding the New Security Environment* (Guilford, CT: McGraw Hill, 2002), p. 84.

23. Shlaim, "Failures in National Intelligence Estimates," p. 356.

24. Richard H. Shultz, "The Era of Armed Groups." In P. Berkowitz, ed., *The Future of American Intelligence* (Stanford, CA: Hoover Institution Press, 2005), p. 2. Emphasis in original.

25. Scheuer, *Through Our Enemies' Eyes*, p. 193.

26. Bergman, *The Secret War with Iran*, pp. 222–235. Bergman makes the case for heavy Iranian involvement in the rise of al-Qa'ida.

27. For Scheuer's view of "obsolete experts" and state sponsorship of terrorism, see Scheuer, *Through Our Enemies' Eyes*, pp. 20–23. The issue of state support for terrorism has always been controversial at the CIA and was fraught with difficulty even during the Cold War. In the early 1980s, for example, CIA Director Casey, for example, was highly critical of the Directorate of Analysis's failure to link the Soviets to international terrorism after reading a book by Claire Sterling, *The Terror Network: The Secret War of International Terrorism* (New York: Holt, Rhinehart & Winston, 1981). Long after chastising the analysts for their intellectual blindness, Casey discovered that Sterling's information linking the USSR to these terrorist operations had come solely from a disinformation operation by the CIA's own Directorate of Operations— CIA disinformation had blown back to the director himself. See Bob Woodward,

Veil: The Secret Wars of the CIA 1981–1987. (New York: Simon & Schuster, 1987), pp. 124–129.

28. Commission, *The 9/11 Commission Report*, p. 340.

29. Parker and Stern, "Blindsided?" p. 606.

30. Jan W. Rivkin and Michael A. Roberto, "Managing National Intelligence (A): Before 9/11," in *Harvard Business School*, Case #706-463 (Boston, MA: Harvard Business School Publishing, 2006), p. 8.

31. Commission, *The 9/11 Commission Report*, p. 128. Abdul Basit (widely known by his alias, Ramzi Yousef) was the convicted mastermind and coconspirator of the 1993 World Trade Center bombing and the Manila Air/Bojinka plots.

32. Wright, *The Looming Tower*, p. 211.

33. Walter Laqueur, *No End to War: Terrorism in the Twenty-First Century* (New York: Continuum, 2004), p. 78. On the same page, Laqueur records that in the modern age suicide terrorism has been used by Muslim (both Shiite and Sunni), Christian, Sikh, Hindu, Jewish, and atheist groups.

34. Mazzetti, "CIA Lays out Errors It Made before Sept. 11," page A1.

35. See Peter R. Neumann and M. L. R. Smith, "Missing the Plot? Intelligence and Discourse Failure." *Orbis*, (2005), pp. 95–107, passim.

36. Laqueur, *No End to War*, p. 236. As Laqueur goes on to ask, why not call Eichmann "an activist demographer . . . To call a terrorist an 'activist' or a 'militant' is to blot out a dividing line between a suicide bomber and the active member of a trade union or a political party or a club."

37. See, for example, Condoleezza Rice, "Campaign 2000: Promoting the National Interest." *Foreign Affairs* (January–February 2000), passim.

38. Quoted in Commission, *The 9/11 Commission Report*, p. 357. Tenet's memo has been declassified and can be accessed via the Intelwire.com site: http://intelwire .egoplex.com/CIA-911-Binder1.pdf, p. 136.

39. Jones is scathing:

> [Tenet] was remarkable for his lack of military, business, leadership or foreign experience. He'd been a loyal Washington staffer for years, a man who got along well with his superiors. Unfortunately, prior to 9/11, Tenet had devoted all his energies not to intelligence collection but to Arab/Israeli peace negotiations. Tenet traveled from capital to capital with a large entourage, including 35 security guards, in a C-141 Starlifter. Tenet's autobiography contains humorous anecdotes about meetings with Yasser Arafat.

40. This issue and the barriers that imposes have been addressed for many years by Steven Aftergood in "Secrecy News," published by the Federation of American Scientists. See www.fas.org.

41. Clarke, *Against All Enemies*, p. 210. Emphasis added. Scheuer agrees on both terrorism's low priority and the decline of the clandestine service generally (related in

the following pages), saying: "Tenet had helped preside over every step of the service's decline during three consecutive administrations—Bush, Clinton, Bush—in a series of key intelligence jobs for the Senate, the National Security Council and the CIA." See Michael Scheuer, "Tenet Tries to Shift the Blame. Don't Buy It." *The Washington Post*, April 29, 2007, page B1. As far as analytical capability assigned to Al-Qa'ida, the Joint Inquiry also found that

> The only substantial infusion of personnel to counterterrorism occurred after September 11, 2001, when the number of CIA personnel assigned to CTC nearly doubled—from approximately 400 to approximately 800—and additional contractors were hired in support of CTC. No comparable shift of resources occurred in December 1998 after the DCI's declaration of war, in December 1999 during the Millennium crisis, or in October 2000 after the attack on *USS Cole*.

See Congress, "Joint Inquiry into Intelligence Community Activities before and after the Terrorist Attacks of September 11, 2001," p. 233.

42. CIA, "OIG Report on CIA Accountability with Respect to the 9/11 Attacks," p. xi. On the other hand, a few weeks before the 9/11 attacks, the CIA's inspector general submitted a report on the CTC to Tenet. It found that the CTC "is a well-managed component that successfully carries out the Agency's responsibilities to collect and analyze intelligence on international terrorism and to undermine the capabilities of terrorist groups." Report quoted in Diamond, *The CIA and the Culture of Failure*, p. 372. That would argue that the analytical failure described later in the chapter must carry more explanatory weight because it indicates that the CTC was deemed up to the threat as it was (mis)perceived.

43. George Tenet, "Worldwide Threat—Converging Dangers in a Post 9/11 World—Testimony of February 6, 2002." In *Senate Select Committee on Intelligence*, U.S. Senate (Washington, DC: 2002).

44. Clarke, *Against All Enemies*, p. 135. Note that such quotations about bin Ladin appearing as a "mere" financier of terrorism in CIA documents is sharply disputed in Pillar, "Good Literature and Bad History," pp. 1030–1031.

45. Coll, *Ghost Wars*, pp. 261 and 79.

46. Commission, *The 9/11 Commission Report*, p. 193.

47. Clarke, *Against All Enemies*, p. 96.

48. Quoted in Zegart, *Spying Blind*, pp. 116–117.

49. George Friedman, *America's Secret War: Inside the Hidden Worldwide Struggle between America and Its Enemies* (New York: Doubleday, 2004), p. 207.

50. Zegart, *Spying Blind*, p. 118.

51. Commission, *The 9/11 Commission Report*, p. 109.

52. Shenon, *The Commission*, p. 188.

53. Quoted in ibid., p. 190.

54. John Miller, Michael Stone, and Chris Mitchell, *The Cell: Inside the 9/11 Plot, and Why the FBI and CIA Failed to Stop It* (New York: Hyperion, 2003), p. 129.

55. Shenon, *The Commission*, p. 190.

56. Miller, Stone, and Mitchell, *The Cell*, p. 125. Emphasis added.

57. They might be well-advised to remember the Rudyard Kipling poem of 1892, "Soudan Expeditionary Force" or "Fuzzy-Wuzzy": "So 'ere's ~to~ you, Fuzzy-Wuzzy, at your 'ome in the Soudan;/ You're a pore benighted 'eathen but a first-class fightin' man." See Rudyard Kipling, *Barrack Room Ballads* (New York: Signet Classics, 2003), p. 12.

58. Commission, *The 9/11 Commission Report*, p. 337.

59. Wright, *The Looming Tower*, p. 264. Emphasis added.

60. Glassé, *The Concise Encyclopedia of Islam*. See entry on "*Hijrah*," pp. 156–157. It is interesting to note that, as the mother of one of the authors—an art historian—noted, the West has similar tales of heroes and spiders' webs, the most famous of which, of course, involves Robert the Bruce (which parallels similar tales involving both King David and Tamerlane).

61. Wright, *The Looming Tower*, pp. 264–265.

62. Friedman, *America's Secret War*, p. 207.

63. Robert Fisk, "Anti-Soviet Warrior Puts His Army on the Road to Peace." *Financial Times*, December 6, 1993.

64. Scheuer, *Through Our Enemies' Eyes*, p. 307.

65. Bernard Lewis, "License to Kill: Osama Bin Laden's Declaration of Jihad." *Foreign Affairs*, 77: 6 (1998), pp. 14–19.

66. Simon Reeve, *The New Jackals: Ramzi Yousef, Osama Bin Laden, and the New Terrorism* (Boston, MA: Northeastern University Press, 1999). See also Yossef Bodansky, *Bin Laden: The Man Who Declared War on America* (Rocklin, CA: Forum, 1999). Reeve mostly draws on FBI sources. Bodansky, in contrast, does not offer footnotes or cite other sources in order to "protect his sources and methods," which does not allow verification of his often bold claims and unconventional interpretations. In several works, for instance, he views bin Ladin as a tool of state sponsors of terrorism and paints the picture of an overarching global Islamic conspiracy led by Shia Iran and regrouping such natural allies as Baathist Syria and Iraq, Sunni Sudan and Pakistan, and even . . . communist China, for good measure, all working together against the West.

67. "Russian Files on al-Qa'eda Ignored," *Jane's Intelligence Digest*, October 5, 2001, p. 4. There are certainly grounds for believing that Russian intelligence services knew a great deal about Ayman al-Zawahiri: According to one source, they actually held him in custody for over six months in 1996, "tried" him for violating the passport regime, and acquitted him . . . Al-Zawahiri then "disappeared" for two weeks before leaving Russia, only to return in 1998 to spend two weeks at an FSB base in Dagestan.

See Michel Elbaz, "Russian Secrets of Al-Qaeda's Number Two—19 July" (Axisglobe .com, 2005); "Unknown History of Jihad—20 July" (Axisglobe.com, 2005); and "Soviet Past of Worldwide Jihad—21 July" (Axisglobe.com, 2005).

68. Charles D. Cremeans, "Basic Psychology for Intelligence Analysts." *Studies in Intelligence*, 15: 1 (1971), p. 111.

69. Hoffman, "The Modern Terrorist Mindset," p. 84.

70. Friedman, *America's Secret War*, p. 2. On the other hand, not everyone associated with Al-Qa'ida and trained as terrorists by them were exactly James Bond clones: According to the *9/11 Commission Report*, one terrorist training course for three men "lasted a week or two in Karachi," where Khalid Sheikh Mohammed "showed [his students] how to read phone books, interpret airline timetables, use the Internet, use code words in communications, make travel reservations and rent an apartment." In short, these training courses were somewhat akin to an orientation program for a study-abroad student, though the trio's training also included "using flight simulator computer games, viewing movies that featured hijackings, and reading flight schedules." See Commission, *The 9/11 Commission Report*, pp. 157–158.

71. U.S. Intelligence estimates between 10,000 and 20,000 fighters between 1996 and 2001. See Commission, *The 9/11 Commission Report*, p. 67.

72. The network structure and operational security measures used by al-Qa'ida are often referred to as "unique." They are nothing of the sort: They follow patterns and methods first established by Russian revolutionaries of the early modern period. See Steven G. Marks, *How Russia Shaped the Modern World: From Art to Anti-Semitism, Ballet to Bolshevism* (Princeton, NJ: Princeton University Press, 2003), pp. 7–37. Certainly the CIA recognizes such a creature. Another piece of evidence for how little good cell-based networks need to change over time is Victor Serge, *What Every Radical Should Know about State Repression: A Guide for Activists* (New York: Ocean Press, 2005), which is a reissued manual originally published in *Bulletin Communiste* in Paris in November 1921. It outlines the tactics developed by Russian revolutionaries to prevent penetration by the Okhrana and latter agencies over the previous forty years (that is, since the founding of the Okhrana—from the Third Section of the Russian Ministry of the Interior—in 1881), and has been reissued for modern "activists" (or delusionals and fantasists with a free-floating sense of grievance and/or a persecution mania: Take your pick). At any rate, when it comes to basic tradecraft there is little new under the sun, and al-Qa'ida's network structure is not Web 2.0.

73. Commission, *The 9/11 Commission Report*, p. 340.

74. Clarke, *Against All Enemies*, pp. 137–138.

75. For a complete list of the quite minor "requirements for a successful attack" see Commission, *The 9/11 Commission Report*, p. 173.

76. Clarke, *Against All Enemies*, p. 192.

77. Commission, *The 9/11 Commission Report*, p. 171. The best overview of how *hawala* works is found in John A. Cassara, *Hide & Seek: Intelligence, Law Enforcement, and the Stalled War on Terrorist Finance* (Washington, DC: Potomac Books, 2006), pp. 144–150.

78. Miller, Stone, and Mitchell, *The Cell*, p. 127.

79. For more on budget cuts after the Cold War, see Snider, *The Agency and the Hill*, pp. 184–187.

80. Clarke, *Against All Enemies*, p. 87.

81. Abraham H. Miller and Nicholas Damask, "Thinking about Intelligence after the Fall of Communism." *International Journal of Intelligence and Counterintelligence*, 6 (1993), p. 163.

82. Coll, *Ghost Wars*, p. 315.

83. The spiritual father of al-Qa'ida was Sayyid Qutb, an Egyptian member of the Muslim Brotherhood. At least through 1985 if not after, the CIA also had no sources whatsoever inside the Muslim brotherhood, the oldest and largest radical Sunni organization. The CTC files on the brotherhood that year were nothing but "old newspaper clippings, a few analytical pieces, and cables from embassies." See Baer, *Sleeping with the Devil*, pp. 98–99 and 112.

84. Wright, *The Looming Tower*, p. 301.

85. Clarke, *Against All Enemies*, p. 199. Tenet agrees in George Tenet and Bill Harlow, *At the Center of the Storm: My Years at the CIA* (New York, NY: HarperCollins, 2007), p. 109. Scheuer disputes this.

86. Coll, *Ghost Wars*, p. 444.

87. Seliktar, *Failing the Crystal Ball Test*, p. 52. For an exploration of whether this is indeed true, see Goldman, *The Ethics of Spying: A Reader for the Intelligence Professional*. Part Four, comparing espionage and intelligence work to other professions, is especially thought provoking. Powers, *The Man Who Kept the Secrets*, pp. v–xi and *passim*, explores this issue in the context of U.S. national power and domestic politics with the lightest touch and most engaging style. He quotes CIA officials as taking the attitude that

> The basic business of the Agency, if ugly in some of its particulars, is necessary too, one of the fatal facts of modern life like taxes, prisons and armies. An outsider naturally resents this argument—it smacks so much of an adult's explanation of the world to a child—but two thousand years of history, in which failures of intelligence were often as destructive as failures of arms, make it hard to dismiss.

88. Miller, Stone, and Mitchell, *The Cell*, p. 133.

89. Authors' conversation with a serving DO officer, November 18, 2005.

90. Miller, Stone, and Mitchell, *The Cell*, p. 134.

91. CIA, "OIG Report on CIA Accountability with Respect to the 9/11 Attacks," p. xix. The CTC officials interviewed by the Joint Inquiry disagreed. See U.S. Congress,

"Joint Inquiry into Intelligence Community Activities Before and After the Terrorist Attacks of September 11, 2001," p. 93.

92. For an overview of how low morale had sunk at the CIA and how risk averse the culture had become, see Coll, *Ghost Wars*, pp. 316–318. See also Jones, *The Human Factor*, passim.

93. Miller, Stone, and Mitchell, *The Cell*, p. 132.

94. Commission, *The 9/11 Commission Report*, pp. 189–190.

95. Miller, Stone, and Mitchell, *The Cell*, p. 134. These conclusions are supported in CIA, "OIG Report on CIA Accountability with Respect to the 9/11 Attacks," pp. xviii–xix. This may still be a problem at the agency, one compounded by a culture of careerism: According to Jones, in 2008:

> Recruiting human sources does not appear to lead to career advancement. It is the lowest form of work within the Agency, and few top managers have ever recruited a good human source. To have recruited human sources in Al-Qa'ida . . . a case officer would have had to be in the field for years, away from Agency stations and HQs. He'd have returned to a dead career, with no management experience and with none of the connections at HQs necessary for personal advancement. A person who wants to advance in the organization does so through lengthy service at HQs, with rare assignments overseas.

See Jones, *The Human Factor*, p. 359.

96. Commission, *The 9/11 Commission Report*, p. 92.

97. Quoted in Reuel Marc Gerecht, "The Counterterrorist Myth." *Atlantic Monthly*, July–August 2001.

98. Amy B. Zegart, "September 11 and the Adaptation Failure of U.S. Intelligence Agencies." *International Security*, 29: 4 (2005), p. 104.

99. Thomas Powers, "The Trouble with the CIA." *New York Review of Books*, January 17, 2002, p. 4.

100. U.S. Congress, "Joint Inquiry into Intelligence Community Activities before and after the Terrorist Attacks of September 11, 2001," p. 343.

101. Coll, *Ghost Wars*, p. 7. One of the authors is reminded of a conversation with a USMC intelligence officer in Jordan, who described an Iraqi as "a Fundamentalist in the sense that he can't be bribed with *money*."

102. Miller, Stone, and Mitchell, *The Cell*, p.129.

103. Gerecht, "The Counterterrorist Myth."

104. Baer, *Sleeping with the Devil: How Washington Sold Our Soul for Saudi Crude*, p. 97. He goes on to say that "most case officers were middle-aged, Caucasian Protestant males with liberal-arts degrees. If they had any experience, it was in the military. Few spoke Arabic, and the ones who did spoke it badly."

105. Quoted in Zegart, *Spying Blind*, page 94.

106. Daniel Byman, "Strategic Surprise and the September 11th Attacks." *Annual Review of Political Science* 8(2005), p. 157.

107. Bamford, *Body of Secrets*, p. 648.

108. Powers, "The Trouble with the CIA," p. 4.

109. Friedman, *America's Secret War*, p. 2.

110. Friedman, *America's Secret War*, p. 2. Similarly, on the day before the attacks, the NSA intercepted messages in which Al-Qa'ida suspects said things such as, "The match is about to begin," and, "Tomorrow is zero hour." These were not translated until September 12 (presumably the cycle was somewhat accelerated by the attacks). However, more than thirty similar cryptic warnings had been intercepted in the months before 9/11, and these warnings were not followed by attacks. See Betts, *Enemies of Intelligence*, p. 107.

111. Byman, "Strategic Surprise and the September 11th Attacks," page 151.

112. Pillar, "Good Literature and Bad History," p. 1022.

113. Betts, *Enemies of Intelligence*, p. 105. This case attempts to show that, as one of authors' masters at boarding school used to intone with deep irony: "If this isn't a failure, it is certainly an invitation to greater effort."

114. Commission, *The 9/11 Commission Report*, p. 341. This is sharply disputed as a "gross" mischaracterization by Pillar but widely accepted elsewhere. See Pillar, "Good Literature and Bad History."

115. Laqueur, *No End to War*, p. 122.

116. CIA, "OIG Report on CIA Accountability with Respect to the 9/11 Attacks," p. xvii.

117. Shenon, *The Commission*, p. 139. See also Charles F. Parker and Eric K. Stern, "Bolt from the Blue or Avoidable Failure? Revisiting September 11 and the Origins of Strategic Surprise." *Foreign Policy Analysis*, 1: 3 (2005), p. 311. Parker seems to take Tenet's side, saying, "The attacks on September 11th could be seen as vindication for Tenet's vigilance."

118. Shenon, *The Commission*, p. 139. Given the amount of self-pleading by Tenet on this issue, a short amplification of it is required. In his memoirs, Tenet attempts an interesting spin on the lack of an NIE. He says that he

... decided that the usual intelligence reporting in the form of Presidential Briefs, finished intelligence reports, National Intelligence Estimates, and the like was insufficient for conveying the seriousness of the threat. So I began sending personal letters to the president [that is, both Clinton and Bush] and virtually the entire national security community, explicitly laying out why I was concerned about the looming terrorist attacks. I knew that all senior officials had full in-boxes—only something out of the ordinary would get their attention. Even one such letter would have been an unusual step. During my tenure, I wrote eight of them. . . . I believed the only way to get their attention was to tell them what I knew and what concerned me, and to do so over and over and over again.

See Tenet and Harlow, *At the Center of the Storm*, p. 122. Given how Tenet treated the frantic e-mail from Michael Scheuer discussed in the following paragraphs, this passage is deeply ironic. It also, of course, turns on its head the intelligence cycle (how were such letters going to affect tasking and collection against Al-Qa'ida in the Intelligence Community?), and runs counter to the idea—which permeates the literature—that NIEs are the primary method of providing focus and warning to the U.S. government. The CIA Inspector General's Report certainly gave no credence to this self-pleading. See CIA, "OIG Report on CIA Accountability with Respect to the 9/11 Attacks," pp. vi and viii. Tenet's defense of, "I was so concerned, over a period of years, I threw out all usual intelligence procedures: sadly, Government (parties otherwise unnamed) didn't listen." It is the self-portrait of a would-be Cassandra but is instead a classic piece of hindsight bias and rationalization. As we discuss in the following pages, the Inspector General's Report is clear: "Neither the DCI nor the DDCI followed up these warnings and admonitions by creating a documented, comprehensive plan to guide the counterterrorism effort at the Intelligence Community level." See ibid., p. vii.

119. Commission, *The 9/11 Commission Report*, p. 261.

120. As the author of a CIA manual on strategic surprise and warning clearly states as a section heading, "Policymakers need evidence on which they can act." See Grabo, *Anticipating Surprise*, p. 139.

121. Commission, *The 9/11 Commission Report*, p. 342. The commission cites "Bin Ladin Threatening to Attack US Aircraft [with antiaircraft missiles]" (June 1998), "Strains Surface between Taliban and Bin Ladin" (January 1999), "Terrorist Threat to US Interests in Caucasus" (June 1999), "Bin Ladin to Exploit Looser Security During Holidays" (December 1999), "Bin Ladin Evading Sanctions" (March 2000), "Bin Ladin's Interest in Biological, Radiological Weapons" (February 2001), "Taliban Holding Firm on Bin Ladin for Now" (March 2001), "Terrorist Groups Said to Be Cooperating on US Hostage Plot" (May 2001), and "Bin Ladin Determined to Strike in the US" (August 2001).

122. Turner, *Why Secret Intelligence Fails*, p. 109.

123. Zegart, *Spying Blind*, p. 86.

124. John Solomon, "CIA Warned of Attack 6 Years before 9/11." Associated Press, April 16, 2004.

125. Betts, "Analysis, War, and Decision," p. 88.

126. Zegart, *Spying Blind*, p. 115.

127. Brzezinski, *Power and Principle*, p. 397.

128. Quoted in Zegart, *Spying Blind*, p. 86.

129. Shenon, *The Commission*, p. 314. According to Betts, in the post 9/11 world bureaucratic defensiveness adds this headline-service mentality, and intelligence bureaucrats "pass all information on to avoid 'later accusations that data was not taken seriously. As one official complained, this behavior is . . . 'preparing for the next 9/11 commission instead of preparing for the next 9/11.'" See Betts, *Enemies of Intelligence*, pp. 111–112.

130. Grabo, *Anticipating Surprise*, p. 164.

131. CIA, "OIG Report on CIA Accountability with Respect to the 9/11 Attacks," p. viii. Responding to criticism after public release of the CIA–Inspector General report in 2007,

> Former director Tenet issued a three-page statement that omitted any discussion of CIA or Intelligence Community analysis of the terrorist threat prior to 9/11. When confronted with evidence of an across the board failure by the analytical community to address a threat that Tenet himself believed worthy of a declaration of war, Tenet had nothing to say.

See Diamond, *The CIA and the Culture of Failure*, p. 372.

132. Ibid., pp. 370–371.

133. Ehud Sprinzak, "The Lone Gunman." *Foreign Policy* November–December (2001),p. 72.

134. Ibid.

135. Falkenrath, "The 9/11 Commission Report: A Review Essay," p. 178.

136. For example Uri Bar-Joseph and Rose McDermott, "Change the Analyst and Not the System: A Different Approach to Intelligence Reform." *Foreign Policy Analysis* 4(2008), pp. 127–145.

137. For example, Zegart, "September 11 and the Adaptation Failure of U.S. Intelligence Agencies."

138. Byman, "Strategic Surprise and the September 11th Attacks," p. 157.

139. U.S. Congress, "Joint Inquiry into Intelligence Community Activities before and after the Terrorist Attacks of September 11, 2001," p. 342.

140. Ibid., p. 233.

141. Commission, *The 9/11 Commission Report*, p. 91. See also Zegart, *Spying Blind*, pp. 68–69.

142. Zegart, *Spying Blind*, p. 69.

143. Turner, *Why Secret Intelligence Fails*, p. 104.

144. Russell, *Sharpening Strategic Intelligence*, p. 126.

145. Russ Travers, "The Coming Intelligence Failure." *Studies in Intelligence*, 01: 1 (1997), p. 3.

146. Coll, *Ghost Wars*, p. 419.

147. Lowenthal, *Intelligence*, p. 87.

148. Commission, *The 9/11 Commission Report*, p. 251.

149. U.S. Congress, "Joint Inquiry into Intelligence Community Activities before and after the Terrorist Attacks of September 11, 2001," p. 338.

150. Ibid., p. 336. This is confirmed in CIA, "OIG Report on CIA Accountability with Respect to the 9/11 Attacks," p. viii.

151. Kent, "Words of Estimative Probability."

152. Coll, *Ghost Wars*, p. 10.

153. Scheuer, *Through Our Enemies' Eyes*, p. 215.

154. Wright, *The Looming Tower*, p. 194.

155. Kent, "Words of Estimative Probability," p. 7. Emphasis added.

156. Scheuer, *Through Our Enemies' Eyes*, p. 206. For an interesting and historically well-grounded exploration of the implications of Al-Qa'ida's world view for deterrence, see Jonathan M. Schachter, "The Eye of the Believer: Psychological Influences on Counter-Terrorism Policy-Making" (Santa Monica, CA: RAND Graduate School, 2002), pp. 79–102.

157. Scheuer discusses bin Ladin's character traits in Scheuer, *Through Our Enemies' Eyes*, pp. 75–81.

158. Wright, *The Looming Tower*, p. 262. The noseless bear was one of four animals in the zoo that survived Taliban rule; a second was a lion that the Taliban had blinded with a grenade.

159. Ibid.

160. Quoted in Coll, *Ghost Wars*, p. 362.

161. Quoted in Scheuer, *Through Our Enemies' Eyes*, p. 124.

162. Seliktar, *Failing the Crystal Ball Test*, p. 174.

163. Milani, *The Making of Iran's Islamic Revolution*, p. 22.

164. Lipsky, "A Primer for Spies," p. A19.

165. Ralph Peters, "Our Old New Enemies." *Parameters*, 29: 2 (1999), pp. 28–30.

166. Handel, "Intelligence and the Problem of Strategic Surprise," p. 34.

167. James Turner Johnson, *The Holy War Idea in Western and Islamic Traditions* (University Park: Pennsylvania State University, 1997), p. 15.

168. Kristen Renwick Monroe and Lina Haddad Kreidie, "The Perspective of Islamic Fundamentalists and the Limits of Rational Choice Theory." *Political Psychology*, 18: 1 (1997), p. 27. Emphasis added. For more on the degree to which terrorists—even suicide terrorists—are *actually* rational, see especially Louise Richardson, *What Terrorists Want: Understanding the Enemy, Containing the Threat* (New York: Random House, 2007).

169. Huizinga, *Homo Ludens*, p. 91.

170. Seliktar, *Failing the Crystal Ball Test*, pp. 187–188.

171. Peters, "Our Old New Enemies," pp. 28–30.

172. Scheuer says that many of bin Ladin's demands are "substantive, tangible issues" in Shenon, *The Commission*, p. 189. Scheuer expands on this theme in Scheuer, *Through Our Enemies' Eyes*, pp. 45–74.

173. An excellent recent discussion of how to approach the concept of "theory of victory" is Colin S. Gray, "Defining and Achieving Decisive Victory" (Carlisle, PA: The Strategic Studies Institute of the U.S. Army War College, 2002), passim. However, the authors disagree with Gray's characterization of Al-Qa'ida's theory. For a discussion of the Islamic fundamentalist views of rational choice versus that of the average Muslim, see Monroe and Kreidie, "The Perspective of Islamic Fundamentalists and the Limits of Rational Choice Theory," pp. 31–41.

174. Commission, *The 9/11 Commission Report*, p. 345. As the commission points out on the same page, in 1994, a private plane was also crashed into the south lawn of the White House.

175. Coll, *Ghost Wars*, p. 275.

176. Commission, *The 9/11 Commission Report*, p. 345. For an accessible discussion of the logic of religious terrorism and violence, see Mark Juergensmeyer, *Terror in the Mind of God: The Rise of Global Religious Violence* (Berkeley: University of California Press, 2000), passim.

177. Weiner, *Legacy of Ashes*, p. 471.

178. Commission, *The 9/11 Commission Report*, p. 92. A *New York Times* article published about six months after the 9/11 Commission Report noted that the figure for Arabic Studies majors in 2003 had only risen to twenty-two. See Frederick P. Hitz, *Why Spy? Espionage in an Age of Uncertainty* (New York: St. Martin's Press, 2008), p. 69.

179. Wright, *The Looming Tower*, pp. 121–122.

180. Scheuer, *Through Our Enemies' Eyes*, p. 80.

181. Brugioni, "The Unidentifieds," p. 9.

182. Laqueur, *No End to War*, p. 132. He talks, of course, about Edward W. Said, *Orientalism: Western Conceptions of the Orient* (London: Penguin Books, 1995). Note that Said was a secularist of Christian descent but nevertheless felt that he had an explicit duty to defend Islam against its detractors.

183. Laqueur, *No End to War*, p. 133.

184. Robert Lempert, "Can Scenarios Help Policymakers Be Both Bold and Careful?" In F. Fukuyama, ed., *Blindside: How to Anticipate Forcing Events and Wild Cards in Global Politics* (Washington, DC: Brookings Institution Press, 2007), p. 113.

185. Quoted in Coll, *Ghost Wars*, p. 405.

186. Tenet and Harlow, *At the Center of the Storm*, p. 115.

187. Commission, *The 9/11 Commission Report*, p. 343.

188. For example, their remit included the actions of doomsday cults like Aum Shinrikyo that spread sarin nerve agent on the Tokyo subways system in 1995; see ibid., p. 198.

189. Zegart, *Spying Blind*, p. 84.

190. Russell, *Sharpening Strategic Intelligence*, pp. 124–125.

191. Zegart, *Spying Blind*, p. 91.

192. According to Gates, each of the CIA's four directorates (the Directorate of Operations, or DO; the Directorate of Intelligence, which does analysis, or DI; the Directorate of Science and Technology, or DS&T; and the Directorate of Administration, or D1) have "four distinct, bureaucratic cultures"; Gates, *From the Shadows*, p. 32. It seems apparent from the passage that follows that the preference for secret information in the DI is amplified in the DO. Note that the CIA was reorganized following 2001 and departments were changed. See the official CIA website, available at www.cia.gov/library/publications/additional-publications/the-work-of-a-nation/history/key-events.html.

193. Zegart, *Spying Blind*, p. 91. Emphasis added.

194. U.S. Congress, "Joint Inquiry into Intelligence Community Activities before and after the Terrorist Attacks of September 11, 2001," p. 338.

195. Shenon, *The Commission*, p. 189. Scheuer illuminates the parallels between bin Ladin and America's Founders and various Christian religious figures on pp. 3–14.

196. Ibid., p. 190. Confirmed in Steve Kroft, "Bin Laden Expert Steps Forward." *60 Minutes* (CBS News, August 22, 2005).

197. Heaven forfend! Shenon, *The Commission*, p. 190.

198. Ibid., p. 193. Confirmed by Wright, *The Looming Tower*, pp. 353–354.

199. Shenon, *The Commission*, p. 190.

200. Klug, "Bin Laden Expert Steps Forward." Though awkwardly phrased, this quotation is correctly quoted.

201. Commission, *The 9/11 Commission Report*, p. 109. See also Zegart, *Spying Blind*, p. 78.

202. U.S. Congress, "Joint Inquiry into Intelligence Community Activities before and after the Terrorist Attacks of September 11, 2001," pp. 339–340.

203. Quoted in Zegart, *Spying Blind*, p. 78. Emphasis added.

204. Wright, *The Looming Tower*, p. 353; Shenon, *The Commission*, p. 138. The Joint Inquiry even found that similar attitudes affected the analysis/tasking/collection interface: "A manager in the CTC confirmed to the Staff that CIA operations officers in the field resented being tasked by analysts because they did not like 'to take direction from the ladies from the Directorate of Intelligence.'" See U.S. Congress, "Joint Inquiry into Intelligence Community Activities before and after the Terrorist Attacks of September 11, 2001," p. 64.

205. Wright, *The Looming Tower*, pp. 353–354. This is confirmed in Shenon, *The Commission*, p. 190.

206. CIA, "OIG Report on CIA Accountability with Respect to the 9/11 Attacks," pp. xx–xxi.

207. Shenon, *The Commission*, p. 194.

208. As *60 Minutes* demonstrates, one of Scheuer's last proposals involved a cruise missile attack against a hunting camp in Afghanistan where bin Ladin was believed to be meeting with members of the royal family of the United Arab Emirates. The attack would have decimated the entire camp. When asked by the interviewer if this bothered him, he responds:

> The world is lousy with Arab princes . . . And if we could have got Usama bin Ladin, and saved at some point down the road 3,000 American lives, a few less Arab princes would have been OK in my book . . . Sister Virginia used to say, "You'll be known by the company you keep." That if those princes were out there eating goat with Usama bin Ladin, then maybe they were there for nefarious reasons. But nonetheless, they would have been the price of battle.

See Kroft, "Bin Laden Expert Steps Forward." ibid

209. Shenon, *The Commission*, p. 194.

210. Tenet and Harlow, *At the Center of the Storm*, p. 113. This, of course, raises the question of priorities: If the CIA is truly "at war" with Al-Qa'ida (as quoted in Commission, *The 9/11 Commission Report*, p. 357.), why is Alec Station—a primary weapon of that war—being run by a GS-13 with no paramilitary training six management layers down from the DCI? One may also ask how the Intelligence Community can be at war with an enemy that never rated an NIE.

211. Shenon, *The Commission*, p. 194.

212. Kroft, "Bin Laden Expert Steps Forward." Just to close the story: Scheuer left the CIA in 2004 and continues to make unofficial contributions to our national understanding of Al-Qa'ida; the CIA shut down the bin Ladin unit in 2006, but the hunt was given a new boost by President Obama, and bin Ladin was eventually killed in a U.S. raid into Pakistan in 2012.

213. Janne E. Nolan and Douglas J. MacEachin, *Discourse, Dissent, and Strategic Surprise: Formulating U.S. Security Policy in an Age of Uncertainty* (Washington, DC: Institute for the Study of Diplomacy, Edmund A. Walsh School of Foreign Service, Georgetown University, 2006), p. 104.

214. Philip A. True, "Be Forewarned: Surprises Are Inevitable." *The Washington Post*, June 5, 2002, p. A23.

215. Scheuer wrote in a *Washington Post* editorial:

> But what troubles me most is Tenet's handling of the opportunities that CIA officers gave the Clinton administration to capture or kill bin Ladin between May 1998 and May 1999. Each time we had intelligence about bin Ladin's whereabouts, Tenet was briefed by senior CIA officers at Langley and by operatives in the field. He would nod and assure his anxious subordinates that he would stress to Clinton and his national security team that the chances of capturing bin Ladin were

solid and that the intelligence was not going to get better. Later, he would insist that he had kept up his end of the bargain, but that the NSC had decided not to strike. Since 2001, however, several key Clinton counterterrorism insiders (including NSC staffers Richard A. Clarke, Daniel Benjamin and Steven Simon) have reported that Tenet consistently denigrated the targeting data on bin Ladin, causing the president and his team to lose confidence in the hard-won intelligence. "We could never get over the critical hurdle of being able to corroborate Bin Ladin's whereabouts," Tenet now writes. That of course is untrue, but it spared him from ever having to explain the awkward fallout if an attempt to get bin Ladin failed.

In any case, as Scheuer goes on to say: "The hard fact remains that each time we acquired actionable intelligence about bin Ladin's whereabouts, I argued for preemptive action." See Scheuer, "Tenet Tries to Shift the Blame. Don't Buy It," p. B1. See also Louis J. Freeh's memoirs, in which the former FBI director simply puts the blame to the Clinton administration's inability or unwillingness to act against bin Ladin; Freeh, *My FBI*.

216. Commission, *The 9/11 Commission Report*, p. 195.

217. Ibid., pp. 195–196. Emphasis added.

218. Graham Allison, "Conceptual Models and the Cuban Missile Crisis." *American Political Science Review*, 63: 3 (1969), pp. 689–718, p. 712.

219. Grabo, *Anticipating Surprise*, p. 142.

220. Quoted in Commission, *The 9/11 Commission Report*, p. 357.

221. U.S. Congress, "Joint Inquiry into Intelligence Community Activities before and after the Terrorist Attacks of September 11, 2001," p. 60. Emphasis added.

222. The Joint Inquiry also said, "Analysts at NSA commented to the Joint Inquiry that CTC viewed them as subordinate—'like an ATM for signals intelligence.'" See ibid., p. 64.

223. Zegart, *Spying Blind*, pp. 113–114. Emphasis added.

224. Mazzetti, "CIA Lays out Errors It Made before Sept. 11," p. A1.

225. Joseph W. Martin, "What Basic Intelligence Seeks to Do." *Studies in Intelligence*, 14: 2 (1970), p. 107.

Chapter 7

1. See Taleb, *The Black Swan*.

2. Kahn's carefully enumerated list of future-oriented policy research goals runs:

(1) To stimulate and stretch the imagination and improve the perspective; (2) To clarify, define, name, expound, and argue major issues; (3) To design and study alternative policy 'packages' and contexts; (4) To create propaedeutic and heuristic expositions, methodologies, paradigms, and frameworks; (5) To improve intellectual communication and cooperation, particularly by the use of historical

analogies, scenarios, metaphors, analytic models, precise concepts, and suitable language; (6) To increase the ability to identify new patterns and crises and to understand their character and significance; (7) To furnish specific knowledge and to generate and document conclusions, recommendations, and suggestions; (8) To clarify currently realistic policy choices, with emphasis on those that that retain efficiency and flexibility over a broad range of contingencies; (9) To improve the "administrative" ability of decision-makers and their staffs to react appropriately to the new and unfamiliar.

See Paul Dragos Aligica and Kenneth R. Weinstein, eds., *The Essential Herman Kahn: In Defense of Thinking* (New York: Lexington Books, 2009), in particular, Chapter 12, "The Objectives of Future-Oriented Policy Research." This basic insight from *Constructing Cassandra* seems to fulfill objectives 1, 2, 4, 5, and 6.

3. Cooper, *Curing Analytical Pathologies*, p. 26. Emphasis added.

4. It is hoped that the mere identification of these organizational dispositions is a partial solution to them, a sort of "immunizing awareness" (the equivalent of John Kenneth Galbraith's "immunizing memory" in economic behavior). As Lebow says: "From Max Weber on, good social scientists have recognized that any regularities in behavior must be understood in terms of their cultural setting and *endure only as long as it remains stable and the regularities themselves remain unrecognized by relevant actors.*" Richard Ned Lebow, "Counterfactuals, History and Fiction." *Historical Social Research—Special Issue: Counterfactual Thinking as a Scientific Method*, 34: 2 (2009), p. 57. Emphasis added. Cassandras, moreover, might be actively sought and treated more as "canaries in the coal mine" rather than as annoyances.

5. Bathurst, *Intelligence and the Mirror*, p. 88.

6. Diagnosing tasking in intelligence work becomes a variation on the verdict that Nobel Prize–winning physicist Richard Feynman offered on NASA's models during the investigation into the *Challenger* Space Shuttle disaster: "GIGO—garbage in, garbage out"; see Richard P. Feynman and Ralph Leighton, *What Do You Care What Other People Think?* (New York: W. W. Norton & Company, 2001), pp. 137–138.

7. Much the best general disquisition of this problem of overconfidence is found in Taleb, *The Black Swan* and *Fooled by Randomness*.

8. Thomas S. Kuhn, "Logic of Discovery or Psychological Research." In I. Lakatos and A. Musgrave, eds., *Criticism and the Growth of Knowledge* (Cambridge, UK: Cambridge University Press, 1970), p. 9. The use of this analogy brings to mind but is not a repeat of the arguments made in S. Gazit, "Estimates and Fortune Telling in Intelligence Work." *International Security*, 4 (1980), pp. 36–56.

9. Thomas U. Berger, "Norms, Identity and National Security in Germany and Japan." In P. Katzenstein, ed., *The Culture of National Security* (New York: Columbia University Press, 1996), p. 326.

10. By feedback, we are speaking here of a loose linkage because strategic surprises are not pure Perrow-like "Normal Accidents" (see Perrow, *Normal Accidents: Living with High Risk Technologies*, passim). The feedback loop described here is not a system of tightly linked components in a strict—and again, mechanistic or positivist—sense, though some parallels are intriguing. To take only one example: "Review" of analysts' work is a form of "safety feature" that contributes to the "accidents" (that is, surprises) by acting as a mechanism of involuntary consensus and suppression of both nuance and dissent. Handel explores this possible linkage in Michael I. Handel, *War, Strategy and Intelligence* (London: Routledge, 1989), pp. 272–274. Allison also briefly explores this idea in Allison and Zelikow, *Essence of Decision*, p. 159.

11. See Soros, *Alchemy of Finance*, pp. 317–322. Self-altering predictions, after all, cannot occur in the natural sciences, but they are the essence of strategic warning in many circumstances!

12. Betts, "Analysis, War, and Decision," p. 88. Emphasis in original.

13. Berkowitz and Goodman, *Best Truth*, p. 69.

14. For an extended discussion of its potentials flaws as an actual representation of the intelligence process, see Hulnick, "What's Wrong with the Intelligence Cycle."

15. Powers, "The Trouble with the CIA," p. 4.

16. Ruble, "Occasional Paper #283."

17. Jones, *The Human Factor*.

18. Kent, *Strategic Intelligence*, p. 157.

19. Paul Bracken, Ian Bremmer, and David Gordon, eds., *Managing Strategic Surprise: Lessons from Risk Management and Risk Assessment* (New York: Cambridge University Press, 2008), p. 308.

20. Betts, "Analysis, War, and Decision," p. 88. Emphasis in original.

21. John F. Schmitt, "A Systemic Concept for Operational Design"; retrieved on May 30, 2007, from the Air University website, www.au.af.mil/au/awc/awcgate/usmc/mcwl_schmitt_op_design.pdf.

22. Robert W. Pringle, "Trust Operation." In J. Woronoff, ed., *Historical Dictionary of Russian & Soviet Intelligence* (Lanham, MD: The Scarecrow Press, 2006), pp. 268–269. This approach drew on the rich history of the Okhrana's provocation and counterintelligence operations, some of the mechanics of which are detailed in Serge, *What Every Radical Should Know about State Repression*. A less extreme form might take an approach to analysis that the CIA took to certain cultural projects of the anti-Soviet Left in the 1950s and 1960s, as detailed in Frances Stonor Saunders, *Who Paid the Piper? CIA and the Cultural Cold War* (London: Granta Books, 2000); and *The Cultural Cold War: The CIA and the World of Arts and Letters* (New York: The New Press, 2001).

23. See, for example, Forecasting World Events, available at http://forecastwe.org/.

24. On why being customer centric leads to the demise of incumbent leaders in business, see Clayton M. Christensen, *The Innovator's Dilemma* (HarperCollins, 2000).

25. Fingar, *Reducing Uncertainty*.

26. Gresham's Law is an economic term that proposes that when two currencies are in circulation side by side, bad currency—that which is debased—tends to drive out sound, pure currency.

27. Alexander Wendt, *Social Theory of International Politics*. In S. Smith, ed., Cambridge Studies in International Relations (Cambridge, UK: Cambridge University Press, 1999), p. 154.

28. It is likely that Trotsky was consciously and somewhat ironically drawing on the rich Russian tradition of literary sketches of hunting trips and the Russian landscape; compare Turgenev's *Notes of a Hunter* or *Sketches from a Hunter's Album*.

29. Leon Trotsky, *My Life: An Attempt at an Autobiography* (New York: Pathfinder Press, 1970), p. 498. Emphasis added. For an accessible discussion of the "larger" factors that prevented Trotsky from succeeding Lenin, see Richard Pipes, *Three "Whys" of the Russian Revolution* (New York: Vintage Books, 1995), pp. 77–84.

30. Trotsky, *My Life*, pp. 494–495. Emphasis added.

31. Stephen Jay Gould, *Wonderful Life* (New York: W. W. Norton, 1989), p. 51. A full and rewarding exposition of Gould's view of contingency and history is presented in chapter V, pp. 292–324.

32. Quoted in David Darling, *Life Everywhere: The Maverick Science of Astrobiology* (New York: Basic Books, 2001), p. 124.

33. Leon Trotsky, *History of the Russian Revolution* (London: Pluto Press, 1977), p. 715, referring to the "Kornilov Affair"; quoted in Ann Talbot, "Chance and Necessity in History: E. H. Carr and Leon Trotsky Compared." *Historical Social Research*, 34: 2 (2009), p. 91.

34. For an excellent recent survey of how this is possible in the broader context of American power, see G. J. David Jr. and T. R. McKeldin III, eds., *Ideas as Weapons: Influence and Perception in Modern Warfare* (Dulles, VA: Potomac Books, 2009).

BIBLIOGRAPHY

Note: Primary sources drawn on in the text that were actual intelligence products (NIEs, SNIEs, sections from PDBs, internal CIA memos, and so on), are cited in the endnotes on the preceding pages but do not appear in the bibliography below. This bibliography does contain, however, the published collections of such documents from which those primary sources were drawn; these collections are mentioned in their respective footnotes alongside the intelligence products in each case. Where such primary documents were not found in published collections, their source is given in the appropriate endnote.

Abella, Alex. *Soldiers of Reason: The RAND Corporation and the Rise of the American Empire* (New York: Harcourt, 2008).

Agrell, Wilhelm. "When Everything Is Intelligence—Nothing Is Intelligence." *The Sherman Kent Center for Intelligence Analysis Occasional Papers*, 1: 4 (2002).

Alexseev, Mikhail A. *Without Warning: Threat Assessment, Intelligence and Global Struggle* (New York: St. Martin's Press, 1997).

Aligica, Paul Dragos, and Kenneth R. Weinstein, eds. *The Essential Herman Kahn: In Defense of Thinking* (New York: Lexington Books, 2009)

Allen, Edward R. "The Validity of Soviet Economic Statistics." *Studies in Intelligence*, 4: 3 (1960), pp. 1–8.

Allen, George W. *None So Blind: A Personal Account of the Intelligence Failure in Vietnam* (Chicago: Ivan R. Dee, 2001).

Allison, Graham. "Conceptual Models and the Cuban Missile Crisis." *American Political Science Review*, 63: 3 (1969), pp. 689–718.

———. "An Intelligence Agenda." *The New York Times*, December 21, 1980, p. 17.

Allison, Graham T., and Zelikow, Philip. *Essence of Decision: Explaining the Cuban Missile Crisis* (New York: Longman, 1999).

Allison, Rupert (writing as Nigel West). *Historical Dictionary of Cold War Counterintelligence* (Lanham, MD: Scarecrow Press, 2007).

Amuchastegui, Domingo. "Cuban Intelligence and the October Crisis." *Intelligence and National Security*, 13: 3 (1998), pp. 88–119.

Anderson, Dwayne. "On the Trail of the Alexandrovsk." *Studies in Intelligence*, 10: 1 (1966), pp. 39–43.

Andrew, Christopher M. "American Presidents and Their Intelligence Communities." In D. A. Charters, A. S. Farson, and G. P. Hastedt, eds., *Intelligence Analysis and Assessment* (London: Frank Cass, 1996).

———. *For the President's Eyes Only: Secret Intelligence and the American Presidency from Washington to Bush* (New York: HarperCollins, 1995).

Appelbaum, Henry R., and John Hollister Hedley. "US Intelligence and the End of the Cold War." *Studies in Intelligence*, 9 (2000), pp. 11–18.

Arani, S. "Iran: From the Shah's Dictatorship to Khomeini's Demagogic Theocracy." *Dissent*, 27 (1980), pp. 9–27.

Arjomand, Said Amir. "Iran's Islamic Revolution in Comparative Perspective." *World Politics*, 38 (1986), pp. 383–414.

Armstrong, Scott. "Carter Held Hope Even after Shah Had Lost His Way." *The Washington Post*, October 25, 1980.

———. "Failing to Heed the Warning of Revolutionary Iran." *The Washington Post*, October 26, 1980, p. A1.

———. "U.S. urged 'Crackdown on opposition.'" *The Washington Post*, October 28, 1980.

Armstrong, Willis C., William Leonhart, William McCaffery, and Herbert C. Rothenberg. "The Hazards of Single Outcome Forecasting." *Studies in Intelligence*, 28: 3 (1984), pp. 57–74.

Aslund, Anders. "The CIA vs. Soviet Reality." *The Washington Post*, May 19, 1988, p. A25.

Baer, Robert. *Sleeping with the Devil: How Washington Sold Our Soul for Saudi Crude* (New York: Crown Publishers, 2003).

Bamford, James. *Body of Secrets: Anatomy of the Ultra-Secret National Security Agency* (New York: Anchor Books, 2002).

Bar-Joseph, Uri, and Rose McDermott. "Change the Analyst and Not the System: A Different Approach to Intelligence Reform." *Foreign Policy Analysis* 4(2008), pp. 127–145.

Barnett, Michael N., and Martha Finnemore. "The Power, Politics and Pathologies of International Organizations." *International Organization*, 53: 4 (1999), pp. 699–732.

Bathurst, Robert B. *Intelligence and the Mirror: On Creating an Enemy* (London: Sage, 1993).

Bearden, Milt, and James Risen. *The Main Enemy: The Inside Story of the CIA's Final Showdown with the KGB* (New York: Random House, 2003).

Becker, Abraham S. "Intelligence Fiasco or Reasoned Accounting? CIA Estimates of Soviet GNP." *Post-Soviet Affairs* (1994).

Belotserkovsky, Vadim. "Letter to the Future Leaders of the Soviet Union." *Partisan Review*, 2 (1975), pp. 260–271.

Berger, Thomas U. "Norms, Identity and National Security in Germany and Japan." In P. Katzenstein, ed. *The Culture of National Security* (New York: Columbia University Press, 1996).

Bergman, Ronen. *The Secret War with Iran*, trans. R. Hope (New York: Free Press, 2008).

Berkowitz, Bruce D. "US Intelligence Estimates of Soviet Collapse: Reality and Perception." In F. Fukuyama, ed., *Blindside: How to Anticipate Forcing Events and Wild Cards in Global Politics* (Washington, DC: Brookings Institution Press, 2007).

Berkowitz, Bruce D., and Allen E. Goodman. *Best Truth: Intelligence in the Information Age* (New Haven, CT: Yale University Press, 2000).

———. *Strategic Intelligence for American National Security* (Princeton, NJ: Princeton University Press, 1989).

Berkowitz, Bruce D., and Jeffery T. Richelson. "CIA Vindicated: The Soviet Collapse Was Predicted." *The National Interest*, 41 (1995), pp. 36–46.

Betts, Richard K. "Analysis, War, and Decision: Why Intelligence Failures Are Inevitable." *World Politics*, 31: 1 (1978), 61–89.

———. *Enemies of Intelligence* (New York: Columbia University Press, 2007).

———. *Surprise Attack: Lessons for Defense Planning* (Washington, DC: Brookings Institution, 1982).

———. "Surprise, Scholasticism, and Strategy: A Review of Ariel Levite's Intelligence and Strategic Surprises." *International Studies Quarterly*, 33: 3 (1989), 329–343.

Bill, James A. *The Eagle and the Lion: The Tragedy of American–Iranian Relations* (New Haven, CT: Yale University Press, 1988).

———. "Iran and the Crisis of '78." *Foreign Affairs*, 57: 2 (1978–1979), pp. 323–342.

Birman, Igor. *Secret Incomes of the Soviet State Budget* (The Hague: Martinus Nijhoff, 1981).

———. "The Soviet Economy: Alternative Views." *Russia*, 12 (1986), pp. 60–74.

Bodansky, Yossef. *Bin Laden: The Man Who Declared War on America* (Rocklin, CA: Forum, 1999).

"Bolstering Russia's Image—and Its Intel?" Stratfor, Feb 1, 2008; available at www.stratfor.com/geopolitical_diary/geopolitical_diary_bolstering_russias_image_and_its_intel.

Bozeman, Adda B. "Iran: US Foreign Policy and the Tradition of Persian Statecraft." *Orbis*, 23 (1979), pp. 387–402.

———. "Political Intelligence in Non-Western Societies." In R. Godson, ed., *Comparing Foreign Intelligence: The US, the USSR and the Third World* (McLean, VA: Pergamon Brassey, 1988).

Bracken, Paul, Ian Bremmer, and David Gordon, eds. *Managing Strategic Surprise: Lessons from Risk Management and Risk Assessment* (New York: Cambridge University Press, 2008).

Brooks, David. "The C.I.A: Method and Madness." *The New York Times*, February 3, 2004, 23.

Brooks, Stephen G., and William C. Wohlforth. "Power, Globalization and the End of the Cold War: Re-evaluating a Landmark Case for Ideas." *International Security*, 25: 3 (2000), pp. 5–53.

Brugioni, Dino A. *Eyeball to Eyeball* (New York: Random House, 1991).

———. "The Unidentifieds." In H. B. Westerfield, ed., *Inside CIA's Private World: Declassified Articles from the Agency's Internal Journal 1955–1992* (New Haven, CT: Yale University Press, 1995).

Brzezinski, Zbigniew K. *Power and Principle: Memoirs of the National Security Adviser 1977–1981* (New York: Farrar, Straus, Giroux, 1983).

———. "Tragic Dilemmas of Soviet World Power: The Limits of a New-Type Empire." *Encounter*, 61 (1983), pp. 10–17.

Bukharin, Oleg A. "The Cold War Atomic Intelligence Game, 1945–70." *Studies in Intelligence*, 48: 2 (2004), pp. 1–11.

Bundy, McGeorge. *Danger and Survival: Choices about the Bomb in the First Fifty Years* (New York: Random House, 1988).

Byman, Daniel. "Strategic Surprise and the September 11th Attacks." *Annual Review of Political Science* 8(2005), pp. 145–170.

Calhoun, Craig, ed. "Cargo Cults." *Dictionary of the Social Sciences* (Oxford, UK: Oxford University Press, 2003)

Callum, Robert. "The Case for Cultural Diversity in the Intelligence Community." *International Journal of Intelligence and Counterintelligence*, 14: 1 (2001), pp. 25–48.

Carver, George A. Jr. "Intelligence in the Age of Glasnost." *Foreign Affairs*, 69: 3 (1990), pp. 147–166.

Cassara, John A. *Hide & Seek: Intelligence, Law Enforcement, and the Stalled War on Terrorist Finance* (Washington, DC: Potomac Books, 2006).

Chang, Laurence, and Peter Kornbluh, eds. *The Cuban Missile Crisis 1962: A National Security Archive Reader* (New York: The New Press, 1998)

Cherkashin, Victor, and Gregory Feifer. *Spy Handler: Memoir of a KGB Officer* (New York: Basic Books, 2005).

Christensen, Clayton M. *The Innovator's Dilemma* (HarperCollins, 2000).

"CI Centre Course 105: John Walker Case." In *Counter-Intelligence Centre Podcasts*, 7:32. (Washington, DC: The Counter-Intelligence Centre, 2007).

CIA. "A Compendium of Analytic Tradecraft Notes, Volume I" (Langley, VA: Product Evaluation Staff of the Directorate of Intelligence, Central Intelligence Agency, 1995).

———. *A Consumer's Guide to Intelligence* (Washington, DC: Office of Public Affairs, Central Intelligence Agency, 1994).

———. *A Consumer's Guide to Intelligence* (Washington, DC: Office of Public Affairs, Central Intelligence Agency, 1999).

———. Economic Research (ER) 77-10436U, *Soviet Economic Problems and Prospects.* (Langley, VA: CIA, 1977).

———. *Factbook on Intelligence* (Washington DC: Office of Public Affairs, Central Intelligence Agency, 1997).

———. *Handbook of Economic Statistics* (Washington, DC: The Central Intelligence Agency, 1989).

———. "A Look Back... Remembering the Cuban Missile Crisis" *CIA Featured Story Archive* (Washington, DC: CIA, 2007), available at www.cia.gov/news-information/featured-story-archive/2007-featured-story-archive/a-look-back-remembering-the-cuban-missile-crisis.html.

———. "OIG Report on CIA Accountability with Respect to the 9/11 Attacks." Office of the Inspector General, editor. (Washington, DC: Central Intelligence Agency, 2005).

CIA Office of Research and Reports, "Cuba 1962: Khrushchev's Miscalculated Risk." EP SC 64-5, February 13, 1964.

Clark, Robert M. *Intelligence Analysis: A Target-Centric Approach* (Washington, DC: CQ Press, 2004).

Clarke, Richard A. *Against All Enemies: Inside America's War on Terror* (New York: Free Press, 2004).

Cline, Ray S. "Is Intelligence Over-Coordinated?" *Studies in Intelligence* (Fall 1957).

CNN. "Inside the CIA: An Interview with Former CIA Analyst Melvin Goodman." In *Cold War* (Cable News Network, 1998).

Codevilla, Angelo M. *Informing Statecraft: Intelligence for a New Century* (New York,: The Free Press, 1992).

Cogan, Charles G. "The In-Culture of the DO." *Intelligence and National Security*, 8: 1 (1993), pp. 78–86.

Coll, Steve. *Ghost Wars: The Secret History of the CIA, Afghanistan, and bin Laden, from the Soviet Invasion to September 10, 2001* (New York: Penguin Books, 2005).

"Commission on the Roles and Capabilities of the United States Intelligence Community." (Washington, DC: Permanent Select Committee on Intelligence, U.S. House of Representatives, US Government Printing Office, 1996).

———. "Preparing for the 21st Century: An Appraisal of U.S. intelligence: Report of the Commission on the Roles and Capabilities of the United States Intelligence Community." In *Commission on the Roles and Capabilities of the United States Intelligence Community* (Washington, DC: US Government Printing Office, 1996).

———. "A Compendium of Analytic Tradecraft Notes, Volume I" (Langley, VA: Product Evaluation Staff of the Directorate of Intelligence, Central Intelligence Agency, 1995).

Conquest, Robert. *Harvest of Sorrow: Soviet Collectivization and the Terror-Famine* (London: Pimlico, 1986).

Coogan, P. T. "America's Strategic Blunders: Intelligence Analysis and National Security Policy, 1936–1991." *Journal of Military History*, 66: 1 (2002), 275–276.

Cooper, Jeffery R. *Curing Analytical Pathologies: Pathways to Improved Intelligence Analysis* (Langley, VA: Central Intelligence Agency, Center for the Study of Intelligence, 2005).

Cornelius, Peter, Alexander Van de Putte, and Matti Romani. "Three Decades of Scenario Planning in Shell." *California Management Review*, 48: 1 (2005), pp. 92–109.

Cox, Michael, ed. *Rethinking the Soviet Collapse: Sovietology, the Death of Communism and the New Russia* (London: Pinter, 1998).

———. "Whatever Happened to the USSR? Critical Reflections on Soviet Studies." In M. Cox, ed., *Rethinking the Soviet Collapse: Sovietology, the Death of Communism and the New Russia* (London: Pinter, 1998).

Crane, Susan A. "(Not) Writing History: Rethinking the Intersections of Personal History and Collective Memory with Hans Von Aufsess." *History and Memory*, 8 (1996), pp. 5–29.

Cremeans, Charles D. "Basic Psychology for Intelligence Analysts." *Studies in Intelligence*, 15: 1 (1971), pp. 109–114.

Croom, Herman L. "The Exploitation of Foreign Open Sources." *Studies in Intelligence*, 13 (Summer 1969), pp. 129–136.

Darling, David. *Life Everywhere: The Maverick Science of Astrobiology* (New York: Basic Books, 2001).

Daugherty, William J. "Behind the Intelligence Failure in Iran." *International Journal of Intelligence and Counterintelligence*, 14: 4 (2005), pp. 449–484.

David G. J. Jr., and T. R. McKeldin III, eds. *Ideas as Weapons: Influence and Perception in Modern Warfare* (Dulles, VA: Potomac Books, 2009).

Davies, Philip H. J. "Intelligence Culture and Intelligence Failure in Britain and the United States." *Cambridge Review of International Affairs*, 17: 3 (2004), pp. 495–520.

Davis, Jack. "Combating Mind-Set." *Studies in Intelligence*, 36: 5 (1992), pp. 33–38.

———. "Strategic Warning: If Surprise Is Inevitable, What Role for Analysis?" *Occasional Papers*, 2: 1 (2003).

Diamond, John. *The CIA and the Culture of Failure: US Intelligence from the End of the Cold War to the Invasion of Iraq* (Stanford, CA: Stanford University Press, 2008).

"DNI Brings Private Firms Into Intelligence Sharing Effort." *Intelligence Online*, August 25, 2006.

Donovan, Michael. "National Intelligence and the Iranian Revolution." *Intelligence and National Security*, 12: 1 (1997), pp. 143–163.

Dujmovic, Nicholas. "Fifty Years of Studies in Intelligence." *Studies in Intelligence*, 49: 4 (2005), pp. 1–15.

Dulles, Allen W. *The Craft of Intelligence* (Guilford, CT: The Lyons Press, 2006).

Eberstadt, Nicholas. *The Tyranny of Numbers: Mismeasurement and Misrule* (Washington, DC: American Enterprise Institute Press 1995).

Elbaz, Michel. "Russian Secrets of Al-Qaeda's Number Two—19 July." Axisglobe.com, 2005.

———. "Soviet Past of Worldwide Jihad—21 July." Axisglobe.com, 2005.

———. "Unknown History of Jihad—20 July." Axisglobe.com, 2005.

Eliot, George. *Felix Holt, The Radical* (New York: Harper & Brothers, 1866).

Ellison, Dawn. "One Woman's Contribution to Social Change at CIA." *Studies in Intelligence*, 46: 3 (2002), pp. 45–53.

Engelberg, Stephen. "CIA Says It Has Restored Link to Campuses to Get More Advice." *The New York Times*, January 19, 1986, p. 1.

Falkenrath, Richard A. "The 9/11 Commission Report: A Review Essay." *International Security*, 29: 3 (2004–2005), pp. 170–190.

Felix, Christopher. *A Short Course in the Secret War*, 4th ed . (Lanham, MD: Madison Books, 1963).

Ferguson, Gregor. *Coup d'État: A Practical Manual* (Poole, Dorset, UK: Arms and Armour Press, 1987).

Ferguson, Niall. "Political Risk and the International Bond Market between the 1848 Revolution and the Outbreak of the First World War." *Economic History Review*, 59: 1 (2006), pp. 70–112.

Feyerabend, Paul. *Against Method* (London: Verso, 1993).

Feynman, Richard P., and Ralph Leighton. *What Do You Care What Other People Think?* (New York: W. W. Norton & Company, 2001).

Fingar, Thomas. *Reducing Uncertainty: Intelligence Analysis and National Security* (Stanford, CA: Stanford University Press, 2011).

Firth, Noel E., and James H. Noren. *Soviet Defense Spending: A History of CIA Estimates 1950–1990* (College Station: Texas A&M University, 1998).

Fischer, Benjamin B. *At Cold War's End: US Intelligence on the Soviet Union and Eastern Europe* (Washington, DC: History Staff, Center for the Study of Intelligence, 1999).

Fisk, Robert. "Anti-Soviet Warrior Puts His Army on the Road to Peace." *Financial Times*, December 6, 1993.

Freeh, Louis J. *My FBI: Bringing Down the Mafia, Investigating Bill Clinton, and Fighting the War on Terror* (New York: St. Martin Griffin, 2005).

Friedman, George. *America's Secret War: Inside the Hidden Worldwide Struggle between America and Its Enemies* (New York: Doubleday, 2004).

Fursenko, Aleksandr, and Timothy Naftali. *One Hell of a Gamble: Khrushchev, Castro and Kennedy, 1958-1964* (New York: W. W. Norton, 1997).

Gaddis, John Lewis. *We Now Know: Rethinking Cold War History* (New York: Oxford University Press, 1997).

Gates, Robert M. "Discussion." In R. Godson, ed., *Intelligence Requirements for the 1990s: Collection, Analysis, Counterintelligence and Covert Action* (Lexington, MA: Lexington Books, 1989).

———. *From the Shadows: The Ultimate Insider's Story of Five Presidents and How They Won the Cold War* (New York: Simon and Schuster, 1996).

———. "An Opportunity Unfulfilled: The Use and Perception of Intelligence at the White House." *Washington Quarterly* (Winter 1989).

———. "The Prediction of Soviet Intentions." *Studies in Intelligence*, 17: 1 (1973), pp. 39–46.

———. "Remarks to DDI Analysts and Managers on 7 January, 1982." Cited in John A. Gentry, "Intelligence Analyst/Manager Relations at the CIA." In D. A. Charters, S. Farson, and G. P. Hastedt, eds., Intelligence Analysis and Assessment (London: Frank Cass, 1996), pp. 140–141.

Gazit, S. "Estimates and Fortune Telling in Intelligence Work." *International Security*, 4 (1980), pp. 36–56.

Geddes, B. "How the Cases You Choose Affect the Answers You Get: Selection Bias in Comparative Politics." In J. A. Stimson, ed., *Political Analysis: An Annual Publication of the Methodology Section of the American Political Science Association* (Ann Arbor: University of Michigan Press, 1990).

Gentry, John A. "Intelligence Analyst/Manager Relations at the CIA." In D. A. Charters, S. Farson, and G. P. Hastedt, eds., *Intelligence Analysis and Assessment* (London: Frank Cass, 1996).

George, Roger Z. "Fixing the Problem of Analytical Mindsets: Alternative Analysis." In R. Z. George and R. D. Kline, eds., *Intelligence and the National Security Strategist: Enduring Issues and Challenges* (Lanham, MD: Rowman & Littlefield Publishers, 2006).

Gerecht, Reuel Marc. "The Counterterrorist Myth." *Atlantic Monthly*, July–August 2001.

Gertz, Bill. "CIA Officials 'Cooked Books,' Ex-Analyst Says." *The Washington Times*, March 27, 1991, p. A3.

Ginor, Isabella, and Gideon Remez. *Foxbats over Dimona: The Soviets' Nuclear Gamble in the Six-Day War* (New Haven, CT: Yale University Press, 2007).

Glassé, Cyril. *The Concise Encyclopedia of Islam* (New York: HarperCollins, 1991).

Gleichauf, Justin F. "A Listening Post in Miami." *Studies in Intelligence*, 46: 10 (2001), pp. 49–53.

Godson, Roy. *Intelligence Requirements for the 1980's: Elements of Intelligence* (Washington, DC: National Strategy Information Center, 1979).

Gold, Bill. "The Shah Was Also Surprised." *The Washington Post*, November 19, 1979, p. B10.

Goldman, Jan, ed. *The Ethics of Spying: A Reader for the Intelligence Professional* (Lanham, MD: Scarecrow Press, 2006).

Goodman, Melvin A. "9/11: The Failure of Strategic Intelligence." *Intelligence and National Security*, 18: 4 (2003), pp. 59–71.

———. "Ending the CIA's Cold War Legacy." *Foreign Policy*, 106: 106 (1997), pp. 128–143.

Gottesman, A. Edward. "Two Myths of Globalization." *World Policy Journal*, XXIII: 1 (2006), pp. 37–45.

Gould, Stephen Jay. *Wonderful Life* (New York: W. W. Norton, 1989).

Gowers, Andrew. "Review of *The Eagle and the Lion: The Tragedy of American–Iranian Relations*, by James A. Bill." *The Financial Times*, May 26, 1988, p. 26.

Grabo, Cynthia M., *Anticipating Surprise: Analysis for Strategic Warning* (Lanham, MD: University Press of America, 2004).

Graham, Daniel O. "Analysis and Estimates." In R. Godson, ed., *Intelligence Requirements for the 1980's: Elements of Intelligence* (Washington, DC: National Strategy Information Center, 1979).

Gravalos, M. E. O. "Pitfall of a Latin Quirk." *Studies in Intelligence*, 7: 4 (1963), pp. 31–32.

Gray, Colin S. "Defining and Achieving Decisive Victory." Carlisle, PA: The Strategic Studies Institute of the U.S. Army War College, 2002.

Gribkov, Anatoli I., and William Y. Smith. *Operation Anadyr: US and Soviet Generals Recount the Cuban Missile Crisis* (Chicago, IL: Edition Q, 1994).

Haas, Peter M. "Introduction: Epistemic Communities and International Policy Coordination." *International Organization*, 46: 1 (1992).

Haines, Gerald K., and Robert E. Leggett, eds. *CIA's Analysis of the Soviet Union 1947–1991: A Documentary Collection* (Washington, DC: Center for the Study of Intelligence, 2001).

Halliday, Fred. "The Iranian Revolution and Great Power Politics: Components of the First Decade." In N. R. Keddie and M. J. Gasiorowski, eds., *Neither East nor West: Iran, the Soviet Union and the United States* (New Haven, CT: Yale University Press, 1990).

Handel, Michael I. "Intelligence and the Problem of Strategic Surprise." In R. K. Betts and T. G. Mahnken, eds., *Paradoxes of Strategic Intelligence* (London: Frank Cass, 2003).

———. *War, Strategy and Intelligence* (London: Routledge, 1989).

Hansen, James H. "Soviet Deception in the Cuban Missile Crisis." *Studies in Intelligence*, 46: 1 (2002), pp. 49–58.

Hedley, John Hollister. "Twenty Years of Officers in Residence." *Studies in Intelligence*, 49: 4 (2005), pp. 31–41.

Hedstrom, Peter, and Richard Swedberg. "Social Mechanisms: An Introductory Essay." In P. Hedstrom and R. Swedberg, eds., *Social Mechanisms: An Analytical Approach to Social Theory* (Cambridge, UK: Cambridge University Press, 1998).

Helgerson, John L. *CIA Briefings of the Presidential Candidates, 1952–1992* (Laguna Hills, CA: Aegean Park Press, 2000).

Helms, Cynthia. *An Ambassador's Wife in Iran* (New York: Dodd, Mead & Company, 1981).

Helms, Richard, and William Hood. *A Look over My Shoulder: A Life in the Central Intelligence Agency* (New York: Ballantine, 2003).

Henshel, Richard L. "The Boundary of the Self-Fulfilling Prophecy and the Dilemma of Social Prediction." *The British Journal of Sociology*, 33: 4 (1982), pp. 511–528.

Herman, Michael. *Intelligence Power in Peace and War* (Cambridge, UK: Royal Institute of International Affairs, 1996).

Herman, Robert G. "Identity, Norms and National Security: The Soviet Foreign Policy Revolution and the End of the Cold War." In P. Katzenstein, ed., *The Culture of National Security* (New York: Columbia University Press, 1996).

Heuer, Richards J. *The Psychology of Intelligence Analysis* (Langley, VA: Center for the Study of Intelligence, CIA, 1999).

———. *Quantitative Approaches to Political Intelligence: The CIA Experience* (Boulder, CO: Westview Press, 1978).

Heuer, Richards J., and Randolph H. Pherson. *Structured Analytic Techniques for Intelligence Analysis* (Washington, DC: CQ Press, 2011).

Hewett, Tom, Emile Morse, and Jean Scholtz. "In Depth Observational Studies of Professional Intelligence Analysts." (Washington, DC: The US National Institute of Standards and Technology, 2004).

Hill, Ron. "Social Science, 'Slavistics' and Post-Soviet Studies." In M. Cox, ed., *Rethinking the Soviet Collapse: Sovietology, the Death of Communism and the New Russia* (London: Pinter, 1998).

Hitz, Frederick P. *Why Spy? Espionage in an Age of Uncertainty* (New York: St. Martin's Press, 2008).

Hoagland, Jim. "CIA–Shah Ties Cloud Iran Data." *The Washington Post*, December 17, 1978, p. A21.

———. "CIA Will Survey Moslems Worldwide." *The Washington Post*, January 20, 1979, p. A1.

Hoffman, Bruce. "The Modern Terrorist Mindset." In R. D. Howard and R. L. Sawyer, eds., *Terrorism and Counterterrorism: Understanding the New Security Environment* (Guilford, CT: McGraw Hill, 2002).

Holland, Max. "The 'Photo Gap' That Delayed Discovery of Missiles." *Studies in Intelligence*, 49: 4 (2005), pp. 15–30.

Hollywood, John, Diane Snyder, Kenneth McKay, and John Boon Jr., *Out of the Ordinary: Finding Hidden Threats by Analyzing Unusual Behavior* (Santa Monica, CA: The RAND Corporation, 2004).

Horelick, Arnold L. "The Cuban Missile Crisis: An Analysis of Soviet Calculations and Behavior." *World Politics*, 16: 3 (1964), pp. 363–389.

House Committee on International Relations. *United States Policy toward North Korea: Testimony of Nicholas Eberstadt, American Enterprise Institute for Public Policy Research*. September 24, 1998.

House Permanent Select Committee on Intelligence—Review Committee. *An Evaluation of CIA's Analysis of Soviet Economic Performance 1970–1990* (Washington, DC: U.S. Government Printing Office, November 18, 1991.

Hudson, Valerie M., ed. *Culture & Foreign Policy* (Boulder, CO: Lynne Rienner Publishing, 1997).

Hughes, Thomas L. *The Fate of Facts in a World of Men: Foreign Policy and Intelligence-Making* (New York: The Foreign Policy Association, 1976).

Huizinga, Johan. *Homo Ludens: A Study of the Play Element in Culture* (Boston, MA: Beacon Press, 1955).

Hulnick, Arthur S., "What's Wrong with the Intelligence Cycle?" *Intelligence and National Security*, 21: 6 (2007), 959–979.

"Intelligence and Crisis Forecasting." *Orbis*, 27: 4 (1989), pp. 817–848.

Jasny, Naum. *Essays on the Soviet Economy* (New York: F. A. Praeger, 1962).

Jeffreys-Jones, Rhodri. "The Socio-Educational Composition of the CIA Elite: A Statistical Note." *Journal of American Studies*, 19: 1 (1985).

———. "Why was the CIA established in 1947?", in R. Jeffreys-Jones and C. M. Andrew, editors, *Eternal Vigilance? 50 Years of the CIA* (London: Frank Cass, 1997).

Jervis, Robert. "Minimizing Misperception." In M. G. Bonham and M. J. Shapiro, eds., *Thought and Action in Foreign Policy* (Stanford, CA: Center for Advanced Studies in the Behavioral Sciences, 1973).

———. *Perception and Misperception in International Politics* (Princeton, NJ: Princeton University Press, 1976).

———. "What's Wrong with the Intelligence Process?" *International Journal of Intelligence and Counterintelligence*, 1 (1986), pp. 28–43.

Johnson, Daniel. *White King and Red Queen: How the Cold War Was Fought on the Chessboard* (New York: Houghton Mifflin Company, 2008).

Johnson, James Turner. *The Holy War Idea in Western and Islamic Traditions* (University Park: Pennsylvania State University, 1997).

Johnson, Loch K. "The DCI and the Eight-Hundred-Pound Gorilla." In R. Z. George and R. D. Kline, eds., *Intelligence and the National Security Strategist: Enduring Issues and Challenges* (Lanham, MD: Rowman & Littlefield Publishers, 2006).

Johnson, Thomas R., and David A. Hatch. *NSA and the Cuban Missile Crisis* (Fort Meade, MD: U.S. National Security Agency, 1998).

Johnston, Rob. *Analytic Culture in the US Intelligence Community: An Ethnographic Study* (Washington, DC: Center for the Study of Intelligence, Central Intelligence Agency, 2005).

———. "Developing a Taxonomy of Intelligence Analysis Variables." *Studies in Intelligence*, 47: 3 (2004).

Joint Chiefs of Staff. "Military Deception: Joint Publication 3-13.4" (Washington, DC: Joint Chiefs of Staff of United States Department of Defense, 2006).

Jones, Ishmael. *The Human Factor: Inside the CIA's Dysfunctional Intelligence Culture* (New York: Encounter Books, 2008).

Juergensmeyer, Mark. *Terror in the Mind of God: The Rise of Global Religious Violence* (Berkeley: University of California Press, 2000).

Kalugin, Oleg, and Fen Montaigne. *The First Directorate* (New York: St. Martin's Press, 1994).

Kam, Ephraim. *Surprise Attack: The Victim's Perspective* (Cambridge, MA: Harvard University Press, 1988).

Karabell, Zachary. "Inside the US Espionage Den: The US Embassy and the Fall of the Shah." *Intelligence and National Security*, 8: 1 (1993), pp. 44–59.

Katzenstein, Peter. *The Culture of National Security* (New York: Columbia University Press, 1996).

Kaufmann, Walter. *The Portable Nietzsche* (New York: Penguin Books, 1982).

Kendall, Willmoore. "The Function of Intelligence." *World Politics*, 1 (1949), pp. 540–552.

Kennedy, David M. "Sunshine and Shadow: The CIA and the Soviet Economy, Case C16-91-1096.0." (Cambridge, MA: Kennedy School of Government, Harvard University, 1991).

Kent, Sherman. "A Crucial Estimate Relived." *Studies in Intelligence*, 8: 2 (1964), pp. 1–18.

———. "The Need for an Intelligence Literature." *Studies in Intelligence*, 1 (1955): 1.

———. "Preface—1966." In *Strategic Intelligence for American World Policy* (Princeton, NJ: Princeton University Press, 1966).

———. "Sherman Kent and the Board of National Estimates: Collected Essays." (Washington, DC: Center for the Study of Intelligence, Central Intelligence Agency).

———. *Strategic Intelligence for American World Policy* (Princeton, NJ: Princeton University Press, 1949).

———. "Words of Estimative Probability." *Studies in Intelligence* (Fall 1964).

Kerbel, Josh. "Thinking Straight: Cognitive Bias in the US Debate about China." *Studies in Intelligence*, 48: 3 (2004).

Khong, Yuen Foong. *Analogies at War: Korea, Munich, Dien Bien Phu, and the Vietnam Decisions of 1965* (Princeton, NJ: Princeton University Press, 1992).

Khrushchev, Nikita Sergeevich. *Khrushchev Remembers*. S. Talbott, trans. (New York: Little Brown & Company, 1970).

Kinch, Penelope. "The Iranian Crisis and the Dynamics of Advice and Intelligence in the Carter Administration." *The Journal of Intelligence History* 6 (Winter 2006), pp. 75–87.

Kipling, Rudyard. *Barrack Room Ballads* (New York: Signet Classics, 2003).

Kissinger, Henry. *The White House Years* (Boston, MA: Little, Brown and Company, 1979).

Kroft, Steve. "Bin Laden Expert Steps Forward." *60 Minutes*. CBS News, August 22, 2005.

Knapp, Frank A. Jr. "Styles and Stereotypes in Intelligence Studies." *Studies in Intelligence*, 8: 2 (1964), pp. A1–A5.

Knorr, Klaus. "Failures in National Intelligence Estimates: The Case of the Cuban Missiles." *World Politics*, 16 (1964), pp. 455–467.

Kotkin, Stephen. *Armageddon Averted: The Soviet Collapse 1970–2000* (Oxford, UK: Oxford University Press, 2001).

Kowert, Paul, and Jeffrey Legro. "Norms, Identity and Their Limits, A Theoretical Reprise." In P. Katzenstein, ed., *The Culture of National Security: Norms and Identity in World Politics* (New York: Columbia University Press, 1996).

Kuhn, Thomas S. "Logic of Discovery or Psychological Research." In I. Lakatos and A. Musgrave, eds., *Criticism and the Growth of Knowledge* (Cambridge, UK: Cambridge University Press, 1970).

Kuhns, Woodrow J. "Intelligence Failures: Forecasting and the Lessons of Epistemology." In R. K. Betts and T. G. Mahnken, eds., *Paradoxes of Strategic Intelligence* (London: Frank Cass, 2003).

Kurzman, Charles. *The Unthinkable Revolution in Iran* (Cambridge, MA: Harvard University Press, 2004).

Labedz, Leopold. "Democratic Centralism." In A. Bullock and S. Trombley, eds., *The New Fontana Dictionary of Modern Thought* (London: HarperCollins, 1999).

Lakatos, Imré, and Alan Musgrave. *Criticism and the Growth of Knowledge* (Cambridge, UK: Cambridge University Press, 1970).

Lantis, Jeffery S. "Strategic Culture and National Security Strategy." *International Studies Review*, 4: 3 (2002), pp. 87–114.

Laqueur, Walter. *No End to War: Terrorism in the Twenty-First Century* (New York: Continuum, 2004).

——. *A World of Secrets: Uses and Limits of Intelligence* (New York: Basic Books, 1985).

Lebow, Richard Ned. "Counterfactuals, History and Fiction." *Historical Social Research—Special Issue: Counterfactual Thinking as a Scientific Method*, 34: 2 (2009), pp. 57–73.

——. "The Cuban Missile Crisis: Reading the Lessons Correctly." *Political Science Quarterly*, 98: 3 (1983), pp. 431–458.

Lebow, Richard Ned, and Janice Gross Stein. "Back to the Past: Counterfactuals and the Cuban Missile Crisis." In P. E. Tetlock and A. Belkin, eds., *Counterfactual Thought Experiments in World Politics* (Princeton, NJ: Princeton University Press, 1996).

Lempert, Robert. "Can Scenarios Help Policymakers Be Both Bold and Careful?" In F. Fukuyama, ed., *Blindside: How to Anticipate Forcing Events and Wild Cards in Global Politics* (Washington, DC: Brookings Institution Press, 2007).

Levite, Ariel. "Intelligence and Strategic Surprises." PhD dissertation, Cornell, 1983.

——. *Intelligence and Strategic Surprises* (New York: Columbia University Press, 1987).

Lewis, Bernard. "License to Kill: Osama Bin Laden's Declaration of Jihad." *Foreign Affairs*, 77: 6 (1998), pp. 14–19.

Lipsky, Seth. "A Primer for Spies." *The Washington Post*, March 12, 1979, p. A19.

Loeb, Vernon. "Back Channels: The Intelligence Community." *The Washington Post*, November 19, 1999, p. A43.

Lowenthal, Mark M. *Intelligence: From Secrets to Policy* (Washington, DC: CQ Press, 2002).

——. "Open-Source Intelligence: New Myths, New Realities." In R. Z. George and R. D. Kline, eds., *Intelligence and the National Security Strategist: Enduring Issues and Challenges* (Lanham, MD: Rowman & Littlefield Publishers, 2006).

Lundberg, Kirsten. "CIA and the Fall of the Soviet Empire: The Politics of 'Getting It Right.'" (Cambridge, MA: Kennedy School of Government, Harvard University, 1994).

Luttwak, Edward N. *Coup d'État: A Practical Handbook* (Cambridge, MA: Harvard University Press, 1979).

——. *Strategy: The Logic of War and Peace*, 2nd ed. (Cambridge, MA: Harvard University Press, 2002).

——. *The Rise of China Versus the Logic of Strategy* (Cambridge, MA: Harvard University Press, 2012).

MacEachin, Douglas J. *CIA Assessments of the Soviet Union: The Record Versus the Charges* (Washington, DC: Center for the Study of Intelligence, 1996).

MacEachin, Douglas J., Janne Nolan, and Kristine Tockman. "Iran: Intelligence Failure or Policy Stalemate?" In *Discourse, Dissent and Strategic Surprise: Formulating American Security in an Age of Uncertainty* (Washington, DC: Institute for the Study of Diplomacy, Georgetown University, 2004).

Mahl, Thomas E. *Desperate Deception: British Covert Operations in the United States, 1939-44* (London: Brassey's, 1999).

Marks, Steven G. *How Russia Shaped the Modern World: From Art to Anti-Semitism, Ballet to Bolshevism* (Princeton, NJ: Princeton University Press, 2003).

Marrin, Stephen. "CIA's Kent School: Improving Training for New Analysts." *International Journal of Intelligence and Counterintelligence*, 16: 4 (2003), pp. 609–637.

———. "CIA's Kent School: A Step In the Right Direction." *International Studies Association Conference*. New Orleans, LA: ISA Archive Online, 2002.

———. "Intelligence Analysis and Decisionmaking: Proximity Matters." PhD dissertation, University of Virginia, 2009.

———. "Intelligence Analysis: Turning a Craft Into a Profession." In *2005 International Conference of Intelligence Analysis* (McLean, VA: Mitre Corporation, 2005).

Marsh, Henry S., and Jennie A. Stevens. "Surprise and Deception in Soviet Military Thought, Part I." *Military Review*: June (1982), pp. 1–11.

Martin, David C. *Wilderness of Mirrors* (Guilford, CT: The Lyons Press, 2003).

Martin, Joseph W. "What Basic Intelligence Seeks to Do." *Studies in Intelligence*, 14: 2 (1970), pp. 103–113.

Matlock, Jack F. "Western Intelligence and the Collapse of the Soviet Union, 1980–1990: Ten Years That Did Not Shake the World (review)." *Journal of Cold War Studies*, 6 (Spring 2004), pp. 99–101.

Matthias, Willard C. *America's Strategic Blunders* (University Park: Pennsylvania State University Press, 2001).

Maxfield, Myles, Robert Proper, and Sharol Case. "Remote Medical Diagnosis: Monitoring the Health of Very Important Patients." *Studies in Intelligence*, 23: 1 (1979), pp. 9–14.

May, Ernest R., and Philip D. Zelikow, eds., *Dealing with Dictators: Dilemmas of US Diplomacy and Intelligence Analysis, 1945-1990* (Cambridge, MA: MIT Press, 2006).

Mazzetti, Mark. "CIA Lays out Errors It Made before Sept. 11." *The New York Times*, August 22, 2007, A1.

McAuliffe, Mary S. *CIA Documents on the Cuban Missile Crisis 1962* (Washington, DC: History Staff of the Central Intelligence Agency, 1992).

McDonald, James Kenneth. "CIA and Warning Failures." In L. C. Jenssen and O. Riste, eds., *Intelligence in the Cold War: Organisation, Role, International Cooperation*

(Oslo: Norwegian Institute for Defence Studies, 2001).[English spelling here; checked]

McDonald, John. *Strategy in Poker, Business & War* (New York: W. W. Norton & Company, 1996).

McDonald, Walter. "African Numbers Game." *Studies in Intelligence*, 8: 4 (1964), 11–20.

McKnight, David. *Espionage and the Roots of the Cold War: The Conspiratorial Heritage* (New York: Frank Cass, 2002).

Mercado, Stephen C. "Reexamining the Distinction between Open Information and Secrets." *Studies in Intelligence*, 49: 2 (2005).

Mikoyan, Sergo. "Eroding the Soviet 'Culture of Secrecy': Western Winds behind Kremlin Walls." *Studies in Intelligence*, 11 (Fall–Winter 2001).

Milani, M. M. *The Making of Iran's Islamic Revolution: From Monarchy to Islamic Republic* (Boulder, CO: Westview Press, 1988).

Miller, Abraham H., and Damask, Nicholas. "Thinking about Intelligence after the Fall of Communism." *International Journal of Intelligence and Counterintelligence*, 6 (1993), pp. 250–270.

Miller, John, Michael Stone, and Chris Mitchell. *The Cell: Inside the 9/11 Plot, and Why the FBI and CIA Failed to Stop It* (New York: Hyperion, 2003).

Mitchell, Rebecca, and Stephen Nicholas. "Knowledge Creation in Groups: The Value of Cognitive Diversity, Transactive Memory and Open-mindedness Norms." *Electronic Journal of Knowledge Management*, 4: 1 (2006), pp. 67–74.

Monroe, Kristen Renwick, and Lina Haddad Kreidie. "The Perspective of Islamic Fundamentalists and the Limits of Rational Choice Theory." *Political Psychology*, 18: 1 (1997), pp. 19–43.

Moskoff, William. "Review Essay: CIA Publications on the Soviet Economy." *Slavic Review*, 40: 2 (1981), pp. 269–272.

Moynihan, Daniel Patrick. "Report of the Commission on Protecting and Reducing Government Secrecy." U. S. Senate, ed. (Washington, DC: U.S. Government Printing Office, 1997.

———. "The Soviet Economy: Boy, Were We Wrong!" *The Washington Post*, July 11, 1990, p. A19.

Mullin, Dennis. "Nobody Can Overthrow Me—I Have the Power." *U.S. News & World Report*, June 26, 1978.

Munson, Harlow T., and W. P. Southard. "Two Witnesses for the Defense." *Studies in Intelligence*, 8: 4 (1964), pp. 93–98.

National Commission on Terrorist Attacks upon the United States. *The 9/11 Commission Report: Final Report of the National Commission on Terrorist Attacks upon the United States* (New York: W. W. Norton, 2004).

National Public Radio. "Difference between a Secret and a Mystery When it Comes to Intelligence Failures." In *All Things Considered* (September 18, 2002); available at http://www.npr.org/programs/atc/transcripts/2002/sep/020918.adelman.html.

Naveh, Shimon. *In Pursuit of Military Excellence: The Evolution of Operational Theory* (London: Frank Cass, 2004).

Neumann, Peter R., and M. L. R. Smith. "Missing the Plot? Intelligence and Discourse Failure." *Orbis* (2005), pp. 95–107.

Nolan, Janne E., and Douglas J. MacEachin. *Discourse, Dissent, and Strategic Surprise: Formulating U.S. Security Policy in an Age of Uncertainty* (Washington, DC: Institute for the Study of Diplomacy, Edmund A. Walsh School of Foreign Service, Georgetown University, 2006).

Novak, Michael. "The Silent Artillery of Communism." In L. Edwards, ed., *The Collapse of Communism* (Stanford, CA: Hoover Institution Press, 2000).

Nye, J. S. "Peering into the Future." *Foreign Affairs*, 77 (1994), pp. 82–93.

Olmsted, Kathryn S. "Blond Queens, Red Spiders, and Neurotic Old Maids: Gender and Espionage in the Early Cold War." *Intelligence and National Security*, 19: 1 (2004), pp. 78–94.

Onuf, Nicholas. "Constructivism: A Users Manual." In V. Kubalkova, N. Onuf, and P. Kowert, eds., *International Relations in a Constructed World* (Armonk, NY: M. E. Sharpe, 1998).

———. "Review of The New Culture of Security Studies." *Mershon International Studies Review*, 42: 1 (1998), pp. 132–134.

Orlov, Alexander. *The March of Time* (London: St. Ermin's Press, 2004).

———. "The U-2 Program: A Russian Officer Remembers." *Studies in Intelligence* (Winter 1998–1999), pp. 5–14.

Parker, C. F., and Stern, E. K. "Blindsided? September 11 and the Origins of Strategic Surprise." *Political Psychology*, 23: 3 (2002), pp. 601–630.

———. "Bolt from the Blue or Avoidable Failure? Revisiting September 11 and the Origins of Strategic Surprise." *Foreign Policy Analysis*, 1: 3 (2005), pp. 301–332.

Parkinson, C. Northcote. *Parkinson's Law, or The Pursuit of Progress* (London: Penguin, 1957).

Perrow, Charles. *Normal Accidents: Living with High Risk Technologies* (Princeton, NJ: Princeton University Press, 1999).

Peter, Lawrence J., and Raymond Hull. *The Peter Principle: Why Things Always Go Wrong* (London: Souvenir Press, 1969).

Peters, Ralph. "Our Old New Enemies." *Parameters*, 29: 2 (1999).

Petersen, Martin. "Making the Analytic Review Process Work." *Studies in Intelligence*, 49 (2005): p. 1.

Pillar, Paul R. "Good Literature and Bad History: The 9/11 Commission's Tale of Strategic Intelligence." *Intelligence and National Security*, 21: 6 (2006), pp. 1022–1044.

———. *Terrorism and U.S. Foreign Policy* (Washington, DC: The Brookings Institution, 2001).

Pipes, Richard. "The Fall of the Soviet Union." In L. Edwards, ed., *The Collapse of Communism* (Stanford, CA: Hoover Institution Press, 2000).

———. *Three "Whys" of the Russian Revolution* (New York: Vintage Books, 1995).

———. *Vixi: Memories of a Non-Belonger* (New Haven, CT: Yale University Press, 2003).

Powers, Thomas. *The Man Who Kept the Secrets: Richard Helms and the CIA* (New York: Alfred A. Knopf, 1979).

———. "The Trouble with the CIA." *New York Review of Books*, January 17, 2002.

Pringle, Robert W. "Arms Control Intelligence." In J. Woronoff, ed., *Historical Dictionary of Russian & Soviet Intelligence*, pp. 16–17 (Lanham, MD: The Scarecrow Press, 2006).

———. "Trust Operation." In J. Woronoff, ed., *Historical Dictionary of Russian & Soviet Intelligence*, pp. 268–269 (Lanham, MD: The Scarecrow Press, 2006).

Putin, Vladimir, Nataliya Gevorkyan, Natalya Timakova, and Andrei Kolesnikov. *First Person: An Astonishingly Frank Self-Portrait by Russia's President Vladimir Putin*, trans. C. A. Fitzpatrick (New York: PublicAffairs, 2000).

Quandt, William B. "The Middle East Crises." *Foreign Affairs*, 58 (1980), pp. 540–562.

Quiggin, Thomas. *Seeing the Invisible: National Security Intelligence in an Uncertain Age* (Singapore: World Scientific Publishing, 2007).

Ramazani, R. K. "Iran's Revolution: Patterns, Problems and Prospects." *International Affairs*, 56: 3 (1980), pp. 443–457.

Randal, Jonathan. "Exile Leader Shifts View on U.S.–Iran Ties; Iranian Exile Leader Shifts Stance on U.S." *The Washington Post*, January 1, 1979, p. A1.

———. "Khomeini: From Oblivion to the Brink of Power." *The Washington Post*, January 21, 1979, A23.

———. "Views differ on Islamic role in republic." *The Washington Post*, February 4, 1979.

Ranelagh, John. *The Agency* (London: Weidenfeld and Nicholson, 1986).

Reeve, Simon. *The New Jackals: Ramzi Yousef, Osama Bin Laden, and the New Terrorism* (Boston, MA: Northeastern University Press, 1999).

Rice, Condoleezza. "Campaign 2000: Promoting the National Interest." *Foreign Affairs* (January–February 2000).

Richardson, Louise. *What Terrorists Want: Understanding the Enemy, Containing the Threat* (New York: Random House, 2007).

Richelson, Jeffrey T., *The US Intelligence Community* (Boulder, CO: Westview Press, 2008).

Richelson, Jeffrey T., Thomas Blanton, and William Burr. "Dubious Secrets." *The National Security Archive*: Electronic Briefing Book No. 90 (2003); available at www .gwu.edu/~nsarchiv/NSAEBB/NSAEBB90/index.htm.

Richter, James. *Khrushchev's Double-Bind: International Pressures and Domestic Coalition Politics* (Baltimore, MD: The Johns Hopkins University Press, 1994).

Rivkin, Jan W., and Michael A. Roberto. "Managing National Intelligence (A): Before 9/11." In *Harvard Business School Case # 706-463* (Boston, MA: Harvard Business School Publishing, 2006).

"The Roar of the Crowd," *The Economist*, March 26, 2012.

Robin, Ron. *The Making of the Cold War Enemy: Culture and Politics in the Military-Intellectual Complex* (Princeton, NJ: Princeton University Press, 2001).

Robinson, Neil. *Ideology and the Collapse of the Soviet System: A Critical History of the Soviet Ideological Discourse* (Aldershot, UK: Elgar Publishers, 1995).

Roosevelt, Kermit. *Countercoup: The Struggle for the Control of Iran* (New York: McGraw-Hill, 1979).

Rosen, Stephen Peter. "Net Assessment as an Analytic Concept." In A. W. Marshall and H. S. Rowen, eds., *On Not Fooling Ourselves* (Boulder, CO: Westview Press, 1991).

Rosenfeld, Stephen S. "Knowing the Outs as Well as the Ins." *The Washington Post*, December 7, 1979, p. A17.

Rouleau, Eric. "Khomeini's Iran." *Foreign Affairs*, 59: 1 (1980), pp. 1–20.

Rubin, B. *Paved with Good Intentions: The American Experience in Iran* (New York: Oxford University Press, 1980).

Ruble, Blair A. "Occasional Paper #283, U.S. Assessments of the Soviet and Post-Soviet Russian Economy: Lessons Learned and Not Learned" (Washington, DC: Woodrow Wilson International Center for Scholars, 2002).

"Russian Files on al-Qa'eda Ignored." *Jane's Intelligence Digest*, October 5, 2001, page 4.

Russell, Richard L. *Sharpening Strategic Intelligence: Why the CIA Gets It Wrong and What Needs to Be Done to Get It Right* (New York: Cambridge University Press, 2007).

Rutland, Peter. "Who Got It Right and Who Got It Wrong? And Why?" In M. Cox, ed., *Rethinking the Soviet Collapse: Sovietology, the Death of Communism and the New Russia* (London: Pinter, 1998).

Saffo, Paul. "Six Rules for Effective Forecasting." *Harvard Business Review*, July–August 2007, pp. 1–11.

Said, Edward W. *Orientalism: Western Conceptions of the Orient* (London: Penguin Books, 1995).

Sakwa, Richard. "Russian Political Evolution: A Structural Approach." In M. Cox, ed., *Rethinking the Soviet Collapse: Sovietology, the Death of Communism and the New Russia* (London: Pinter, 1998).

Saunders, Frances Stonor. *The Cultural Cold War: The CIA and the World of Arts and Letters* (New York: The New Press, 2001).

———. *Who Paid the Piper? CIA and the Cultural Cold War* (London: Granta Books, 2000).

Schachter, Jonathan M. "The Eye of the Believer: Psychological Influences on Counter-Terrorism Policy-Making" (Santa Monica, CA: RAND Graduate School, 2002).

Schemmer, Benjamin F. "The Intelligence Community's Case against Turner." *The Washington Post*, April 8, 1979, D1.

Scheuer, Michael. "Tenet Tries to Shift the Blame. Don't Buy It." *The Washington Post*, April 29, 2007.

———. *Through Our Enemies' Eyes: Osama bin Laden, Radical Islam, and the Future of America* (Washington, DC: Potomac Books, 2006).

Schmitt, John F. "A Systemic Concept for Operational Design," 2008. Available at www.au.af.mil/au/awc/awcgate/usmc/mcwl_schmitt_op_design.pdf.

Schroeder, Gertrude. "Soviet Reality Sans Potemkin." *Studies in Intelligence*, 12: 2 (1968), pp. 43–51.

Schum, David A., and Jon R. Morris. "Assessing the Competence and Credibility of Human Sources of Intelligence Evidence: Contributions from Law and Probability." *Law, Probability and Risk*, 6: 1–4 (2007), pp. 247–274.

Schwartz, Peter, *Inevitable Surprises: Thinking Ahead in a Time of Turbulence* (New York: Gotham Books, 2004).

Schweitzer, Peter. *Victory: The Reagan Administration's Secret Strategy That Hastened the Collapse of the Soviet Union* (New York: Atlantic Monthly Press, 1994).

Sciolino, Elaine. "Iran's Durable Revolution." *Foreign Affairs*, 61: 4 (1983), pp. 893–920.

Scott, William F. "The Face of Moscow in the Missile Crisis." *Studies in Intelligence*, 37: 5 (1966), pp. 105–109.

Seliktar, Ofira. *Failing the Crystal Ball Test: The Carter Administration and the Fundamentalist Revolution in Iran* (Westport, CT: Praeger, 2000).

———. *Politics, Paradigms, and Intelligence Failures: Why So Few Predicted the Collapse of the Soviet Union* (Armonk, NY: M. E. Sharpe, 2004).

Senate Committee on Foreign Relations. *Estimating the Size and Growth of the Soviet Economy: Hearing Before the Committee on Foreign Relations*, 101st Congress, 2nd session (Washington, DC: U.S. Government Printing Office, 1990).

Serge, Victor. *What Every Radical Should Know about State Repression: A Guide for Activists* (New York: Ocean Press, 2005).

Shackley, Theodore. *Spymaster: My Life in the CIA* (Dulles, VA: Potomac Books, 2006).

Shenon, Philip. *The Commission: An Uncensored History of the 9/11 Investigation* (New York: The Hachette Book Group, 2008).

Sherwin, Ronald G., and Barton Whaley. "Understanding Strategic Deception: An Analysis of 93 Cases." In D. C. Daniel and K. L. Herbig, eds., *Strategic Military Deception* (New York: Pergamon Press, 1982).

Shlaim, Avi, "Failures in National Intelligence Estimates: The Case of the Yom Kippur War." *World Politics*, 28: 3 (1976), 348–380.

Shreeve, Thomas W. "The Intelligence Community Case Method Program: A National Intelligence Estimate on Yugoslavia." In R. Z. George and R. D. Kline, eds., *Intelligence and the National Security Strategist: Enduring Issues and Challenges* (Lanham, MD: Rowman & Littlefield Publishers, 2006).

Shulsky, Abram N., and Gary J. Schmitt. *Silent Warfare: Understanding the World of Intelligence* (Washington, DC: Brassey's, 2002).

Shultz, George P. *Turmoil and Triumph: My Years as Secretary of State* (New York: Charles Scribner's & Sons, 1993).

Shultz, Richard H. "The Era of Armed Groups." In P. Berkowitz, ed. *The Future of American Intelligence* (Stanford, CA: Hoover Institution Press, 2005).

Sick, Gary. *All Fall Down: America's Tragic Encounter with Iran* (New York: Random House, 1985).

Smith, Abbot E. "On the Accuracy of National Intelligence Estimates." *Studies in Intelligence*, 13: 4 (1969), pp. 25–35.

Smith, Michael Douglas. "The Perils of Analysis: Revisiting Sherman Kent's Defense of SNIE 85-3-62." *Studies in Intelligence*, 51: 3 (2007), pp. 29–32.

Smith, Thomas Bell. *The Essential CIA* (Privately printed, 1975).

Snider, L. Britt. *The Agency and the Hill: CIA's Relationship with Congress,1946–2004* (Washington, DC: The Center for the Study of Intelligence, Central Intelligence Agency, 2004).

Solomon, John. "CIA Warned of Attack 6 Years before 9/11." Associated Press, April 16, 2004.

Soros, George. *Alchemy of Finance: Reading the Mind of the Market* (New York: Touchstone Books, 1988).

"Soviet National Security Policy: Responses to the Changing Military and Economic Environment, SOV 88-10040CX" (Washington, DC: Directorate of Intelligence, Office of Soviet Analysis, Central Intelligence Agency, 1988).

Sprinzak, Ehud. "The Lone Gunman." *Foreign Policy* November–December (2001), pp. 72–73.

Steiner, James E. *Challenging the Red Line between Intelligence and Policy* (Washington, DC: Institute for the Study of Diplomacy, School of Foreign Service, Georgetown University, 2004).

Stennis, John, *et al.* "Investigation of the Preparedness Program, Interim Report on the Cuban Military Buildup by the Preparedness Investigating Subcommittee" (Washington, DC: Committee on Armed Services, U.S. Senate, 88th Congress, 1st Session, 1963).

Sterling, Claire. *The Terror Network: The Secret War of International Terrorism* (New York: Holt, Rhinehart & Winston, 1981).

Stopford, John M., Susan Strange, and John S. Henley. *Rival States, Rival Firms: Competition for World Market Shares* (Cambridge, UK: Cambridge University Press 1991).

Sullivan, William. *Mission to Iran* (New York & London: W. W. Norton & Company, 1981).

Suvorov, Viktor. *Aquarium* (London: Hamish Hamilton, 1985).

Taheri, A. *Nest of Spies: America's Journey to Disaster in Iran* (New York: Pantheon Books, 1988).

———. *The Spirit of Allah: Khomeini and the Islamic Revolution* (Bethesda, MD: Adler & Adler, 1985).

Talbot, Ann. "Chance and Necessity in History: E. H. Carr and Leon Trotsky Compared." *Historical Social Research*, 34: 2 (2009), pp. 88–96.

Taleb, Nassim Nicholas. *The Black Swan: The Impact of the Highly Improbable* (New York: Random House, 2007).

———. *Fooled by Randomness: The Hidden Role of Chance in Life and in the Markets* (New York: Texere, 2004).

Tehranian, M. "Communication and Revolution in Iran: The Passing of a Paradigm." *Iranian Studies*, 13 (1980), pp. 5–30.

Tenet, George. "Worldwide Threat—Converging Dangers in a Post 9/11 World—Testimony of February 6, 2002." In *Senate Select Committee on Intelligence*. (Washington, DC: 2002).

Tenet, George, and Bill Harlow. *At the Center of the Storm: My Years at the CIA* (New York: HarperCollins, 2007).

Terechow, William. "The Soviet Atlas as a Source." *Studies in Intelligence*, 10: 2 (1966), pp. 37–42.

Tetlock, Philip E. *Expert Political Judgment: How Good Is It? How Can We Know?* (Princeton, NJ: Princeton University Press, 2005).

Thomas, Stafford C. "The CIA's Bureaucratic Dimensions." *International Journal of Intelligence and Counterintelligence*, 12: 4 (1999), pp. 399–413.

Tinsley, Catherine H. "Social Categorization and Intergroup Dynamics." In B. Fischhoff and C. Chauvin, eds., *Intelligence Analysis: Behavioral and Social Scientific Foundations* (Washington, DC: Committee on Behavioral and Social Science Research to Improve Intelligence Analysis for National Security, National Research Council, 2011).

Trachtenberg, Marc. *History & Strategy*. Princeton Studies in International History and Politics (Princeton, NJ: Princeton University Press, 1991).

Travers, Russ, "The Coming Intelligence Failure." *Studies in Intelligence*, 01: 1 (1997).

Treverton, Gregory F. *Reshaping National Intelligence for an Age of Information* (Cambridge, UK: Cambridge University Press, 2003).

———. "Risks and Riddles." *Smithsonian*, June 2007; available at www.smithsonianmag .com/people-places/presence_puzzle.html.

Treverton, Gregory F., and James Klocke. *The Fall of the Shah of Iran* (Cambridge, MA: Harvard University, 1988).

———. "Iran, 1978–1979: Coping with the Unthinkable." In E. R. May and P. D. Zelikow, eds., *Dealing with Dictators: Dilemmas of US Diplomacy and Intelligence Analysis, 1945–1990* (Cambridge, MA: MIT Press, 2006).

Trotsky, Leon. *History of the Russian Revolution* (London: Pluto Press, 1977).

———. *My Life: An Attempt at an Autobiography* (New York: Pathfinder Press, 1970).

True, Philip A. "Be Forewarned: Surprises Are Inevitable." *The Washington Post*, June 5, 2002, A23.

Turist, Amerikanskiy. "A Note on Casual Intelligence Acquisition." *Studies in Intelligence*, 2: 3 (1958), pp. 71–74.

Turner, Michael A. "Issues in Evaluating U.S. Intelligence." *International Journal of Intelligence and Counterintelligence*, 5: 3 (1991), pp. 275–285.

———. *Why Secret Intelligence Fails* (Dulles, VA: Potomac Books, 2005).

Turner, Stansfield. *Burn before Reading: Presidents, CIA Directors, and Secret Intelligence* (New York: Hyperion, 2005).

———. "Intelligence for a New World Order." *Foreign Affairs*: Fall (1991), 150–166.

———. "Purge the CIA of KGB Types." *The New York Times*, October 2, 1991.

———. *Secrets and Democracy: The CIA in Transition* (New York: Harper and Row, 1986).

U.S. Congress, ed. "Joint Inquiry into Intelligence Community Activities before and after the Terrorist Attacks of September 11, 2001." (Washington, DC: U.S. Senate Select Committee on Intelligence and U.S. House Permanent Select Committee on Intelligence Together with Additional Views, 2002).

Wallerstein, Immanuel. *Unthinking Social Science: The Limits of Nineteenth-Century Paradigms* (Philadelphia: Temple University Press, 2001).

Walton, Timothy. *Challenges in Intelligence Analysis: Lessons from 1300 BCE to the Present* (Cambridge, UK: Cambridge University Press, 2010).

Ward, Steven R. "Evolution Beats Revolution in Analysis: Counterpoint to "The Coming Revolution in Intelligence Analysis." *Studies in Intelligence*, 46: 3 (2002), pp. 29–36.

Warner, Michael, and Kenneth J. McDonald. *US Intelligence Reform Studies since 1947* (Washington, DC: Strategic Management Issues Office and the Center for the Study of Intelligence of the CIA, 2005).

Watanabe, Frank. "Fifteen Axioms for Intelligence Analysis." *Studies in Intelligence*, Semiannual Edition: 1 (1997).

Watt, D. Cameron. "The Historiography of Intelligence in International Review." In L. C. Jenssen and O. Riste, eds., *Intelligence in the Cold War: Organisation, Role and International Cooperation* (Oslo: Norwegian Institute for Defence Studies, 2001).

Weber, Max, *Economy and Society* (Berkeley: University of California Press, 1978).

Weiner, Tim. *Legacy of Ashes: The History of the CIA* (New York: Doubleday, 2007).

———. "Naiveté at the CIA: Every Nation's Just Another U.S." *The New York Times*, June 7, 1998.

Weldes, Jutta. "Bureaucratic Politics: A Critical Constructivist Assessment." *Mershon International Studies Review*, 42: 2 (1998), pp. 216–225.

———. *Constructing National Interests: The United States and the Cuban Missile Crisis* (Minneapolis: University of Minnesota Press, 1999).

Wendt, Alexander. "Anarchy Is What States Make of It: The Social Construction of Power Politics." *International Organization*, 41: 3 (1992), pp. 335–370.

———. "On Constitution and Causation in International Relations." *Review of International Studies*, 24: 5 (1998), 101–118.

———. *Social Theory of International Politics.* In S. Smith, ed., Cambridge Studies in International Relations (Cambridge, UK: Cambridge University Press, 1999).

West, Nigel. "KGB." In N. West, ed., *Historical Dictionary of Cold War Counterintelligence*, pp. 172–173 (Lanham, MD: The Scarecrow Press, 2007).

Westerfield, H. Bradford, ed. *Inside CIA's Private World: Declassified Articles from the Agency's Internal Journal 1955–1992* (New Haven, CT: Yale University Press, 1995).

"What's in a Name? (Technology Quarterly)." *The Economist*, March 10, 2007, pp. 27–28.

Wilbur, Donald N. "Clandestine Service History: Overthrow of Premier Mossadeq of Iran (CS Historical Paper 208)" (Washington, DC: Central Intelligence Agency, 1954).

Wilhelm, John Howard. "The Failure of the American Sovietological Economics Profession." *Europe-Asia Studies*, 55: 1 (2003), pp. 59–74.

Windrem, Robert, and Victor Limjoco. "9/11 Commission Controversy." *Deep Background: NBC News Investigates*, January 30, 2008, available at http://deepbackground.msnbc.msn.com/archive/2008/01/30/624314.aspx.

Wirtz, James J. "Miscalculation, Surprise, and U.S. Intelligence." *Studies in Intelligence*: Special November 2002 Issue, pp. 85–93.

Wixson, Andrew. "Portrait of a Cuban Refugee." *Studies in Intelligence* (Summer 1964), pp. 35–41.

Wohlstetter, Roberta. "Cuba and Pearl Harbor." *Foreign Affairs*, 43: 4 (1965), pp. 690–707.

———. *Pearl Harbor: Warning and Decision* (Stanford, CA: Stanford University Press, 1962).

Wolf, Markus, and Anne McElvoy. *Man without a Face: The Autobiography of Communism's Greatest Spymaster* (New York: PublicAffairs, 1997).

Woodward, Bob. *Veil: The Secret Wars of the CIA 1981–1987* (New York: Simon & Schuster, 1987).

Wright, Lawrence. *The Looming Tower: Al-Qaeda and the Road to 9/11* (New York: Random House, 2006).

Wright, Robin. *In the Name of God* (New York: Simon & Schuster, 1989).

Xenakis, Christopher I. *What Happened to the Soviet Union? How and Why American Sovietologists Were Caught by Surprise* (Westport, CT: Praeger Publishers 2002).

Zegart, Amy B. "September 11 and the Adaptation Failure of U.S. Intelligence Agencies." *International Security*, 29: 4 (2005), pp. 78–111.

———. *Spying Blind: The CIA, the FBI, and the Origins of 9/11* (Princeton, NJ: Princeton University Press, 2007).

Zubok, Vladislav, and Constantine Pleshakov. *Inside the Kremlin's Cold War: From Stalin to Khrushchev* (Cambridge, MA: Harvard University Press, 1996).

INDEX

Abdul Basit, 197, 318n31
ad hoc terrorists, 43, 200
Adelman, Ken, 30, 95
advocacy (principle), 42, 44
Afghanistan: al-Qa'ida in, 205, 206; Soviet
  invasion, 77, 113, 202, 207, 210, 284n8;
  Taliban, 209, 210, 219, 220, 244, 306n172,
  327n158
Agrell, Wilhelm, 55
Ajax (Operation), 81, 93
Albright, Madeleine, 74
Alec Station, 201, 206, 220, 225–230
Alekseyev, Aleksandr Ivanovich, 161
Alexseev, Mikhail A., 110, 111, 127–28, 131,
  288n48, 315n294
Allen, George, 31, 274n128, 288n47
Allison, Graham, 67, 96, 180; on Cuban
  Missile Crisis, 8–9, 135, 146, 148,
  151, 164, 175, 189, 304n140, 305n162,
  313n274; *Essence of Decision*, 8–9, 135;
  on government politics model, 8–9,
  239; on McCone, 170; on organizational
  behavior model, 8, 239, 307n194,
  313n274; on probability, 115; on rational
  actor model, 8
al-Qa'ida, 194, 195–218, 321nn70,71,
  322n83, 328n173; CIA's misjudgments
  regarding, 3, 24, 39, 43, 75, 180, 191,
  192, 212–24, 226, 228–33, 237, 247,
  266n23, 319nn42,44, 324n110; merger
  with Egyptian Islamic Jihad, 197–98;
  monetary resources, 197, 206; network

structure of, 321n72; and suicide
  missions, 197, 198, 222. *See also* bin
  Ladin, Usama; Embassy attacks in 1998;
  September 11th attacks; World Trade
  Center attack of 1993
al-Zawahiri, Ayman, 197, 320
Ames, Aldrich, 78, 244, 276n162
Amuchastegui, Domingo, 174
Anadyr (Operation), 147, 155–157, 160, 181,
  303n120
analogical reasoning, 154, 302n107
Andrew, Christopher, 92
Andropov, Yuri, 113, 121, 187
Angleton, James Jesus, 54, 270n64
Agranat Commission, 9
anthropologists, 85, 97, 272n108
Anticipating Surprise, 20, 133, 149, 315n301
Arjomand, Said, 99
Arrow, Kenneth, 292n123
Ashcroft, John, 212–13
Assange, Julian, 107
Atta, Mohamed, 206
Aum Shinrikyo, 328n188
Azpillago Lombard, Florentino, 162

Baer, Robert, 323n104
Baker, James, 130
Ball, George, 179–80, 311n240
Bamford, James, 211, 306n170
Bamian (World Heritage site), 220
Barnett, Michael, 28

361